Africa in Transition

Africa
in Transition

Geographical Essays edited by

B. W. HODDER and D. R. HARRIS

METHUEN & CO LTD
11 NEW FETTER LANE LONDON EC4

First published 1967
© *1967 B. W. Hodder and D. R. Harris*
Printed in Great Britain
by Ebenezer Baylis and Son, Ltd
The Trinity Press, Worcester, and London

Distributed in the U.S.A.
by Barnes and Noble, Inc.

Contents

Preface

Among the chief causes of the recent upsurge of interest in African affairs has been the unprecedented speed and scale of political change in the continent. The post-war race to independence began in 1951, reached a climax between 1960 and the end of 1962 when twenty-two new sovereign states appeared on the map of Africa, and had nearly run its course by 1966 when all but nine territories had attained fully independent status. Individually many of these new African states are small and appear to have little economic or demographic significance. But taken together they form a politically powerful group representing nearly one-third of the total voting strength of the United Nations. Furthermore, the success or failure of African governments in dealing with a wide range of economic, social and political problems will have implications reaching far beyond the shores of Africa. Economic development, problems of national cohesion and stability, the most appropriate form of government, tribalism, the ideological conflict between the Western and Communist worlds, the continued existence of white minority governments, and the prospects for regional co-operation or African unity: these are some of the critical issues with which independent African governments are having to grapple. Only the most ingenuous observer would suggest that the way in which these complicated and often intractable problems are tackled is of concern only to Africans; it is possible that the continuance of apartheid and white supremacy in southern African may lead to a major racial conflict with world-wide repercussions. Interest in Africa today is also part of a general concern with the 'developing' or 'third' world, of which all African nations except South Africa are members. It is widely accepted that economic development in these countries is the responsibility not only of African governments but also of the peoples of the developed world; for only with external capital, technical aid and new trading opportunities can the economies of African countries reasonably be expected to prosper.

This widening and deepening of world interest in the continent has been reflected in a rapid increase in the volume and range of writings on African affairs since the early 1950's. In the field of geographical studies alone a number of new and important texts have appeared, dealing either with

1*

Africa as a whole or with one of its major regions; and a flood of scientific papers, many of them based on detailed field research, has appeared in professional geographical journals over the last twenty years.

The present volume brings together essays by several authors, all of whom are concerned with teaching the geography of Africa in the University of London. The common aim has been to analyse, within a regional framework, the background to some of the many problems and issues with which Africans themselves are most deeply concerned today but which have so far received relatively little attention in the geographical literature. A uniform treatment has been deliberately avoided, so that the essays differ widely in emphasis and focus attention upon quite different themes. Each essay is thus a personal and individual study of a part of Africa of which the author has first-hand experience, and nowhere has there been any attempt to write the comprehensive geography of Africa or its regions. This volume, in fact, must be regarded as being only complementary to existing regional texts. Select bibliographies, however, are included at the end of each essay to assist further exploratory reading about this most rapidly changing of the world's continents.

London, July, 1967   B.W.H. and D.R.H.

Acknowledgements: The authors wish to express their gratitude to Dr. A. M. O'Connor, Mr. D. Hilling and Dr. P. W. Porter for reading sections of the manuscript and for making a number of valuable suggestions.

Figures

The authors wish to express their gratitude to Trevor Allen of the University College Cartographic Unit for drawing Figures 1-11, 17-18, 20-26 and 28-31; to G. Davenport of Birkbeck College for Figures 12-16 and 19; and to Mrs. E. Wilson, Miss S. Hall and Miss E. Crux of the Drawing Office of the London School of Economics for Figures 32-41.

Both in the maps and in the text the spelling of place-names follows the *Times Atlas of the World*, Vol. IV, 1956.

Introduction : *The African Scene*

Introduction: *The African Scene*

By THE EDITORS

The Diversity of Africa

Of all the generalizations commonly made about Africa one of the least valid is that Africa is lacking in diversity. There are four main reasons why this assumption should so often be made. In the first place, our knowledge of this vast continent is both recent and slight: many of the simplest geographical facts about Africa, especially to the south of the Sahara, were not known to Europeans until well into the nineteenth century; and systematic scientific or historical investigation is, for most of Africa, strictly a twentieth-century phenomenon. Secondly, the sheer size of Africa – over $11\frac{1}{2}$ million square miles (about 30 million km²) and so the largest continent after Asia – is not easily apprehended, and this question of scale is probably responsible for much current misunderstanding about many aspects of African life and environment. A simple but significant difference between Africa and Europe, for instance, is that the units of comparison are so very much larger in Africa. The Sahara, the tropical rain forests, the high plains or plateaux, the rift valleys of East Africa, the Congo and Chad basins, the Nile valley: all these refer to physical units vastly larger than anything to be found in Europe. Thirdly, the fact that a greater part of Africa than of any other continent lies within the tropics has encouraged the belief that it is – physically at least – the most homogeneous. Finally, Africa is a strikingly compact continent with few coastal indentations; with a coastline of only 16,100 miles (25,800 km) it readily gives the impression of being both smaller and more uniform than it really is.

However, Africa is no less varied in its natural and cultural features than any other continent. There is some truth in the statement that 'in its structure as in its relief, Africa is the continent of simplest forms and provides a marked contrast with the complexity of Eurasia' (Fitzgerald, 1961:1); indeed most of Africa is remarkable for the undisturbed nature of its ancient blocks, which outcrop over approximately one-third of the continent's surface. In the west and centre they form extensive low plateaux at about 2000 ft (650 m), and in the east and south vast high plateaux averaging 4000 ft (1300 m) above sea level. But, although these huge expanses are characteristic features of the African landscape, their level surfaces are interrupted by the steeply folded and sharply eroded mountain ranges of the northern and southern extremities of the continent; the mountain massifs of the Sahara and parts of East Africa, which include the towering peaks of Tibesti, Ruwenzori, Elgon, Kilimanjaro and Kenya; and the rugged blocks of Ethiopia. In its climate and vegetation Africa ranges from hot desert to equatorial rain forest and from Mediterranean woodland and scrub to the whole complex of tropical savannas. Soils, too, vary widely, often over quite small distances, and include a variety of lateritized soils, together with brown earths, the rich alluvial soils of the river floodplains and deltas, and different types of volcanic soil.

Great diversity also characterizes Africa's population: in its geographical distribution; in the patterns of urbanization and forms of settlement; and

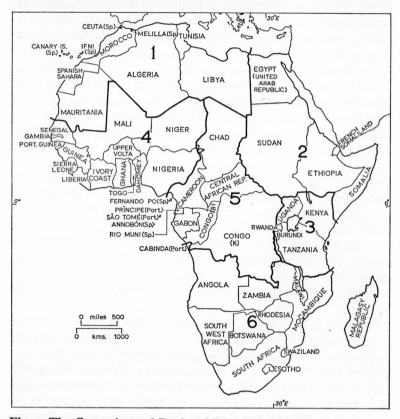

Fig. 1. The Countries and Regional Divisions of Africa

The numbers refer to essays in the text. The existence of Biafra is at present (mid-1967) ignored owing to its uncertain future.

above all in its ethnic composition. There are a number of important non-African minorities, notably European and Asian, but the Africans themselves are at least as varied as the indigenous peoples of any other continent. However African peoples are classified, the pattern is immensely complex: there are many hundreds of tribes, some eight hundred languages, and numerous religions. The indigenous peoples of Africa are of many different physical types, at different levels of economic, social and political development, and they have reacted in differing ways to the impact of European influences. Just as there is no one 'African' landscape or environment, so there is no such person as a typical 'African'.

Finally, Africa is politically the most diverse of all the continents. Divided into over fifty political units, it already commands almost one-third of the total votes in the United Nations; and this fact gives the continent a much more important role in world affairs than its relatively small population of some 310 million would otherwise suggest. Of the fifty-one territories in Africa today, thirty-seven are now (1967) independent and the still-dependent territories are clustered in southern Africa with a few outliers farther to the north. African mainland territories range in size from some 770 square miles (2000 km²) in Ifni to over 965,000 square miles (2½ million km²) in the Republic of Sudan, and they vary from forest states like Gabon to savanna and desert states like Chad and Mauritania and to almost wholly mountainous countries such as Lesotho and Ethiopia. Fourteen states are completely landlocked.

The regional division of Africa adopted in this book is indicated in Fig. 1 and Table 1. The main criterion used in making this division has been simply the experience and mutual convenience of the contributors, but the areas adopted nevertheless correspond quite closely to conventional areal terminologies.

1. *North Africa:* Libya, Tunisia, Algeria, Morocco, Mauritania and the Spanish territories of Melilla, Ceuta, Ifni and Spanish Sahara. Physically and culturally most of this area belongs to the Mediterranean and Moslem worlds, although several of the territories reach deep into the Sahara. Geographically the two most important units are the fold mountains of the Atlas system and the Sahara with its extensive plateaus and great mountain massifs such as the Ahaggar. The Saharan interiors of Libya and Algeria have recently acquired considerable economic significance from the exploitation of oil and natural gas resources. Because of its historical and political relations with its northern neighbours, Mauritania is included here in North Africa, although its strongest economic ties are with West Africa.

2. *Northeast Africa:* Egypt (United Arab Republic), Sudan, Ethiopia, Somalia and French Somaliland. This area comprises two main elements: the Nile Valley lands of Egypt and Sudan; and the mountains and deserts of Ethiopia and the Horn of Africa.

3. *East Africa:* Kenya, Uganda, Tanzania, Rwanda and Burundi. This is essentially the East African plateau together with the great lakes and high mountain ranges and peaks associated with the rift valley systems.

4. *West Africa:* Senegal, Gambia, Portuguese Guinea, Guinea, Sierra Leone, Liberia, Ivory Coast, Mali, Upper Volta, Ghana, Togo, Dahomey, Nigeria, Niger. This area includes all countries lying to the west of Lake Chad and south of North Africa. With fourteen states – all independent except for Portuguese Guinea – this is politically the most diverse of the African regions here discussed.

5. *Equatorial Africa:* Chad, Cameroun, Central African Republic, Spanish Guinea, Gabon, Congo Brazzaville and Congo Kinshasa. These countries are best thought of as (a) the countries that formerly comprised French Equatorial Africa: Chad, Central African Republic, Gabon and Congo Brazzaville, together with Cameroun; (b) the former Belgian Congo, now Congo Kinshasa; and (c) Spanish Guinea together with the Spanish offshore islands of Fernando Po and Annobón and the Portuguese islands of São Tomé and Principé.

6. *Southern Africa:* Angola (with Cabinda), Zambia, Malawi, Moçambique, Rhodesia, Botswana, South West Africa, South Africa, Lesotho, Swaziland and the Malagasy Republic (Madagascar). This area comprises all of Africa south of Equatorial and East Africa, together with the island state of Malagasy. White settlers and white supremacy governments are important elements in several of these countries. As a whole they can be divided into (a) the still-dependent Portuguese territories of Angola (with Cabinda) and Moçambique and the British territory of Swaziland; (b) the independent African-controlled territories of Zambia, Malawi, Botswana and Lesotho; (c) the mandated territory of South West Africa; and (d) Rhodesia and the Republic of South Africa.

The Opening Up of Africa

It is a truism that the most important geographical dichotomy in Africa is between those parts of the continent lying to the north and south of the Sahara. Historically as well as physically, North Africa has a closer affinity with Mediterranean Europe than with the rest of Africa. Extensions of Phoenician, Greek, Roman and Moslem civilizations flowered there and it provides, indeed, a unique area for the study of cultural contact and succession. Beyond the Sahara to the south, however, relatively little is known of Africa's early history. Contacts across the Sahara were not lacking, although these affected chiefly the northern fringes of the savanna or sudanic belt stretching across the continent from the Atlantic to the Upper Nile; and in these northern savanna lands arose a succession of often powerful indigenous states whose very life lay in their ability to trade across the Sahara with the Mediterranean world. Contacts with sub-Saharan Africa were also made southward along the Nile valley; from Arabia across to Ethiopia or Somalia and thence through the East African highlands; and by Arab dhows which reached the east coast at least as early as the tenth century A.D. Our knowledge of early states or civilizations farther to the south is as yet only fragmentary, but it is already quite sufficient to refute the common assumption that Africa south of the Sahara has no history. Core areas of ancient African states are now known to have existed, for example, in Buganda, Kongo, Zulu and Merina (Malagasy); and many of the earliest civilizations in southern Africa may well have been both extensive and advanced. Africa has clearly not always been the passive recipient, 'her history no more than the product of external impact. Africa has contributed to world cultural integration in the past, no less then the present' (Herskovits, 1962:147). But to European eyes the continent south of the Sahara remained a dark and mysterious world until long after the earliest Portuguese ventures around the coast in the fifteenth century; indeed much of it remained unknown until the last quarter of the nineteenth century.

One of the central questions of African history is why, in spite of the continent's relatively close proximity to Europe, the opening up of Africa south of the Sahara to European knowledge and influence was so long delayed. Explanations of this paradox usually appeal to the deterrent effects of the physical environment. The coasts of this compact continent are generally rectilinear, with no large and deep embayments encouraging penetration. Most of the interior is plateau country and the plateaus usually reach close to the coast, restricting the coastal plain, providing falls on the lower stretches of most rivers and silting up many of the river mouths. Penetration inland has also been discouraged by the high incidence of disease. Landing on the coast itself has usually been difficult because of the heavy surf, sandy beaches, mangrove swamps and forests. Strongly running coastal currents have frequently discouraged contacts by sea. The barrier of the Sahara – this great stretch of desert which covers over a quarter of the continent and extends right up to the west coast of the West African bulge – has restricted movement southward by land and sea; and even the Nile route southward through the desert ends either in the *sudd* swamps of Bahr-el-Ghazal or in the fastnesses of the Ethiopian mountains.

Although these physical factors undoubtedly helped to delay European penetration, their significance has often been exaggerated. According to one writer, over-emphasis on their importance has been 'largely responsible for the fiction of an Africa that for centuries lay dormant, out of contact with the rest of the world, impervious to the impulses emanating from centres of civilization' (*ibid*: 14). It has been pointed out that other largely tropical areas – in Central America and in Southeast Asia – had similar physical difficulties (Oliver and Fage, 1962:13), and Africa was closer to Europe than was either the American or the Asian tropics. Other non-physical reasons must clearly be sought to account satisfactorily for the relatively late European penetration of Africa south of the Sahara.

Prominent among these is the lack of any strong motive for European involvement. At least until well into the slaving era, European overseas commerce concentrated upon the Far Eastern trade in spices and other items, and many of the earliest European coastal settlements in Africa – including those at the Cape of Good Hope – were related to this overriding interest. Furthermore, even when slave-trading became important, Europeans had little incentive to penetrate inland. Indigenous African states at or near the coast were only too ready to act as middlemen for European traders, but they were on the whole unwilling to allow any direct penetration inland by Europeans: 'most of the African peoples were organized into states and communities powerful enough to deter invaders and migrants from overseas until late in the nineteenth century . . . It was in large measure the progress already made by the Africans in earlier centuries that enabled them to resist the modern age for so long' (*ibid*: 13–14).

It was thus not until the second half of the nineteenth century that any substantial opening up of sub-Saharan Africa began. Although the Portuguese discovered much of the coast in the fifteenth century, and even penetrated up the Zambezi in the early part of the sixteenth century, and although there was considerable Dutch settlement in the Cape region during the seventeenth century, none of these contacts led to large-scale penetration of the interior. Until well into the nineteenth century European settlements were for the most part restricted to small coastal trading stations.

During the nineteenth century, however, European explorers began to make significant advances into tropical Africa south of the Sahara. First among them were Mungo Park, Clapperton and Lander in West Africa. During the middle years of the century exploration extended even farther inland and included the great trans-Saharan and West African sudanic journeys of Barth. Meanwhile, between 1841 and 1863, Livingstone, Burton, Speke and Grant opened up the southeast of the continent and from 1871 to 1877 Stanley carried through his famous trans-continental journey and other travels in central Africa. As a result of these explorations many of the great puzzles of African geography were solved. In particular, the courses of the rivers Niger, Nile, Congo and Zambezi were traced within the space of half a century, and by the 1880's the main drainage and relief features of the continent were known to Europeans. During the same period missionaries and administrators took an increasing part in the process of extending European influence. Exploration and evangelism frequently led to trade. And it was soon realized that profitable trade depended on the maintenance of a *pax* which in turn could not be assured without administrative intervention and control in the hinterland areas. Consequently, as the explorers, missionaries, traders and administrators came from several different European countries, Africa soon became a field for the conflicting ambitions of the major European colonial powers.

From Colonialism to Independence

The Colonial Impact

Within the last hundred years Africa has experienced two periods of rapid and climactic change. The first occurred during the decade 1884–1894, when much of the continent was parcelled out among the competing European powers, and the second during the decade 1956–1966, when most African countries achieved their independence. It was during the earlier period of change that the political outline of the present pattern of independent states was first laid down.

The comparative study of colonial policies and their differing impacts on African life and economy has only recently begun (Newbury, 1961). Yet this is a vital field of study because no analysis of the contemporary problems of independent African states can afford to ignore the colonial origin of so many of these problems. Africa was the most completely colonized of the continents and the very identity of many African states, as well as their current problems, originate in their different colonial histories. An understanding of the principal differences between European colonial policies in Africa, and especially of British and French colonialism, is therefore essential. While both Britain and France had nurtured grand designs in Africa – the idea of a French Africa stretching from the Mediterranean to the Congo and the British ambition to paint the map red from Cairo to the Cape – there were important contrasts in their colonial policies.

Of all forms of colonization in Africa, the British is the most difficult to generalize about, partly because it refers to such large areas of the continent but also because of Britain's essentially pragmatic and decentralized approach to colonial administration. In certain areas, such as Kenya and southern Africa, European settlement was an important factor in formulating and carrying out policies, whereas in the West African territories, for example, there was no substantial white settlement – either for agriculture of for mining – to influence policy. In all its African territories, however, Britain was responsible for establishing peace and security, including the setting up of effective local police forces; and there was heavy British investment in the African colonies. Furthermore, Britain early became committed to encouraging evolution from colonial to commonwealth or independent status, although this proved to be easier in those territories where white settlement was inconsiderable than where there were large numbers of expatriate white colonists. Through a system of indirect rule Britain maintained the indigenous cultures as far as possible. Control was established without undue usurpation of power. Indirect rule proved to be an economical system, in that it allowed large areas to be administered by relatively few officials, but because it depended upon the strength and coherence of traditional tribal societies its effectiveness was very much reduced in those areas where local institutions were weak.

Unlike British colonialism, French policy in Africa was, until after the Second World War, committed to the ideal of assimilation rather than eventual self-government by Africans. African territories were simply regarded as part of France Overseas. French colonial administration was therefore more direct and highly centralized than its British equivalent. It depended upon relatively large numbers of administrators and gave little encouragement to local cultures or languages. Emphasis was on the creation of a small African élite; there was little in the way of a colour bar in French Africa; and Frenchmen were often to be found in some of the more lowly occupations. White settlement was numerically important only in French North Africa, although significant minorities were to be found in Dakar (Senegal) and in the small plantation areas of Cameroun and Malagasy. During the post-war years, however, France moved in three distinct stages from a policy of assimilation to one of association. These stages were expressed in the 1944 Brazzaville Conference; in the 1956 *loi cadre*, followed by the 1958 New Constitution; and in 1960 by the amending of the New Constitution to allow complete independence.

Unlike the British and French colonial occupation of Africa, Belgian control was confined to one large territory – the Congo – in the very heart of the continent. Highly centralized like that of the French, but aimed eventually, like British administration, at some form of self-government, Belgian colonial policy was essentially long-term and theoretical in its approach. It argued that many years of evolution and careful tuition would be necessary before Africans could properly assume control in the Congo. Priority was given to economic and social development; educational policy was broadly based at the elementary level; there was little growth of an élite among the African population; and political expression and experience was denied to European and African alike until just before independence.

Among the remaining forms of European colonialism in Africa, that of the Portuguese is still of importance because it affects large areas which represent the last considerable bastions of colonialism on the continent. Like that of the French, Portuguese policy has been aimed at assimilation, all territories being regarded as part of the Portuguese Union and administered directly from Lisbon. With substantial numbers of white settlers, especially in Angola, there is little apparent colour bar, and racial intermixture is an official goal. The Spanish colonial system is very similar to that of the Portuguese but applies only to small and unproductive territories. Finally, the German and Italian colonial impact, although directed at considerable territories, was limited in time by the defeat of the metropolitan countries in the First and Second World Wars respectively.

With the exception of Liberia, all countries in Africa have experienced in some way and to some degree the impact of one or more periods of European colonialism, even Ethiopia being for a few years under Italian rule. The nature of this impact can best be seen in the light of three significant generalizations. First, it was initially very slight: conscious attempts at economic, social and political development were the exception rather than the rule for some thirty-five years after partition. Secondly, it took place in a society that was by no means homogeneous or static. Africans have commonly been highly selective in their acceptance of European ideas and techniques, some African societies being much more receptive to change than others. While for analytical convenience it is useful to isolate the European impact, it should be emphasized that it could only operate within the dynamic context of tribalism and indigenous forms of religion. Islam, secure in the north and spreading rapidly southward into Negro Black Africa, proved to be a rich and sturdy cultural tradition strong enough to withstand that of Europe. Indeed European administrators soon realized that they could not afford to ignore existing realities in formulating policies: 'the attempt to bridge the centuries without adequate study of other mentalities, traditions and beliefs, is more likely to lead to failure than to success' (Lugard, 1926: 14). Thirdly, while the prospect of economic gain was certainly a principal motive in the European scramble for Africa, it was not the only one. The concept of 'trusteeship' was frequently an element and sometimes an important element in European-African relations. And this was no mere rationalization; for a great many administrators sincerely held the view that they had 'a duty to humanity to develop the vast economic resources of a great continent'.

On the other hand, it would be misleading to underestimate the magnitude of the European impact on African societies. Everywhere it brought about a sudden social upheaval of often dramatic proportions: 'until the very recent penetration by Europe the greater part of Africa was without the wheel, the plough or the transport animal; almost without stone houses or clothes, except for skins; without writing and so without history. Mentally and physically the Africans were helpless before a European intrusion all the more speedy and overwhelming because it came at a time when science had given Europe such immense material power' (Perham, 1951:132). The social changes that have taken place in Africa during and since the colonial period have been compared with those that occurred in Western Europe when peasants and craftsmen were replaced by agricultural labourers and factory workers. In Africa, however, these changes have been both more sudden and of external origin. They have arisen from the unrestrained impact of European civilization upon African societies, and from the resultant contacts between widely disparate levels of technical advancement, methods of administrative organization and codes of conduct.

The Advance towards Independence

The second great period of change in Africa took place in the decade 1956–1966, during which years most African countries passed from some form of dependent status to independence. It is the speed as much as the reality of independence in Africa that needs to be stressed. To read the literature of the 1940's and early 1950's dealing with the move towards independence in Africa is a salutary experience, because almost without exception the writers of the day were pleading for time in which to prepare Africa for independence. In 1944 one authority argued against any abrupt removal of the 'colonial yoke', calling for a gradual withdrawal within an unspecified but generous time limit (Herskovits, 1944: 112). A few years later Huxley noted that Europeans had destroyed much of what was good or harmonious in African culture without being given the time to put anything stable or constructive in its place; she was sceptical about the African being able to find his way without further tutelage, and argued against leaving him to his own devices (Huxley, 1949: 114–128). As late as 1955, Belgian authorities were still talking in terms of a thirty-year transitional period to independence for their Congo territory.

As it turned out, all were thinking and writing within far too generous a time-scale and were unaware of the magnitude of the forces that were so soon to succeed in asserting the national sovereignty of most African colonial territories.

The Population of Africa

Precise statements about the population of Africa are seldom possible, because the census data are so uneven and unreliable, but the total population today is believed to be about 310 millions. The overall density is thus about 14 per square mile (10 per km²), which is less than half the world's average density and the second lowest of any inhabited continent. Although Africa comprises about 22 per cent of the world's land surface (excluding Antarctica) it contains only 8 per cent of the world's population.

This low density of population is the most important demographic fact about Africa. In the following essays frequent reference is made to the social, political and economic implications of this low density and to the fact that the development of some African countries is held back by insufficient numbers of people. But there are certain areas of high population density where the opposite situation prevails. The distribution of population over the continent is in fact very uneven, the greatest concentrations being found in the Atlas lands of Northwest Africa, the lower Nile valley, sections of West Africa, discontinuous areas in the lakes region of East Africa, and parts of South Africa (Fig. 2).

Considered by countries the most populous African state is Nigeria, with some 55 million, or little less than 20 per cent of the total. A small group of countries have populations of between 10 and 20 million. But most African states contain under 5 million inhabitants, and no less than nineteen countries have less than 2 million each (Table 1). The population base of most African countries is indeed very small and this fact has a significant effect on their prospects of achieving economic development and political independence.

Africa is the least urbanized of the inhabited continents, there being only sixty-five towns with populations of over 100,000. With the exception of South Africa and Egypt the rural population of all countries in the continent exceeds 70 per cent of the total. Towns are, however, of particular importance in any study of contemporary Africa. A number of writers point to the fact that many major problems of social, economic and political change are focused in the towns (Steel, 1961), and that 'towns are the most active agents of emancipation' (Scipio, 1965:37). With the exception of Addis Ababa in the Ethiopian highlands, all the larger towns of Africa with populations over 300,000 are in the densely peopled areas, although the heavily populated lakes region of East Africa does not yet have a town of major size. Much of the urban settlement is, however, of European origin. Only in the Moslem lands of the north along the Mediterranean coast and in parts of West Africa is there a well developed indigenous urban tradition.

It is in studying the dynamics of African population that the lack of reliable data is felt most keenly. A rapid change in the rate of population growth can however be anticipated from the generally high birth, death and infant mortality rates now prevailing, which, for the continent as a whole, have reached about 47, 23 and 50–100 per 1000 respectively. With improved sanitation and disease control, rates of increase are already mounting rapidly in many countries. Although this may be beneficial in the

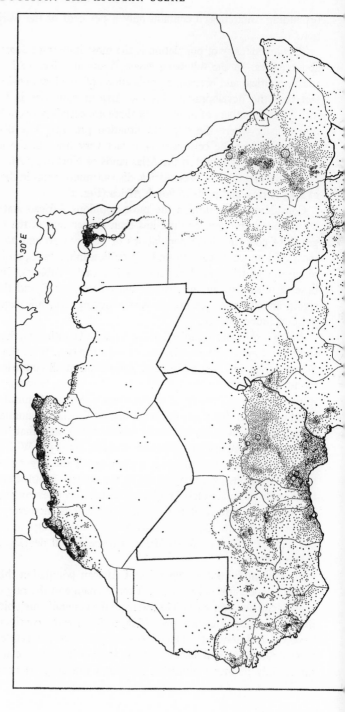

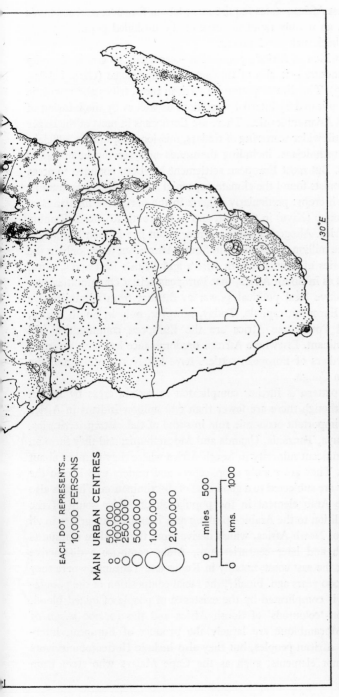

EACH DOT REPRESENTS...
10,000 PERSONS

MAIN URBAN CENTRES

○ 50,000
○ 100,000
○ 250,000
○ 500,000
○ 1,000,000
○ 2,000,000

0   miles   500
0   kms.   1000

Fig. 2. Distribution of Population (after Nel, 1959)

sense that most African states require more labour for successful economic development, an unduly rapid increase of the unskilled population may actually hold back such development.

The composition of Africa's population – especially its ethnic diversity and tribal structure – is also of fundamental importance (Oxford Atlas, 1965: 102–103). The diverse pattern of African races, tribes and linguistic groups is complicated by internal migrations as well as by the infusion of European and Asian minorities. There are Europeans in most of the larger towns and a still wider scattering of traders, missionaries, miners, officials, advisers and technicians, including thousands now serving independent African states. But most European settlement has been confined to areas where the colonists found the climate congenial and conditions favourable for raising cash crops: particularly Algeria in the north, the highlands of Kenya and Congo (Kivu) in the east, and in the south Rhodesia, Zambia and South Africa. Altogether there are now about five million Europeans in Africa, three million of whom are in South Africa. But it was only in the former territories of French North Africa and British East and Central Africa, as well as in South Africa, that European settler communities ever exercised effective local political power as distinct from administrative control from European capitals. Today, however, only in South Africa, Rhodesia and Portuguese Africa are the European communities still politically dominant. Elsewhere African predominance has been asserted; and large numbers of European settlers have left North Africa and the former Belgian Congo.

The racial pattern is further complicated in certain areas by Indian minorities. Although there are fewer than one million Indians in Africa they fulfil an important economic role in some of the eastern territories, notably in Kenya, Tanzania, Uganda and Moçambique; and they form an even more significant minority in South Africa where they number about half a million. They are mainly shopkeepers and traders who live in the cities and they are subjected to a good deal of discrimination. There is also a considerable Arab element in the population of Africa south of the Sahara. In addition to the Arabic-speaking and Islamized majorities in all the countries of North Africa, which derive from the Moslem conquests of the seventh and later centuries A.D., Arabs comprise a distinctive minority along the east coast, notably in Kenya and Tanzania, where they settled over 1,000 years ago. Finally, the racial composition of the popula-tion of Africa is complicated by the existence of people of mixed blood. The 1½ million 'coloureds' of South Africa and the 100,000 *mistos* of Angola and Moçambique are largely the product of European inter-mingling with African peoples, but they also include Hottentot survivors and other minor elements, such as the Cape Malays who stem from

Indonesian slaves imported by the Dutch in the seventeenth and eighteenth centuries.

Problems of Independence

Although it is convenient to treat the economic and political problems of independence as distinct, the newly independent nations of Africa have in recent years become fully aware that to make such a distinction is often arbitrary and misleading. Economically all African states except South Africa are part of the 'developing' world. In many, annual income per capita is as low as £20 and only in South Africa does it exceed £100. Today only about 3 per cent by value of the world's goods and services originates in Africa, and the economic backwardness this represents is a crippling legacy inherited by all independent African states. The determination to break out of this poverty into material prosperity was always an important and sometimes a decisive motive in the drive for political independence. But just as surely, no independent African nation can expect a sustained period of political stability unless at the same time effective economic development takes place and its benefits are passed on to the bulk of the population. Once generated, the 'revolution of rising expectations' cannot be ignored with impunity.

Economic Development

Some of the problems of economic development in Africa relate to difficulties of the physical environment. In particular, lack of water and poverty of soils are commonly believed to set fundamental limitations on African development and they are sometimes put forward as the main reasons why Africa is so little developed today. Certainly in this most tropical of all continents moisture is more often a limiting factor to plant growth than is temperature. Dry climates are in fact more extensive in Africa – which contains about one-third of the world's deserts and semi-deserts – than in any other continent. According to one estimate, precipitation is 'scanty' in about 75 per cent of sub-Saharan Africa and in more than half of the continent water is the principal factor limiting economic advance. Not only is there inadequate precipitation in these dry areas, but they suffer also from great fluctuations of rainfall within individual seasons and from year to year. About 20 per cent of the continent has a 'tropical savanna' climate, characterized by a short rainy season and a long dry season, and a great deal of such rain as there is is erratic and torrential. About 8 per cent of Africa has a 'tropical rainforest' climate, marked by a ten to twelve-month rainy season, but most of this area is too wet for optimum human utility.

It is true, also, that many African soils, especially those that are intensely lateritized, suffer from very poor nutrient status and structure, and that there are proportionately fewer young and fertile alluvial soils than in any other continent. Soil erosion, too, has become a serious problem in many areas.

Yet it is easy to exaggerate the limiting effect on African development of poor soils and inadequate moisture. Most indigenous agricultural systems show successful adaptation to both these deficiencies, although their productivity tends to be low. If the empirically acquired skills of traditional African agriculture can be successfully combined with modern techniques of water conservation and soil improvement these deficiencies can be largely overcome and productivity greatly increased. In particular, local water supplies can be regularized and augmented by small-scale irrigation schemes and other hydraulic works which are relatively cheap and easy to construct, while in a few favoured countries large multi-purpose schemes, such as the Volta River Project in Ghana, are proving economically feasible. Similarly, although much remains to be learned about African soils, there is little doubt that the fertility of many of them can be substantially raised by the judicious application of appropriate modern artificial fertilizers.

A further disadvantage in the natural resource base of many African countries is the low economic value of the vegetation, much of which has been degraded by centuries of burning, grazing and shifting cultivation. About 27 per cent of Africa has a forest cover – a lower percentage than in South America – but much of this is in fact forest-savanna woodland, the trees of which are not generally suitable for lumbering. Nor are the trees of the tropical rain forest itself comparable in utility to those of mid-latitude forests and they are usually uneconomic to exploit because of the very varied species composition of the stands. Many of the savanna grasses, too, have only a low nutritive value for domestic livestock.

Although there are considerable problems associated with the exploitation of Africa's resources of water, soils and vegetation, there is much in the physical environment of the continent that is advantageous to economic development. Most important is the wealth of water power and the presence of minerals, including fissionable raw materials. Africa's water power resources are thought to exceed 40 per cent of the world's potential, about 18 per cent of which – or 45 per cent of Africa's total – is to be found in the Congo basin alone. While the usefulness of the great rivers of Africa – the Nile, Zambezi, Limpopo, Orange, Congo and Niger – as routes of communication is severely restricted by the cataracts and gorges along their lower courses, these and many lesser rivers have, for this very reason, a high potential value for reservoir construction and hydro-electric power generation. Coal is generally scarce and of poor quality, but the production of petroleum and natural gas is increasing rapidly, especially in the Libyan and Algerian Sahara and the Niger delta. Most of Africa, however, consists of ancient basement rocks in which large reserves of petroleum and natural gas are unlikely to be found. The deposits of fissionable material in the Congo's Shinkolobwe area comprise unusually rich uranium ores and they held a leading position in world production during and immediately after World War II. In South Africa fissionable material is recovered as a by-product from gold refining; and many other countries, including Nigeria, Zambia, Moçambique, Gabon and Tunisia, are now known to have valuable deposits of fissionable ores.

Africa is also a storehouse of non-energy-producing minerals, although as yet only a small proportion of these is exploited. There are particularly large reserves of bauxite, chromium, cobalt, copper, diamonds, gold, iron, manganese, niobium, phosphates, platinum and tantalum. So far most of the production is for export, and it is as a means of earning foreign exchange and tax revenue, as well as of providing employment, that mining will continue for some time to be of great importance in Africa. Most of the minerals extracted are not yet used as raw materials in African industry, although in some cases they are concentrated and refined by primary processing plants. In Africa as a whole mining comes second only to agriculture in value of production; and in some countries, for instance Sierra Leone, it completely dominates the cash economy. In 1961 minerals accounted for about 36 per cent of the total value of all African exports. Employing altogether approximately 100,000 non-Africans, mining is the most highly organized and capitalized sector of the modern economy and it has sometimes been the decisive initiator of economic growth. South Africa, South West Africa, Zambia, Rhodesia and Congo Kinshasa normally produce more than three-quarters by gross value of Africa's total mineral output, and South Africa alone accounts for over two-fifths of this total.

Much has still to be learned about the physical environment and resource base of African countries, in many of which even such fundamental tasks as geological survey and topographical mapping remain to be accomplished. But enough is known to encourage the belief that physical factors seldom raise insuperable barriers to economic development and that some areas at least are richly endowed with natural resources awaiting exploitation.

In considering the human resources necessary for economic development it is apparent that over much of Africa there are too few people to provide an adequately large domestic market and labour supply. On the other hand low population density can have real advantages for economic development in that it demonstrates the need for the most economic use of labour and so may stimulate the introduction of labour-saving devices, as it did for instance in the former Belgian Congo. However the rate of growth of population represents, potentially at least, a severely limiting factor. With an average annual rate of population increase of about 2·5 per cent, Africa is already beginning to share the experience of so many developing countries in which the benefits of economic development are dissipated by the rapidity of population growth.

The question of whether Africa's population is adequate for sustained economic development has a qualitative as well as a quantitative aspect. The irrational belief that Africans are in some innate way inferior to the peoples of other continents has absolutely no scientific basis, despite the fact that it is still implicitly assumed or even explicitly stated in many discussions on African affairs. But it is true that generally low standards of health and education seriously inhibit economic, social and political change. In tropical Africa most people are habitually affected by one or more of the major endemic diseases – such as malaria, sleeping sickness, bilharzia and yellow fever – which sap energy, reduce initiative, and lower efficiency. Quite apart from overriding humanitarian motives there are strong economic arguments for extending and intensifying the health programmes of the World Health Organization and other bodies. Lack of education and elementary technical skills are also serious obstacles to economic development. At present about three-quarters of the African population is illiterate, and until the level of literacy and technical skill can be effectively raised, developments, especially industrialization and the modernization of agriculture, will be gravely impeded.

Shortage of capital, too, is a major obstacle to economic advance. With the exception of South Africa, all African nations lack sufficient capital adequately to finance their own development and they are obliged to borrow from the industrially advanced countries and the United Nations. Most of the foreign capital flowing into Africa today is in the form of loans and grants from the former colonial powers to their ex-dependencies, but this kind of foreign aid is often criticized as having unwelcome political implications.

The natural and human resources of Africa, with all their inherent limitations and opportunities, provide a very uneven basis for economic advance in the two main directions of agricultural improvement and industrialization. Agriculture is the dominant activity in most countries, but it comprises a wide range of different systems, from the temporary clearings of the shifting cultivator to the highly capitalized and mechanized plantation. About 60 per cent of Africa's agricultural land is devoted primarily to subsistence crops. Commercial crops are produced in modified traditional systems in Senegal, Ghana, Nigeria, Uganda and Ethiopia; and large-scale plantations characterize the production of rubber in Liberia, palm products, rubber and cocoa in the Congo, sisal and tea in East Africa, and sugar in Angola and Uganda. European-owned companies and estates account for a high percentage of commercial agricultural output in Kenya, Rhodesia and South Africa, and until recently they did so too in Algeria, Morocco and Tunisia. Peasant cultivation of irrigated crops is dominant in Egypt, while a large proportion of Sudanese cotton is raised under a unique partnership system. Commercial livestock production is as yet relatively unimportant although there are some 120 million cattle in Africa.

The need to increase agricultural production, both for export and for domestic consumption, is widely recognized, but so far little success has been achieved. To a considerable extent this is a problem of reforming indigenous and European-imposed systems of land tenure, but Africa has also been the scene of a number of dramatic failures to accelerate economic growth by large-scale schemes of agricultural development. The Ground-nut Scheme in East Africa, the Niger Project in Nigeria and the Poultry Scheme in Gambia are notorious examples of failures which have been ascribed to a whole range of causes varying from soil poverty and uncertain rainfall to the economics of mechanization. Less publicity, however, has been given to the more successful schemes, both large and small, such as the Gezira Scheme of the Sudan and the peasant *paysannat* schemes of the Congo.

In all but a few African countries, notably South Africa, Rhodesia and Egypt, manufacturing industry has reached only rudimentary levels of development. This is largely due to lack of capital, skilled labour, and domestic and external markets. But it is also due, as is much of the low agricultural output, to inadequate transportation.

Africa has nearly 30,000 miles (45,780 km) of railways of different gauges, but relatively dense networks exist only in the former French territories of North Africa and in South Africa, which alone possesses over a quarter of the total length of track. The most complete road systems are also in South Africa and the more populous parts of the Mediterranean littoral. On the other hand, the best waterways for navigation are in tropical Africa: the Congo and its tributaries, the Niger and Benue, the Great Lakes of East Africa, and the Nile. In these and many other parts of the continent, however, the economic infrastructure is being gradually built up, particularly by modernizing communications: road and rail networks are being extended; waterways, coastal approaches and ports are being improved; power potential, especially in hydro-electricity, is being developed; and most large cities in Africa are now on international air routes.

But perhaps the most fundamental economic problem in Africa today arises from the fact that the economies of a majority of African countries depend upon what has been called the colonial pattern of trade: their prosperity is excessively dependent upon the export of a few primary

2

products – mostly minerals and agricultural produce such as cocoa, cotton and palm oil – and they are obliged to import most of the manufactured goods they require. Their economies are subject to damaging fluctuations in the world prices of a very limited number of products and there are virtually no established overseas markets for such manufactured goods as they do produce. There is a pressing need for developing African countries to gain more effective access to existing channels of world trade, but this may prove impossible unless the industrially developed nations make a determined effort to lower existing commercial barriers. Even then there remains the difficulty that many African states are suspicious of trading agreements, or of entering into such groupings as the *EEC*, on the grounds that they only represent a form of neo-colonialism.

National Unity
The problem of creating an effective sense of national unity in any African state is not simply a political matter: it is also part of a wider complex of economic, social, historical and psychological issues. The obstacles to national unity are many and varied. In Congo Kinshasa, for example, they include the sheer size of the country, the low density of population, the fragmented tribal pattern of the population, the lack of any established élite, the poverty of internal communications, and the strikingly peripheral distribution of mineral resources and economic development. A further fundamental difficulty is that few African states today have any traditional awareness of their identity as independent political units. Although, as we have seen, a number of large and independent African states did exist in pre-European times, no modern nation in Africa south of the Sahara coincides either with the territorial extent of one of these early states or even with a tribal area. Tribalism, in fact, far from providing the basis of national identity, is one of the most powerfully divisive forces in the continent today. It accounts for the early federalist forms of government in Nigeria, Congo and Uganda; the troubles in the Buganda Province of Uganda in 1966; and the attempted secession of Biafra from Nigeria in 1967. It delayed progress towards independence in many countries, especially for example in Kenya, where it provided a major hindrance in the prolonged and intricate negotiations over the extension of authority to the Africans.

The force of tribalism may be gradually lessening throughout Africa, but tribal allegiances, expressed through loyalty to the chief, still outweigh the idea of national loyalty in many newly independent African countries. However, the effectiveness of tribalism in delaying the growth of national unity varies greatly from area to area and, like so much else in Africa, is not susceptible to easy generalization. While strongly centralized political institutions have long existed among certain tribes, such as the Yoruba of West Africa, many other tribes lack a tradition of centralized authority; and this directly affects the degree to which a population is prepared to accept national as distinct from tribal control.

The problem of how best to overcome the divisive effects of tribalism and foster the growth of national unity is reflected in the form of government adopted by independent African states. The most significant political development of recent years has been the rapid emergence of the one-party system, in its various guises, as the most widely adopted form of government. Many Western observers regard this trend as an undesirable feature of contemporary African politics, implying as it does a revolt against the 'Westminster model' of parliamentary democracy and carrying with it the seeds of totalitarian dictatorship. It is also suggested that opposition to the one-party state can only be expressed through violence; and it is argued that this explains the large number of military coups which have taken place in African countries since independence. Between 1960 and 1966 twelve elected African governments were replaced by military juntas.

On the other hand, it is not impossible for a one-party state to provide for a peaceful change of government: in Tanzania, for example, such provisions are written into the constitution. Military coups, moreover, have not been confined to the one-party states, having occurred also in Nigeria, for long described as one of the most democratic countries in Africa. Many political parties, in fact, appear to be evolving a new form of government that is neither totalitarian nor strictly in the tradition of multi-party parliamentary democracy, but rather something in between. And indeed there is much in the traditional mould of African political institutions – notably the desire to identify leadership with a person rather than a party – that argues against the 'democratic' multi-party system. As one commentator has put it: 'a multi-party system in an unsophisticated society places a frightful premium on political irresponsibility' (Quigg, 1964:327). Others argue for the one-party state in Africa on the grounds that African society generally lacks rigid class divisions (on which competing political parties are so often based in developed societies) and that a multi-party system in an African nation tends to crystallize along tribal lines, as is so clearly the case in Nigeria.

Boundary Problems

The emergence of independent states in Africa has been remarkable not only for the speed of political change but also because it has resulted in very few boundary changes. In recent years Tangier and Spanish Morocco, including the southern zone of the former Spanish protectorate (Tarfaya), have been incorporated in Morocco; British Togoland and British Northern Cameroons have disappeared into Ghana and Nigeria respectively; British

Somaliland has become part of Somalia; and Eritrea and Ethiopia have federated. For the most part, however, colonial boundaries have, despite all their imperfections, been accepted as the territorial frameworks for independence in modern Africa. It was early recognized that independence would only ever be granted by the several colonial powers on the basis of existing territorial units, and that serious economic difficulties – in, for example, communications, currencies, and trading associations – lay in the way of any immediate attempt to redraw the political boundaries of Africa. However arbitrary these political units may have been as geographical entities, they already existed on the ground and on maps, and it was within their limits that the newly independent African governments had to foster the sense of nationhood.

The national boundaries of independent Africa are therefore substantially the same as the political divisions of colonial Africa. Nevertheless numerous boundary problems exist, although it is doubtful whether the arbitrary nature of any African boundary is the root cause of friction between the states it divides. Usually a boundary only becomes politically significant when friction is generated by some other cause: 'Il n'y a pas de problèmes de frontières. Il n'est que des problèmes de Nations' (Ancel, 1938: 196).

Some of Africa's boundary problems arise from the large number and complex pattern of state territorial limits. Even before the recent phase of rapid political change Africa had the longest land boundaries of any continent: 28,670 miles (45,872 km) as compared with 26,113 miles (41,784 km) in Asia (Boggs, 1940). Africa is in fact the most politically fragmented continent. Many of its states have five or six neighbours; the Sudan has eight and Congo Kinshasa no less than nine. Furthermore, the pattern of nation states reflects the compactness of the continent and the fact that it has the shortest coastline in relation to area: only Egypt, Morocco, Somalia and South Africa command more than one sea-front. Most of the littoral states have only a narrow coastal front and widen as they extend inland, the most extreme example being Congo Kinshasa. In addition fourteen states – Mali, Niger, Upper Volta, Chad, Central African Republic, Uganda, Zambia, Rhodesia, Malawi, Rwandi, Burundi, Botswana, Swaziland and Lesotho – are completely landlocked. This is a greater number than exist in the whole of the rest of the world. They occupy almost a quarter of the continent and contain just under 15 per cent of its population, so that the problems associated with landlocked states are nowadays peculiarly African ones. The complexity of the political map is further increased by the persistence of European-administered coastal enclaves and offshore islands, notably Cabinda, Spanish Guinea (Rio Muni), São Tomé, Principé, Annobón, Portuguese Guinea, Spanish Sahara, Ifni,

Ceuta, Melilla and French Somaliland – most of which are Portuguese and Spanish territories on or off the west coast where the impact of Iberian maritime expansion was first felt. Some problems, particularly of communications, also arise from the awkward shape of certain states, as with the bow-tie shape of Mali, the L-shape of Somalia, the narrow waist across Zambia, the Katanga pedicle of Congo Kinshasa and the Caprivi strip of South West Africa.

Boundary problems also arise from the nature of the territory through which they have been drawn. Many countries, especially in West Africa, represent colonial extensions from coastal strips or nodes and, as is well illustrated by Nigeria and Gambia, their frontiers reflect the former concentration of trading interests at the coast, the difficulties of inland penetration, and the desire of the Europeans to control river mouths. The adoption of watersheds as African boundaries was indeed largely due to the fact that early exploration was concentrated along the rivers; and it was not unusual for colonial powers to agree to adopt a watershed as a boundary before it had even been located or mapped. Where a river or stream was itself chosen as a boundary, problems have often arisen. In the western Sudan between Darfur and Wadai, for example, people move to the wadis during the seven to eight months' dry season; yet the boundary between Sudan and the former territories of French Equatorial Africa was sited for much of its length along the Wadi Kaja and the Wadi Tini. Rather than functioning as a divide, therefore, it acts as a magnet along which and across which there is considerable movement (Barbour, 1961: 322).

Still more significant are the problems that arise where boundaries pass through homogeneous tribal territories. Some of the most striking examples of this phenomenon are provided by those boundaries which bisect the tribal lands of the Hausa, Ewe, Zande, Bakongo, Masai and Somali peoples. Some of the problems associated with these peoples are discussed in later chapters, and Barbour has considered elsewhere the interesting case of the Azande who are dispersed along the Nile–Congo watershed, 29 per cent of them in Sudan, 68 per cent in Congo Kinshasa, and 3 per cent in the Central African Republic (*ibid*: 319).

To overcome the problems associated with national boundaries in Africa it has often been suggested that they should be redrawn 'more in accordance with geographical realities'. This may appear desirable in theory, but in practice it is virtually impossible to demarcate any wholly satisfactory boundary line and it is difficult to avoid the conclusion – which is supported by more detailed discussion in several of the following essays – that the state boundaries of Africa must remain substantially as they are. There is in fact no widespread desire for a fundamental revision of the political map and some African leaders see in the existing pattern of arbitrary boundaries an opportunity actually to promote co-operation: 'we must use the existing pattern of states as an instrument for unifying Africa and not as an instrument for dividing Africa' (Nyerere, 1963: 5). The need to overcome boundary problems has been repeatedly invoked in support of policies of closer co-operation or unification, especially where traditional migration and trade continues to take place across a boundary line.

Perhaps the main reason why there are relatively few serious border disputes in Africa at present is that most of the boundaries do not yet mark the effective limits of national territory: they still function as rather ill-defined frontier zones. Very many African states are divided by these incompletely controlled buffer zones, across which much human movement takes place. Indeed the actual concept of a formal boundary line is essentially of European colonial origin in Africa. The traditional African concept was one of frontier marches: in North Africa, for example, the geographical limits of the Moslem states were only vaguely circumscribed according to the allegiance of the people (*umma* or 'community of believers') to their spiritual rulers. Today, however, the state and its boundaries provide the framework for nation-building throughout Africa, and, as existing frontier zones shrink to become lines of firm authority, it is likely that border disputes will increase in number and severity.

Internal regional and provincial boundaries give rise to problems comparable to those associated with the international boundaries of Africa. However, apart from the work of Prescott (1965) and a few other scholars, internal boundary problems have as yet been little studied. In view of the need to overcome the strong centrifugal forces at work within many African states the overriding problem associated with internal boundaries is the extent to which they help or inhibit the development of a sense of national unity. In Nigeria the military government established in 1966 at first abolished all regional boundaries in the vain hope of dissolving traditional regional allegiances, but in 1967 the country was re-divided into twelve new state units. In Kenya internal divisions resulted in the delineation of six new, essentially ethnic, regions, each of which was originally intended to exercise a measure of administrative autonomy. A seventh, northeastern region was later added as a concession to the Somali problem. But it is now clear that the projected powers of the seven regions will not be fully exercised, although the divisions still remain. As planning units they suffer from the major disadvantage that in a country where water is crucial they cut across the main drainage basins (McMaster, 1966: 4). When Congo Kinshasa became independent in 1960 it consisted of six large, strongly contrasted provinces, but this number was increased to twenty-two, and later reduced to eleven, in an attempt to break down regional poliarities. In Libya a similar but abortive attempt was made to foster a sense of nationhood by replacing the three large and long-established provinces of Tripolitania, Cyrenaica and Fezzan by ten smaller administrative regions.

World Interest in Africa

One of the principal reasons for the present intensity of international interest in Africa is the actual and potential value to the world of the continent's resources, especially its minerals and agricultural products. In addition to a wide range of metallic and non-metallic minerals Africa is now known to possess large reserves of energy-producing minerals, notably the huge deposits of uranium ore at Shinkolobwe in Congo Kinshasa, and the production of oil and natural gas is increasing rapidly in Algeria, Libya and Nigeria, from where much of it is exported to Western Europe. Trade in primary agricultural products – notably cocoa, coffee, groundnuts, cotton, hides and skins, and palm oil – is also of great importance to a number of Western countries. African trade is in fact essentially oriented to the North Atlantic Basin: 80 per cent of its exports by value and 75 per cent of its imports are with Maritime Europe or Anglo-America. Furthermore, it is now widely appreciated in the developed world that the potentially large African market cannot be utilized to the full while living standards there remain so low. Yet economic development cannot proceed in Africa unless world markets for African products are both secure and rising, or unless alternative market opportunities are provided. This cardinal problem of economic development is therefore not one that can be solved by any individual African nation acting alone. It is a continental and world problem which can only be resolved by joint agreement on trade, such as the proposals now being put forward by *UNCTAD* (United Nations Trade and Development Conference, 1964).

Complementary to the problem of trade is the question of aid. Most economic aid has been sporadic and quite inadequate for the needs of the recipient countries. Much of it has been channelled through the World Bank which at first concentrated on the modernization and extension of transport facilities but has more recently begun to finance the development of electric power potential and the commodity-producing sectors of the economy, notably agriculture, irrigation and mineral production. The World Bank also provides technical assistance and it has set up the International Development Association as an affiliate organization with the purpose of making 'soft' loans available to developing countries. Financial aid is also given through other United Nations agencies, such as the United Nations Special Fund, through the British Development Corporation, and through the French Fonds d'Aide et de Co-opération (*FAC*) and Fonds d'Investissement pour le Développement Economique et Social des Territoires d'Outre Mer (*FIDES*). The United States has assisted many African countries, and the Soviet Union has provided aid to Egypt, Ethiopia, Somalia and Guinea. China, too, has a stake in Africa, having advanced credits to Ghana, Guinea and Tanzania. Aid has also been provided by ex-colonial powers, such as West Germany, Italy and Belgium, which no longer have any territorial possessions in the continent, and both the Middle Eastern Arab states and Israel have shown greatly increased interest in independent Africa. While the need for aid – through trade, loans or technical assistance – is undisputed, difficulties often arise over the political motives of the donor nations. Aid is perhaps seldom if ever given for entirely non-political reasons and it is not surprising that the recipient nations often interpret the quickening interest in Africa shown by the developed countries as a form of neo-colonialism.

Another, less important, reason for the outside world's interest in Africa is the strategic significance of the continent, which can be regarded as the

Fig. 3. Africa, 1967 (dates indicate year of attaining independence)

politically fragmented outer fringe of Mackinder's 'World Island'. Mackinder first described Africa as a 'Southern Heartland' and later fore-saw a possible geopolitical link with South America (Mackinder, 1942); but Cohen expects Africa to remain part of the 'Trade-Dependent Mari-time World' and also suggests that the character of the continent as a political shatterbelt may be accentuated by an increase of Indian influence along the eastern margin (Cohen, 1964). However, judged by more prac-tical criteria, such as the anxiety of world powers to obtain military bases, overflying rights and access to vital raw materials, it appears that the strategic importance of Africa may be declining (Scipio, 1965).

Lastly there is the world's intense and increasing interest in the political affairs of Africa. This arises partly from the sheer pace of recent political change (Fig. 3) and partly from the numerical significance of African votes in the United Nations. But it is also due to the fact that the issue of colour prejudice seems most likely to come to a head in Africa. The most explosive political situation in the continent at present is the clash between the independent, African-controlled states and the white minorities that rule both South Africa and the remaining colonial territories, particularly Angola and Moçambique, and Rhodesia. The continuance of these white minority governments in southern Africa is – to the newly independent African nations – a constant and unwelcome reminder of their colonial past. And, although political change has occurred on an unprecedented scale during the last decade, Africa is likely to remain in its present unsettled phase of transition from colonial domination to national independence based on universal suffrage until the remaining white minority govern-ments have given way to majority rule throughout the continent.

TABLE I.I *Area and Population of African Countries*
(*data from* United Nations Demographic Yearbook 1965, *New York, 1966*)

	Area (1,000 km²)	Estimated Population 1964 (thousands)	Population Density (per km²)
1. North Africa			
Libya	1,760	1,599	1
Tunisia	164	4,565	28
Algeria	2,382	10,975	5
Morocco	445	12,959	29
Mauritania	1,031	900	1
Spanish Sahara	266	48	0
Ifni	2	52	35
Ceuta (city)	–	78	4,130
Melilla (city)	–	78	6,527
Total	6,050	31,214	
2. Northeast Africa			
Egypt (U.A.R.)	1,000	28,900	29
Sudan	2,506	13,180	5
Ethiopia	1,222	22,200	18
Somalia	638	2,420	4
French Somaliland	22	70	3
Total	5,388	66,770	
3. East Africa			
Kenya	583	9,104	16
Uganda	236	7,367	31
Tanzania	940	10,325	12
Rwanda	26	3,018	115
Burundi	28	2,650	95
Total	1,813	32,464	
4. West Africa			
Senegal	196	3,400	17
Gambia	11	324	29
Portuguese Guinea	36	525	15
Guinea	246	3,420	14
Sierra Leone	72	2,240	31
Liberia	111	1,041	9
Ivory Coast	322	3,750	12
Mali	1,202	4,485	4
Upper Volta	274	4,650	17
Ghana	239	7,537	32

TABLE I.I—*continued*

	Area (1,000 km²)	Estimated Population 1963 (thousands)	Population Density (per km²)
Togo	57	1,603	28
Dahomey	113	2,300	20
Nigeria	924	56,400	61
Niger	1,267	3,237	3
Total	5,070	94,912	

5. *Equatorial Africa*

	Area (1,000 km²)	Estimated Population 1963 (thousands)	Population Density (per km²)
Chad	1,284	3,300	3
Cameroun	475	5,103	11
Central African Republic	623	1,320	2
Spanish Equatorial Africa	28	263	9
São Tomé and Principé	1	58	58
Gabon	268	459	2
Congo Brazzaville	342	826	2
Congo Kinshasa	2,345	15,300	7
Total	5,366	26,629	

6. *Southern Africa*

	Area (1,000 km²)	Estimated Population 1963 (thousands)	Population Density (per km²)
Angola (with Cabinda)	1,247	5,084	4
Zambia	753	3,600	5
Malawi	119	3,900	33
Moçambique	783	6,872	9
Rhodesia	389	4,140	11
Botswana	570	543	1
South West Africa	824	564	1
South Africa	1,221	17,474	14
Lesotho	30	733	24
Swaziland	17	288	17
Malagasy	587	6,180	11
Total	6,540	49,478	

Total Africa	30,258	310,000	

References and Select Bibliography

ALLAN, W. 1965. *The African Husbandman*, Oliver and Boyd, Edinburgh and London.

ANCEL, J. 1938. *Les frontiéres*, Paris.

BARBOUR, K. M. 1961. A geographical analysis of boundaries in inter-tropical Africa. In BARBOUR, K. M., and R. M. PROTHERO (eds.). 1961. *Essays on African Population*, Routledge, London: 303–323.

BARTH, H. 1857. *Travels and Discoveries in North and Central Africa*, London.

BAUMANNN, H. and D. WESTERMANN. 1948. *Les peuples et les civilisations de l'Afrique*, Hachette, Paris.

BIEBUYCK, D. (ed.). 1963. *African Agrarian Systems*, Leopoldville.

BOGGS, S. W. 1940. *International Boundaries*, New York.

BREZEZINSKI, Z. 1963. *Africa and the Communist World*, University Press, Stanford.

BUCHMAN, J. 1962. *L'Afrique noire indépendante*, Presses Universitaires, Paris.

CARTER, G. M. 1960. *Independence for Africa*, Praeger, New York.

COHEN, S. B. 1964. *Geography and Politics in a Divided World*, Methuen, London.

CORNEVIN R. 1962. *Histoire de l'Afrique*, Presses Universitaires, Paris.

DUMONT, R. 1962. *L'Afrique Noire est Mal Partie*, Hachette, Paris.

FAGE, J. D. 1958. *An Atlas of African History*, Arnold, London.

FITZGERALD, W. 1961. *Africa*, Methuen, London, 9th ed.

FORDHAM. P. 1965. *The Geography of African Affairs*, Penguin Books, Harmondsworth.

FORTES, M. and E. E. EVANS-PRITCHARD (eds.). 1940. *African Political Systems*, Oxford University Press, London.

GONCHAROV, L. 1963. New forms of colonialism in Africa. *Journal of Modern African Studies*, Vol. 1: 467–474.

HAILEY, Lord. 1957. *Africa Survey, Revised 1956*, Oxford University Press, London.

HAMDAN, G. 1963. The political map of the new Africa. *Geographical Review*, Vol. 53: 418–439.

HANCE, W. A. 1964. *The Geography of Modern Africa*, Columbia University Press, New York.

HERSKOVITS, M. J. 1944. Native self-government. *Foreign Affairs*, Vol. 23: 491–504.

1962. *The Human Factor in Changing Africa*, Routledge, London.

HERTSLETT, Sir E. 1909. *The Map of Africa by Treaty*, London, 3rd ed.

HODGSON, R. D. and E. A. STONEMAN. 1963. *The Changing Map of Africa*, Van Nostrand, New York.

HOVET, T. 1963. *Africa in the United Nations*, Evanston, Ill.

HUXLEY, E. 1949. British aims in Africa. *Foreign Affairs*, Vol. 28: 116–128.

KIMBLE, G. H. T. 1960. *Tropical Africa*, Twentieth Century Fund, New York, 2 vols.

LEGUM, C. (ed.). 1961. *Africa, A Handbook to the Continent*, Methuen, London.

LUGARD, F. D. *Lord*. 1926. The white man's task in tropical Africa. *Foreign Affairs*, Oct., in Quigg, 1964: 5–16.

MACKINDER, *Sir* H. J. 1942. The round world and the winning of the peace. *Foreign Affairs*, Vol. 21: 595–605.

MBOYA, T. 1963. *Freedom and After*, Cassell, London.

—— 1963. The party system and democracy in Africa. *Foreign Affairs*, Vol. 42: 172–181.

MCEWAN, J. M. and R. B. SUTCLIFFE (eds.). 1965. *The Study of Africa*,

MCMASTER, D. N. 1966. Kenya. *Focus*. Methuen, London.

MURDOCK, G. P. 1959. *Africa, Its Peoples and Their Culture History*, McGraw Hill, New York.

NEL, A. 1959. Some problems in compiling a population map of Africa. *Journal for Geography*, Vol. 1: 66–68 and map.

NEWBURY, C. W. 1961. *The Western Slave Coast and Its Rulers*, Clarendon Press, Oxford.

NYERERE, J. 1963. A United States of Africa. *Journal of Modern African Studies*, Vol. 1: 1–6.

OLIVER, R. and J. D. FAGE. 1962. *A Short History of Africa*, Penguin Books, Harmondsworth.

OXFORD REGIONAL ECONOMIC ATLAS OF AFRICA. 1965. London.

PERHAM, M. 1951. The British problem in Africa. *Foreign Affairs*, Vol. 30: 131–144.

—— 1963. *The Colonial Reckoning*, Fontana, London.

PHILLIPS, J. 1959. *Agriculture and Ecology in Africa*, Faber, London.

POST, K. W. J. 1964. *The New States of West Africa*, Penguin Books, Harmondsworth.

POTEKHIN, I. I. 1963. Land relations in African countries. *Journal of Modern African Studies*, Vol. 1: 39–59.

PRESCOTT, J. R. V. 1965. *The Geography of Frontiers and Boundaries*, Hutchinson, London.

QUIGG, P. W. (ed.). 1964. *Africa: A Foreign Affairs Reader*, New York.

REYNER, A. S. 1964. *Current Boundary Problems in Africa*, Pittsburgh.

SCIPIO. 1965. *The Colonial Legacy*, London.

SELIGMAN, C. G. 1957. *Races of Africa*, London, 3rd ed.

STAMP, *Sir* L. D. 1963. *Africa, A Study in Tropical Development*, Wiley, New York, Revised Edition.

STEEL, R. W. 1961. The towns of tropical Africa. In BARBOUR and PROTHERO, *op. cit:* 249–278.

WORTHINGTON, E. B. 1958. *Science in the Development of Africa*, London.

1 North Africa *(excluding Egypt)*

1 North Africa (*excluding Egypt*)

By D. R. HARRIS

Geographical Diversity in Unity

The expressions Near East, Middle East and Far East slip readily off European tongues to denote familiar if vaguely circumscribed geographical areas. Looking westward, through Arab eyes, the lands of North Africa fall naturally into a comparable sequence: *el-Maghreb-el-Adna*, the Near West; *el-Maghreb-el-Ausat*, the Middle West; and *el-Maghreb-el-Aqsa*, the Far West. These three 'Wests' emerged as distinct regions of the Arab world soon after the Islamic conquest in the seventh century A.D. and they coincide closely with the independent North African states of today. Libya and Tunisia comprise *el-Maghreb-el-Adna*, Algeria *el-Maghreb-el-Ausat* and Morocco and Mauritania *el-Maghreb-el-Aqsa*.[1]

To the Arabs the Maghreb as a whole was and is clearly differentiated from the rest of Moslem Africa. Neither the Egyptians, nor the Islamized peoples living along the southern fringe of the Sahara, have had close and enduring political links with the Maghreb, although briefly in the past Cairo has exercised loose sovereignty over the eastern Maghreb and Morocco has extended a tenuous hold as far as the middle Niger.

The cultural distinctiveness of North Africa, which sets it apart from the rest of the continent, springs partly from this history of independent political evolution. But it has been accentuated by the role of the Sahara as a racial transition zone between the Negro populations of West and Central Africa and the mainly white inhabitants of the Maghreb. There has been a Negroid element present in the population of North Africa from prehistoric times but white people have formed a majority since at least the beginning of recorded history. The unique character of the Maghreb also arises from the fact that it is the only part of Africa to have experienced intimate and sustained contact with Europe, through trade and war, since classical antiquity. The resulting interchange of ideas, skills and people benefited civilization on both shores of the Mediterranean and made of the Maghreb a cultural salient in Africa from which many new influences filtered southward across the Sahara.

[1] Historically *el-Maghreb-el-Aqsa* has either included or excluded Mauritania and the Spanish colonies of Ifni and Spanish Sahara according to variations in the extent of Moroccan control over the westernmost desert.

The cultural uniqueness of North Africa finds its echo in the physical isolation of the Maghreb at the northwestern confines of the continent. The Atlas mountain system, with its intermontane basins and high plateaus, stretches from southwestern Morocco to Tunisia and forms the rugged core of the region. Northward only a narrow and discontinuous strip of lowland separates the mountains from the Mediterranean. At either end of the mountain core, in western Morocco and eastern Tunisia, fertile coastal plains incline gently towards the sea. Southward the last ridges of the Atlas overlook the gravel, sand and rock surfaces of the Sahara which stretch uninterruptedly from the Atlantic coast of Mauritania to the Mediterranean coast of Libya. Environed by sea and desert, North Africa is known to the Arabs as *djezira-el-Maghreb*, the island of the West. It is an apt description of this region in which, thanks both to the Saharan barrier and the proximity of Europe, different cultural elements have blended to form a pattern of life and landscape unique in Africa.

In its continental context, and particularly when compared with tropical Africa south of the Sahara, the Maghreb exhibits striking physical and cultural homogeneity. But on closer examination this apparent unity dissolves into a complex of diverse landscapes and subtly differing ways of life. Within a physical environment that itself displays great variety of climate and surface form, successive peoples have spread and intermingled, gradually building up the cultural mosaic that characterizes the region today.

LINEAMENTS OF THE LAND

The seven political units that comprise the Maghreb – Libya, Tunisia, Algeria, Morocco, Ifni, Spanish Sahara and Mauritania – occupy just over one-fifth of the African continent, but almost 90 per cent of this enormous area lies within the arid wastes of the Sahara. Together the seven territories share over 4500 miles (7240 km) of Mediterranean and Atlantic coastline, and, appearing to turn their backs on the desert, all have their administrative capitals on or very near the coast (Fig. 4). However, the greater part of both the Mediterranean and the Atlantic littoral is inhospitable to shipping. Much of the coast is either cliffed, or low, sandy and exposed. There are few offshore islands or natural harbours to provide shelter – the magnificent deep-water port of Bizerta being the principal exception – and the countries of the Maghreb have traditionally been land-based rather than dependent upon sea power. Indeed it was not until the French occupation in 1912 that the capital of Morocco shifted from the imperial cities of the interior – Fez, Meknès and Marrakesh – to the coast. The only extensive shoreline offering sheltered anchorage and easy access to the interior is in eastern Tunisia, stretching from the Gulf of Tunis to the island of Djerba, and it was there

Opposite: **Fig. 4. North Africa** (The Maghreb)

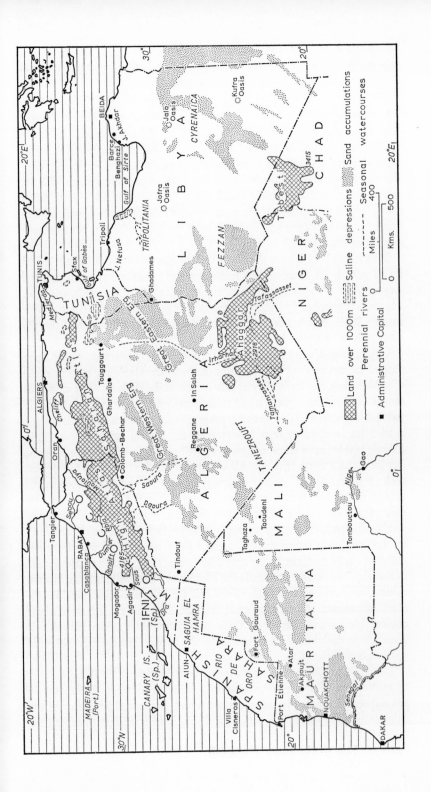

that the first and only sea-borne empire ever to arise in North Africa was founded by the Phoenicians in the first millennium B.C.

The Inner Maghreb

The mountain core of the Maghreb and the fringing coastal lowlands occupy only a tenth of the total area of North Africa but contain an overwhelming majority of its population. This zone, which can be thought of as the inner Maghreb, is made up of the Atlas mountain system with its associated plateaus and plains, and although it reaches some 1200 miles (1930 km) from southern Morocco eastward to the Gulf of Gabès it seldom exceeds 200 miles (320 km) in depth from the coast inland to the northern margin of the Sahara.

This crumpled fringe at the northwestern extremity of the African shield forms part of the complex of Alpine mountain chains that surrounds the western Mediterranean basin. The rugged arc of the Rif Atlas in northern Morocco is matched by the lofty crescent of the Baetic Cordillera in southeastern Spain, and in northern Tunisia the fold lines of the Tell Atlas die away only to reappear in the mountains of Sicily

Uplift, folding and faulting in Tertiary and Quaternary times have shaped the major structural features of the inner Maghreb, but the rocks of which they are built vary much in age and lithology. The principal ranges of the Atlas system trend from southwest to northeast in roughly parallel alignment. They become progressively younger in age from the Anti-Atlas in southwestern Morocco to the central spine of the High, Middle and Saharan Atlas, and on to the Rif and Tell Atlas overlooking the Mediterranean coast (Fig. 5). All except the Anti-Atlas consist of folded rock of Mesozoic age, chiefly resistant limestones and sandstones in the central ranges and softer schists and slates in the Rif and Tell Atlas. By contrast the Anti-Atlas is a fractured massif of much more ancient rocks: Archaean quartzites and Palaeozoic limestones and sandstones. Within and on the margins of the mountain complex there are other blocks of ancient resistant rocks thought to be fragments of a once extensive Hercynian peneplain. The largest of these is the Moroccan Meseta which has deflected some of the northwestern folds of the Middle Atlas into an atypical north-south alignment. Along persistent fracture lines, at the edges of these ancient blocks and elsewhere, there have been outpourings of volcanic lavas whose dark hues stand out against the predominantly light-coloured sedimentary rocks of the mountains.

Tertiary and Quaternary earth movements have resulted in subsidence as well as uplift. Downwarped troughs, filled with great thicknesses of alluvial sediments, are found scattered round the coastal periphery of the Atlas mountain system. The largest and most numerous occur beneath the

Opposite: **Fig. 5. The Inner Maghreb**

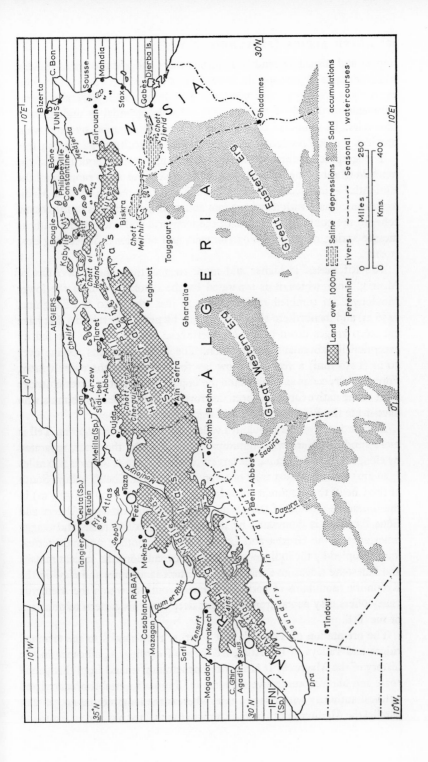

steppes and coastal lowland of Tunisia; others underlie the plains of Bône and Mitidja in Algeria and the lower valleys of the rivers Sebou and Sous in Morocco. Surface water permeates readily into their generally coarse sediments so that these troughs have valuable potential as underground reservoirs. In semi-arid central Tunisia their exploitation by deep wells provides a much needed supply of water for agricultural and urban use.

Topographic contrasts between the three major structural units of the inner Maghreb – the Rif and Tell Atlas, the central Atlas ranges and the Anti-Atlas – are accentuated by the gradual progression from a Mediterranean climate with its winter rain and mild temperatures in the coastal zone, to the continental régime of the semi-arid and arid interior with its meagre spring rains, scorching summers and occasional desiccating dust storms.

The Rif massif is higher and more rugged than the Tell Atlas of Algeria, from which it is separated by the desolate plain of the lower Moulouya. Its tumbled ramparts rise to just over 8000 ft (Tidighine, 2456 m) and its northern slopes are gashed by numerous streams that have cut steep gorges down to the Mediterranean. These streams are fed by exceptionally abundant precipitation. The higher summits receive over 50 in (1250 mm) a year and snow lies for several months every winter. Forests of fir, cedar and oak clothe the upper slopes, but at lower altitudes most of the native forest has been destroyed by the Berber inhabitants who have made the Rif their stronghold since prehistoric times.

Eastward, across the Moulouya valley, the relief of the Algerian Tell is more subdued. Narrow, longitudinal ranges parallel the coast, separated by elongated alluvial plains, the largest of which extends for over 200 miles (320 km) from the coast west of Oran to the lower Cheliff valley. South of the Cheliff the mountains broaden and rise to over 6500 ft (1985 m) in the limestone bastion of the Ouarsenis massif; and between Algiers and Bône the coast is dominated by the ancient crystalline rocks and craggy limestones of the Greater and Lesser Kabylies, another mountain retreat long occupied by the indigenous Berbers. Beyond Bône the ancient massifs and limestone ridges give way to less resistant sandstones and clays in the Kroumirie mountains of northern Tunisia, south of which the Medjerda valley offers easy access from the coast deep into this eastern termination of the Tell.

The orientation of Tunisia's east coast, at right-angles to the terminal ridges and valleys of the Atlas, has been of cardinal significance in the history of the Maghreb. It has invited penetration inland from that genial coast and allowed successive invaders of Tunisia to establish centralized political authority with relative ease; whereas the longitudinal ranges that parallel the Mediterranean from Bizerta to Ceuta have blocked access to the interior, denied extensive hinterlands to the coastal towns of Algeria, and encouraged political fragmentation.

With its rocky coast, steep slopes and scanty vegetation the landscape of the Tell has a distinctly Mediterranean aspect. Uncleared remnants of forest remain only on the highest massifs, nourished by over 40 in (1000 mm) of rain a year. The lower hills, where they are not cultivated, carry open woodland of pine and evergreen oak or a meagre cover of aromatic shrubs and herbs. Following heavy rain, surface runoff is rapid and the marks of intense erosion scar many hillsides. Despite the long summer drought, rainfall is generally sufficient to allow cultivation without irrigation. Semiarid conditions only prevail in the Moulouya valley, the Oran–Cheliff plain and along the southern margin of the Tell where annual precipitation falls below 16 in (400 mm).

Between the southern foothills of the Rif and the northern ranges of the Middle Atlas the narrow Taza corridor provides the only lowland route between Algeria and the fertile plains of Atlantic Morocco. From the beginning of the Christian era to the Second World War it has funnelled the movement of invading armies. Near its western approach are the ruins of the Roman provincial capital of Volubilis as well as the modern city and former Islamic capital of Fez.

At the farthest limit of the Maghreb the lowland of Atlantic Morocco lies enclosed between the western slopes of the Atlas and the coast. However, it has not been a cultural cul-de-sac because, since earliest times, important routes have linked it with other populous regions, across both the desert to the south and the Strait of Gibraltar to the north. It is a productive area of diverse topography, crossed by the longest and fullest rivers of the Maghreb, which, together with substantial reserves of underground water, have made possible the development of large-scale irrigation schemes. Backing the dune-bordered coast is a series of rich alluvial plains. The most northerly is the Gharb, occupying the flood-plain of the river Sebou; farther down the coast the lower Chaouïa plain forms the immediate hinterland of Casablanca; and south of the Oum er Rbia the Doukkala plains stretch for 150 miles (240 km) to Mogador. These level grainlands give way inland to more varied relief. Three ancient Hercynian massifs are interposed between the coastal plains and the Atlas. Largest is the Moroccan Meseta, which extends from the coast between Rabat and Casablanca to the Middle Atlas, and rises inland from a low cultivated plateau to a rugged wilderness of wooded foothills. The much smaller Hercynian fragments of the Rehamna and the Djebilet adjoin the middle courses of the rivers Oum er Rbia and Tensift, the upper courses of which flow across irrigated alluvial plains – the Tadla and the Haouz – which nestle close to the foot of the Atlas. Dominating the Haouz plain, at the point where once prosperous trans-Saharan trade routes terminated after crossing the High Atlas, stands the former capital of Marrakesh. The elaborate architecture of its palaces and mosques evokes the splendour of its imperial past and it remains today the principal city of southern Morocco. The northern half of the Atlantic lowland enjoys a Mediterranean climate with over 16 in (400 mm) annual rainfall, and most of it is intensively cultivated. At one time it supported extensive forests of cork oak, but today only the degraded woodland of Mamora, north of Rabat, remains to suggest the former abundance of this valuable tree. South of the Oum er Rbia semi-arid conditions prevail and dry-farmed cereal lands are interspersed with patches of irrigation wherever sufficient surface or ground water is available.

Together the Middle and High Atlas constitute the most formidable mountain barrier in North Africa. Over 400 miles (640 km) long and seldom less than 50 miles (80 km) wide, they isolate the Atlantic lowland core of Morocco which, behind their sheltering wall, has developed a tradition of political independence from the rest of the Maghreb. They have also served as a vast mountain refuge for the native Berber population, a cultural enclave in which tribal ways of life persist. Physically the mountains divide the relatively well-watered Atlantic façade from the barren steppe and desert to east and south, just as in another 'Far West' the American Sierra Nevada cuts off the Nevada desert from the 'Mediterranean' lands of coastal California.

Dividing the Atlantic and Mediterranean catchments of the Sebou and the Moulouya, the Middle Atlas forms a complex mountain mass rising to heights of over 10,500 ft (Bou Naceur, 3290 m). The highest peaks crown folded ridges that overlook the semi-arid Moulouya valley to the east, but westward these are replaced by limestone plateaus whose whiteness is relieved by green spreads of oak and cedar forest and the dark patches of occasional small volcanic cones and lava flows. In the summer semi-nomadic Berber tribesmen pasture their flocks in the mountains, the higher slopes of which are snow-covered for several months every winter.

Southward, beyond the narrowing divide that separates the headwaters of the Moulouya and the Oum er Rbia, the mountain barrier attains its most spectacular development in the massive bulk of the High Atlas. Stretching nearly 500 miles (800 km), from Cape Ghir on the Atlantic coast to the eastern flank of the Moulouya valley, and reaching heights of over 13,000 ft (Tubkal, 4165 m), the High Atlas is the greatest mountain range in Africa west of the Ruwenzori. At its western end barren limestone ridges and tabular masses of ancient crystalline rocks rise abruptly above both the Haouz plain to the north and the Sous valley and Anti-Atlas to the south. Occasional fault-bordered depressions cut transversely across the range and are followed by roads and tracks, the most important of which links Marrakesh with the Sous valley. Beyond the pass of Telouet at the watershed between the Tensift and the Dra, the High Atlas broadens into a series of sharply folded ridges with precipitous scarps and the highest peaks bear the marks of former glacial erosion; but northeastward it gradually narrows and declines in height as the Algerian border is approached.

In Algeria the trend of the High Atlas is intermittently continued in a series of much lower fold mountains – the Ksour, Amour and Ouled Naïl ranges – known collectively as the Saharan Atlas. They are separated from the coastal Tell by the High Plains, a great spread of semi-arid intermontane plateaus and basins some 500 miles (800 km) long and 100 miles (160 km) wide. From their western end, where they reach over 4000 ft (1220 m) in the plateau of Dahra, the High Plains gradually fall in height eastward and end in the Hodna basin, a huge enclosed depression, the bottom of which is little over 1000 ft (305 m) above sea level. The surface of the High Plains consists of alluvial debris, sparsely covered by alfa and other coarse grasses, and only occasionally do the remnants of worn-down fold mountains project through the thick mantle of alluvium to break the monotony of the featureless landscape. Most of the area has no drainage outlet to the sea and at the centre of each basin of internal drainage there are vast saline depressions or *chotts*, the largest of which are the Chott ech Chergui and the Chott el Hodna (Fig. 5). During rainy periods the *chotts* are transformed into large shallow lakes which give way, as the water is absorbed and evaporated, to saline mud flats and swamps.

East of the Hodna basin the High Plains end against the uplifted block of the Aurès massif. This mountain fastness, with its narrow gorges, sheer cliffs and barren upper slopes which rise to over 7500 ft (Chélia, 2328 m), is, like other inaccessible massifs of the Atlas, a traditional home of Berber tribesmen. It lies athwart the Saharan Atlas but its northern ridges adjoin the southernmost folds of the Tell and enclose several alluvial plains studded with salt flats. Close to the Tunisian border the two Atlas ranges merge. The dominant southwest-northeast orientation of the mountains is prolonged south of the Medjerda valley as the High Tell or Dorsale of Tunisia. Its rugged folds die away eastward and find their final expression in the hilly Cape Bon peninsula which projects to within 90 miles (145 km) of Sicily.

In semi-arid central Tunisia, south of the Dorsale, the Atlas system is so attenuated that only isolated massifs rise above the expanse of alfa-covered alluvial basins which is known as the High Steppe. The longitudinal ridges north and south of the Chott Djerid mark the last outcrop of the Atlas folds and also the boundary between the steppe and the desert. East of the High Steppe the mountains give way completely to a monotonous gravelly plateau – the Low Steppe – which is underlain by subsidence troughs of great value as reservoirs of exploitable ground water. The Low Steppe is crossed by several seasonal watercourses which only flow after heavy rain. They normally fan out and evaporate in relatively small salt flats, or *sebkas*, before reaching the sea. As the east coast is approached the Low Steppe finally merges into the Sahel, an intensively cultivated alluvial plain which is the hinterland for the flourishing coastal cities of Sousse and Sfax.

At the other extremity of the inner Maghreb the third major structural unit of the Atlas mountain system – the Anti-Atlas – picks out in bold relief the northwestern edge of the Sahara. It is made up of extremely ancient folded rocks, the buckled edge of the African shield, which have been uplifted to form a sharp-crested asymmetrical range rising to over 8000 ft (Aklim, 2531 m). Its steepest scarps overlook the fertile wedge of the Sous valley which drains west to the Atlantic at Agadir. Across the head of the valley a plateau of volcanic lavas narrowly joins the Anti-Atlas with the southern slopes of the High Atlas before the ranges are separated again, farther east, by the upper course of the Dra. Along the southeastern face of the Anti-Atlas bare sunbaked slopes are trenched by gorges from which cultivated palm groves protrude like green tongues into the desert.

On close examination the physique of the inner Maghreb displays great diversity, but the Atlas mountain system confers a pattern of unity on the region as a whole. The mountains provide the articulated skeleton which is fleshed out by the intermontane plateaus and peripheral plains. If the physical unity of the inner Maghreb arises from its tectonic homogeneity as a zone of geologically recent Alpine folding, that of the outer Maghreb derives more from climate. Although the relief of the Sahara is controlled very largely by the rigid basement of resistant rocks that underlies it, this does not differentiate it from other parts of the African shield extending farther south in the continent. It is the extreme aridity of its climate that gives such marked geographical unity to this greatest of the world's deserts. Yet within its parched confines there exists surprising variety of surface form and feature.

The Sahara

The simplest and most convenient way of delimiting the Sahara is by means of the 4 in (100 m) isohyet of mean annual precipitation. This somewhat arbitrary line gains significance as a geographical boundary because it corresponds with other physical divisions between the inner and the outer Maghreb. It closely parallels the southern edge of the Atlas folds, skirting the desert slopes of the Anti-Atlas and Saharan Atlas and running along the northern margin of the Chotts Melrhir and Djerid. In Libya it excludes from the desert the coastal lowlands of Tripolitania, nearly reaches the Mediterranean coast at the Gulf of Sirte and continues eastward in Cyrenaica south of the Jebel Akhdar. Along the margin of the inner Maghreb it also corresponds closely with the southern limit of occurrence of alfa grass (*Stipa tenacissima*), which characterizes so much of the semi-arid steppe zone, and with the northern limit of productive date palm groves.

The extreme aridity of most of the outer Maghreb, which reaches almost total drought in the far southwest of Algeria and in parts of southern Libya, is accentuated by the irregularity of the rainfall. Over most of the northern desert the meagre rains occur spasmodically, although chiefly in autumn and winter, but in the central Sahara there is no regular seasonal pattern: a heavy fall in one day may be followed by several years of absolute rainless-ness. In the southern desert summer rains are usual, but this régime only affects the fringe of the outer Maghreb in southern Mauritania and south-eastern Algeria. These rigorous conditions, combined with very high temperatures and frequent violent winds, are reflected in the absence or extreme sparseness of vegetation and in a division of the population into settled cultivators, who occupy oases dependent upon permanent supplies of ground water, and nomadic pastoralists whose herds feed on such seasonal pastures as become available after rain.

Another consequence of the aridity of the Sahara is that its surface is not divided into a series of integrated drainage basins. Only along the margin of the Atlas and around the periphery of the Ahaggar massif are there long, well-defined watercourses (Fig. 4). These *oueds* or *wadis* are normally dry and, even after heavy rain, floods seldom travel their whole length. It is likely that they are the fossilized relics of a system of watercourses which drained the Sahara during wetter 'pluvial' phases of the Pleistocene epoch. Today none except the Dra reaches the sea, but several shorter *wadis* extend to the Atlantic coast in Spanish Sahara and Mauritania and to the Mediterranean coast in Tripolitania. The inland watercourses terminate in saline depressions or lose themselves in sandy and gravelly accumulations of alluvium. Longest and largest is the Saoura which rises at the eastern end of the High Atlas and pursues its irregular, intermittently palm-fringed course for some 600 miles (960 km) into the heart of the desert before fading out south of Reggane. For most of this distance it is followed by the Tanezrouft road, a long-established trade route which crosses the Sahara to reach the 'big bend' of the river Niger just upstream of Gao. None of the concentric watercourses that drain the Ahaggar massif flows as frequently or as far as the Saoura, but the former course of the Irharhar can be traced northward right across the Great Eastern Erg as far as the inland depression occupied by the Chotts Melrhir and Djerid. Most of this depression is now below sea level and there is little doubt that at one time it formed a vast western extension of the Gulf of Gabès. Several proposals have been put forward to cut a channel from the coast and flood the depression, thus opening a huge area of the northern desert to the sea, but expense and the uncertainty of economic benefit have so far prevented the realization of this ambitious project.

Lacking the variety of colour and form with which a plant cover and a pattern of active stream drainage endows more humid and hilly regions, the landscape of the Sahara shows its diversity most clearly in the contrasted textures of its barren surfaces. Smooth gravel-covered plains known as *reg* probably cover the greatest area. These 'desert pavements' are littered with wind-polished rock fragments and it is relatively easy to travel across them, by camel or motor vehicle. The Tanezrouft plain, which extends over a huge area west of the Ahaggar massif and is crossed by the road from the Saoura to the Niger, is the largest and most desolate of them. Scarcely less extensive are the sand accumulations. They vary from almost flat surfaces where level bedrock is veneered by a thin cover of sand, as in parts of eastern Libya, to massive dune formations or *ergs*, such as the Great Western and Great Eastern Ergs of Algeria (Fig. 4). The wind causes frequent minor changes in the topography of active dune systems, but in some areas, particularly Mauritania, there are large areas of dead dunes, the surface of which has been partly fixed by vegetation, making crossings of them less hazardous. Where neither gravel nor sand obscures it the surface of the desert commonly consists of exposed bedrock or *hamada*. This is often smooth enough to afford easy crossing, although some *hamadas* are rocky wildernesses littered with boulders and pitted by erosion hollows.

These varied desert surfaces characterize the low plains and level plateaus that make up most of the outer Maghreb. Only in the far southeast of Algeria is the monotony broken. Here the Ahaggar massif rears above the desert to a height of over 9000 ft (Tahat: 2918 m), its ancient crystalline and recent volcanic rocks eroded into a lunar landscape of extreme ruggedness. The deep valleys that radiate from the massif have long given shelter to a population of Berber-speaking oasis cultivators and it has also functioned as a mid-desert crossroads for several trans-Saharan trade routes, notably the Hoggar road from Ghardaïa south of the Saharan Atlas to Kano in northern Nigeria. Lower tributary massifs partly surround the Ahaggar: to the north the Tassili-n-Ajjer and to the south the Adrar des Iforas and the Aïr, which extend across the Algerian frontier into Mali and Niger. The other great mountain massif of the Sahara – Tibesti, whose volcanic peaks reach well over 10,000 ft (Emi Koussi: 3415 m) – adjoins the southern border of Libya, but most of it lies outside the Maghreb in neighbouring Chad (Fig. 4).

Despite its compelling aridity and desolate landscapes, in which cultivation is confined to the immediate vicinity of isolated *wadis*, wells and springs, the Sahara contains a wealth of known mineral resources which greatly enhance its economic and political significance in the modern world. Although men have been living in and travelling across the desert since prehistoric times, salt is the only mineral that was exploited on a considerable scale before the present century. Large salt deposits were systematically mined for many centuries at such places as Taghaza and Taoudeni in the western desert and traded south to the salt-hungry Negro populations of the upper Niger. Salt was indeed an essential item in the flourishing trans-Saharan commerce of medieval and early modern times. But it was not until after the Second World War that systematic prospecting began to reveal the remarkable variety of mineral wealth in the Sahara. The most extensive and valuable deposits are of oil and natural gas and their exploitation is already revolutionizing the economic prospects of Algeria and Libya, although some of the proven deposits, such as the huge reserves of natural gas in the Ahnet Basin south of In Salah, lie well beyond the present range of economic exploitation (Fig. 10). At present iron ore is the only other mineral being extracted on a large scale – at Fort Gouraud in northern Mauritania – but valuable deposits awaiting future exploitation include iron near Tindouf, copper at Akjoujt and nickel, tin and wolfram in the Ahaggar massif (Fig. 11).

The Coastal Zones of Libya and southern Mauritania

The hinterlands of the coast in Tripolitania, Cyrenaica and southern Mauritania are the only parts of the outer Maghreb that lie outside the Sahara and receive more than 4 in (100 mm) mean annual rainfall. The two more humid enclaves along the Libyan coast are effectively separated by the approach of Saharan conditions to the sea around the desolate shores of the Gulf of Sirte. This desert barrier, some 300 miles (480 km) wide, has had a profoundly divisive effect throughout Libya's history. It has always been easier to travel from Tripolitania to Tunisia and from Cyrenaica to Egypt than between the two Libyan provinces and they have indeed often owed separate political allegiance to their respective neighbours.

The Tripolitanian coastal zone consists of a low plain, the Djeffara, which is an eastward continuation of the coastal plain that stretches from Gabès in southern Tunisia. It is about 50 miles (80 km) wide at the Libyan frontier and is backed by a crescentic range of hills, the Jebel Nefusa, which gradually curves towards the coast until it cuts off the plain east of Tripoli. The Djeffara experiences a semi-arid climate with a winter rainfall régime, and, in the immediate vicinity of the coast, it is intensively cultivated.

Inland towards the encircling hills it becomes much drier and less productive. The Nefusa hills rise to over 2600 ft (800 m) and present a steep scarp to the north overlooking the coastal plain. They are partly covered by low-growing scrub, and ancient olive groves cluster round the villages of their Berber-speaking inhabitants. Southward the slopes of the Nefusa dip gently towards the desert.

The Cyrenaican coastal zone is dominated by the compact upland of the Jebel Akhdar which thrusts bluntly into the Mediterranean east of the Gulf of Sirte. It is somewhat lower than the Tripolitanian upland and has a steep seaward-facing scarp cut by deep gorges. However, its limestone heights receive more rainfall (14–26 inches or 350–650 mm) than the Tripolitanian hills (8–20 inches or 200–500 mm) and support open woodlands of scrub oak and juniper in which livestock are grazed. Cultivation is largely restricted to patches of deeper soil on the lower slopes and along the narrow coastal strip.

Along the Mauritanian coast, from a point about half way between Port Étienne and Nouakchott southward to the Senegal valley, there is a gradual increase in mean annual rainfall from 4 in (100 mm) to over 12 in (300 mm). Here, on the desert fringe of the West African savanna lands, the rains are concentrated into a short summer season and acacia trees – from which gum arabic is extracted for export – are scattered sparsely over the landscape. Flat clay plains, often mantled by sand dunes, stretch inland from the coast and terminate against low west-facing sandstone scarps. The presence of ground water at slight depth beneath the plains makes possible some local irrigation from wells, but most of the inhabitants depend for their subsistence on their herds of livestock which forage among the shrubs and coarse grasses that partly cover the dunes and clayey depressions.

Patterns of Culture

The diversity of landscape that gives the physical geography of the Maghreb its distinctive character is matched by the complexity of its cultural geography. A mosaic of different languages, dialects and ways of life underlies the political unity of each modern North African state and generates persistent tensions which are only slowly being resolved. This complexity is a heritage from the successive occupation of North Africa by many different peoples of contrasted cultures. The variegated social and economic fabric of the present has been woven out of the tangled skeins of the region's troubled past.

The primary cultural contrasts are between the Arabic-speaking majority, and minorities speaking Berber, French, Spanish or Italian; between the overwhelming majority of the population that is racially Caucasoid or white, and the scattered Negroid peoples; between the Mohammedan masses and the much smaller communities of Jews and Christians; between sedentary cultivators and nomadic or semi-nomadic pastoralists; and between relatively sophisticated town dwellers and the rural folk of the *bled* or countryside. None of these groups is completely self-contained and there is much cultural intermingling, but the basic divisions persist and profoundly influence the social and economic structure of the modern Maghreb.

The Ethnic Pattern

In classical times the un-Romanized occupants of the lands at the fringe of the Empire were known as *barbari*: the 'barbarians'. Thus the term Berber came to be applied by Europeans to the native inhabitants of North Africa. It has precise meaning only in a linguistic sense, although it is sometimes misleadingly given a racial connotation. The Berbers are in fact racially Caucasoid, with occasional Negroid admixture, and do not differ physically in any major respect from the Arab and European populations of the Maghreb. However, in so far as they have retained their own language against the pervasive spread of Arabic, so have they also tended to conserve traditional ways of life that set them apart from the non-Berber communities. The present distribution of Berber speakers therefore reveals a distinctive and persistent cultural pattern (Fig. 6).

The Berber language is related to Ancient Egyptian and is usually classified as a member of the Hamitic linguistic stock.[1] Today it comprises a large number of distinct dialects, not all of which are mutually intelligible. This is a characteristic feature of an ancient language without written texts,[2] but it has been accentuated by the geographical isolation of the principal Berber groups.

By far the greatest number of Berber-speakers live today in the Atlas mountains of Morocco. They are divided into several tribal confederations of which the most important are the Chleuh, who occupy the Anti-Atlas, the High Atlas and the intervening Sous valley; the Rifians of the eastern Rif Atlas; and the Beraber of the Middle Atlas. Many smaller tribal groups, such as the Tekna, Drawa, Filala, Warain and Zekara, also live within the mountains. Altogether about 40 per cent of the Moroccan population is Berber-speaking. The original inhabitants of the Canary Islands – the Guanche – also spoke a Berber dialect. In Algeria Berbers occupy a much less extensive area but they nevertheless make up about 30 per cent of the

[1] G. P. Murdock includes also Chadic, Cushitic and Semitic languages in the Hamitic stock, which is alternatively known as the Afroasiatic or Hamitic-Semitic stock (Murdock, 1959: 14).

[2] A crude alphabet, which probably owed its origin to Phoenician influence, was formerly used for rock inscriptions by the Berber-speaking Tuareg of the central Sahara.

population. They are most numerous in the densely-peopled Kabylie mountains east of Algiers. Other distinct groups are the Menasser of the coastal Tell west of Algiers; the Chaouïa of the Aurès massif; and the inhabitants of the north Saharan oases of Touggourt, Ouargla, Mzab, Gourara and Figuig. Only small and isolated pockets of Berber-speakers remain in Tunisia and Libya. They comprise less than 2 per cent of Tunisia's population and are restricted to the island of Djerba and to the sandstone plateau in the desert south of Gabès known as the Monts des Ksour which is the home of the partly troglodytic tribes of Matmata and Djebalia. In Libya probably less than 5 per cent of the population consists of Berber-speakers. They occupy the Jebel Nefusa of Tripolitania as well as some of the oases of the interior such as Jofra and Jalo (Fig. 6).

Almost all these Berber groups are sedentary farmers living in compact and sometimes fortified villages in the mountains or oases, but some, such as the Beraber of the Middle Atlas, also practise seasonal transhumance. The only fully nomadic Berber-speaking pastoralists are the Tuareg of the central Sahara. They are thinly scattered over an immense triangular tract of desert stretching from the plateaus of Aïr and Adrar des Iforas, across the Ahaggar massif and north towards the oasis of Ghadames. Although they themselves despise cultivation and settled life they control a large number of Negro serfs – known as Haratin or Bella – and Sudanese slaves, who live in the oases and on whose agricultural produce the Tuareg depend to supplement the meagre supplies of milk and meat from their herds. In southern Mauritania there are two remnant tribes of partly Berber-speaking semi-nomadic pastoralists: the Tasumsa and the Idaouich (Fig. 6).

Ever since the cohesion of the Berber peoples of North Africa was shattered by the Arab invasions of the seventh and later centuries A.D., relations between these two major ethnic groups have been troubled. Frequently they have been in open warfare and the Arabs have seldom succeeded in imposing effective governmental authority over the belligerent Berber tribesmen. In Morocco the conflict was tacitly recognized by division of the country into the *bled el-makhzen*, or lands of government, and the *bled es-siba*, or lands of dissidence. Hostility between Berber and Arab long persisted because of differences in language and in methods of maintaining social order rather than because of religious opposition. The traditional Berber system of government is based on representative councils in which authority rotates and the aggrandizement of power by one member is easily checked. The Arab tradition on the other hand is authoritarian, with power concentrated in the hands of the individual rulers of village, tribe and nation. As a result the Berbers have seldom succeeded in organizing and maintaining centralized political control over

Opposite: **Fig. 6. The Maghreb: Present Distribution of Berber and Teda Speech,** after Briggs, 1960; Capot-Rey, 1953; Despois, 1964; Mikesell, 1961; and Murdock, 1959)

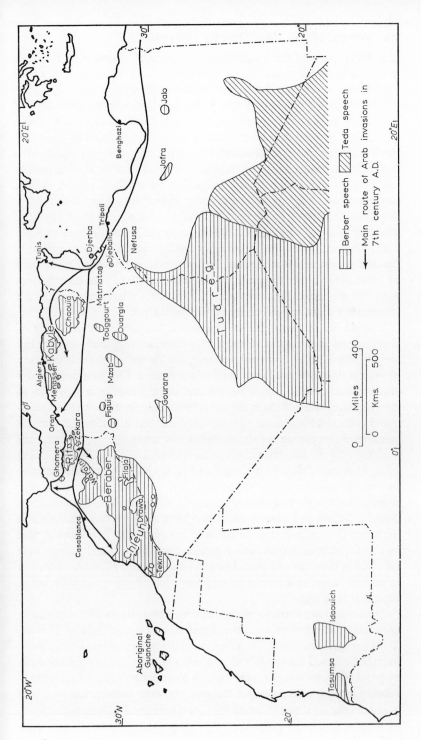

Berber speech   Teda speech

Main route of Arab invasions in
7th century A.D.

0   Miles   400

0   Kms.   500

20°W   20°E   20°E   20°E

30°N   30°   30°   30°   20°   20°   0°   0°

Aboriginal
Guanche

Casablanca   Ghomera   Oran   Algiers   Tunis   Djerba   Tripoli   Benghazi

Rif   Menasser   Kabyle   Djebala   Nefusa   Jalo

Beraber   Chaouia   Matmata   Jofra

Zekara   Figuig   Mzab   Touggourt   Ouargla

Chleuh   Filala   Gourara

Drawa   Tuareg

Tekna

Idaouich

Tasumsa

3

substantial parts of the Maghreb. And, conversely, because each tribe is prepared to defend to the limit its own territorial independence, they have stubbornly resisted the imposition of alien authority.

Nevertheless throughout North Africa Berber speech has gradually lost ground to Arabic until today its distribution is reduced to a relict pattern of survival in mountain strongholds and desert refuges. The spread of Arabic has been aided and outdistanced by the even more successful diffusion of Mohammedanism. Nominally at least all Berbers are followers of the Prophet and accept the five 'pillars' of Islam: faith, prayer, fasting, almsgiving and pilgrimage. The majority indeed are pious and faithful in observing the fast of Ramadan, although they have never taken kindly to the duty of almsgiving when it has assumed the guise of a head or tribal tax. In fact while Islam as a faith is accepted, as an authoritarian system of law and government it is rejected. Surviving traces of pagan animism, such as belief in the power of *jinns* (demons) and the cult of local saints (*marabouts*) whose sacred shrines become the object of pilgrimages, add to the unorthodox character of Berber Mohammedanism.

Outside the Berber areas the population consists overwhelmingly of Arabic-speaking orthodox Moslems whose lives are regulated – more or less strictly – by Koranic law. Few, however, are 'Arabs' in the sense that they are direct descendants of immigrants from Arabia. The great majority are the Arabized descendants of Berbers and other pre-Islamic occupants of the Maghreb. Most of them are sedentary, living in the towns and cultivated lowlands, but a distinctive minority are semi-nomadic and nomadic pastoralists, occupying the steppe and desert zones. Among the latter are such tribes of the Saharan margin as the Nememcha, Arab Gheraba, Ouled Naïl, El Arbaa, Ouled Sidi Cheikh and Beni Guil (Fig. 7), who migrate to summer pastures in the steppe and Tell; as well as the truly Saharan nomads, such as the Chaamba of the north-central desert and the Moors of Spanish Sahara and Mauritania. The Moors are a striking example of a nomadic, originally Berber people who adopted both Islam and Arabic as a result of contact with Arab invaders. Berber words and phrases have survived in the otherwise pure Arabic spoken by most Moorish tribes, and in central Mauritania certain vassal groups have even retained Berber as their first language.

At the opposite extreme of the Saharan Maghreb, in southern Libya, there exists a still more curious cultural minority: the Teda or Toubou. Their present homeland is the Tibesti massif but they also range northward into the Fezzan. They are difficult to classify racially, having predominantly Negroid characteristics combined with a blood group pattern that suggests relationship not with Sudanese Negroes but with Berbers. Linguistically however they are clearly differentiated from both the Arabic-speaking white and Negro populations and from the Berber Tuareg (Fig. 6). Their language consists of several closely related dialects belonging to the Kanuric or Central Saharan linguistic stock, to which the languages of certain other Negroid groups living south and east of Tibesti also belong. In religion and way of life they fairly closely resemble their neighbours and traditional enemies the Tuareg. They were converted to Islam probably in the late eighteenth century but many pagan beliefs still underlie the Moslem veneer. Most of the Teda live a pastoral nomadic life, although they customarily spend part of each year in the agricultural oases which are cultivated for them by Haratin serfs and Sudanese Negro slaves.

The remaining elements that make up the ethnic mosaic of the Maghreb are the communities of Jewish and European origin. The Jews are most numerous in the coastal cities of Morocco, Algeria and Tunisia. These groups derive mainly from the Sephardic Jews who were expelled from Spain after the Christian reconquest of Andalusia. Before the European occupation of North Africa they fulfilled a key role in the economic life of the Moslem communities by engaging in such activities as banking, money-lending and tax-collecting which were either proscribed by the Koran or regarded as degrading by devout Moslems. Their linguistic ability also assured them an important place as middlemen in the early contacts between Europeans and Arabs, and under European protection they gradually adopted French, Spanish or Italian as their domestic language while speaking Arabic in the market-place. Hebrew is maintained as a ritual language only.

The Sephardic Jews constitute only a minority – although an influential one – of North African Jewry. The majority, who call themselves *Plishtim* (Palestinians) and claim to be descendants of original migrants who came direct from Palestine, are scattered throughout the Maghreb, some living as merchants and craftsmen in urban ghettos, some as petty traders or peasant farmers in rural areas, and some as artisans in desert oases such as Ghardaïa. The *Plishtim* are generally poorer and more conservative than the Sephardic Jews, and, although some may be descendants of ancient Jewish immigrants, most of them are probably descended from early Berber converts to Judaism who were later dispersed by the Arab conquest.

Since they gained their independence the Arab states of the Maghreb have shown tolerance towards their Jewish communities, whose financial and technical skill they value, and consequently there has been relatively little emigration. Only in Libya, where anti-Jewish riots accompanied the creation of the state of Israel, have most of the Jews left the country. In Tunisia emigration has reduced the Jewish population by about a third, and in Algeria and Morocco the loss has been still less significant. Today the total Jewish population of the Maghreb probably amounts to about 500,000.

Europeans have occupied a significant but fluctuating place in the cultural composition of North Africa since Roman times. Their role has varied from that of conqueror, administrator and colonist to that of merchant, mercenary and slave. Their present numbers and distribution chiefly reflect the pattern of French, Spanish and Italian colonization in the nineteenth and twentieth centuries, with substantial changes as a result of emigration since the withdrawal of European political control. The great majority of Europeans live in towns, particularly in the coastal cities, where they work as business men, administrators and skilled labourers. The European rural population is now very small and even before independence it represented only about 10 per cent of the total European population, which had, by 1956, reached a peak of about 1·8 millions (approximately 1,000,000 in Algeria, 500,000 in Morocco, 250,000 in Tunisia and 50,000 in Libya). Since independence emigration has reduced this total by over 80 per cent, to little more than 250,000.

Most of the Europeans living in the Maghreb are French, either by birth or naturalization. Many of the French are locally born descendants of settlers who came from southern France and Corsica, while others are naturalized Spaniards and Italians. Very few are first generation settlers who were born in France. Before independence the French communities of Algeria, Morocco and Tunisia constituted a governing, land-owning and merchant class which lived in social isolation from the Arab and Berber masses. Although Christian and Moslem lived side by side with relatively little antagonism there was no fusion of the two groups; few Moslems became naturalized Frenchmen and mixed marriages were extremely rare. However, the dominant French minority exerted an influence on the cultural geography of the three territories out of all proportion to their numbers. They transformed the larger coastal cities, expropriated and increased production on the better agricultural land, and established military and civil authority from the coast deep into the desert, building in the process an extensive road and rail system which has proved a valuable inheritance to the newly independent states. Another valuable legacy of the colonial period is the French language which is still taught in a majority of schools.

The Spanish and Italian elements comprise less than 10 per cent of the total European population. They are approximately equal in number but concentrated respectively at the western and eastern ends of the Maghreb adjacent to their home countries. The Spanish are most numerous in northern Morocco – the former protectorate of Spanish Morocco – where they live almost exclusively in the towns, notably in the two remaining Spanish territorial enclaves of Ceuta and Melilla, and in Tangier and Tetuán. Rural colonization was never encouraged in Spanish Morocco and the people of the interior were little affected by colonial rule, although Spanish was quite widely accepted; it is still spoken as a second language by some Berber tribesmen of the Rif. Spaniards are quite numerous in the rest of Morocco and in Algeria, particularly in coastal towns such as Casablanca and Oran, and small numbers of civil and military personnel administer the Spanish territories of Ifni and Spanish Sahara.

Italians are an important element only in the populations of Tunisia and Libya. In Tunisia they live chiefly in Tunis itself and in the fertile Cape Bon peninsula. In Libya they are largely confined to Tripolitania, where most of them live in the towns and only a few remain on the farms that were established during the Italian occupation. The Italian population of Cyrenaica is negligible because all Italian civilians were evacuated by their government during the desert fighting of the Second World War and very few have been allowed to return.

In addition to the French, Spanish and Italian minorities several other European nationalities are represented by small populations in North Africa. Of these only the Maltese and Greek fishermen and traders, who are to be found in most of the ports of the eastern Maghreb, add significantly to the pattern of ethnic diversity.

The Rural Pattern
The fundamental division in the rural economy of the Maghreb is between sedentary agriculture and nomadic or semi-nomadic pastoralism. However, these categories are not mutually exclusive and a variety of intermediate forms, such as mountain transhumance and semi-sedentary cultivation, add diversity to the traditional pattern of rural ways of life in the inner Maghreb (Fig. 7). In the Sahara the distinction between nomadic pastoralists and sedentary oasis farmers is more absolute, for, although the nomads depend on the oases for part of their food supplies, most of them still despise cultivation and leave it to their Haratin serfs and Sudanese slaves.

Along the northern margin of the desert pure pastoral nomadism gradually gives way to the semi-nomadism that characterizes so much of the steppe zone. The boundary between these two ways of life is indeed much more vague and variable than can be indicated on Figure 7. A few tribes, such as the Beni Guil of the Dahra plateau and adjacent areas in eastern Morocco, are almost pure pastoralists who supplement the produce of their herds with dates and grain from the oases of Figuig; but others, such as the Berber-speaking Aït Atta of southern Morocco and the Ouled Sidi Cheikh, Ouled Naïl and Nememcha of Algeria, pasture their herds in the High Atlas, Saharan Atlas and Aurès mountains during the summer; while still others, such as the El Arbaa of Laghouat and the Arab Gheraba of

Touggourt, migrate deep into the steppe and Tell zones seeking summer pastures and casual employment as harvest labourers.

Within the steppe zone semi-nomadic pastoralism is still the dominant way of life, although, as a result of both the French colonial policy of *fixation au sol* and the drift of population to the towns, which has intensified since independence, an increasing number of tribes have become sedentary. This is facilitated by the fact that, unlike the true nomads, semi-nomads spend only part of the year on the move with their animals and have fixed settlements where they practise some agriculture and to which the whole tribe returns at harvest and other festive times. The trend towards a fully sedentary life is most advanced in the steppes and plains of central and southern Tunisia and coastal Libya, the Algerian High Plains and the Moulouya lowland of eastern Morocco. It has affected very little the semi-nomads of the desert fringe south of the Anti-Atlas in southern Morocco and Spanish Sahara. As semi-nomadic tribes become more sedentary they turn increasingly to agriculture; communal use of land gives way gradually to private land ownership; and the traditional tents – which are of Arab origin and made of strips of camel's and goat's hair or wool – are replaced either by permanent houses or, when the semi-nomads remain impoverished, by temporary huts known as *gourbis*.

The mountain massifs of the inner Maghreb are for the most part occupied by sedentary Berber-speaking farmers who live in compact villages, the houses of which are sometimes huddled protectively around a fortified granary of *ksar* which acted in the past as a defensive stronghold. The villages are usually located on the higher, uncultivable ground and overlook irrigated and dry-cultivated fields of cereals, vegetables and tree crops. In those parts of the Anti-Atlas and High Atlas occupied by the Chleuh and other Berber tribes, in the western and central Rif, in the Greater Kabylie and in scattered smaller massifs, such as the northern Monts des Ksour occupied by the Matmata, the whole population of each village is sedentary; but elsewhere, notably in the Middle Atlas and eastern Rif, among the Chaouïa of the Aurès and the Djebalia of the southern Monts des Ksour, and in the Jebel Nefusa, livestock play a more important part in the rural economy and part of the village population migrates with the animals to higher pastures in the summer and to the lowlands in the winter. The practice of seasonal transhumance by some of the mountain Berbers probably dates back to prehistoric times, but the mobility of certain tribes, such as the Beraber of the Middle Atlas, was increased by the adoption of tents as a result of contact with invading pastoral nomads during the late classical and medieval periods. Since European occupation suppressed tribal warfare there has been a tendency for the higher fortified villages to be abandoned in favour of more convenient valley sites and for

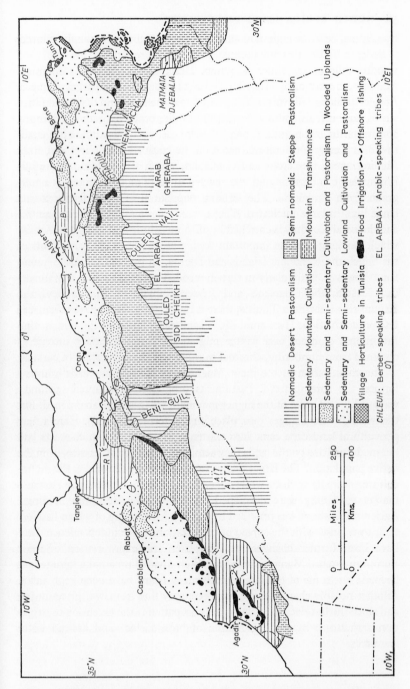

Fig. 7. The Inner Maghreb: Rural Ways of Life (after Despois, 1964)

Nomadic Desert Pastoralism

Semi-nomadic Steppe Pastoralism

Sedentary Mountain Cultivation

Mountain Transhumance

Sedentary and Semi-sedentary Cultivation and Pastoralism in Wooded Uplands

Sedentary and Semi-sedentary Lowland Cultivation and Pastoralism

Village Horticulture in Tunisia

Flood Irrigation

Offshore fishing

CHLEUH: Berber-speaking tribes

EL ARBAA: Arabic-speaking tribes

Miles

Kms.

transhumance to the high mountain pastures to be correspondingly reduced·

Sedentary life also predominates in the more humid lowlands and wooded hills of the inner Maghreb. Here, in the Atlantic lowland of Morocco, in most of the Algerian Tell and in northern and eastern Tunisia, Arabic-speaking cultivators living in villages, hamlets and dispersed farmsteads raise cereals and a wide variety of other crops by both dry-farming and irrigation techniques. Along the east coast of Tunisia there is a tradition of intensive horticulture, based on the cultivation of olives and other Mediterranean tree crops and vegetables, which stems from the original Phoenician colonization and was revived in early modern times by immigrants from Andalusia. The farming population of these fertile coastal lands lives in large nucleated villages which serve as local market centres and the rural economy is enriched by offshore fishing and sponge gathering, which has long been an important source of wealth to the inhabitants of the Sahel, the Kerkenna Islands and Djerba. In parts of the more humid zone, however, particularly in certain wooded uplands such as the Moroccan Meseta, the Ouarsenis and Lesser Kabylie of Algeria, and the Kroumirie of northern Tunisia, there is more emphasis on pastoralism and less on cultivation. Here rural life is semi-sedentary and the tent is used for limited summer and winter migrations. Supplementary income is obtained from lumbering, charcoal burning and the harvesting of cork.

The colonization of the inner Maghreb by Europeans partially transformed the rural pattern. Pastoralists progressively adopted sedentary ways of life and some of the higher mountain villages were abandoned. But the most drastic changes took place on the fertile lowlands. Here a new agricultural landscape came into existence where European colonists laid out modern farms on the lands they acquired, legally or otherwise, from the native population. The larger estates were commonly devoted to the monoculture of cereals or vines, while mixed farming and – near the chief towns – market gardening were developed on the smaller European holdings. Agricultural labour was provided by the Moslems, many of whom had lost their own lands with the spread of colonization. Since independence there have been further changes resulting from the expropriation of most European estates. Many of these have been divided up among local tenant farmers, but some of the larger mechanized farms have been kept intact. Another notable change in the rural economy that has taken place during and since the last decade of European occupation is the extension of irrigation agriculture by the exploitation of both surface and ground water resources.

The Urban Pattern

The separation of urban and rural life is an ancient and enduring cultural feature of the Maghreb. In the hierarchy of settlement forms there is a gap between the city and the village, hamlet or farmstead. The word 'town' has no Arabic equivalent in the Maghreb and most settlements of a size intermediate between the city (*medina*) and the village (*dshar*) are recent European creations. Urban life has in fact only flourished under the influence of alien invaders – Romans, Arabs, Frenchmen – and it has been and remains sharply differentiated from rural and tribal ways of life. Berber social organization, which favours the maintenance of small politically and economically independent units, has hindered the growth of towns. So too has the practice of holding weekly open air markets at convenient tribal meeting points, instead of establishing permanent trading centres which, in other parts of the world, have commonly served as the nuclei of market towns.[1]

The distribution of cities in the Maghreb betrays their alien origins. Most are located on the coast where small trading stations founded by foreign merchants have, in favourable sites, grown into substantial ports. In the interior, cities are restricted to the lowlands where foreign conquerors could impose their authority. Thus the tradition of urban life is most strongly developed at the eastern and western ends of the inner Maghreb, in the accessible lands of the Tunisian Sahel and the Atlantic lowland of Morocco. It is tenuous in inland Algeria and in the Sahara finds expression only in the unique nucleated villages or 'towns' of the larger oases.

The most striking contrast in the morphology of North African cities is between the compact irregularity of the Arab *medinas* and the more open formality of the European additions. The *medina* is often still surrounded by its medieval wall and dominated by a fort or *kasba* as well as by the great mosque. Lesser mosques mark the wards into which the city is divided and the houses, built around interior courtyards, present blank outer walls to the maze of narrow streets and alleys that connect them. A functional division of the city is apparent in the segregation of Jewish and other minorities in separate quarters and in the complex partitioning of the market or *souk* according to the trades represented. Under vaulted alleys near the great mosque cluster the quiet shops of the candlemakers, incense dealers, booksellers, tailors and jewellers; farther away, lining separate streets, are the noisier premises of the leather workers and shoe makers, smiths and carpenters; while the periphery of the *souk* is occupied by the

---

[1] This check to urbanization has operated most effectively in the Berber highlands of Morocco; see M. W. Mikesell (1958).

3*

dirtier trades and those that require most space: the butchers and tanners, potters, weavers and dyers, and the stalls for bread, vegetables and other foodstuffs. Several *medinas*, such as those of Fez and Tunis, have been important religious and intellectual centres since medieval times when Islamic universities grew up in association with their principal mosques. These and other cities, such as Rabat, Meknès and Marrakesh, also became dynastic capitals and their imperial past is perpetuated today in their richly ornamented palaces and elaborate gardens.

The effect of European colonization on the urban pattern of the Maghreb was to modify the Arab *medinas*, greatly enlarge many of the ports, and create new towns, chiefly in the interior. The coastal cities from which the Europeans could best control colonial trade became important administrative centres, grew rapidly and eclipsed less favoured ports and inland markets. Casablanca, the fastest growing city in Africa, expanded from a population of about 20,000 in 1900 to over a million by the early 1960's. Likewise Algiers and Tunis have experienced phenomenal growth to reach populations of over 900,000 and 700,000 respectively. Among other ports that have flourished and expanded under European control are Safi, Tangier, Oran, Bougie, Bône, Bizerta, Sousse, Sfax, Tripoli and Benghazi, all of which benefited from the construction of railways linking them with their populous hinterlands.

Europeanization of North African towns has generally taken the form of extensions beyond the *medinas*, although in Algeria, where the Europeans at first built their houses within these old centres, many of the original *medinas* have lost their identity in the modern city that has overwhelmed them. In Tunisia and particularly in Morocco, where it was declared policy to establish European settlements adjacent to, but separate from, native towns, the *medinas* are often intact and relatively little altered. The early European extensions are usually characterized by a rectilinear plan, focusing on one or more central squares linked by tree-lined avenues which serve as the commercial and administrative hub of the modern town. Farther out are the sprawling residential suburbs occupied by Europeans and upper-class Moslems, and on the edge of the urban area the huddled shacks of the *bidonville* or shanty town where unemployed townsfolk and job-seeking migrants from the countryside eke out a squalid living.

The newest elements in the urban pattern of the Maghreb are the towns founded by Europeans and those that have been created or significantly enlarged since independence. European foundations are few and mainly in Algeria, which was less thoroughly urbanized by the Arabs than its neighbours but was first to experience French colonization. The port of Philippeville was founded in 1838, within a decade of French intervention, and later other towns, such as Sidi-bel-Abbès, Tiaret and Sétif, were built as administrative and market centres in the interior. As a modern system of road and rail communications was developed by the French, former villages such as Constantine in the Tell, or Biskra and Colomb-Bechar at the edge of the desert, grew into considerable towns.

Since independence the principal cities of the Maghreb have continued to receive a stream of migrants from the impoverished countryside, but it is the development of mineral resources, particularly oil and natural gas, that is adding the most novel element to the urban pattern. At the oil fields in the Sahara new towns such as Hassi Messaoud and Edjelé are being built, while at the coastal terminals of the pipelines refineries, as at La Skhira north of Gabès, and petrochemical works, as at Arzew east of Oran, act as new focii for industrial and urban growth. In Mauritania exploitation of the rich haematite deposits at Fort Gouraud is leading to the rapid expansion of Port Étienne at the terminus of the new railway built to export the iron ore. And the stimulus of independence, backed by royalties from iron and oil, has encouraged the governments of both Mauritania and Libya to construct brand new capitals at Nouakchott and Beida.

The Cultural Succession

Just as the structural pattern of the Maghreb incorporates rocks from many different levels of the geological succession so does its cultural pattern combine ingredients from a succession of cultures. The superimposition, blending and persistence in modified form of African, Asian and European ways of life has produced the complex cultural mosaic of today.

From a wealth of archaeological evidence in the form of stone tools, pottery and rock art it is clear that both the Atlas lands and the Sahara sheltered considerable prehistoric populations. In Palaeolithic and Meso-lithic times, prior to 5000 B.C., these earliest inhabitants of the Maghreb subsisted by hunting, fishing and gathering. During phases of glaciation in the northern hemisphere, humid 'pluvial' conditions visited North Africa and plant and animal life was probably abundant in all but parts of the central Sahara. The racial composition of this primary population is un-certain, but it evidently included both Negroid and Caucasoid elements.

The succeeding Neolithic period is marked by the arrival of the first agriculturalists. There is some evidence that from about 5000 to 2500 B.C. the Sahara experienced a 'subpluvial' climate, with moister conditions than at present, and that it supported savanna vegetation and a rich 'Ethiopian' fauna of lion, elephant, rhinoceros, hippopotamus, crocodile, giraffe, antelope, ostrich and other animals now restricted to tropical Africa. Into this hunter's land intruded herdsmen who raised cattle and probably culti-vated grains. Rock paintings, such as the magnificent frescoes of the Tassili-n-Ajjer massif, suggest that these earliest herdsmen were racially

Negroid. However, the Neolithic population of the northern Sahara and the Atlas lands was racially Caucasoid.

Some time during the third millennium B.C. it appears that the Saharan climate shifted towards arid conditions such as prevail today, the 'Ethiopian' fauna and the vegetation on which it depended gradually disappeared – its elimination hastened no doubt by the depredations of hunters and herdsmen – and cultivation contracted, with the diminishing water supply, until it came to resemble the intermittent oasis agriculture of today. It is possible that at this time too the separation of herdsmen from cultivators marked the beginnings of pastoral nomadism in the desert, although its full development awaited the later introduction of the horse and the dromedary from Southwest Asia. By the close of prehistoric times, therefore, the Sahara had already assumed its modern character as a transitional zone and partial barrier between the predominantly Caucasoid occupants of the Maghreb and the Negro populations of tropical Africa; and within it the traditional dichotomy between oasis cultivators and pastoral nomads had already begun to emerge.

Berber Foundations

In the northern Maghreb the Neolithic period also saw the emergence of ways of life that have persisted, with modification, to the present. From about 4000 B.C. the Caucasoid inhabitants of the Mediterranean littoral and Atlas lands acquired a knowledge of agriculture and adopted a more sedentary life than when they depended exclusively on hunting, fishing and gathering. The crops and domestic animals on which their new economy was based – the most important of which were barley and wheat, sheep, goats and pigs – were introduced from Southwest Asia via Egypt. Somewhat later cattle, horses, asses, and a knowledge of both the plough and metalworking were introduced from the same area. These early North African farmers and pastoralists, who were subsequently referred to by classical authors as 'Libyans', were the ancestors of the modern Berbers. At the beginning of historical times, about 1000 B.C., they occupied most of the northern Maghreb. They had even colonized the Canary Islands, where, as the aboriginal Guanche, they preserved unaltered a primitive Neolithic culture until the Spanish conquest of the islands in the late fifteenth century; but they had not yet penetrated far into the Sahara.

It was, therefore, during the three millennia of the Neolithic that the Berber foundations of the North African cultural complex were laid down. The fundamental pattern of tribal life, based on permanent farming villages with supplementary seasonal transhumance among some tribes, originated at that time. Some classical authors describe the 'Libyans' as nomads but these descriptions probably refer only to transhumant semi-nomads. It is unlikely that any of the Berbers practised fully nomadic pastoralism until post-classical times, when the availability of the dromedary and the example of invading Arab nomads encouraged some tribes, such as the Tuareg, to adopt this novel way of life in the Sahara. Prehistoric Berbers did however originate trans-Saharan trade, employing human porters and ox- and horse-drawn carts, before camel caravans came into use in late classical times.

Thus when the first Phoenician merchant adventurers reached the North African coast somewhat before 1000 B.C. they found the littoral and the mountainous interior occupied by Berber-speaking tribesmen who lived in compact villages, cultivated grains, raised livestock and hunted the 'Ethiopian' fauna which had survived in these more humid lands north of the desert. The imprint of Berber culture was indelibly fixed by this time, and despite the later impact of more advanced peoples it has not yet been effaced over much of the northern Maghreb.

The Empires of Carthage and Rome
The earliest seafarers to visit the North African coast from the eastern Mediterranean may have been Minoans and Egyptians, but they have left no trace of permanent settlement and it was the Phoenicians who founded the first colonies in the Maghreb. Coasting westward they gradually established a series of trading stations at approximate intervals of a day's voyage, from Tripolitania to beyond the Strait of Gibraltar. Carthage, which was founded in 814 B.C. just north of the present site of Tunis, commanded the entrance to the western Mediterranean through the Sicilian Channel, and Gades, on the site of modern Cadiz, gave the Phoenicians strategic control of Gibraltar and the Atlantic sea route by which they obtained tin and lead from Brittany and Cornwall. In the sixth century B.C., when Phoenicia was conquered by the Babylonians, the western colonies became independent of the homeland and were welded into a single empire under the control of Carthage. Greek traders, who had founded Cyrene in 631 B.C. and four other colonies in Cyrenaica, were prevented from penetrating farther west along the North African coast and the Romans were excluded by treaty from all lands where the Carthaginians had established trading stations. By 400 B.C. their empire embraced – besides the North African littoral from the Gulf of Sirte to southwestern Morocco – the Spanish coast from Gades to Cape Nao, the Balearic Islands, Sardinia, Malta and most of Sicily. The stage was set for the inevitable conflict with Rome which was to lead, by the close of the third Punic War in 146 B.C., to the total destruction of Carthage (Fig. 8).

With the exception of Carthage itself, Punic settlements in North Africa did not develop extensive hinterlands. They functioned as centres of

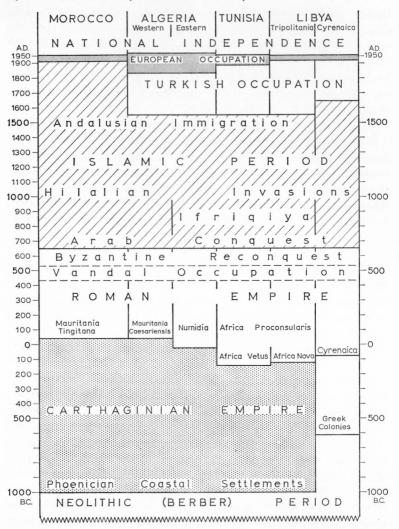

Fig. 8. The Northern Maghreb: The Cultural Succession through Historical Times

entrepôt trade rather than as bridgeheads for colonization. So secretive were the Carthaginians about their commercial dealings that little is known of their African trade. The principal local products obtained from Berber tribesmen were probably timber, wool and skins, purple *Murex* dye, ivory and ostrich feathers. There can be little doubt that the Carthaginians also tapped the trans-Saharan trade routes previously established by the

Berbers. Indeed this may well have been the motive that led to the founding of the three cities – Sabratha, Oea (Tripoli) and Lepcis – whence Tripolitania gets its name. These three trading stations, grouped unusually close together, must have thrived on something more profitable than purely local trade. Their geographical position would have favoured the interception of trans-Saharan routes, such as that via Ghadames oasis and the Ahaggar massif, and it may be that their wealth derived from gold and slaves imported from the Fezzan and perhaps from tropical West Africa.[1]

Beyond its Tunisian heartland the Carthaginian empire consisted of little more than isolated coastal colonies separated by extensive tracts of Berber territory. Rather than extend their power inland by conquest the Carthaginians preferred to foster their commercial interests by treaty with the Berber chieftains of the interior. In northern Tunisia and the Sahel, however, Punic settlement wrought major changes in the cultural landscape. On to the Berber substratum of cereal cultivation and animal husbandry the Phoenicians grafted horticultural skills derived from the eastern Mediterranean. They introduced tree crops such as the olive, fig, pomegranate, almond and walnut; the grape vine and a knowledge of wine-making; and probably new techniques of irrigation and agricultural terracing. In the hinterland of Carthage a pattern of small-scale intensive farming was initiated which is reflected in the tradition of specialized horticulture that still characterizes the area (Fig. 7). The adoption in this and other areas of stone-built houses, in place of huts made of mud-brick and straw, may also have been due to the Carthaginians and it is likely that the Punic language was itself quite widely accepted. Outside the territory under direct Carthaginian control the diffusion of new crops and techniques, customs and beliefs, probably proceeded very slowly. But the millennium of Punic occupation provided ample opportunity for even the more remote Berber tribes to experience some modification in their way of life, particularly perhaps as a result of the practice of employing tribesmen as mercenary soldiers in the Carthaginian army. When the Romans ultimately defeated Carthage and succeeded to empire in North Africa, the Berber foundations of culture had been widely but unevenly overlaid by Punic influence. The northern Maghreb had by then been irrevocably drawn into the orbit of Mediterranean civilization.

At first the extension of Roman dominion in Africa was restricted to northern and eastern Tunisia, which became the province of Africa Vetus, and its purpose was simply to prevent a revival of Carthaginian power. However, the hostility of Berber chieftains and the ambitions of Roman commanders and land speculators led inevitably to wider conquest. The

[1] The nature and extent of Carthaginian trade with the interior is fully considered by E. W. Bovill (1958: 16–30).

cities of Tripolitania were soon added to the empire, as the province of Africa Nova, and in 74 B.C. Cyrenaica became a separate province to which the island of Crete was added a few years later. In 25 B.C. the Emperor Augustus united Tunisia and Tripolitania into the enlarged province of Africa Proconsularis and at the same time annexed the Berber chiefdoms of eastern Algeria to form the province of Numidia. Finally, in A.D. 46, the Emperor Claudius created in western Algeria and Morocco the provinces of Mauritania Caesariensis and Mauritania Tingitana – so-called from their capitals at Caesarea (Cherchell) and Tingis (Tangier) – and the Roman occupation of North Africa was complete (Figs. 8 and 9).

For the first four centuries of the Christian era the northern Maghreb flourished under the aegis of the *Pax Romana*. Then in A.D. 429 the Vandals, who had recently invaded Spain, were invited to assist in quelling a series of Berber revolts that were undermining the failing authority of Rome. Not only did they do so but in ten years they had dispossessed the Romans throughout most of North Africa and were in command of Carthage. The century of Vandal occupation did not, however, bring about any significant cultural change and in A.D. 533 the Byzantine general Belisarius success-fully reconquered the lost North African provinces, where the declining Roman tradition was upheld for another century until the Arab onslaught burst upon the Maghreb from the east.

At the apogee of Roman power, early in the third century A.D., the southern frontier of Africa Proconsularis coincided closely with the natural boundary between the steppe and the desert. Farther west, in Numidia and Mauritania Caesariensis, it reached only into the High Plains, while in Mauritania Tingitana it extended just south of Volubilis to encircle the fertile plain of the Gharb (Fig. 9). The frontier itself consisted of an elaborate defensive system, known as the *limes*, which comprised not only stretches of *fossatum* – or artificial ditch and wall – linking natural barriers such as the *chotts* and the Aurès massif, but also a supporting network of roads, camps and forts. This complex system of defence in depth was manned chiefly by *limitanei*: retired legionaries and Romanized Berbers who were granted land in exchange for military service at the frontier and who established self-sufficient colonies, many of which outlasted the collapse of Roman authority. In the western Maghreb the *limes* protected the coastal lowlands from attack by unconquered mountain tribes, but in the east it was designed mainly to repel raids by desert nomads. Such raids became progressively more frequent during the Roman period because it was then that the dromedary was introduced into North Africa and as a result many Saharan tribesmen increasingly adopted a pastoral nomadic way of life. The maintenance of the *limes* in the eastern Maghreb was one of the most remarkable achievements of Roman rule. Based on elaborate

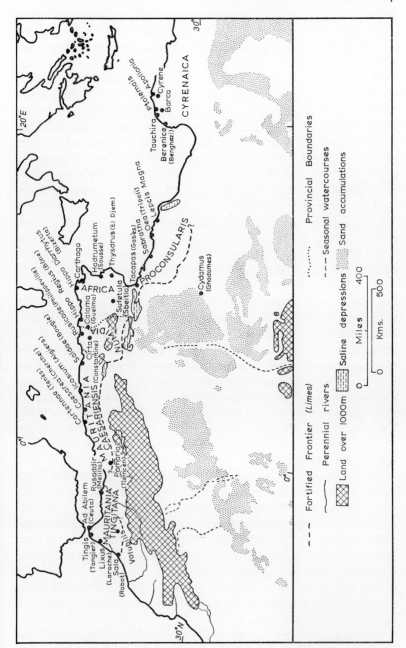

Fig. 9. Roman North Africa in the Early Third Century, A.D.

irrigation works, it marks the most southerly extension of nearly continuous settlement that has been achieved in North Africa and its example provides a challenge to modern plans for agricultural development along the margin of the desert.

Although irrigation was practised by both Carthaginians and Berbers, the Romans greatly extended irrigation agriculture within their North African provinces as well as along the *limes*. Their skill as hydraulic engineers is evident not only from the impressive remains of aqueducts and cisterns which supplied the towns, but also from the dams and wells by which surface and ground water was exploited for cultivation, many of which have been restored to active use in recent times. The most distinctive contribution of the Romans to the agricultural landscape was, however, the large commercial estate or *latifundium*. Soon after the destruction of Carthage, Roman speculators began to buy land in the new African provinces and to create huge estates which were worked by slaves and by tenant farmers or *coloni*. The monoculture of olive, grape vine, wheat and barley for export to Rome progressively replaced the Punic pattern of small-scale, horticultural, mixed farming. By the second century A.D. it had become declared policy to extend the cultivated area in order to satisfy the growing demands of the Roman market. As a result, by means of both irrigation and dry farming, cultivation was pushed farther into the semi-arid interior than at any time before or since. By perfecting dry-farming techniques for conserving soil moisture the Romans extended olive cultivation in central Tunisia right up to the limit set by the 8 in (200 mm) isohyet of mean annual rainfall and were thus able to support flourishing towns, such as Sufetula (Sbeitla), in areas that appear barren and unproductive today. Traces of Roman olive groves, observed and photographed from the air, have in fact stimulated modern French and Tunisian attempts to extend cultivation in the interior.

The Romans also had a profound effect on the urban landscape of North Africa. Not only did they re-design and enlarge most of the coastal settlements founded by the Phoenicians and Greeks, but inland they established a network of new towns linked by an elaborate road system. Although the typical Roman grid plan is seldom recognizable in the form of modern North African towns, the intimate relationship that exists between classical and contemporary urban patterns is revealed by the close juxtaposition of Roman sites with present-day towns and roads. Roman urbanization was, however, largely restricted to the lowlands, just as was modern European settlement in the Maghreb.

Little is known of the extent to which Latin and, later, Christianity were adopted in North Africa during the Roman occupation. Probably only a small minority of the inhabitants became completely assimilated into

Roman life, and there is evidence that Punic was still widely spoken in Numidia in the fifth century A.D.[1] Berber veterans of the Roman army would have carried a knowledge of the foreign language and faith back to their tribes – there is proof of such influence in the use by many Berber groups of the Julian calendar – but the Roman period remained essentially a colonial one during which alien authority was imposed on the Berber-Punic cultural complex without completely transforming it.

The Impact of Islam

Less than ten years after the death of Mohammed, the Arabs of the Abbassid caliphate in Baghdad launched their attack on North Africa. Byzantine resistance was easily overcome. Cyrenaica and the Fezzan fell in A.D. 642, Tripolitania in 647, and Tunisia, Algeria and Morocco soon after. By 711 the Arabs had crossed the Strait of Gibraltar and embarked on their conquest of Spain. Arabization proceeded slowly at first, especially in the Berber highlands, but it was later accelerated both by the invasion of 'Hilalian', Arabic-speaking pastoral nomads from the eleventh century onwards and by the arrival of Moslem refugees from Andalusia in the fifteenth, sixteenth and early seventeenth centuries (Fig. 8).

The initial Arab occupation of the Maghreb was a political conquest rather than a mass migration. It was accomplished by soldiers and missionaries, not by land-hungry settlers, and at first its effects were confined to the lowlands. Existing towns were quickly Arabized and many new ones founded, but the rural tribes were little affected. By 800 two centres of political power had emerged in the accessible lowlands at either end of the Maghreb. From Tunisia, which became known as Ifriqiya after the former Roman province of Africa Proconsularis, the Arabs administered both Tripolitania and eastern Algeria, at first from the newly founded cities of Kairouan and Mahdia, and later from Tunis, close to the site of Carthage. From Morocco, which was first effectively united by the Almoravid dynasty during the eleventh century, control was exerted over western Algeria and at times also over Andalusia, at first from the Byzantine centres of Tangier and Ceuta, and later from Fez and Marrakesh which were founded in 807 and 1062 respectively. At the peak of their power in 1102 the Almoravids – who were converted Berbers from the Mauritanian desert – commanded all Moslem Spain and the western Sahara in an empire that reached from the river Ebro to the Senegal.

Arabs and Arabized Berbers also established dynasties independent of Baghdad in Ifriqiya. One of these, the Fatimids, who had founded

---

[1] For example, St Augustine of Hippo Regius (Bône) requested that Punic-speaking bishops should be appointed to Numidian dioceses in order that they should be intelligible to their congregations.

Mahdia, conquered Egypt from the Abbassids in 969 and set up their new capital at Cairo, leaving Ifriqiya to be administered by their vassals the Zirids. In the middle of the eleventh century the latter declared their independence of Cairo and, in revenge, the Fatimids unleashed against them two large and warlike tribes of bedouin nomads from central Arabia, the Beni Hilal and the Beni Sulaim. The Arab historian Ibn Khaldun records that these pastoralists descended on the Maghreb 'like a swarm of locusts destroying everything in their path'. Their incursions were the first and most massive in a series of 'Hilalian' invasions that continued with diminishing frequency for several centuries. How many nomads moved into North Africa at this time is unknown – conservative estimates suggest about 250,000 – but they were certainly more numerous than the original Arab conquerors and they carried the new faith and language deep into the rural Maghreb. By 1400 they had occupied much of the northern Sahara, spread over the Tunisian Steppes and the High Plains of Algeria, and passed through the Taza corridor into the Atlantic lowland of Morocco. In their search for fresh pastures and new camping grounds they dispossessed many of the inhabitants of the plains, but they did not dislodge most of the mountain Berbers.

The pre-eminent effect of the Arab conquest and the Hilalian invasions was to make Mohammedanism and Arabic the dominant religion and language of the Maghreb. Their acceptance by the indigenous pagans and Christians was accelerated by intermarriage between the relatively small number of Arab invaders and native women. By the third or fourth generation the immigrants had been thoroughly assimilated into the local population and their new faith and language widely adopted. The ease with which Arabic spread may imply that Punic was still being spoken in Tunisia and other parts of the eastern Maghreb at the time of the conquest. Punic is as closely related to Arabic as Spanish is to French and the assumption that its use survived the Roman period makes the ready acceptance of Arabic speech and culture in the eastern Maghreb more intelligible. This assumption would also help to explain why the Berber language has been more completely eliminated from Tunisia and coastal Libya than from Algeria and Morocco (Fig. 6).

The replacement of Berber – and possibly in some areas of Latin – by Arabic took place first in the lowlands. In the highlands, where the indigenous Berbers, with their tradition of tribal democracy, resisted the imposition of authoritarian Arab rule, Arabic was adopted only slowly if at all. The survival today of Berber speech in mountainous Morocco and Algeria is a measure of how successfully the highlands have resisted Arabization, although, since the achievement of independence from France, the stature of Arabic has been enhanced and the rate of its adoption by the mountain Berbers has been accelerated. Today there are few tribes that are not in part at least bilingual and it is likely that Berber dialects will be abandoned in many areas within the next few generations.

The present distribution of Berber speech in the inner Maghreb has resulted from its persistence in already occupied mountain strongholds which were avoided by the invading Arabs, rather than from the retreat of lowland Berbers into highland refuges. However, the presence of Berber-speakers in the Sahara did result from their being driven out of more favoured areas by the tide of Arab advance. The initial Arab conquest drove some Berber tribes out of Libya and Tunisia into the oases of the northern Sahara where they survive today (Fig. 6). Ouargla, for example, was occupied by Berbers in the ninth century. But the Hilalian invasions caused greater displacement. They resulted in the expulsion of the ancestral Tuareg from their homeland in Tripolitania into the central Sahara. There the Tuareg adopted a predatory, pastoral nomadic way of life modelled on that of the bedouin invaders and they subjugated the indigenous Negroes, who became the Haratin or serf class on whom they depend for agricultural produce. Although they are now strict Moslems the Tuareg betray their derivation from the formerly Christian territory of Tripolitania by retaining the cross as their most prized decorative motif.

The Hilalian invasions also had a disastrous effect on cultivation and settled life in the inner Maghreb. Despising agricultural and urban civilization the bedouin nomads seized cultivated land and allowed it to revert to rough pasture; they let irrigation works fall into ruin and so facilitated the spread of malaria; and they destroyed most of the remaining forests by unrestricted grazing, browsing and burning, thus inducing widespread soil erosion. They encouraged some Berber tribes, such as the Beraber of the Middle Atlas and the Chaouïa of the Aurès massif, to become more nomadic, generally disrupted the economy of the *bled* and undermined the commercial basis of urban life. Along the coast ports reverted from trade to piracy and inland many towns were deserted. In central Tunisia, for example, the once flourishing Roman town of Thysdrus (El Djem), which boasted the third largest amphitheatre in the Empire, was abandoned, and even Kairouan, the holy city and first capital of Ifriqiya, was reduced to a minor provincial centre.

In contrast to the devastating effects of the Hilalian invasions, the migration of Moslem refugees from Andalusia had beneficial consequences for the Maghreb. Ejected from Spain during and after the Christian reconquest, most of the Andalusians settled in the towns, where they brought about a partial revival of skilled crafts, commerce and civilized life, particularly in the old urban centres of northern Morocco and Tunisia. They imported a more refined form of Arabic which sharpened the distinction – still apparent today – between the classical Arabic spoken by sophisticated townsmen and the rough speech of the rural tribes; and they improved agriculture by introducing from Spain new crops and superior techniques of cultivation. North African agriculture had already been enriched by the initial Arab occupation, which resulted in the introduction of new irrigation devices and of such crops as rice, sugar cane, bitter orange, lemon, apricot, spinach, pepper, ginger, indigo, saffron, mulberry and cotton; but those Andalusians who settled outside the towns took this process a stage further by introducing an assembly of American crops that had already been carried to Spain by Europeans, notably maize, beans, squash, tomato and tobacco, as well as opuntia cactus and agave which are still widely used as hedge plants. In particular Andalusian farmers did much to revive the failing tradition of intensive village horticulture in northern and eastern Tunisia. The Christian reconquest of Spain also drove many Sephardic Jews into the Maghreb where they contributed to the renaissance of trade and urban life.

By the mid-sixteenth century Arab conquest, Hilalian invasion and Andalusian immigration had transformed the cultural make-up of North Africa. Their combined effect had been to create the dualism between Arab and Berber society, which is such a striking feature of the modern Maghreb, and to deepen the gulf that separates urban from rural life. It only remained for European colonization in the nineteenth and twentieth centuries to add the last major element to the cultural mosaic of today. But in the intervening centuries the central and eastern Maghreb was to experience yet another phase of alien rule.

Turkish Interlude

Christian hostility towards the Moslems did not end with the capture of Granada in 1492. Although Moslem rule had been extinguished throughout the Iberian peninsula, under the impetus of the reconquest the Portuguese and Spanish carried the war into North Africa. Already in 1415 the Portuguese had launched a successful attack against Ceuta and by the early sixteenth century they also controlled Tangier and had established a string of fortresses reaching down the Atlantic coast of Morocco as far as Agadir. At the same time the Spanish had seized Melilla, Oran, Algiers, Bougie, Tunis and Tripoli. But the Iberian powers were by now engaged in more profitable adventures overseas and, in Morocco, the native Arabo-Berber dynasties soon regained control of all the coastal settlements except Mazagan, which remained Portuguese until 1790, Ceuta, which was ceded to Spain by Portugal in 1668, and Melilla. Today both Ceuta and Melilla remain Spanish and are administered as *plazas de soberanía* from Cadiz and Malaga.

The result of Iberian intervention in the Maghreb was to perpetuate hostility between Christians and Moslems for over three centuries and to provoke raids by the notorious corsairs or 'Barbary pirates' who became the scourge of European shipping in the Mediterranean. After expelling the Portuguese the Moroccans retained their independence, but only at the expense of losing economic and social contact with Europe. The country relapsed into isolation, preserving a degenerate medieval civilization into the twentieth century. In the central and eastern Maghreb, however, the consequence of Spanish attacks was three centuries of Turkish rule.

When, in the mid-sixteenth century, the Arabs appealed to their co-religionists for assistance in driving the Spanish out of North Africa, the Ottoman Turks not only accomplished this task but overstayed their welcome and remained as rulers. They first secured Tripoli, Tunis and Algiers as naval bases and by 1557 had divided the eastern and central Maghreb into three *ojaks* or regencies administered from these three capitals. Although they continued to recognize the sovereignty of the Turkish government at Constantinople the three regencies soon acquired a large measure of independence and became in effect self-governing colonies within the Ottoman Empire. Hereditary dynasties ruled by Beys were founded in Tripoli and Tunis, whereas Algiers became an oligarchic republic ruled over by a Dey who was elected for life. The present political geography of the central and eastern Maghreb originated at this time when the frontiers that divide Tripolitania, Tunisia and Algeria were first laid down. Cyrenaica, however, did not come under Turkish rule until 1640 when a Bey was installed at Benghazi (Fig. 8).

One of the first consequences of the Turkish conquest was an intensification of maritime activity, both privateering and legitimate trade. Algiers became the centre of this commerce, which was largely in the hands of Moslems of European origin, and the city's pre-eminence among the Mediterranean ports of the Maghreb dates from this time. Oran, Bône, Tunis and Tripoli flourished likewise, but Turkish rule had little effect on the peoples and economy of the interior. The Turkish language was never adopted outside the small ruling class, which itself tended to become increasingly Arabized, and Turkish administration beyond the major cities remained rudimentary.

However, the Turkish period did affect the interior in one way, by stimulating a brief revival of trans-Saharan trade, particularly in Libya. This arose mainly from the demand for Negro slaves in Turkey and Egypt, as well as in the Maghreb itself. The principal source of supply was the Bornu country west of Lake Chad, with whose Moslem ruler the Turks of Tripoli established friendly relations, and most of the slaves were marched across the desert by way of the ancient caravan route that passed between the Ahaggar and Tibesti massifs, before being sold in the markets of Tripoli and Benghazi. It was not until the middle of the nineteenth century that a breakdown in relations between Tripoli and Bornu led to the collapse of this barbarous trade.

The general outcome of the Turkish interlude was to prolong the isolation of North Africa from advancing European technology, to help preserve outmoded ways of life, and to accentuate the disparity between the wealthy coastal cities and the impoverished countryside. As a result, when European intervention came, its impact on the cultural patterns of the Maghreb was all the more sudden and disruptive.

European Occupation

The incident which led to the French assault on Algiers in 1830 occurred when the last Dey, provoked by insults to his religion, struck the French Consul with a fly-whisk. This breach of diplomatic etiquette was to have far-reaching consequences, for it provided the French with a pretext for embarking on their career of conquest in North Africa. They declared that their aim was to put an end to piracy, but the Barbary corsairs had long since ceased to offer any real threat to European shipping, and the chief reasons for the French action seem to have been the refusal of the Dey to allow them to maintain a privileged trading station near Bône and the hope of winning military credit for the weak restoration government of Charles X. The French also claimed that they were coming to liberate the Algerian Arabs from their despotic Turkish rulers, but, after ten years of indecision, they set about the direct conquest and colonization of the whole country and thus inaugurated the modern age of imperialism in the Maghreb.

The subjugation of Algeria by the French army proved to be an infinitely harder task than had been anticipated and it involved appalling cruelty to the Arab and Berber populations. Resistance was most desperate and prolonged among the Berbers, particularly in the Kabylie and Aurès massifs, and it was not until 1884 that 'pacification' of the whole country was completed. Mohammedanism was undermined by the conversion of mosques into churches and the rural economy was dislocated by the confiscation of tribal lands. By 1846 there were already 100,000 French *colons* settled on the more fertile parts of the Tell and by the early twentieth century European colonists had expropriated about 40 per cent of Algeria's cultivated land. Memories of the barbarities of the French conquest, and resentment of the injustices which flowed from it, go far to explain the tenacity with which Algerians fought for their freedom in the rising that began in the Aurès in 1954 and culminated in the withdrawal of the French and the proclamation of an independent Algerian republic in 1962.

Even before the French had fully consolidated their hold on Algeria they began to extend their control over the neighbouring territories. In 1881, acting to forestall claims by Britain and Italy, they occupied Tunisia. Two expeditionary columns entered the country but there was no resistance and the occupation was a diplomatic rather than a military coup. Tunisia became a protectorate, with the Bey retaining nominal authority, and, although French officials soon took over effective control of administration and European colonists eventually occupied up to 20 per cent of the cultivated area, land was not actually expropriated, mosques were not converted into churches, and there was no memory of cruel oppression to add bitterness to the struggle that led to the achievement of Tunisian independence in 1956.

Having secured Algeria's eastern flank against occupation by competing European nations, it was inevitable that the French should seek to extend their control to the west also. At the beginning of the twentieth century Morocco was almost the only African state that still retained its independence. Occupying a key strategic position at the entrance to the Mediterranean it excited the cupidity of all the major European powers. In 1904 France gained the agreement of Italy and Britain to French ascendancy in Morocco in exchange for recognizing their predominance in Libya and Egypt respectively. At the same time France concluded a secret treaty with Spain which divided Morocco into northern and southern zones of influence. After further diplomatic manoeuvres with Germany and the intervention of French troops to quell a series of tribal disorders, France officially established a protectorate over Morocco in 1912 and signed a convention with Spain defining the limits of the Spanish zone.

The French occupation of Morocco was delayed both by the First World War and by the resistance of the Berbers. At first it was limited to the plateaux east of the Moulouya and to the Atlantic lowland. In 1914 these two areas were linked by occupation of the Taza corridor and construction was begun of the railway that now connects Casablanca, Algiers and Tunis. 'Pacification' of the mountain tribesmen proceeded very slowly and was not completed in the Anti-Atlas and along the Saharan margin until 1934. The military campaigns were, however, carried out with a minimum of cruelty by the first French Resident General, Marshal Lyautey, who had genuine respect for Moroccan culture which he wished to modernize rather than supplant. European colonists occupied a much smaller proportion of the cultivated land than in Algeria or Tunisia – approximately 8 per cent – and, thanks largely to Lyautey's beneficent influence, the French régime had gone far to achieve his aims when Morocco regained its independence under King Mohammed V in 1956.

In northern Morocco the Spanish encountered even greater difficulty than the French in establishing their control. The Berbers of the Rif put up exceptionally stubborn resistance and were only defeated with the help of the French in 1926. During the Spanish civil war and the Second World War the Spanish completely neglected their protectorate and their tardy efforts to develop it after 1945 were soon terminated by its reintegration into the independent Moroccan kingdom in 1956. At the same time Tangier, which had been under international administration since 1923, was incorporated into Morocco.

Although by 1900 French troops had entered most of the oases in the Algerian Sahara and had established communication across the desert with French outposts near Lake Chad, European occupation of the western Sahara was delayed until after the conquest of Morocco. In 1934 the French occupied Tindouf, and, by despatching troops from Senegal to link up with columns from Morocco, brought Mauritania and the caravan routes of the western desert under their control. In the same year the Spanish took possession of Ifni, which had been ceded to them by Morocco in 1860 but never actually occupied, and also made effective their occupation of Tarfaya (the southern zone of their Moroccan protectorate) and adjacent Spanish Sahara, the extent of which had been agreed with the French in the convention of 1912. Tarfaya was returned to the independent Moroccan government in 1958, but the two administrative units into which Spanish Sahara is divided – Saguia el Hamra and Rio de Oro – remain Spanish. Mauritania achieved its independence in 1960 when the African territories of the former French Community were emancipated.

The Italian seizure of Libya completed European occupation of the Maghreb (Fig. 8). The initial invasion took place in 1911 with the capture of Tripoli and by 1914 the Italians were in control of the whole country; but during the first world war the Tripolitanians and the Sanusi tribesmen of Cyrenaica drove the Italians back to the coastal cities. Between 1921 and 1932 Italy brutally reconquered the country, causing great loss of life and arousing lasting bitterness. Ambitious colonization schemes were initiated but the new 'Pax Romana' was soon ended by the campaigns of the Second World War, after which Libya was administered by British military authorities until 1951. In that year the United Kingdom of Libya, under its new hereditary ruler King Idris I, became the first African state to attain post-war independence.

Contemporary Problems

With their emergence from colonial tutelage the independent nations of North Africa face formidable problems of economic betterment and political organization. Like other newly independent African states their central dilemma is how to match the 'revolution of rising expectations' that everywhere accompanies independence with tangible improvements in living standards for a majority of the population. To achieve this they must not only promote economic development but also foster a strong political sense of national identity. As a result of their historical experience of both European and Moslem civilization the countries of the Maghreb have a more highly developed sense of nationhood than many other young African states, but, with rapidly increasing populations living at or near subsistence level, their economic problems are as acute as those in most other 'developing' parts of the continent.

The Economic Situation

North Africa's fundamental economic problem is to raise the standards of life of its impoverished inhabitants – most of whom are both undernourished and underemployed – sufficiently fast to outpace the effects of excessive population growth. The present demographic structure of the Maghreb is part of the colonial legacy. When Europeans first occupied North Africa its total population was probably between 6 and 7 million. By 1964 it had grown to approximately 31·2 million (Morocco: 12,959,000, Algeria: 10,975,000, Tunisia: 4,565,000, Libya: 1,559,000, Mauritania: 900,000, Melilla (city): 78,000, Ceuta (city): 78,000, Ifni: 52,000, Spanish Sahara: 48,000) and it continues to increase at a rate of over 2 per cent per annum, or more than half a million each year.

The gradual extension of European methods of disease control to the Arab and Berber populations has been the primary cause of this population explosion. In the past, high mortality rates counteracted high fertility and effectively checked population growth, but since the notorious killing diseases of North Africa – typhus, cholera, smallpox, malaria, plague and venereal diseases – have been either eliminated or greatly reduced, continuing high fertility has resulted in a massive increase of population. Furthermore, the rate of population growth will probably accelerate in the foreseeable future because mortality rates are likely to be reduced still more and because in each country over half the population is now under twenty years of age.

Certain factors tend to diminish population increase locally, but a general reduction in fertility is improbable. Since independence some attempt has been made to promote birth control, particularly in Tunisia. However, traditional Moslem attitudes, which favour early marriage and large families, together with easy divorce and, among some of the more conservative communities, polygamy, prevent birth control from being generally adopted as a means of reducing excessive population increase. Male migration from densely populated rural areas, both to the larger towns and overseas to France and elsewhere, has also slowed down population growth locally in recent decades, but its overall effect has been slight and is further decreasing as the migration of whole families tends to replace that of single men.

All the countries of North Africa are experiencing rates of population increase far in excess of the opportunities available for full-time employment of their adult populations. But only certain rural areas of the Maghreb suffer from acute 'overpopulation', in the sense that they support exceptionally high densities of population at very low standards of living and generate an outward flow of migrants. Most important of these are the mountain massifs and desert oases occupied by Berber-speaking farmers, notably the Kabylie mountains and north Saharan oases of Algeria, the eastern Rif, western High Atlas and Anti-Atlas of Morocco, the southern Monts des Ksour of Tunisia, and the Jebel Nefusa of Tripolitania. Rural overpopulation is less acute in the lowlands, although excessively high densities characterize parts of the Atlantic lowland of Morocco, particularly the Doukkala plains, as well as the Tunisian Sahel and the island of Djerba. Migrants from these overpopulated parts of the *bled* have in turn created urban overpopulation by crowding into the *bidonvilles* of the larger towns where most of them find at best only part-time employment.

Faced with the consequences of mounting demographic pressure the first economic need of the nations of the Maghreb is to expand employment, particularly in the overpopulated countryside and in the cities most swollen by the influx of rural migrants. Agricultural development, mineral exploitation, industrialization and, to a lesser extent, tourism offer the main hopes of alleviating mass underemployment and raising living standards. But shortages of capital and skilled manpower impose severe restrictions on economic initiative and oblige the newly independent governments of North Africa to plan carefully the development of their limited resources.

Agricultural Development

The improvement of farming methods and the increase of agricultural output, both of local food supplies and cash crops for export, probably offers the best hope of improving living standards in the more populous states of the Maghreb. In Libya and Mauritania, however, where population density remains relatively low and valuable deposits of petroleum and iron ore are being exploited, revenues from these resources are capable of raising living standards more rapidly than is agricultural development.

Despite the massive movement of people from the countryside into the towns which had, by 1960, increased the urban population of Morocco, Algeria and Tunisia to approximately 25 per cent of the total, over 65 per cent of the working population in these countries is still employed in agriculture. Much cultivation remains on a subsistence basis, but agricultural products have nevertheless in recent years comprised about 75 per cent by value of Algeria's exports, 55 per cent of Tunisia's and 40 per cent of Morocco's. Capital investment in agriculture can therefore be justified as a means of both raising local production above subsistence level and earning much needed foreign revenue.

Agricultural development in the Maghreb since independence, as well as during the last decade of European occupation, has taken the dual form of intensified production on lands already cultivated and extension of the cultivated area, the latter mainly by means of irrigation schemes. Both approaches have been hindered by social and physical restraints, chiefly archaic systems of land tenure and inadequate water resources.

Traditional Moslem law in North Africa recognizes three main types of tenure: *melk* lands, the freehold of which is owned privately by individuals or families; *habou* lands which, although they may be privately owned, are inalienable and provide revenue for religious and charitable purposes such as the upkeep of mosques and schools; and *arch* lands which are held in communal ownership by tribes, mainly in the steppe and desert zones, and which are also inalienable. The great extent of both *habou* and *arch* tenure in the Maghreb has kept unproductive much land which might otherwise have been subject to private purchase and development. However, both during and since the period of European occupation the traditional pattern of land ownership has been substantially changed. First the European colonists, in the course of taking over most of the better land by confiscation and purchase, greatly extended the proportion owned as private freehold. Large private estates were created on which cash crops were raised, often by mechanized methods, and many of the dispossessed Moslems joined the ranks of the unemployed. Since independence most European-owned land has been expropriated and much of it divided among local farmers. Extensive tracts of *habou* and *arch* lands are also being opened to settlement by individual farmers and in some areas, such as semiarid central Tunisia, voluntary cooperatives are being set up to run newly-established perimeters of irrigation.

Following the expropriation of European farms and the progressive revision of traditional forms of Moslem land tenure, the success of further agricultural development now depends chiefly on the modernization of techniques of cultivation and the provision of more water for irrigation. Considerable progress was achieved during the colonial period, particularly by the French, who pioneered the discovery and exploitation of underground water resources and embarked on a modest programme of reservoir construction. Surface water is only available in sufficient quantity for large-scale permanent irrigation in the more humid Tell of Algeria and Tunisia and the Atlantic coastal plain of Morocco. Barrage and diversion dams have been built along the larger perennial rivers, notably in the drainage basins of the Oum er Rbia, Sebou, Tensift and Moulouya in Morocco, the Cheliff in Algeria and the Medjerda in Tunisia. Several of these form part of multi-purpose schemes which provide hydro-electric power and flood control facilities, as well as water for irrigation, industry and urban use. But more significant than the few large-scale installations are the thousands of smaller hydraulic works that are being constructed, many of them on the sites of former Roman dams. At minimum cost they substantially improve local water supplies and also help to check soil erosion. Small-scale, low cost improvements in the use of underground water, such as the provision of diesel and wind pumps for wells, have similarly yielded good returns, but in certain areas, where large reserves of good quality underground water have been discovered, more ambitious development schemes are under way. Chief among these are the exploitation by deep wells of the Quaternary subsidence troughs of central Tunisia and of the aquifers that bring artesian water within reach of modern well-boring equipment throughout much of the northern Sahara. One such development scheme in southern Tunisia envisages the linking together of the old oases along the northern edge of the Chott Djerid by a series of new oases using artesian water and producing high quality *deglat* dates and other fruit for export.

Although the most successful method of raising agricultural output in North Africa has so far proved to be the harnessing of new supplies of surface and underground water, the provision of new and improved crops, livestock, fertilizers and agricultural implements is likely to be of equal or greater importance in the future. All the governments of the Maghreb have embarked on experimental farming programmes and many new crops and techniques are being tried out. Among the more successful are the introduction of improved varieties of tree fruits, the development of both irrigated and dry-framed fodder crops to raise the productivity of local livestock, and the rationalization of the alfa and esparto grass industries. Ambitious tree-planting programmes have also been initiated in an effort to check the severe soil erosion that has depleted the soil cover over so much of North Africa. Drought-resistant trees, particularly Aleppo pine and introduced species of eucalyptus, are being extensively planted in the Tell and steppe zones and efforts are being made to control unrestricted browsing by goats, which has for so long prevented the natural regeneration of trees and shrubs. One of the first acts of the independent government of Tunisia was to order a mass slaughter of goats and to ban goat herding throughout all but the driest parts of the country.

Oil, Ores and Industrialization

Agricultural development, chiefly by means of relatively cheap, small-scale technical improvements following tenurial reform, can make the most direct contribution to raising living standards among the rural mass of the population. But to alleviate conditions in the overcrowded cities and to provide jobs for the continuing flow of migrants, which, despite improvements in agriculture, can be expected from the acutely overpopulated mountains and oases of the interior, a great expansion of non-agricultural employment will be necessary. This is only likely to be achieved by vigorous exploitation of North Africa's mineral resources, notably the deposits of oil and natural gas discovered since 1956, accompanied by industrialization to the full extent that limited supplies of capital and skilled labour will allow.

Mineral exploitation is chiefly important as a means of earning foreign revenue for investment in industry and other forms of development. It does not provide jobs for a significant number of unskilled workers. In the first decade of oil and natural gas exploitation in the Algerian Sahara, for example, the number of nomads and oasis dwellers employed as labourers was 10,000 at the most, or less than 2 per cent of the population of the desert itself. Nor is there any prospect of a considerable increase. As a source of revenue for capital investment, however, oil and natural gas is already of unparalleled importance to Libya and Algeria and could become so to other North African territories if continuing exploration results in the discovery of new major deposits.

The most spectacular accretion of wealth from oil exploitation has occurred in Libya. The first wells were brought into production in 1961 and by 1965 annual oil revenues had risen to £280 million, a value which greatly exceeded the previous total income of the country. Following the pattern set by Iraq and other underdeveloped oil-producing nations, 70 per cent of this revenue is earmarked for economic development. But so far comparatively little of it has been spent because development is held back by the lack of other natural resources, the shortage of skilled labour and the inevitably slow process of initial planning. Libya's first five-year plan (1964–68) provides for public works of all kinds, particularly housing and road-building, and it includes several major projects such as the building of a new city to replace Barce, over half of which was destroyed by a severe earthquake in February, 1963, and the construction of a new capital at Beida. All the wells at present producing are located in the oil fields of the Sidra Basin and Serir and are connected by pipeline to coastal terminals at Sidra, Lanuf, Brega and Tobruk, but there are also proven reserves in western Tripolitania and Fezzan, which, because of their relatively poor quality and distance from the coast, remain uneconomic (Fig. 10). Libya's total reserves exceed 1000 million tons and between 1961 and 1965 Libyan oil production increased from less than 1 million to over 58 million tons. It is probable that a continuing rapid rise in output will be achieved for some time to come.

In Algeria, where the first discovery of Saharan oil was made at Edjelé in January, 1956, production has not increased quite so dramatically. From a total of about 1 million tons in 1959 output rose to 26 million in 1965. The producing wells are located in two areas with combined proven reserves of some 1000 million tons: the Fort Polignac Basin southeast of the Great Eastern Erg, which is linked by pipeline to the Tunisian coast at La Skhira, and the Central Basin between the Great Western and Great Eastern Ergs, which is connected by pipeline to the Algerian port of Bougie (Fig. 10). The oil field at Hassi Messaoud in the Central Basin comprises Africa's largest known deposit of crude oil, with proven reserves of about 480 million tons. As exploitation has proceeded, Hassi Messaoud has developed into a considerable town, lavishly equipped with air-conditioned houses, cinemas, libraries and other amenities for the highly paid, mostly European technicians who work the oil field. The crude oil is lighter and contains less sulphur than the heavy black oils of the Middle East and it can be used in its natural state to drive the diesel engines that are employed in drilling for both oil and water. Some of it is refined locally to provide cheap petroleum products and it is used to generate electricity which is supplied to Ouargla and other nearby oases. Transport facilities have also been revolutionized. Surfaced roads now link the oil fields with the oases and there is a regular air service to Algiers.

As well as the oil deposits discovered in these two areas immense reserves of natural gas have been found in the Algerian Sahara. In 1956 one of the world's largest gas fields was found at Hassi R'Mel, northwest of Ghardaïa oasis, and it is now linked by pipeline to the coast at Arzew, Oran and Algiers (Fig. 10). The gas not only provides a cheap local supply of power but is also liquefied and exported in refrigerated tankers to several European countries. Huge reserves of natural gas have also been found in the Fort Polignac Basin and in the Ahnet Basin northwest of the Ahaggar massif (Fig. 10), but the latter are too remote for economic exploitation at present. Altogether Algeria's reserves of oil and natural gas represent a natural resource of enormous potential value, which, in 1965, already earned the country £36·5 million in foreign revenues.

As yet neither oil nor natural gas has been found in significant quantities outside Algeria and Libya. In Morocco small amounts of oil are produced

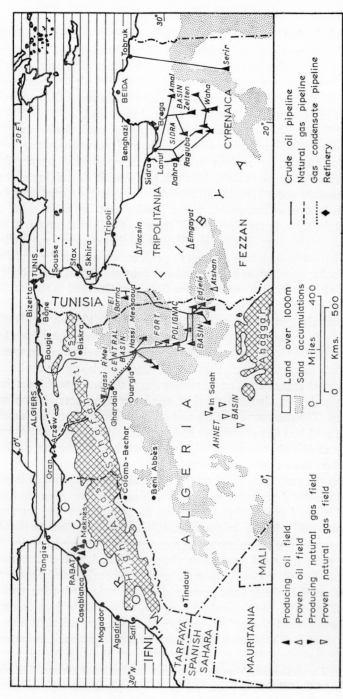

Fig. 10. The Maghreb: Oil and Natural Gas

4

near Meknès, but, despite extensive search, hopes of finding deposits in the Saharan province of Tarfaya have been abandoned. Even more, intensive prospecting in Tunisia has revealed only one substantial oil field at El Borma (Fig. 10). It produces sufficient for Tunisia's domestic needs and a modest surplus for export. In both Spanish Sahara and Mauritania prospecting continues but has not yet proved successful.

In addition to oil and natural gas other varied and valuable mineral resources exist in North Africa (Fig. 11). Many of them remain untapped, particularly in the Sahara, because the costs of exploitation are prohibitively high, but in Mauritania, Morocco and Tunisia the mining of iron ore, phosphate and other minerals provides an important source of export revenue. The most remarkable recent development has taken place in Mauritania. Here, in the Kedia d'Idjil range east of Fort Gouraud, is one of the richest iron ore deposits in Africa. It consists of 150 to 200 million tons of haematite ore which averages 63 per cent iron content. Its exploitation is being financed by an international consortium which has built a 400-mile long railway to export the ore from Fort Gouraud to the coast at Port Étienne. By 1965 the annual export target of 6 million tons, worth approximately £30 million, was reached for the first time. A substantial share of this revenue accrues to the Mauritanian government, which has thus acquired sufficient capital to finance economic development on a scale that should ultimately benefit the whole of the country's sparse population. Already work at the mines, on the railway and in the new townships at Port Étienne and Fort Gouraud provides employment for several thousand labourers. The construction of the new capital at Nouakchott, the launching of a road-building programme and the exploitation of valuable copper deposits at Akjoujt, are also providing opportunities for regular employment where none existed previously.

Just as the economic prospects of Libya and Algeria depend so largely on oil and natural gas and those of Mauritania on iron ore, Morocco looks to the increased export of phosphate and its derivatives as the country's main source of capital for development. Morocco has long been the world's leading exporter of phosphate and it competes with the Soviet Union for second place in world production after the United States. The main Moroccan deposits are located near the towns of Khouribga and Youssoufia (Louis Gentil) on the Atlantic coastal plain and in 1964 production reached 10·2 million tons. In the same year exports of phosphate from Safi and Casablanca earned some £41·3 million or over a quarter of Morocco's foreign revenue. Phosphate is also Tunisia's most valuable mineral export. The principal mines lie north of the Chott Djerid depression to the west of Gafsa and a total annual output of over 2 million tons assures Tunisia's place as the world's fourth largest producer. Phosphate mining is associated

Opposite: **Fig. 11. The Maghreb: Principal Mineral Deposits**

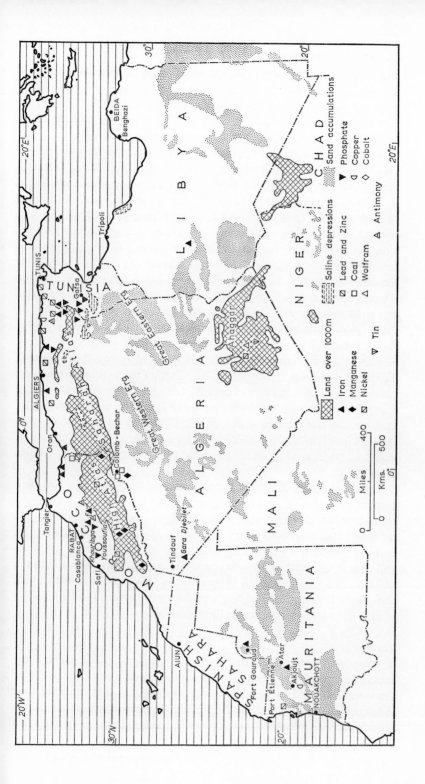

with ambitious programmes of industrialization in both Morocco and Tunisia where plants for the manufacture of superphosphate fertilizer, sulphuric acid and other chemicals have been built at Safi and Sfax. They contribute not only to export earnings but also provide the fertilizer that is essential for the improvement of domestic agriculture.

At present no other minerals make a major contribution to the supply of capital available for economic development in North Africa, although appreciable quantities of iron, lead, zinc, manganese and coal are mined in the inner Maghreb and there are large unexploited mineral resources in the Sahara, notably of iron ore at Gara Djebilet near Tindouf (Fig. 11).

Until the discovery of Saharan oil and natural gas revolutionized the situation by providing both capital and local sources of power, there were few opportunities for large-scale industrialization in North Africa. Now the basis exists for some development of heavy industry, at least in Algeria, Libya and perhaps Tunisia. This is at first likely to be restricted to the oil industry itself, except for the installations based on phosphate exploitation. A complex of petrochemical works is being established at Arzew on the Algerian coast and there is a large refinery at Algiers. Refineries also exist near Casablanca and Rabat in Morocco, at Bizerta in Tunisia and at Brega in Libya (Fig. 10). Further petrochemical works are planned by the governments of both Algeria and Libya. Eventually other heavy industries may be developed using local resources such as, for example, the manufacture of iron and steel based on the iron ore and coal deposits near Tindouf and Colomb-Bechar. However, none of the major industrial projects so far realized goes far to satisfy the need for unskilled employment.

The development of light industries, particularly those processing agricultural products, offers a better prospect of providing jobs for the untrained urban dwellers and rural migrants. Since independence the number of factories engaged in food-processing and the manufacture of building materials – particularly flour mills, fish and vegetable canneries and cement and brick works – has been increased in Tunisia and Morocco and also, to a lesser extent, in Algeria. But in Libya and Mauritania, with their smaller populations and restricted domestic markets, the development of light industry has as yet made little headway.

Tourism

The opportunities for alleviating mass underemployment and raising living standards through the encouragement of tourism are much more restricted than those afforded by agricultural development, mineral exploitation or industrialization. However, in Tunisia and Morocco the tourist industry already makes a substantial contribution to foreign exchange earnings and there is considerable potential for its development also in Algeria and Libya.

The most remarkable rise in tourism has taken place in Tunisia. Capitalizing on the unexcelled beaches of its eastern coast and the prodigious wealth of Roman and medieval Moslem remains in the interior, the Tunisian government has launched a vigorous campaign to improve tourist facilities. As a result the annual number of visitors increased from 25,000 to over 150,000 in the first ten years of independence. This rapid rate of increase is likely to be sustained as direct air services between European cities and Tunis are improved and in the near future Tunisia may well become one of the greatest tourist magnets in the Mediterranean. By the 1970's it is estimated that Tunisia will be receiving over £30 million annually from tourism and that it will have become the country's principal means of earning foreign currency.

Morocco is less well endowed with tourist attractions. Although its imperial cities and the spectacular mountain and desert scenery of the interior are a great asset, its Atlantic coast is swept by the cool waters of the Canaries current and it lacks warm-water beaches comparable to those of Tunisia. Nevertheless the number of visitors to the country has risen steeply in recent years and the prospects for further expansion of tourism are good.

The Political Situation

None of the nations of the Maghreb can hope to solve its economic problems unless it achieves and maintains political unity. Without a purposive sense of nationhood the sustained effort necessary to raise living standards will not be made, and without a measure of political stability the foreign loans and investment on which so many development plans depend will not become available. The growth of national unity among the states of the Maghreb is not as fragile as it is in many other young African nations, but in their drive towards nationhood the North African states are nevertheless hindered by internal political stresses of varying severity. Their external relations are also to some extent prejudiced by frontier disputes which have arisen since independence, and by differing political alignments with the outside world, both within and beyond Africa.

Internal Stresses

Weaknesses in national unity arise from the major ethnic and geographical divisions of the Maghreb. The ancient cleavage between Arab and Berber finds expression in the internal politics of Algeria and, to a lesser extent, in Morocco; while that between Caucasoid and Negroid races is most apparent in Mauritania. In Libya the strong separatist tendencies of

Tripolitania and Cyrenaica result more from the strictly geographical division of the country.

Tunisia, the most securely united of North Africa's independent states, lacks a significant Berber minority and its territory is small and compact enough to be governed directly from Tunis without arousing any marked regional antagonisms. During its first decade of independence it has also profited from the stability that comes from uninterrupted political leadership by one man, President Bourguiba, who led the independence struggle against the French and who now, more than any other North African leader, personifies the aspirations of his young nation.

In Algeria the bitter eight-year war of independence conducted by the *Front de Libération Nationale* (F.L.N.) welded the country, for the first time in its history, into a united nation. But the enduring ethnic and geographical divisions that have so often in the past made of Algeria a marchland between the more easily unified realms of Morocco and Tunisia have shown signs of reasserting themselves since independence. In 1963 the Berber population of the Kabylie massif rose in rebellion against the newly installed government of independent Algeria. The rising was suppressed and the leaders sentenced to death, but hostility between Berber and Arab persists. It stems from their traditionally contrasted patterns of social organization and is accentuated by the fact that the most acute conditions of rural overpopulation are found in the Berber-occupied mountain massifs. To submerge the sturdy tradition of Berber separatism – which has already survived two thousand years of Roman, Arab, Turkish and French rule – in loyalty to the new ideal of nationhood is likely to remain the most difficult problem of internal politics facing independent Algeria.

Unlike republican Tunisia and Algeria, Morocco is a constitutional monarchy with a long history as an independent kingdom. The French occupation can be viewed as a relatively brief interruption of Moroccan sovereignty, which has held sway for many centuries over the political core area of the Atlantic coastal lowland, and, to a varying extent, over the fringing Atlas mountains and western Sahara as well. Consequently there is a strong tradition of loyalty to the monarchy, which has been, since independence, directed first towards King Mohammed V, the revered leader of his people in the struggle against the French, and then towards his son, King Hassan II. The Berber tribes of the mountains continue to express their contempt for centralized government by flouting its authority from time to time, as for example by refusing to pay taxes, but they do not endanger the monarchy, which indeed draws much of its support from the rural areas. Such organized opposition as there is to the king and his somewhat authoritarian government feeds rather on the grievances of the underprivileged masses living in the overcrowded cities. Provided their economic prospects can be improved this does not represent a lasting threat to national unity.

To a much greater degree even than Morocco, Libya depends for the preservation of its political unity upon its constitutional monarch. King Idris I, who has presided over his country's fortunes since 1951, is respected in all three of Libya's disparate provinces as the symbol of national independence. But apart from his personal prestige there is little to check the polarization of the country around its two historical nuclei: the Djeffara plain and Tripoli as the core of Tripolitania, and the Jebel Akhdar and Benghazi as the heart of Cyrenaica, with the desert province of Fezzan uneasily divided between them. The decision to build a new national capital at Beida in Cyrenaica is an attempt to sidestep the competing claims of the two provincial capitals but, as the desert barrier along the Gulf of Sirte rules out the possibility of a central location, the new city will do little to assuage separatist tendencies. In 1963 it was proposed to increase national cohesion by replacing the three traditional provinces by ten smaller regions, but the scheme was undermined by regional prejudices and has not yet been fully implemented. The best hope for establishing Libyan unity on a lasting basis probably lies in expanding the network of modern communications to link the provinces more closely together. Oil revenues now make this possible, but it is likely to be many years before the ancient loyalties that bind most Libyans either to Tripolitania or to Cyrenaica are submerged in a larger loyalty to Libya itself.

The main internal problem of Mauritania is not to curb political separatism but to foster national awareness among the nomadic tribes that make up a large part of its widely dispersed population. There is, however, a radical division between the Caucasoid element in the population, which is of mixed Arab and Berber origin, and the Negroid peoples, most of whom are sedentary and occupy the Senegal valley in the extreme south. The white element forms a majority and dominates the administration of the country, but there is much racial mixing and little or no discrimination, so that racial tensions do not threaten the growth of national unity. One of the first and most imaginative acts of the newly independent government, faced with the formidable task of creating a Mauritanian nation, was to undertake the construction of the new capital at Nouakchott to supersede the old administrative capital, St Louis, which was not even in Mauritania but across the river in Senegal. Financed by revenue from the iron mines at Fort Gouraud and located at a point mid-way along the coast between the desert north and the more humid south, Nouakchott symbolizes the hopeful attempt to build a viable Mauritanian state.

In the neighbouring territory of Spanish Sahara, which, with the enclaves of Ifni, Ceuta and Melilla, constitutes the last vestige of European political control in North Africa, there is neither an effective nationalist movement nor any immediate prospect of independence. The Spanish government is unwilling to relinquish its claims, particularly since active prospecting for oil and other mineral deposits began, and since Morocco and Mauritania attained their independence the colony has become inextricably involved in the territorial disputes that bedevil relations between the three countries.

External Relations

Despite public commitment to the ideal of pan-Maghreb unity each North African state has pursued an essentially nationalistic policy since becoming independent. Frontier disputes have broken out between Algeria and Morocco and between Morocco, Mauritania and the Spanish territories; and differences in the foreign policies of individual states have tended to accentuate the growth of nationalism at the expense of North African unity.

The unresolved border dispute between Algeria and Morocco concerns a stretch of about 400 miles (640 km) of Morocco's southeastern frontier between the meridians 2° and 9° West (Fig. 5). This boundary was never precisely demarcated during the French occupation of North Africa and in 1963 fighting broke out between Moroccan and Algerian troops over frontier posts, at Hassi Beida and Tinjoub, which had remained unoccupied since the withdrawal of the French. The interest of both countries in the area has been intensified by knowledge of the massive iron ore deposits at Gara Djebilet, near Tindouf, a short distance inside present Algerian territory. The Algerians base their claim on the fact that the disputed area was included in Algeria at the date of independence. The Moroccans point out with some justice that one of the main objects of the French, from their conquest of Algeria until their occupation of Morocco in 1912, was to hem Morocco into the smallest possible area of northwest Africa. Consequently Morocco claims that the original treaty of 1845 between France and Morocco, which failed to define the frontier at all precisely and which was reinterpreted in 1901–02 in France's favour, should be disregarded, and the status of all the disputed territory renegotiated.

The frontier dispute with Algeria is part of Morocco's much wider claims to territory in the western Sahara. These find some historical justification in the fact that Morocco has, since the original establishment of the Almoravid empire in the eleventh century, periodically extended its rule over large tracts of the desert. However, in the past the extension of Moroccan sovereignty was regarded more as a spiritual than as a territorial matter. Dominion was claimed wherever the faithful mentioned the name of the Moroccan Sultan in their Friday prayers; although their devotion to him seldom embraced a willingness to pay tribute or taxes. According to such a religious criterion Moroccan sovereignty stretched far beyond the southern boundaries inherited when the country regained its independence in 1956; and the recent discovery of valuable mineral resources in the western Sahara has, from Morocco's standpoint, only sharpened concern over its long-standing claims.

Today the Moroccan government lays official claim to the whole of Mauritania and Spanish Sahara. Before Mauritania became independent in 1960 there was some support among its politicians for integration with Morocco, but this soon faded when it became apparent that international exploitation of the Fort Gouraud iron ore deposits – which Morocco specifically opposed – would provide Mauritania with a secure economic basis for independence. The prospect of closer co-operation with Morocco has also receded since Mauritania began to strengthen its old economic links with West Africa, which have grown out of centuries of trade with the Moslem peoples of the Senegal and Niger valleys. Although the Mauritanian government has not joined any of the West African nations in their tentative moves towards political integration, it has agreed with Senegal, Mali and Guinea on the internationalization of the Senegal river and has joined an inter-state committee, set up with assistance from the United Nations Special Fund, to plan the development of irrigation, hydro-electric power and improved navigation throughout the drainage basin of the river.

At present there seems little chance of Morocco successfully pressing its territorial claims against Mauritania. On the other hand it is unlikely that Spain will succeed indefinitely in maintaining its foothold in Spanish Sahara and Ifni, least of all in the latter, which is geographically and historically so firmly attached to Morocco and whose Spanish garrisons have more than once been attacked by Moroccan irregular troops.

Relations between the nations of the eastern Maghreb are not clouded by active frontier disputes, although Tunisia has raised the question of an extension of its sovereignty southward into Algeria and Libya to obtain a share of the underground water and mineral resources of the Sahara. It is inconceivable, however, that either state would consider such a plea unless it were part of a broader political settlement. The idea of a North African federation has often been canvassed but the past development and present policies of each country are so distinctive that there is little chance of such an ambition being realized in the foreseeable future. The interdependence of Morocco, Algeria and Tunisia was solemnly proclaimed at the Conference for Maghreb Unity held in Tangier in 1958 and it has been reaffirmed since. The possibility of Libya joining an eventual federation has also been sympathetically considered. But it is very unlikely that interdependence will be carried beyond the level of practical cooperation in

4*

economic matters – for which purpose the Maghreb Permanent Consultative Committee was set up in 1964 – to the stage of outright political union.

Similarly, in their political relations with the outside world, the newly independent states of North Africa have put the realities of national interest before the uncertain benefits of common action. All of them subscribe to the aims of the Organization of African Unity, all but Mauritania are members of the Arab League, and they are unanimous in rejecting their colonial past, but they nevertheless pursue separate and sometimes conflicting foreign policies. For example, Algeria, proud of its revolutionary credentials won in the long struggle for independence, has pursued a more vigorously 'anti-imperialist' policy in Africa than its neighbours; while Tunisia has risked expulsion from the Arab League by advocating a tolerant attitude towards Israel. As they continue to follow their own paths to fully independent nationhood in the second half of the twentieth century, the nations of the Maghreb are likely to enhance their special standing in post-colonial Africa. With their unique inheritance of European, Moslem and indigenous African cultures, and with the prospect before them of successful economic growth, they are capable of making a vital contribution to the task of bringing the rest of the continent into a stable relationship with the modern world.

References and Select Bibliography

This list is largely restricted to studies of North Africa as a whole which relate closely to the themes developed in this essay. Comprehensive bibliographies listing works on particular North African countries, regions and problems will be found in several of the books cited here, notably in Depois, 1964, and Capot-Rey, 1953.

BARADEZ, JEAN. 1949. *Fossatum Africae: vue-aérienne de l'organisation romaine dans le Sud-Algérien*, Arts et Métiers Graphiques, Paris.

BARBOUR, NEVILL (ed.). 1962. *A Survey of North West Africa (The Maghreb)*, Oxford University Press, London.

BASSET, ANDRÉ. 1952. *La Langue berbère*, Oxford University Press, London.

BOUSQUET, G. H. 1956. *Les Berbères*, Presses Universitaires de France ('Que sais-je?' series), Paris.

BOVILL, E. W. 1958. *The Golden Trade of the Moors*, Oxford University Press, London.

BRIGGS, L. C. 1960. *Tribes of the Sahara*, Havard University Press, Cambridge, Mass.

CAPOT-REY, ROBERT. 1953. *Le Sahara français*, Presses Universitaires de France, Paris.

CHEVALIER, L. 1947. *Le probléme demographique nord-africain*, Presses Universitaires de France, Paris.

CHOURAQUI, ANDRÉ. 1952. *Les Juifs d'Afrique du Nord*, Presses Universitaires de France, Paris.

CLARKE, J. I. 1959. Studies of semi-nomadism in North Africa. *Economic Geography*, Vol. 35: 95–108.

1961. Economic and political changes in the Sahara. *Geography*, Vol. 46: 102–119.

DESPOIS, JEAN. 1961. Development of land use in Northern Africa. 219–237 in STAMP, L. D. (ed.), *A History of Land Use in Arid Regions*, Unesco, Paris.

1964. *L'Afrique du Nord*, Presses Universitaires de France, Paris, 3rd ed.

DESPOIS, JEAN and RENÉ RAYNAL. 1967. *Géographie de L'Afrique du Nord-Ouest*, Payot, Paris.

DRESCH, JEAN et al. 1963. *Réforme agraire au Maghreb*, Maspéro, Paris.

DUPREE, LOUIS. 1958. The non-Arab ethnic groups of Libya. *Middle East Journal*, Vol. 12: 33–44.

EVANS-PRITCHARD, E. E. 1949. *The Sanusi of Cyrenaica*, Clarendon Press, Oxford.

FISHER, GODFREY. 1957. *Barbary Legend: War, Trade and Piracy in North Africa 1415–1830*, Oxford University Press, London.

GALISSOT, R. 1961. *L'économie de l'Afrique du Nord*, Presses Universitaires de France ('Que sais-je?' series), Paris.

GALLAGHER, C. F. 1964. *North African Problems and Prospects. Part I: Rural Reform and Revolution. Part II: Industrialization and Development*, American Universities Field Staff Reports, New York.

GAUTIER, E. F. 1952. *Le passé de l'Afrique du Nord: Les siècles obscurs*, Payot, Paris, 2nd ed.

GSELL, STÉPHANE. 1913–28. *Histoire ancienne de l'Afrique du Nord*, Hachette, Paris, 8 vols.

HARRISON CHURCH, R. J. 1961. Problems and development of the dry zone of West Africa. *Geographical Journal*, Vol. 127: 187–204.

————. 1962. Port Étienne: a Mauritanian pioneer town. *Geographical Journal*, Vol. 128: 498–504.

HERNANDEZ-PACHECO, E. and F. *et al.* 1949. *El Sahara español, estudio geografico, geologico y botanico*, Madrid.

HOUSTON, J. M. 1954. The significance of irrigation in Morocco's economic development. *Geographical Journal*, Vol. 120: 314–328.

INTERNATIONAL BANK FOR RECONSTRUCTION AND DEVELOPMENT. 1960. *The Economic Development of Libya*, Baltimore.

JULIEN, C. A. 1951–52. *Histoire de l'Afrique du Nord: Tunisie, Algérie, Maroc*, Payot, Paris, 2nd ed., 2 vols.

KHALDUN, IBN. 1925–56. *Histoire de Berbères et des dynasties musulmanes de l'Afrique septentrionale* (trans. by de Slane), Paul Geuthner, Paris, 2nd ed., 4 vols.

LE DUC, G. 1952. *Industrialisation de l'Afrique du Nord*, Armand Colin, Paris.

MCBURNEY, C. B. M. 1960. *The Stone Age of Northern Africa*. Penguin Books, Harmondsworth.

MIKESELL, M. W. 1958. The role of tribal markets in Morocco. *Geographical Review*, Vol. 48: 494–511.

————. 1961. *Northern Morocco: A Cultural Geography*, University of California Publications in Geography, Vol. 14, University of California Press, Berkeley and Los Angeles.

MURDOCK, G. P. 1959. *Africa: Its Peoples and Their Culture History*, McGraw Hill, New York, Chapters 15, 16, 18, 52 and 53.

MURPHEY, RHOADS. 1951. The decline of North Africa since the Roman occupation: climatic or human? *Annals of the Association of American Geographers*, Vol. 41: 116–132.

THOMAS, B. E. 1957. *Trade Routes of Algeria and the Sahara*, University of California Publications in Geography, Vol. 8, University of California Press, Berkeley and Los Angeles.

WARMINGTON, B. H. 1954. *The North African Provinces from Diocletian to the Vandal Conquest*, Cambridge University Press, Cambridge.

————. 1964. *Carthage*, Penguin Books, Harmondsworth.

WILLIMOTT, S. G. and J. I. CLARKE (eds.). 1960. *Field Studies in Libya*, Department of Geography, University of Durham.

ZARTMAN, W. I. 1963. *Government and Politics in Northern Africa*, Praeger, New York.

2 Northeast Africa

2 Northeast Africa

By ANNE M. S. GRAHAM

If any dominant theme can be discerned in the geography of Northeast Africa it is, perhaps, the extent to which man's activities in this generally arid region are dependent upon the opportunities offered by its rivers and rainfall. This is most obvious in the case of the Nile. The waters of this great river provide the main source of livelihood for the peoples of Egypt, and make possible the seasonal occupation of the swamp lands of southern Sudan. Beyond the confines of the Nile valley, rainfall is the main factor influencing cultivation, settlement and opportunities for development. The high and therefore relatively well-watered Ethiopian massif assumes importance not only as a major focus of settlement but because runoff from the highlands brings opportunities for cultivation to the surrounding plains; and even small hill masses at lower elevations form minor foci of settlement. Northeast Africa, with its large expanses of desert, semidesert and savanna, illustrates in a remarkable way man's ingenuity in obtaining a livelihood from an environment that is chronically short of water. Within the region there are wide variations in ways of life ranging from fully nomadic pastoralism to sedentary cultivation. Settled agriculturalists predominate in the well-watered highlands of Ethiopia and in the perennially irrigated lands of Egypt; the Somali Republic is overwhelmingly a country of pastoralists; while the most striking feature in the human geography of the Sudan is its great diversity.

While all the countries of this north-eastern corner of Africa share the environmental hazard of limited water supplies, in other respects it is their individuality that impresses most. A dominant factor in the geography of this region, where Africa merges into the Middle East, has been the proximity of the lands of South West Asia; their varied influences have evoked varied responses in the countries of the area, whose cultural characteristics, in consequence, display little uniformity. Egypt has, throughout most of its long history, formed part of the Levant rather than part of Africa. The Sudan straddles the junction between the Caucasoid north and Negroid south of the continent. Furthermore, while Moslem invaders swept through the surrounding lowlands, Ethiopia in its highland fastness was the only country in Africa to preserve an ancient Christian culture. Even the colonial period brought little cultural uniformity to the region. The French, Italian and British imperial powers exerted very different degrees of authority over the individual territories of the area; indeed Ethiopia, and to a lesser extent Egypt, retained much of their independence. Today Northeast Africa includes both the African country with the longest record of independence (Ethiopia) and one of the continent's last colonial possessions (French Somaliland).

Because of this great diversity within the region Northeast Africa is not considered as a whole in this chapter but instead its constituent territories are discussed in two major divisions: the lands of the Nile (Egypt and

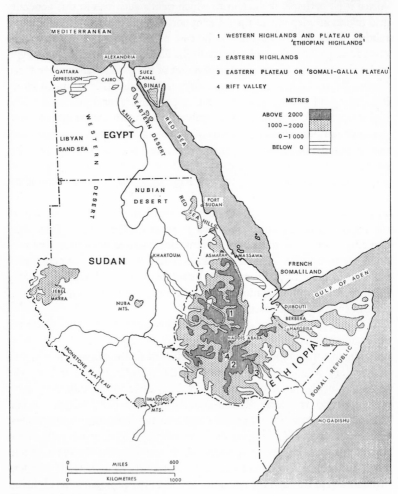

Fig. 12. Northeast Africa

Sudan), and the countries of the Horn of Africa (Ethiopia, French Somali-land and Somalia).

Egypt and Sudan

The Physical Environment

The vast territories of Egypt and Sudan together stretch through 28 degrees of latitude and are traversed throughout their entire north-south length by the Nile. Much of the region is a plain (Fig. 12): the monotony of the topography is only relieved by subtle changes in vegetation which often reflect minor local variations in the availability of moisture.

Rocks of the Basement Complex underlie most of Sudan and extend north into the eastern part of Egypt. Elsewhere younger sediments, mainly limestones and sandstones, predominate. The ancient crystalline rocks form uplands which surround the Sudan on all sides except the north and northwest. Tertiary lavas are important locally, forming the volcanic heights of Jebel Marra and capping parts of the Ethiopian foothills. Else-where the Basement Complex outcrops in isolated clusters of inselbergs, such as the Nuba Mountains. Superficial deposits are widespread. Much of central and eastern Sudan comprises a plain of aggradation. It is down-warped and extremely flat, indeed so flat that the wetter, southern portion is subject to extensive flooding each year. In the west between Jebel Marra and the Nuba Mountains there is a wide belt of ancient sand-dunes, called the qoz, which was formed during an arid phase in the Pleistocene. The crystalline rocks of the southwestern Ironstone Plateau weather to produce red lateritic loams. In the north, however, the desert has only skeletal soils. The Western Desert, which stretches from Sudan almost to the coast of Egypt, has a fairly varied although low topography. There are rocky and gravelly plateaus, massifs, mesas and buttes. In its centre is the formidable sand sea of the Libyan desert. The north is characterized by a series of steep-sided depressions with generally sandy soils. Here underground water comes close to the surface and oases are found, but salinity is a major problem, particularly in the lower southern depressions. In contrast, the eastern bank of the Nile is more mountainous. The Nubian Desert is edged by the Red Sea Hills and merges into the highlands of Egypt's Eastern Desert. Both here and in the Sinai peninsula, mountains rise to over 6,500 ft (2000 m).

Stretching as the region does from the Mediterranean almost to the Equator, its rainfall shows zonal patterns typical of the northern parts of the African continent (Fig. 13). The Mediterranean coast has a scanty winter rainfall. The rains extend only a few miles inland, except where the hills of Sinai and the eastern desert attract occasional storms. Southward there is an area of extreme aridity and the Libyan Desert is in fact one of the driest

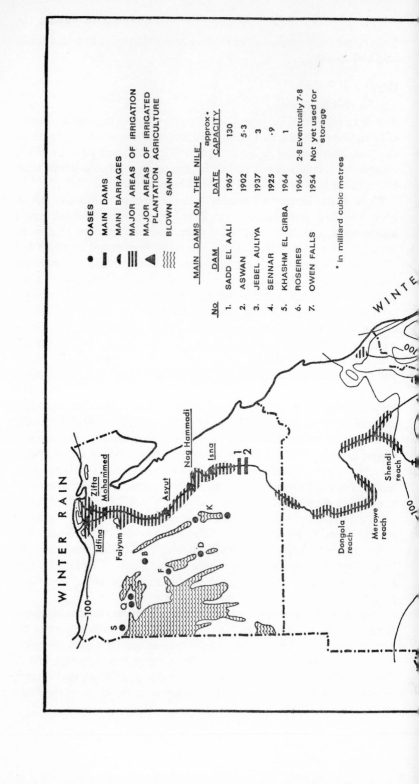

WINTER RAIN

OASES

MAIN DAMS

MAIN BARRAGES

MAJOR AREAS OF IRRIGATION

MAJOR AREAS OF IRRIGATED
PLANTATION AGRICULTURE

BLOWN SAND

MAIN DAMS ON THE NILE

No	DAM	DATE	approx. CAPACITY
1.	SADD EL AALI	1967	130
2.	ASWAN	1902	5.3
3.	JEBEL AULIYA	1937	3
4.	SENNAR	1925	.9
5.	KHASHM EL GIRBA	1964	1
6.	ROSEIRES	1966	2.8 Eventually 7.8
7.	OWEN FALLS	1954	Not yet used for storage

* in milliard cubic metres

Idfina
Zifta
Mohammed
Nag Hammadi
Asyut
Isna
Faiyum
Dongola reach
Merowe reach
Shendi reach

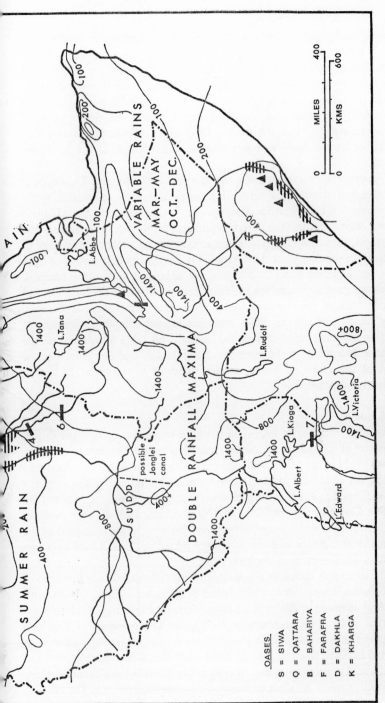

Fig. 13. Northeast Africa: Rainfall, Rivers and Dams (rainfall after Jackson 1961)

areas on earth. Beyond this the influence of the inter-tropical convergence zone is felt. At about latitude 17°N there are short, highly erratic summer rains. Southward, the rainy season becomes longer and more regular in duration, the total rainfall higher and less variable. By the time the southern Sudan is reached, the rains last for about seven months, normally exceed 32 inches (800 mm) and show the double annual maxima typical of equatorial regions. Isohyets do not follow lines of latitude exactly, but swing northward in the east as a result of the influence of the Ethiopian massif.

Vegetation is everywhere adapted to a season of drought. In general it becomes more abundant from north to south in response to rainfall. There is, however, a narrow strip of xerophytic vegetation along the Mediterranean coast. South of the desert, semidesert scrub vegetation shades first into short, then into tall grass savanna. Throughout these zones species of acacia form the dominant trees. Gradually the density and variety of trees increases, however, until the deciduous woodland of the south is reached. Local topographic variations interrupt this pattern and the swamps and flooded areas of the southern Sudan have their own treeless landscapes. Very locally, altitude modifies temperature and rainfall sufficiently to produce montane vegetation as, for example, on Jebel Marra and on the Imatong Mountains of the southeast. Even the low Red Sea Hills, like the coast of the Horn of Africa, attract sufficient winter rains to bear a distinctive vegetation.

Arabization

Knowledge of the early history of the Nile valley is very uneven. Egypt, the centre of an ancient civilization, was from the earliest times part of the known world of the Mediterranean; but the southern Sudan remained part of the Dark Continent until well into the nineteenth century. The northern Sudan formed a zone of contact between the cultures and civilizations of the Middle East and the traditions of Negro Africa. Unlike other states in northern Africa, which are separated from the heart of the continent by the Sahara desert, Egypt and the Sudan are joined to Black Africa by a belt of continuous settlement along the Nile.

The dominant theme in the history of the Nile valley is the process of Arabization. This process, which is still by no means complete, began with the Arab invasion of Egypt in A.D. 639. The new rulers rapidly established political control as far south as Nubia, but the presence of Christian kingdoms astride the Nile in the northern Sudan prevented further substantial advance. Such advance as there was resulted from immigration and commercial penetration rather than from conquest. In the eleventh century a second wave of Moslem expansion from Arabia, known as the Hilalian invasion, gave new impetus to Islamic civilization in Egypt. The fall of Maqurra, the most powerful of the Sudanese Christian kingdoms, in the thirteenth century, and of Soba in the fifteenth, removed the long-standing barrier to Arab advance. The trickle of immigration became a flood. Large numbers of Arabs moved up the Nile and then fanned out into the grasslands to east and west. The dominance in the next four centuries of the powerful Funj kingdom, which at its apogee extended from the Ethiopian foothills to Darfur and constituted one of the great medieval savanna kingdoms of Africa, provided conditions favourable to the continued steady expansion of Islam.

For long the southern Sudan had lain outside the main stream of these events. There were three main stages in the unification of the Sudan, all of great significance in the process of Arabization. The rule of Mohammed Ali in Egypt (1805-1849) saw not only a rapid modernization of that country but also a conquest of the northern Sudan, followed by a dramatic expansion of Egyptian authority into the southern Sudan. This first contact between Moslem and pagan was accompanied by a growth in the slave trade which was to leave a mark on their relationship deep into modern times. The main significance of the second period, when the Sudanese revolted against Egyptian rule, was the development of embryonic Sudanese nationalism based on a movement of religious reform. This endowed northern Sudan with a certain unity which was soon to be tested against the European invader. Finally, British occupation of Egypt in 1882 was followed in 1896 by a military advance into the Sudan. The Condominium agreement of 1899 gave Britain effective authority while Egypt retained the semblance of power, and, as a result of British rule, the outlying areas of the country were brought under the authority of the central government.

Despite this, the effect of the actions of the Condominium government was to foster southern separatism. A policy of separate development was followed, based partly on a consciousness of the profound ethnic differences between north and south and partly on a failure to decide where the political future of the south lay. Only in 1947 was a firm decision taken that the south should form part of a united Sudan. But the delay was at least partially responsible for the grave problems confronting the Sudanese nation on independence in 1956.

Peoples and Ways of Life

While the distribution of the various peoples that make up the population of Sudan and Egypt has been largely determined by historical factors, their ways of life have been intimately affected by the physical environment.

In contrast with the Sudan, the population of Egypt shows a remarkable ethnic uniformity. This is due largely to the fact that the original riverine peoples have so successfully absorbed nomadic immigrants and invaders, in itself perhaps a tribute to the dominant influence of the Nile on the culture and ways of life of the peoples of the area. Because of their position at the gateway to Africa the Hamitic peoples of Egypt experienced the full force of the Arab invasions. For a considerable period, parts of the delta, particularly in the west, lay uncultivated because of the incursions of pastoral nomads who also subjugated the coastlands and the oases. The agriculture of the latter areas has never fully recovered. In the oases, for example, a mere 30,000 feddans[1] are cultivated today. The indigenous peasant population of the riverine area, however, was remarkably resistant to change. Arab settlers entering the valley and the Faiyum eventually adopted the native agricultural system which was so well adapted to the environment. Despite their initial aloofness from village life, they were in due course completely absorbed into the mass of the population. For their part, the Egyptians gradually adopted the Arabic language and the Islamic religion. Some evidence of the strength of the pre-Arab culture is provided by the continued existence – mainly in middle and upper Egypt – of a Coptic Christian minority which at present numbers about two million.

Today over 96 per cent of Egypt's population lives along the Nile. A large majority are peasant cultivators whose activities are described later in this essay. About one-third are town-dwellers. Although the twentieth century has seen a vast influx of people to the cities, urban life has always been of greater importance in Egypt than elsewhere in Northeast Africa. The site of Cairo, an important nodal point, dates from Pharaonic times although the present city is of Arab origin. The principal towns grew up as centres of trade and crafts, housing ethnic minorities which included Copts and Levantine immigrants who were until recently prominent in commerce and industry.

The remaining 4 per cent of the population live mainly along the coast and in the oases. The narrow coastal strip has a winter rainfall of only 5–10 in (125–250 mm), but because temperatures are low this is enough for a little dry farming. Moreover, some use is made of underground well-water and moisture tapped from sand dunes to grow typical Mediterranean perennial crops such as figs and olives, and, in the east, date palms. Flocks of sheep and goats make short transhumant movements into the interior during the wet period. Often part of a tribe has adopted a settled way of life while the rest has remained nomadic. In the west, where most of the population is of Berber-Arab stock, there is comparatively little camel nomadism because the interior of the Libyan desert is too inhospitable for

[1] A feddan is a measure of area used in Egypt and Sudan and is equivalent to 1·038 acres or 0·412 hectares.

even this most hardy of occupations. In the Eastern Desert and Sinai peninsula the rugged uplands receive a little rain. As the ground is impermeable, runoff collects and is used by the nomadic population who have emigrated at various times from Arabia. In general, nomadism is declining, a decline accelerated by the fact that as agriculture is expanded towards the margins of the Nile valley, some of the better grazing lands are lost. There are now fewer than half a million nomads in Egypt.

The effects of Arab immigration into the Sudan were much more complex than in Egypt. The indigenous peoples gradually acquired the Islamic faith and the Arabic language and they tended to adopt the Arab tribal system. On the other hand, Arab stock was absorbed by the indigenous inhabitants and the basis was laid for the complex racial pattern of the modern Sudan. The purer Arabs of modern Sudan are probably descended from those immigrants who occupied the least competed-for desert areas of the country. They remained camel-owning nomads and mixed little with the indigenous inhabitants. In contrast, those Arabs who eventually settled in the riverine areas, or who moved farther south and became cattle-owning nomads, show on the whole much greater racial and cultural mixing. As in Egypt, immigration continued spasmodically and on a decreasing scale. The last arrivals, the Rashaida, entered the Sudan by the Red Sea route as late as the mid-nineteenth century. The process of Arabization has accelerated in the last century, materially aided by increased population mobility which was itself the result of modern communications and economic development.

Ways of life among the Arabized people of northern Sudan range from pure nomadism to fully settled agriculture (Fig. 14). Most people, in fact, engage in some cultivation and possess some livestock. Usually the way of life found in a particular area shows close and obvious adjustment to the natural environment and especially to its water supplies. But sometimes more subtle human factors have clearly played a dominant role. The stronger the Arab traditions of a particular tribe, the more it will despise agricultural pursuits. For example, richer Arabs often employ ex-slaves or other 'inferior' Negroid peoples to grow their necessary food crops. With the exception of the riverine population, which is described separately, the peoples of the desert and semidesert are mainly nomadic. Those of the central zones are predominantly agriculturalists although poor water supplies may necessitate a transhumant rather than a fully settled way of life; while many of those in the south are more completely nomadic.

In general, nomadic movements are along a north-south axis following the seasonal movement of the sun. The driest part of a tribe's territory is grazed during the rains, the better watered parts in the dry season. Occasionally the presence of water supplies around hilly areas or beside rivers

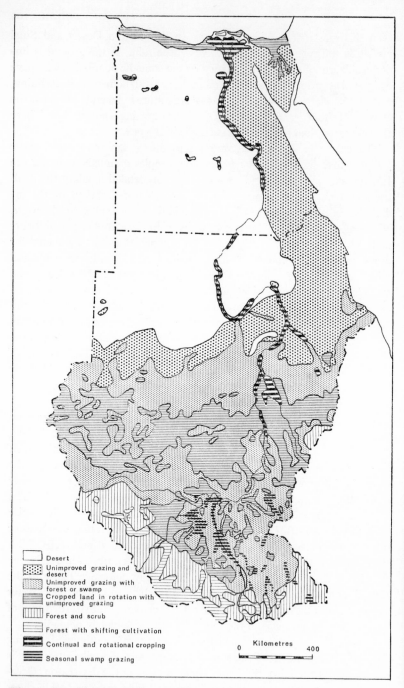

Desert

Unimproved grazing and desert

Unimproved grazing with forest or swamp

Cropped land in rotation with unimproved grazing

Forest and scrub

Forest with shifting cultivation

Continual and rotational cropping

Seasonal swamp grazing

Kilometres

0   400

Fig. 14. Land Use in Sudan and Egypt (slightly modified from Hamdan, 1961, and Barbour, 1961, based on Lebon. For greater detail see Lebon, 1965.)

may alter the prevailing direction of movement. Thus, in the far north, nomads are often forced by the absence of alternative water supplies to spend much of the dry season beside the Nile. In the central Sudan there is a rather different pattern of annual migration towards the White Nile. Tribes pass the rainy season about 30 miles (50 km) from the river. Just when the grasses there dry up, the Jebel Auliya reservoir is emptied and a wide strip of land is exposed which provides fresh grazing for the surrounding tribes.

In the semi-desert areas of western Sudan migration patterns are influenced by the Gizzu. This area lies on the borders of Sudan and, if the late rains have been adequate, provides excellent grazing in early winter. The main dry season is usually spent in the south, often on the margins of the *qoz*, where the tribe has permanent water supplies. It is here, too, that a little cultivation may take place in the summer, while most of the people and the animals go north following the rains. To the south the Baggara utilize the combined resources of sandy *qoz* and clays. Most tribes have a home territory on the boundary between the two soil types. Here clay depressions alternate with cultivated sandy ridges. During the rains the cattle move north to the healthier, fly-free *qoz* where the grasses are palatable although poor in salts. In the dry season they move south and graze the tall coarse grasses of the clay plains, often ending up on the margins of the swamps of the southern clay plains where water and a little fresh grass are available.

In the eastern Sudan, north-south migrations occur over greater distances. There is no *qoz*, but healthy summer grazing is obtained in the Butana, the northernmost part of the clay plains. One tribe travels over 200 miles (320 km) and crosses the Blue Nile, the Dinder and the Rahad in the course of its annual migration from its dry season camp at the edge of the marshes of southern Sudan to its rainy season quarters in Butana. Most of the tribes, however, do not go as far south as this; indeed in the far east a game reserve as well as the Ethiopian boundary prevents their doing so. In their migrations they tend to keep close to the rivers, where pools provide water both while the tribes are in transit and at their ultimate dry season camp. There are some tribes who remain in Butana throughout the year. These utilize the grazing around the few permanent wells in the dry season, while in the rains they take the opportunity to move farther afield to fresh grasses, particularly in the north.

Not all the peoples of northern Sudan have been assimilated into the Arab culture. Some, probably because of their isolation, have managed to maintain their cultural integrity. The Nubians are a white Hamitic people with an admixture of Negroid blood. Despite the fact that the Nile routeway crossed their territory, few Arabs settled there, probably because the rocky desert beyond the river could not provide grazing for their animals. Thus the Nubians have been able to preserve their languages and culture, although they have adopted Islam. In recent years, however, the land of Nubia has been unable to support all its people, and increasing numbers of Nubians have begun to participate in Sudanese life as traders, civil servants and politicians.

The nomadic Beja, another Hamitic people closely akin to the ancient Egyptians, ranged the whole of northeastern Sudan before the coming of the Arabs. Today they are found only in the wild, inhospitable Red Sea area, which includes the barren coast and the rugged country of the Red Sea Hills and the edge of the Ethiopian plateau. In their migrations they make full use of the meagre rainfall, benefiting both from winter showers in the coastal zone and from summer storms in areas to the south.

It is believed that the Negro population of Sudan used to extend much further north than at present. Today, while most of the Arab tribes show evidence of Negroid blood, comparatively pure Negro peoples are rare in the northern Sudan, and are only to be found in remote refuge areas of central Sudan, such as the Ingessana Hills in the southeast, the Nuba Mountains, and especially the hill masses of isolated Darfur. In the last two areas there are also a few peoples showing traces of Nubian origin. Typically these groups remained within the security of their hills, terracing the slopes and cultivating their small fields, continuously making use of intensive agricultural techniques. With the establishment of peaceful conditions they are now leaving the security of the hills and cultivating the surrounding plains where ample land is available.

In southern Sudan there are three main peoples: Nilotes, Nilo-Hamites and Negroes of the Sudanic linguistic group. Most of the Nilotic tribes are cattle herders par excellence. Their animals not only constitute a source of prestige, but are the very focal point of their existence. Inhabiting the swampy clay plains of the south, the Nilotes make short seasonal migrations of less than 100 miles (160 km) in response to the rhythm of the floods. During the rains they retreat to the patches of well-drained, high ground on which their permanent villages are sited. Here they cultivate the millet which together with milk provides their basic diet, while the cattle are crowded on such limited grazing as is available. Then they move gradually down to lower ground, utilizing the fresh grasses which become available as the waters retreat. By the height of the dry season they are established beside the rivers which provide permanent water supplies.

Most of the Ironstone Plateau is unsuitable for cattle because of the presence of the tsetse fly, but Nilotes are found in the lower parts of the northern plateau where the cleared land is comparatively free from the fly. The main inhabitants of the area are, however, Negro tribes who practise shifting cultivation in the woodlands and who, in their agricultural habits, often show intimate understanding of local ecological conditions. Here in the south the rainfall is such that a wide range of crops can be grown. Indeed, the light early rains can be used to raise a quick second crop. Roots such as yam and manioc supplement maize, sorghum and Eleusine millet which form the staple diet. Fields are small, intercropping is normal and the agricultural season long. Hunting and gathering in the surrounding bush supplements harvests.

The peoples of the southeastern Sudan are mainly Nilo-Hamites. Although they are traditionally cattle-keepers, the intermittent occurrence of tsetse fly in this area has caused many tribes to abandon this occupation. Flocks can, however, be kept and there is some cultivation. There is one Nilotic tribe – the Acholi – living in these hills who also lack cattle. In the extreme southeast conditions are similar to the rest of the southern clay plains, and the inhabitants, who are recent Nilo-Hamitic immigrants from the south-east, practise a similar kind of transhumance with their cattle.

The Nile Valley: Past, Present and Future Use

The Nile is a major international river whose waters, derived from rainfall in the highlands of East Africa and Ethiopia, debouch into the Mediterranean over 4000 miles (6440 km) away. In the lower part of its course the river flows through semiarid and arid country. Here it assumes vast importance since the population is dependent on its waters for their livelihood. Yet those countries which rely most completely on the river – Egypt and Sudan – have no control over its headwaters, which are in the territories of other states.

Man's attempts to use the waters of the Nile have progressed through several stages of sophistication. As technical ability has increased so greater controls and modifications have been imposed on the natural régime of the river. A very high proportion of the flow of the Nile is now utilized. Hence, further developments cannot be of merely local significance but will inevitably affect the whole of the river basin.

The highlands of East Africa have an equatorial rainfall régime. The infant waters of the Nile, known first as the Victoria Nile, then the Albert Nile and finally the Bahr el Jebel, have a steady annual flow with two flood periods. The river descends on to the flat clay plains of southern Sudan and enters the immense papyrus swamp of the Sudd where it overflows its ill-defined channel. When it emerges from the swamps its seasonal fluctuations have been partially evened out. More important, evaporation and transpiration have reduced its volume by half. The Bahr el Ghazal, whose tributaries rise mainly in the watershed area which forms the western boundary of Sudan, enters the Sudd from the west but contributes almost

CONTRIBUTION OF THE MAIN TRIBUTARIES TO THE FLOW OF THE NILE AT ASWAN

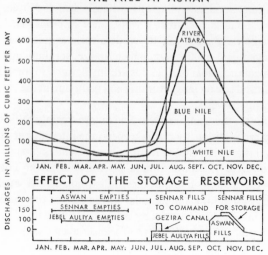

EFFECT OF THE STORAGE RESERVOIRS

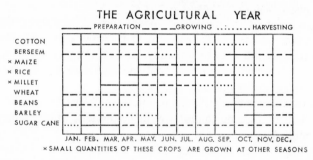

THE AGRICULTURAL YEAR

——— PREPARATION — — — GROWING ..:...... HARVESTING

COTTON
BERSEEM
× MAIZE
× RICE
× MILLET
WHEAT
BEANS
BARLEY
SUGAR CANE

JAN. FEB. MAR. APR. MAY. JUN. JUL. AUG. SEP. OCT. NOV. DEC.
× SMALL QUANTITIES OF THESE CROPS ARE GROWN AT OTHER SEASONS

LABOUR REQUIREMENTS IN AGRICULTURAL FIELD WORK 1960

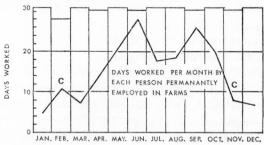

DAYS WORKED PER MONTH BY EACH PERSON PERMANANTLY EMPLOYED IN FARMS

C ADDITIONAL WORK MAINTAINING CANALS IS PERFORMED IN WINTER BUT WAS NOT INCLUDED IN THE GRAPH; NOR WAS ANY ALLOWANCE MADE FOR TIME SPENT CARING FOR LIVESTOCK

Fig. 15. Irrigated Agriculture in Egypt (after Hansen and Marzook, 1965; Hurst, 1952; and Tothill, 1948)

nothing to the Nile's waters. Its inflow is virtually cancelled out by evaporation losses occurring as it flows slowly along its very flat, swampy course.

A reduced Nile leaves the Sudd, but its losses are redressed by the Sobat. This is the most southerly of the three tributaries that enter the Nile from the Ethiopian highlands to the east. These rivers have a marked seasonal régime corresponding to the distribution of rainfall in Ethiopia. The further north the tributary, the greater the seasonal variation in its flow. In the case of the Sobat, seasonal fluctuations are modified by the effect of swamps. The Blue Nile, the largest of the three, has a maximum volume in August which is forty-six times as great as the flow in April, the month of lowest discharge. Northward the Rahad and Dinder, tributaries of the Blue Nile, together with the Atbara, actually cease to flow for several months each year. This is in sharp contrast to the more even régime of the White Nile, whose maximum volume in October is only one and a half times as great as its minimum flow in May.

The régime of the main Nile is dominated by that of the Blue Nile (Fig. 15). The annual flow of the Blue Nile is twice that of the White Nile at Khartoum. The Atbara to the north merely accentuates the Blue Nile's seasonal rhythm. At Aswan at the height of the flood period the White Nile contributes only 10 per cent to the total flow, but during low water when the Blue Nile's volume has shrunk to its minimum it provides 83 per cent. The Atbara is the last source of additional water for the Nile. Further north, rivers from the Ethiopian highlands simply expend themselves in the sandy Sudanese plain. After joining the Atbara the main Nile flows through arid country. Increasing evaporation, percolation into the alluvial bed of the river, and withdrawals for irrigation all reduce the natural flow.

The land surface in Egypt slopes towards the Mediterranean with a gentle gradient of about 5 in per mile (8 cm per km). The bed of the river slopes even more gently, for during its long history the deposition of transported material has slowly raised its bed along the lower course. Thus, the Nile in flood, contained by its levees, flows above the level of the surrounding land over much of its length. In the Nile valley the land slopes away from the river at a gradient of about 8 in per mile (16 cm per km). Throughout its history, the Nile when flooding has deposited most of its load near its banks, only the finer particles being carried farther towards the desert margins; hence the greater elevation of alluvium close to the river. The Nile valley is up to 12 miles (19 km) wide in Lower and Middle Egypt but tapers off gradually towards the south. In northern Sudan the river seldom exceeds a mile and a quarter (2 km) in width and in places the hills close right in towards the river. This fact largely explains why basin agriculture was developed early and over a wide area in Egypt whereas in the Sudan it was only established in scattered pockets.

Agriculture was introduced into Egypt from Southwest Asia about 5000 B.C. After a probable period of cultivation in the marginal hills, early farmers began to raise crops in the Nile valley itself, planting in damp land which was exposed as the floods retreated. Gradually they attempted to improve their fields by regulating the disposal of the flood waters over the ground. Hurst (1952) believes that elementary irrigation techniques may have evolved on the east bank of the Nile, where the hills closely approach the river and where flood waters would have penetrated in tongues up the valleys between the hills. Simple bunds across these low-lying strips of land would regulate the amount and duration of their annual wetting, and such modest banks would be within the capacity of a small and isolated community to organize and construct. Further development of basin agriculture involved major earthworks, cooperation in the distribution of water, and constant attention to maintenance. It therefore required centralized political organization. According to tradition Menes, the first Pharaoh, began to develop a national system of basin cultivation in 3400 B.C. The method was utilized throughout the Nile valley until the end of the nineteenth century, and 20 per cent of Egypt's agricultural land will continue to be irrigated in this way until the Sadd el Aali Dam at Aswan is in full use.

Under the system of basin irrigation, the valley lands on either side of the river are divided into basins. Longitudinal banks confine the Nile to its bed and prevent uncontrolled flooding. Transverse banks across the valley complete the basins and retain the water. As the Nile rises, water enters a canal, the head of which is about 14 ft (4·5 m) above the bed of the river. The canal carries water to the basin, running diagonally across it and then north along the desert margins at a slope less than that of the river. Often a chain of several basins are filled by the same canal, the furthest upstream filling first. Flooding begins towards the end of August and in October the land is ready for sowing. The crops grow throughout the winter and are harvested between April and June. After harvest the land remains fallow until the following flood. The main crops produced under the basin system have changed little with the centuries. Only flax, once the basis of the cloth industry, has been superseded by cotton. Egypt's traditional winter crops include cereals such as wheat and barley and various pulses, as well as the fodder crops which enable animal husbandry to be practised. Since all land in the basins is cultivated each year, a rotation is practised, cereals (and in the past flax) being followed by legumes. The latter are used both for human and animal consumption.

Basin cultivation is adjusted to the same seasonal régime that existed before agriculture replaced the natural vegetation of the Nile valley. Growth follows inundation and is in turn succeeded by increasing aridity. The period of agricultural activity is brief, and since the time of growth coincides with the cool weather the range of crops that can be grown is restricted. Under this system the cultivator's activities follow the rhythm of the Nile and his life is dependent on the rise and fall of the river. The basin system was an attempt by man to utilize the natural flood of the Nile more efficiently by regulating it. But this regulation did not amount to control. If the seasonal rise of the river was particularly small the cultivated area could be reduced by half. If floods were especially high the Nile might break from its retaining walls and devastate the countryside. This uncertain situation became doubly precarious during periods of unstable government, for the system required an active authority to maintain canals and banks. Throughout Egypt's history, political collapse was frequently followed by loss of cultivable land resulting from failure to maintain efficient irrigation works.

Nevertheless, the system has been remarkably self-perpetuating. Ecologically it has distinct merits. The annual flooding deposits a layer of silt about a millimetre thick and provides a fresh supply of plant nutrients to the soil. This single, generous inundation of the land makes salinization unlikely. After harvest, the increasing aridity of the land enforces a fallow season, so avoiding soil exhaustion. As the clay dries out it cracks deeply. With soils thus aerated and exposed to the intense insolation of summer, weeds and plant diseases have difficulty in surviving.

The land that could be irrigated under the basin system was limited to the area that could be commanded by the canals. Under the Pharaohs it seems to have amounted to about six million feddans and thereafter it fluctuated. During periods of prosperity the system was apparently able to support a population of about seven million.

Basin irrigation was not the only method of achieving crop production. Simple lift techniques were used, either to bring water to fields above the level of the floods or to prolong the growing season on land from which the floods had retreated. In this way cultivators were able to grow crops both in the flood period and during the summer months when the water level in the Nile was low. Areas thus irrigated were normally close to the banks of the river, but sometimes shallow wells were also used as sources of water. The amount of land that could be irrigated by these methods was limited by the amount of labour available. The shadoof, the earliest lifting device, which was introduced to Egypt about 1000 B.C., can only irrigate a quarter of a feddan each day. The Archimedean screw and the sagia, introduced later by the Greeks, can water three-quarters of a feddan and up to five feddans a day respectively, but the former is capable of only a very small lift and the latter requires draught animals to operate it. Nevertheless such methods were widely used throughout Egypt and northern and central Sudan to increase agricultural production. By the end of the eighteenth century probably about 20 per cent of Egypt's agricultural land was under perennial irrigation of this type. Much of it was on big estates, where landowners invested in lift irrigation in order to grow commercial crops.

Attempts to develop large-scale perennial irrigation in Egypt began in the 1820's. Mohammed Ali and his successors strove to expand the area under summer cash crops, particularly cotton, in order to make Egypt a major producer of raw materials for Europe's markets and thus promote her entry into the modern world. In a sense the great technological changes in agriculture that followed were Egypt's response to and equivalent of the industrial revolution in Western Europe.

The first efforts to achieve large-scale perennial irrigation were unsatisfactory. Summer canals were excavated, but the Nile was too low at this season for proper gravity flow to occur. Silting reduced the capacity of the canals and an annual corvée of forced labour was necessary to maintain them. In the second half of the nineteenth century an alternative method was tried. A barrage, built across the head of the Nile delta, ponded back the flow of the Nile, raising the water-level until the water was high enough to enter the normal heads of the canals. This scheme enabled the agricultural land of the delta to be converted to perennial irrigation. It also effectively used up the whole flow of the river during the low water period. To achieve further expansion of perennial irrigation it was necessary to store some of the surplus water from the time of flood and to release it during the low water period in order to augment the natural flow of the river. There was no suitable site for a storage reservoir in the wide alluvial valley of the Nile in northern Egypt, but a dam was built at Aswan on the rocky outcrop of the first cataract to the north. This dam, working in conjunction with Asyut barrage which was built at the same time, brought perennial irrigation to Middle Egypt for the first time. The demand for summer water continued to grow. In the years that followed, the Aswan dam was twice raised and new barrages were constructed. In the late 1930's the Jebel Auliya dam was built in the Sudan in order to provide further water storage for Egyptian agriculture. The risk of establishing a reservoir outside the national territory was in this case minimized since Egypt was, at least nominally, a co-administrator of the Sudan.

The control works of the Nile made it possible to use the river's waters throughout the year. The natural flow during the low water period, a quantity of 15·4 milliard m³ was completely devoted to agricultural purposes. Moreover, the combined capacities of the storage reservoirs augmented this natural flow by as much as 50 per cent. Thus the seasonal variations of the river's régime were modified – but not tamed. No water could be withdrawn for storage from the main Nile during the peak of the flood because the river in spate carried so much suspended material that the reservoirs would have quickly silted up. It was partly because of this, and partly because the storage capacity was in any case too small, that nearly half the Nile's flow from the high-water period ran unused into the Mediterranean. Altogether, only just over 60 per cent of the annual volume of the river was being used for irrigation.

Moreover, man had no control over the total amount of water brought down by the Nile in any particular year. While the average annual flow was about 83 milliard m³ as measured at Aswan, it has varied from as little as 42 milliard m³ to as much as 155 milliard m³ during the last hundred years. As more intensive use was made of the Nile's waters these variations had increasingly important consequences. If the river's flow during the low-water period was less than average, then the area to be planted with summer crops had to be reduced and valuable land lay idle until the next flood. Moreover, particularly high floods were far more dangerous under the system of perennial irrigation than under the basin system. No longer could water be allowed to spread freely over the land. Some fields contained standing crops at the time of the flood (Fig. 15) and so the application of water had to be more carefully controlled. Massive embankments were necessary to retain the Nile within its bed, and if the banks were breached or surmounted the damage to crops and settlements could be enormous.

Thus perennial irrigation radically altered the hydrology of the Nile valley. The simple annual sequence of flood followed by increasing aridity was eliminated. Instead the valley remained basically dry with measured amounts of water being applied regularly throughout the year. Water being always available, the growing season was extended to twelve months. Farmers utilized the seasonal variation in temperatures to grow a wide range of crops. Agricultural conditions were described as similar to the Mediterranean in winter, to the American Gulf Coast in spring and early summer, and to the Monsoon lands in late summer and autumn.

There was a great increase in crops requiring high temperatures, including cotton, which had been known since the sixth century B.C., and rice and sugar cane, which were introduced by the Arabs in the Middle Ages. But to view the new crop complex simply in terms of changed relative proportions of plants grown would be to underestimate the magnitude of the innovations that had taken place. The hot weather crops were essentially cash crops. Cotton in particular revolutionized the agricultural economy. Agriculture was now geared to foreign markets, and traditional food crops declined in importance. This decline was accentuated by the introduction in the early nineteenth century of maize, which rapidly ousted

5

wheat and barley as the staple cereal of the peasantry. Grown as a flood crop, it further increased the farmers' activities in the hot season and reduced his reliance on old-fashioned winter crops (Fig. 15). The major agricultural season was now at variance with the natural supply of water available for the land. Cultivation no longer followed flood. Rather, as a result of man's ingenuity, the main crops grew both when the river was at its lowest level and when it was in spate: times when previously very little farming could take place. As a natural consequence of the twelve-month growing season, perennial irrigation facilitated agricultural intensification. Two or even three crops could be grown in a single year and therefore, although topography limited the physical area that could be cultivated in Egypt, the cropped area expanded rapidly. The seasonal farmer who had been free to engage in public works for part of the year was transformed into a peasant who was tied to the soil throughout his lifetime.

This agricultural revolution was not achieved without cost, although many of the problems became apparent only after the passage of time. After the first few years yields declined. This was partly the result of decreasing soil fertility. Since only clear water could be used for perennial irrigation, the water applied to the fields was deficient in silt. In addition, the twelve-month growing season provided a continuous temptation to overcrop. From the beginning of the twentieth century increasing use was made of artificial fertilizers, but yields still remained well below those achieved under basin irrigation. Constant applications of water to the land eventually caused widespread waterlogging and salinization of soils. Damage first became apparent on low-lying sandy areas, particularly the important cotton centre of the Middle Delta, but the trouble spread. Two partial remedies were found. After 1918, artificial drainage was introduced and intricate networks of drains were dug. Secondly, some of the higher canals were eliminated and lift irrigation was substituted as a more satisfactory means of bringing water to the more elevated areas. Perennial irrigation resulted in continually damp soils and perpetually high humidity. These conditions favoured the multiplication of crop pests and diseases. Increasing vigilance and widespread use of insecticides and sprays were necessary to combat these hazards. In developing the system of perennial irrigation man had artifically altered the natural agricultural environment. The system so created could only be maintained by constant recourse to artificial aids.

As time passed, existing arrangements for the use of the Nile became inadequate. The growing population put increasing pressure on the land under perennial cultivation in Lower and Middle Egypt. Yet because of inadequate storage facilities, over 900,000 feddans in Upper Egypt were still under basin irrigation. Lack of water in summer was also holding up schemes to reclaim more land for agriculture. The acreage of the rice crop fluctuated from year to year according to the volume of the natural flow of the Nile in the low-water period.

The Sudan, too, was short of water. The Condominium government had done much to develop its irrigation resources. Basin irrigation had been extended in the north. Pumps were introduced as more efficient substitutes for shadoof and sagia. Cash crops were tried out. In 1925 the Sennar Dam was completed and used to irrigate the new Gezira scheme. As the Sudan's demands for water increased it became necessary to safeguard Egypt's requirements. The 1929 Nile Waters Agreement reserved for Egypt the whole of the natural flow of the river during the low-water period from 15 January to 15 June. At this time the Sudan could only use water which had been stored at the Sennar Dam during the flood period, apart from a very small fixed allowance for pumps. Moreover, any new construction works on the Nile in the Sudan were to be dependent on the agreement of Egypt. After the second world war cotton prices boomed. The Sudan government accordingly planned to develop the Managil extension to the Gezira scheme. The area under pump schemes was expanding rapidly. Private individuals found that investing in these was a most profitable enterprise; by growing cotton they could cover their capital outlay in only three or four years. The Sennar Dam, despite some enlargement, was hard put to provide water for the increased acreage of summer crops. With the approach of independence in 1956, the Sudan government made it plain that it had not been a party to the 1929 Nile Waters Agreement and did not regard itself as bound by it. Acrimonious and intermittent discussions took place between the two countries until, in 1959, a new agreement was reached on the division of the waters.

The old agreement had given full recognition to the fact that Egypt, in contrast to Sudan, was already making extensive use of the Nile's waters; this was of course partly because Egypt was utterly dependent on the Nile for its agriculture whereas the Sudan was not. In 1920 Egypt was using over 40 milliard m³ of water a year whereas the Sudan took a mere 1·5 millard m³. In the years that followed both countries increased their withdrawals: the Sudan to 4 milliard m³ and Egypt to over 48 milliard m³. The Sudan now sought to achieve a division of the remaining waters of the Nile that was based not on ratios of consumption in the past but on the feasibility of future developments. In contrast to Egypt, where cultivable land was in short supply, the Sudan possessed large tracts of irrigable land. The 1959 agreement went some way towards achieving a more equitable distribution of water. The Sudan was allowed an extra 14·5 milliard m³, whereas Egypt's share was increased to only 55·5 milliard m³. If more water eventually became available for use, the two countries were to receive half each,

Egypt had yielded to Sudanese pressure for more water because the government was anxious to obtain Sudan's consent to the High Dam project. This consent was essential, as the water stored behind the dam would flood Sudanese territory. In fact the agreement was achieved only two months before work began on the Dam in January 1960.

Unlike previous control works designed for a single purpose – to provide seasonal water supplies – the High Dam will bring a wide range of benefits to Egypt. The value of agricultural production will be increased by almost one-third. The Dam will permit the perfection and extension of the system of perennial irrigation, to which 700,000 feddans of basin land in Upper Egypt will be converted. Water will be available to put another million feddans of land under cultivation for the first time. The supply of water for summer crops will be ensured; in particular there will be enough for a million feddans of rice. For the dam will not simply provide seasonal storage but will also even out fluctiations in the annual flow of the river, bringing new security to Egyptian agriculture. In order to achieve this century storage, as it is called, a very larger reservoir is required. The New High Dam is to have a capacity of 130 milliard m³. Of this 30 milliard m³ are an allowance for eventual silting. 70 milliard m³ will be available for storing water, part of which will be released for irrigation each year. The amount will vary, for it will be used to supplement the natural flow of the river in such a way that hot weather crops will be assured of adequate water supplies. The remaining 30 milliard m³ of the Dam's capacity will be utilized only in emergencies. In years of exceptionally high water it can hold back the crest of the flood, thus safeguarding Egypt's land from the danger of breaches in the Nile's banks.

The Dam has one other purpose. Its waters will be used to generate sufficient electricity to double Egypt's power supplies. Some of this will be used to drive pumps for lift irrigation, but most will be reserved for industry. Thus the Nile, for so long the foundation of agriculture, will become the basis for economic diversification. It will assume this role at a time when, despite every effort to utilize the countries land and water resources, Egyptian agriculture is supporting a decreasing proportion of the total population, and the urgent need to industrialize is paramount.

The Dam, however, is not without its disadvantages.[1] The middle of a

[1] The High Dam project was not the only means by which century storage could have been achieved. A previous scheme had involved the construction of a series of control works on the headwaters of the Nile. Briefly, Lake Tana and Lake Victoria were to be used as reservoirs for century storage, regulators were to be put on Lake Kioga and Lake Albert, and the Sudd bypassed by means of the Jonglei Canal. A dam on the Fourth Cataract would have provided additional seasonal storage and together with a diversion canal to the Wadi Rayyan, would have given protection against unusually high floods. The plan had previously received the general consent of the Egyptian monarchy, and Uganda had been given £4 million to raise the

desert is not the best place for a reservoir and losses from evaporation are estimated at over 10 millard m³ a year, which represents quite a high proportion of the river's total flow. The reservoir is about 250 miles (400 km) long and of this over 70 miles (some 115 km) lies in Sudan. The area flooded comprises the traditional homeland of the Nubians and over 100,000 people have had to be resettled. This is not the first time that the way of life of the riverine population has been disrupted, but the upheaval has not been so drastic before. Nubia was a barren rocky region with only a narrow strip of cultivable land beside the Nile. Any reduction in the agricultural area upset the precarious balance between men and environment. Thus the flooding, caused first by the construction of the Aswan Dam and later by subsequent enlargement to it, resulted in successive waves of emigration, particularly from the southern area which was the most affected. Some Nubians were resettled on irrigation schemes in southern Egypt or northern Sudan. Others sought employment in service occupations in the towns. Often they left their families behind, supporting them with remittances, so that Nubia came to be called the land of women. Still others remained, moving their villages higher up the banks and cultivating a hurried crop when land was exposed during the seasonal lowering of the level of the reservoir. The construction of the Saad El Aali Dam at Aswan has required the final evacuation of most of Nubia. The Egyptians have been settled in the sugar area of Kom Ombo, only 20–30 miles (35–50 km) from Aswan, while the Sudanese Nubians have had to face a more drastic removal to Khashim El Girba on the Atbara.

EGYPTIAN DEVELOPMENT

Agriculture

Four crops have formed the backbone of Egypt's agriculture ever since perennial irrigation became general. Berseem (clover) occupies the largest area of land and provides the staple foodstuff for the country's livestock. Cotton, the largest single export earner, has an acreage which fluctuates according to world market conditions. Maize not only provides the basic food of the peasantry, but different parts of the plant are used for a wide range of other household purposes. Wheat, the traditional grain, has shown

---

Owen Falls Dam so that Lake Victoria could be used for century storage. The scheme provided a comprehensive method of controlling the flow of the whole Nile basin. It would have involved the close cooperation of all the riparian states: Congo, Uganda, Ethiopia and Sudan. At a time when independent nationalist states were emerging, such agreement would have been hard to achieve and harder still to maintain. For these and other reasons President Nasser's government shelved the scheme, preferring a single control works built within Egypt's own territory. It was considered that the High Dam would provide Egypt with more electricity, be quicker to construct, and require less foreign exchange than the multiple projects of the earlier scheme.

a proportional decline although it is the staple food of the growing urban population as well as of the more prosperous classes. These crops are cultivated throughout Egypt and together occupy at least 70 per cent of the total agricultural acreage. There are regional variations in their distribution but these are not so marked as in the case of secondary crops. Wheat in any case is tolerant of a wide range of conditions, and cotton and maize – because of their value as a cash crop and a foodstuff respectively – are often grown even in areas basically unsuited to them. Irrigation has tended to eliminate regional differences in the availability of water supplies; and the soils, because of their riverine origin, have a fairly uniform chemical composition throughout the valley. Thus the main ecological factors responsible for variations in crop patterns are temperature and the mechanical composition of the soil. Because the Nile drops the heavier particles from its load first, the clay content in the soil generally increases from south to north, although there is a fringe of sandy soil along the east and west margins of the delta. Temperatures, on the other hand, increase from north to south. Cotton, which prefers moderate heat, rich heavy soils and perennial irrigation, declines in both quantity and quality from north to south. The same is true of berseem and maize which dislike extreme heat and low humidities.

The northern part of the delta is a pioneer zone. Because the land is so close to sea-level, drainage is difficult and salinity a major problem. Land reclamation projects based on the operation of flushing have, however, lowered the salt content of the soil and made it possible to grow rice. The population density of the area is low by Egyptian standards. Agriculture is extensive and commercialized. Cotton is grown wherever possible and large acreages of berseem support a livestock industry. The sandy, rather saline lands of the delta fringes grow specialized crops, such as sesame, groundnuts and barley, as well as providing the urban markets to the east and west with vegetable produce.

In contrast, the southern delta and the head of the valley form a long-settled and densely populated region. The normal crop complex is here modified by the need for intensive food production. Maize and wheat are unusually prominent. Fruit and vegetable cultivation together with dairying are traditional, specialized activities whose purpose is to serve the urban centres.

In Middle Egypt, the four main crops continue to be important, but towards the south millet is gradually substituted for maize, and berseem competes with other types of fodder, such as beans, which are important throughout the area. Minor crops like onions, sesame and lentils are concentrated in particular localities where they compete with cotton as a cash crop. In the Faiyum special topographic conditions favour the cultivation of rice and fruit, the former on the low, salty land of the depression, the latter on the higher terraced slopes.

In the far south of the country these changes become most marked. Millet surpasses maize in many places and, especially on poor or sandy soils, barley may replace wheat. Sugar-cane and lentils are more important cash crops than cotton. It is significant, however, that crops such as barley, beans and millet, which are prominent here, are grown in decreasing quantities throughout Egypt as a whole. This region, situated in a narrow part of the Nile valley, remote from the market and without perennial irrigation, has long been an agricultural backwater.

In view of this emphasis on crop production, the large part played by livestock in the farming system is at first sight surprising. Livestock, in fact, are remarkably fully integrated into the rural economy. Animals, particularly donkeys, are still generally required for transport. Cattle and buffaloes are used for draught purposes and provide some meat and milk. The omnivorous goat also supplies milk; and sheep, together with poultry and pigeons, are the main source of meat for the villager. Because trees are few in the agricultural landscape of Egypt, manure is widely used as fuel. There is almost no pasture land but the main leguminous fodder crops, with their nitrogen-fixing properties, fit naturally and admirably into the rotation system. There is, however, a marked seasonal variation in the feeding stuffs available. From November to May there is lush berseem, but during the summer there is little fresh fodder because of competition from field crops. Today there is an increasing trend towards the keeping of cattle and a corresponding decrease in the numbers of sheep and goats. Animal husbandry is in fact one of the most profitable ways of using the land, for Egypt's large population and slowly rising standard of living have created a large demand for its products. Altogether livestock account for about 20 per cent of the total agricultural output. (*See Hamdan, 1961.*)

Land-Labour Relationships

Egypt's principal problem is an imbalance between population and resources. At the end of the eighteenth century the population was about 3 million; it is now about 30 million, yet the cultivated area has increased very little (Table II). Rural population densities exceed 2,000 per square mile (750 per km^2) and include some of the highest agricultural densities in the world.

Many features of the agricultural system are directly attributable to this population pressure on the land. Sophisticated irrigation and drainage techniques have been developed in order to make the best use of limited supplies of land and water. This aspect of agriculture is highly capitalized, the government being the main investor. On the other hand, most agricultural operations are carried out by the peasantry on a small scale using laborious methods and rudimentary equipment. Family farms of 2 to 5 feddans and with the household helping in the fields are normal. Egyptian agriculture is extravagant in the use of labour. Mechanization was slow to appear and has been introduced on only a few large farming enterprises. It is, indeed, on the very crops that are most labour intensive that some of the highest profits are made. For these are the crops – cotton, rice and onions – in the production of which Egypt has an edge over most of her neighbouring competitors.

With the increase in population, per capita production has fallen during most of this century, a situation aggravated by the wars and inter-war depression. In the last twenty years, however, this trend has been reversed. The farming population has been stabilized (agriculture now employs only 57 per cent of the actively engaged population) and this, together with agricultural improvements and the increase in land available for cropping, has stimulated a rise in productivity. However, with existing techniques and cropping patterns, there is considerable seasonal unemployment, mainly during the winter months (Fig. 15).

Because of the intense pressure on the land the majority of cultivators practise a biennial crop rotation. The most common pattern[1] is:

Year One – Berseem-Cotton-Wheat (or other winter crop)
Year Two – Winter crop (from Year One), Maize (or other summer or flood crop), Berseem

Such a rotation, which enables the land to produce a cash crop and two grain crops as well as fodder in the space of two years, naturally tends to exhaust the soil. A less intensive, triennial rotation is practised on government schemes and other progressive holdings in order to maintain fertility. Here only one crop of cotton, maize, and wheat is produced in three years. Crop yields are about 20 per cent higher, but total remuneration per unit of land is lower. The system therefore lacked popular appeal. Yields in Egypt generally compare very favourably with yields elsewhere. Intensive application of labour and fertilizer, controlled application of water and wide use of pesticides have combined to produce this result. (*See Hansen and Marzouk.*)

The pressure of population on the land has had a profound influence on patterns of land ownership and systems of land tenure. During the twentieth century the natural increase in population together with the Moslem

---

[1] Naturally there are regional variations on this pattern. In the rice-growing areas of the Delta a triennial rotation is commonly practised: berseem is followed by cotton; then more berseem is followed by maize or rice; and finally wheat, barley or even flax is followed by more maize or rice. In Upper Egypt, sugar usually remains on the land for three years, giving three harvests. On other fields the two-year rotation involves grains and sometimes legumes.

system of inheritance resulted in the fragmentation of properties which were often already small. From 1896 to 1952, the total area of properties of less than 5 feddans increased by almost 220 per cent while the number of owners increased by 430 per cent. In contrast there was comparatively little change in the size or total number of larger properties. By 1952 the distribution of land was therefore extremely uneven (Table III). Over 60 per cent of all landowners were absentees; there was widespread renting of land; and the system was open to many abuses. Because of the demand for land, rents were high and considerable profit accrued to owners of this scarce resource. Yet there was little security of tenure, leases being normally granted for a year or less. A third of Egypt's farmers were affected by this system. Only 66 per cent were owner operators; 20 per cent were tenants; while the remaining 14 per cent owned some land but had to supplement it by renting. Moreover, since there were only about a million holdings in 1952, a large body of the rural population was unable to obtain any land at all. These were the agricultural workers who usually found employment on the large estates, although often on a seasonal basis only. Because the supply of labour was plentiful, wages were very low. There was little opportunity for labourers to improve their status, for land prices were so high that a feddan cost the equivalent of twenty years' wages.

It was to remedy these abuses that President Nasser's government carried out what has amounted to a social revolution in agriculture. Its main purpose has been a radical redistribution of farm incomes. Large-scale land ownership has been abolished. No individual may own more than 100 feddans nor may he lease out more than 50 feddans. The size of farming units is restricted, an individual owning more than 50 feddans being forbidden to rent additional fields. The surplus lands from the large estates, together with certain other areas which had been requisitioned, amounted to about a million feddans. This was available for redistribution to peasants with under 5 feddans of land. By 1964 over 267,000 agriculturalists had received farms ranging from 2 to 5 feddans according to the quality of the land and the size of their families. Subdivision of properties was forbidden in order to prevent further fragmentation of ownership. As well as increasing the number of peasant proprietors the government improved conditions for the tenant farmer. There is now greater security of tenure, and rents which have been restricted are now at about two-thirds of their former level. The position of labourers who are still landless is, however, unsatisfactory. Without the estates there is less demand for their services, and despite the establishment of a trades union and minimum wage legislation their remuneration remains low.

While the land reforms have multiplied the number of small owners, efforts have also been made to provide them with the benefits of large-scale

5*

organization. The redistributed lands have been grouped together in compulsory co-operatives. These provide agricultural requisites, marketing and credit facilities and certain social services. Perhaps even more important, each farmer's land is made up of three plots, one being situated in each of the large blocks allocated to the main crops under the compulsory triennial rotation. The cooperative, the basic unit of production, is about 1,000 feddans in area; agricultural operations are on a correspondingly large scale and mechanization is common. This type of co-operative is now spreading outside the Land Reform areas. Land is consolidated with the consent of the landowner and without alienation of his rights, in order to achieve the economies of large-scale production within the framework of private ownership.

As a further means of satisfying the demand for land the government has embarked on a programme of land reclamation and it is hoped eventually to increase the cultivated area to over 7·5 million feddans. As higher lifts become economic, more elevated areas along the edge of the valley are being brought under cultivation. Land is being reclaimed along the margins of the delta and to a lesser extent in the Faiyum. Cultivable land close to the river is nevertheless limited. Moreover, despite increasing economies in the use of water the Nile itself is not inexhaustible. The government has been forced to reassess the soil and water resources of the arid regions beyond the valley. Two main areas once supported a greater population than at present, and these, together with other areas, offer good possibilities for development. Aquifers of 'fossil' Quaternary water lie at a shallow depth beneath the oases of the western desert, and some are considered suitable for modern agricultural exploitation. In the coastal areas of the northwest, cultivation is being extended and intensified by making better use of rainfall as well as by summer irrigation from local supplies of ground water. These reclamation schemes, however, are extremely costly and each contributes only a modest increment to the total supply of cultivable land.

Industrialization

Recent industrial development, and the growth of new employment opportunities which have accompanied it, have therefore been of particular importance. This has been much discussed elsewhere so that only a summary is given here. Egypt's manufacturing industries began on a small scale early in the twentieth century. Production was and still is largely geared to agricultural requirements and the processing of agricultural products. Stimulated by protectionist policies which were initiated in the 1930's, industry is now the fastest-growing sector of the economy. After South Africa, Egypt is the most industrialized country in Africa, and the further development of heavy industry is encouraged by large reserves of phosphates, manganese iron and oil in the country. A wide range of both capital and consumer goods are produced, and industrial workers form a well-paid and well-cared-for proletarian élite. With the growth of industry and the expansion of the accompanying services, there has been large-scale migration from the country to the town. Although the traditional life of the village goes on, over 30 per cent of the population has already been absorbed into new urban environments in Egypt.

These attempts to enlarge the resource base have helped to ease Egypt's population difficulties to some extent, but the whole problem has clearly to be tackled much more closely at its source. Since 1962 the government, supported by religious authorities, has adopted a policy of promoting birth control and large numbers of family-planning clinics have been established. But as long as children are an economic asset, as they so clearly are on family farms, and the age of marriage remains low, large families are likely to continue to be the norm among the mass of the population. In any case, even if the present natural increase rate of about 2·5 per cent a year is reduced, the large numbers of young people in the existing population will inevitably result in a large increase in total numbers for many years to come.

SUDANESE DEVELOPMENT
Irrigation
Irrigation in the Sudan has developed very differently from irrigation in Egypt. Partly because it was less vital to the life of the country, large-scale irrigation came late to the Sudan: over half the estimated irrigable area still remains to be exploited (Table IV). Yet while the Sudan has as yet nothing to compare with Egypt's Sadd el Aali Dam, the Roseires Dam will not only enable more intensive use to be made of the existing irrigated areas, but will also provide water for further pump irrigation and new gravity schemes such as that of Kenana. In contrast to Egypt, rural population densities in Sudan are often quite low. Except in the north, they are less than 260 per square mile (100 per km²) in irrigated areas and elsewhere they seldom exceed 130 per square mile (50 per km²). There has occasionally been difficulty in getting enough suitable tenants for new irrigation schemes. Moreover, since irrigation occupies a small place in the structure of the traditional Sudanese economy, new tenants frequently lack previous experience of irrigated agriculture. Because land is abundant, tenants' holdings are often 15 feddans or more in size; crop rotations are extensive; and long fallow periods ensure soil fertility. Only three crops are generally grown: sorghum millet and fodder supply the needs of the farmer's family and livestock; and long-staple cotton is the cash crop. Over-dependence on cotton, which accounts for over 65 per cent by value of the country's

exports, makes the Sudanese economy vulnerable in years of poor harvests and whenever world market prices are unfavourable. The inadequacy of labour is revealed every cotton-picking season when more than 250,000 extra labourers are needed on the irrigation schemes.

It is in the Northern Province of Sudan that conditions are most similar to those in Egypt. Most of the people there are dependent on riverine agriculture, land holdings are small, and intensive crop production is practised. Traditional irrigation methods are important, but pumps have spread rapidly and now command over half the agricultural area. The Nile is not the only source of water. In the east, two seasonal rivers – the Baraka and the Gash, both of which originate in the Ethiopian Highlands – have built up deltas in the Sudanese plain, and here flush irrigation is practised. As the rivers rush down in flood, attempts are made to direct the flow so

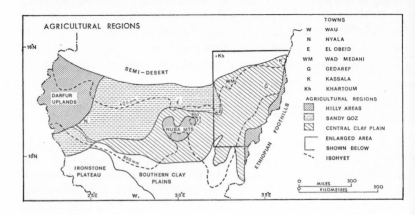

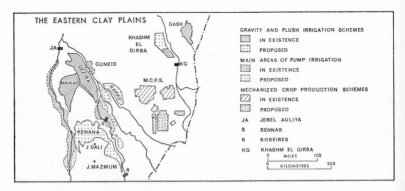

Fig. 16. The Central Sudan (after Sudan Survey, 1953 and Govt. of Sudan, 1957, modified and brought up to date)

that part of the alluvial lands are wetted sufficiently to produce a crop when the floods retreat. Cotton and, in the Gash, castor are grown in the wettest areas, with millet on the drier margins.

It is, however, in the clay plains of the central Sudan that the greatest developments in irrigation have taken place and where the greatest potential for future extensions exists (Fig. 16). In this area of seasonal rainfall irrigation is not essential, but it does provide important benefits. It enables people to achieve a fully-settled way of life and to participate in associated social services; it affords higher and more reliable yields from the land; and it provides opportunities for increasing rural incomes through the raising of cash crops.

The Gezira scheme, which was established on land lying between the Blue and White Niles, has achieved considerable renown. Together with the Manaqil extension, it extends over 1·8 million feddans or about half the land under irrigation in the Sudan. As in much of the rest of the clay plain, physical conditions are here admirably suited to large-scale irrigation. The smooth, gently sloping surface of the land has facilitated canalization, the clay soils are impermeable, and there is little seepage from the canals. Thus underground drainage is unnecessary, although surface drains are needed to prevent flooding after rainstorms. Gravity irrigation of the Gezira area from the Sennar Dam is simple because the land slopes to the northwest. The Blue Nile, which provides most of the water for irrigation, is low in salts; so, too, are the soils of the Gezira, which probably derive from the silt deposited by the river in the past. Salinity, therefore, is not a problem.

In the Gezira proper the size of the standard tenancy is 40 feddans. These large holdings have created a class of prosperous tenant farmers who have used their high cash incomes to become employers of field labour. Over half of each farm remains uncultivated each year, the tenant normally planting 10 feddans of cotton, but only 5 of millet and 2·5 of fodder.[1] Recently there has been a trend both towards smaller holdings which are more easily operated by a single family and, with more water available, towards more intensive cropping systems. Thus on the Manaqil extension, farmers have holdings of 15 feddans, with 5 feddans of cotton, 2·5 of millet and 2·5 of lubia grown in any one year. Both in the Manaqil and in the main Gezira the government and the Gezira Board take between them 60 per cent of the cotton crop to finance the running of the schemes. The farmer keeps the whole of his other crops. Livestock are normall kept, and there are small stands of timber and a few market gardens, but nowhere is the output adequate to satisfy the demands of the prosperous peasantry, so

[1] In the north of the Gezira some crop diversification, particularly the introduction of wheat, has recently taken place.

that additional quantities have to be imported from outside. There is in fact a symbiotic relationship between the Gezira and the surrounding non-irrigated areas. The Gezira not only provides a market for certain products from outside: it also offers seasonal opportunities for employment. The cotton-picking season coincides with the dry season in the non-irrigated areas and the Gezira then offers to the people of these areas attractive prospects not only of wage-earning but also of obtaining grain and grazing.

Although gravity irrigation predominates, pump schemes are also common in central Sudan. The long reservoir behind the Jebel Auliya Dam is full between July and February, and high water levels make lift irrigation possible during this period. Development along the Blue Nile has been slower because the river is deeply entrenched and a very high lift is required, except in the area near the Sennar reservoir. Pump schemes may be owned either by the government or by private entrepreneurs. Because the density of population living close to the river is fairly high, tenants have smallish holdings ranging from about 7·5 to 18 feddans, and only about a third of the land is fallow in any one year.

The Khashm el Girba scheme, while still in the clay plains, is in the far east of the Sudan. This, the most recent scheme to be developed, is noteworthy in several respects. It represents the first attempt to use the waters of the deeply entrenched and highly seasonal river Atbara. While some of the tenancies are allocated to the local nomadic population, this scheme has been chosen for the resettlement of Nubians from the area flooded by the Aswan Dam. Apart from cotton, the range of crops being grown on the tenancies is new, and the government is also running a sugar plantation with wage labour (Table V). The Nubians have, however, encountered certain problems of adaptation. The area is not as dry as northern Sudan and their beloved dates will not grow. Their previous holdings were small and fragmented: their new ones are large and consolidated. In Nubia the soil is light alluvium: in Khasm el Girba it is heavy, sticky clay. The rhythm of agricultural activity to which the Nubians were accustomed was such that temporary jobs could be taken and incomes supplemented by trading: but now no land lies fallow and hard work is required fairly continuously throughout the year. The ex-nomads, too, have had to make abrupt changes in their way of life. Previously the only crop they cultivated was a little rain-grown millet, but this is excluded from the tenancies because it harbours sugar cane pests. The scheme, moreover, makes no provision for fodder for the livestock to which the local people are still devoted. The process of adaptation of the new tenants, which must be successful if the scheme is to flourish, gives the Khashm el Girba project a particular interest.

Non-Irrigated Agriculture in the Central Clay Plains

In the Sudan, the area between latitudes 14° and 10°50′N has long been important for crop production. The rainfall required for non-irrigated agriculture varies with soil types. On the clays, which release only a small proportion of their soil moisture for plant growth, about 18 in (450 mm) of rain are required to mature a crop successfully, whereas on the permeable *qoz* sands as little as 12 in (300 mm) a year may suffice. North of these isohyets agriculture is generally unimportant, although nomads may cultivate occasional crops in places where runoff accumulates. In parts of the eastern clay plains, however, where rainfall exceeds 10 inches (250 mm), water conservation techniques rather similar to those used in Somalia are found and agriculture can support a fairly high density of population. In the south of the central Sudan the proportion of settled agriculturalists again declines, although for different reasons. Here the rainy season is generally unpleasantly humid and unhealthy and the clay soils make movement difficult. As a result, most of the area is used only in the dry season and then only for nomadic grazing.

It is in the central clay plains that the most important developments in rainland cultivation, as well as in irrigated agriculture, have taken place. Here, inadequate supplies of drinking water have always limited the distribution of settlement and determined the land that can be cultivated or grazed. Traditionally, villages were either strung out along the major rivers or clustered at the foot of rocky outcrops where, in the porous piedmont zone, well water was obtainable. Some seasonal expansion into the clay plains was made possible by means of hand-dug *hafirs* (shallow basins excavated in the impermeable clay.) Sited in natural depressions where runoff accumulated, they conserved water for a few months after the rains. In 1945 machinery was first used both to excavate *hafirs* and to dig canals which concentrated runoff into them from a wider catchment area. These *hafirs*, which have an average capacity of about 50,000 cubic feet (1400 m³), are much larger than their predecessors; they are also deeper, and losses from evaporation are consequently less. Each is capable of supporting a permanent settlement of about two hundred families with their domestic animals. Alternatively they can supply much larger numbers of agriculturalists or livestock with water on a temporary basis.

The mechanically excavated *hafirs* have revolutionized water supplies on the clay plains. Quickly and economically constructed, over 500 of them had been excavated by 1961. Even allowing for the fact that some have since failed and that others were used to supplement the water supplies of existing settlements, they have enabled about one-twentieth of the area of Sudan to be fully utilized for the first time. It is true that there has been some misuse of the new land, particularly through overgrazing. This was

probably inevitable, since traditional methods of land use spread spon-
taneously into the plain, unaccompanied by conservation techniques.
Nevertheless there has been a great expansion of crop and livestock production. Meanwhile the pressure of population on the land around traditional
waterpoints has been relieved and, consequently, overcropping and overgrazing have been reduced. The pattern of settlement has become more
dispersed and many people have been able to adopt a fully settled way of
life for the first time.

Although most of the new water points have been used to expand
traditional agriculture and animal husbandry, the remainder have made
possible the introduction of a completely new system of agricultural
exploitation. The Mechanized Crop Production Scheme was started in
1945 in a previously waterless and little-used stretch of the eastern Sudan
near Gedaref. It now occupies over 1 million feddans, of which about
625,000 feddans are cultivated each year. A smaller project has also been
started at Jebel Mazmum and Jebel Dali to the south of the Managil
extension.

The Mechanized Crop Production Scheme is operated by tenants under
the very loose control of the government. But these tenants are quite unlike
the closely supervised peasants on the irrigation schemes. In the rainlands,
holdings are 1000 feddans in extent. The tenant must supply a tractor and
implements and have a reserve capital of at least £2000. Most are wealthy
businessmen who remain in the towns and employ farm managers. In
theory, tenants choose their crops, but market conditions and rainfall limit
their choice. Millet predominates throughout. In the dry north it is the
only crop that can be grown, in the central part some sesame is introduced,
and in the far south there is a little cotton as well. These crops are in fact
precisely the same as those grown by peasant farmers elsewhere in the clay
plains. A modern version of shifting cultivation is practised: a holding is
cultivated continuously for four seasons, then the land lies fallow for four
years while the tenant is moved to another area. The preparation and
sowing of the land are carried out mechanically, but harvesting is done by
hand, because the type of millet eaten in the Sudan cannot be cut by
machine. Unlike the situation in the irrigated areas, the period of high
demand for labour on the schemes occurs at a time when the local farmers,
too, are busy. Hence workers have to be recruited from further afield.
Because each holding requires about 200 men, a total labour force of about
1,300 is needed and this involves considerable organization. The scheme
has stimulated developments in the surrounding areas of traditional agriculture. Local farmers now hire or even buy tractors in order to increase
the size of their holdings and they employ more than half as many labourers
as the Mechanized Crop Production Scheme. Further expansion of the

scheme is envisaged, but it seems likely that, at least for the present, mechanized crop production must be largely confined to the rainfall zone it now occupies. The northern boundaries of the scheme already reach an area where rainfall is inadequate for cultivation in three years out of ten, so that commercial agriculture is financially risky. In the south the high cost of clearing the dense bush discourages expansion. Moreover, in this area early rains may be so heavy that the ground becomes impassable for machinery before planting is complete.

The non-irrigated part of the central clay plains constitutes the granary of Sudan. The surplus millet produced in this area has kept food prices low in the expanding towns and, despite marketing difficulties, some has been exported. The central clay plains as a whole, including the irrigated areas, form the agricultural heartland of the country. The expansion of cultivation which has taken place has had two effects. First, economic opportunities have attracted an influx of migrants. Some of these have come on a temporary basis to work as labourers in the irrigated areas or in the Mechanized Crop Production Scheme. Others have come as permanent settlers, bringing their families and creating farms, particularly in the east where population density was previously low and where the excavation of *hafirs* has opened up virgin lands. Many have come from the far west of Sudan, a remote undeveloped region. Others are West Africans from still further afield who pause to earn a living while making the pilgrimage to Mecca. This east-west migration into the clay plains is facilitated by the railway which traverses the area. Secondly, the extension of agriculture and in particular of agricultural schemes has had a profound effect on the local nomadic population. Seasonal movements have been restricted by the presence of standing crops. The area of natural vegetation has been reduced, although this is partially compensated for by the fact that *hafirs* now allow fuller use to be made of the remaining grazing areas.

Impasse in the Far West and South

The clay plains extend into the western Sudan. Here, too, water supplies have been improved by means of *hafirs*. In the area of the Nuba mountains they have led to a vast expansion of rain-grown cotton. Here the response to new water points has been a little different from elsewhere, for the Nuba prefer to continue to live in their traditional hill-foot villages rather than move out into the plain. Moreover, there has been less immigration, partly because the area is off the main routes and partly because the population density is already unusually high.

The improvement in water supplies has not been confined to the clays. An entirely new source of water is being tapped in the sandy *qoz* regions to the north and west. Much of this area is underlain by water-bearing rocks of the Nubian Sandstone series. Over 150 deep bores descend 400–600 ft (120–200 m) to the aquifer, and provide an important source of water supplementary to the traditional shallow wells which merely tap the perched water table beneath seasonal streams or depressions.[1] Agricultural developments in the *qoz* have not, however, been so striking as in the plains. The light soils are quickly exhausted and easily eroded compared with the almost indestructible clays. A different range of crops is found because of the generally sandy soils. Pennisetum (bulrush millet) often replaces sorghum, and minor crops include sesame, groundnuts and water melons, but never cotton. The most densely populated area is the northern *qoz*, partly because it is crossed by the main east-west routes. Here cultivation to an excessive extent is common, yields are often low and rainfall is marginal for agriculture. But cultivators are not entirely dependent on their field crops. In this part of Sudan the species of acacia which supplies gum arabic (*Acacia senegal*) grows wild, but is carefully protected. Gum collecting, a dry season pursuit, complements agricultural activities. Altogether the Sudan produces over 80 per cent of the world's gum arabic and it forms over 10 per cent by value of the country's exports.

The southern *qoz* is better watered but is little cultivated because the Baggara inhabitants are more interested in pastoralism. These nomads are now prepared to sell their cattle for meat and there is a considerable trade despite the fact that distance to the markets reduces the quality of the stock. The nomads of the White Nile are luckier for they are close to the markets of central Sudan, but both groups produce cheese, which is readily transportable. Elsewhere in the west and far west poor communications prevent the export of livestock products. The very far north is an exception and here, as in the northeast, camels are exported on the hoof to be eaten in Egypt. The trade provides the inhabitants of this most barren region with a useful cash income.

In the far west of the Sudan the mountains of Jebel Marra create a different agricultural region. While much of the surrounding land is stony, with thin, infertile soils, the numerous streams draining from the mountains provide alluvium and irrigation water to supplement the seasonal rainfall. In the mountains themselves the cool temperatures allow temperate crops to be grown on terraced fields. Perennial fruits and winter crops such as tobacco and onions are of local importance. A few small dams have been built with the aim of exploiting the streams more fully, but since there are

---

[1] Some deep bores have been sunk in the semidesert country to the north, but, except in specially favoured locations, it seems unlikely that the low rainfall can provide sufficient recharge for the aquifer. These bores may well have a limited life.

no big rivers or large areas of good soil, developments will have to be on a small scale.

Poor transport is a major factor hindering the development of this and other distant parts of the Sudan. There are almost no all-weather roads. Those built on the clays are impassable in the rains when the ground swells into a sticky morass. On the other hand the sands of the *qoz* and the north are difficult to cross both in the dry season and immediately following rainstorms. The railway maintains a tenuous link between the main towns but it has only recently been extended to the far west. And only in the early 1960's, with the extension to Wau, did it penetrate part of the way into the south. Communications between northern and southern Sudan are particularly difficult since it is necessary to cross the southern clay plains. Here a prolonged season of heavy rains together with annual flooding renders roads impassable and the railway uncertain for much of the year. The main Nile has a regular boat service but the journey is very slow and only small amounts of freight can be handled.

The southern Sudan exports very little, and the people of the flood plain are for the most part outside the money economy. Engrossed in the life of their herds they are unwilling to sell or cull their cattle, even though the animals would have some value as beef if they were scientifically managed. Generally these southerners are unenthusiastic cultivators, and in any case agriculture is limited to the small patches of high well-drained land. Unusually high floods may destroy subsistence crops, particularly in the middle of the region, and it is only in the area adjoining the central clay plains that the southerners produce a grain surplus. Fishing, a widespread part-time occupation, could undoubtedly be expanded. With water control, irrigated agriculture could also be extended in the south, for with its high humidities, high temperatures and ample water the area is particularly suited to rice and sugar-cane cultivation.

Beyond the clays lie the Ironstone Plateau and the hills of southeastern Sudan. Here shifting cultivators live at or near subsistence level. Clearing the woodland vegetation is arduous work. In the plateau, yields are generally low because the lateritic soils are poor in nutrients and are quickly exhausted. In the drier southeast there are some more fertile, alkaline soils, but the broken nature of the country and poor water supplies restrict their use. Partly because of inadequate soils there has been little development of plantation agriculture, and the rainfall is not really high enough for true tropical forest products such as cocoa, rubber or palm oil. Moreover, the onset of the rains is sometimes delayed, with consequent damage to perennial crops. It is unlikely that even products such as tea and coffee, which are much in demand in northern Sudan, could compete successfully with imports from abroad because of labour and transport problems. It is significant that the Zande scheme, the main agricultural project in the south, aimed to raise living standards not so much by increasing the export of commercial crops as by achieving local self-sufficiency. It envisaged that such imports as were essential should be paid for by the export of low-bulk processes products which could withstand delays in transport. However, despite considerable investment and advice, cotton goods were the only source of income to survive the first few years of the scheme.

The population of the south is itself a major hindrance to development. The concept of regular employment is foreign to most of the people. Even if attitudes to work changed, the scattered distribution of population would make it difficult to get any large labour force together. The southerners have had almost no experience of trade, let alone of entrepreneurship. Initiative would have to come from outside. But northerners are reluctant to invest in the south and under present conditions foreign investors are scarcely likely to be attracted to the area, although there has been some aid from international agencies.

The Problem of the South

The south constitutes the main problem area of the Sudan and is likely to remain so for many years to come. While most of the northern peoples are Arabized and have come under the unifying influence of Islam, the diverse peoples of the south have remained ethnically distinct and politically fragmented. Swamps and forests have inhibited communication and contributed towards the perpetuation of separate tribal units. Even the biggest groups, the Dinka and the Azande, lack a unified system of government.

The profound ethnic and cultural differences between south and north in Sudan have been made more acute by a basic problem of lack of contact. Movement between the two areas has always been difficult because of the swamps, and until the nineteenth century even the main Nile was unnavigable. Except along the banks of the Nile, an empty area separates the two regions. This is partly due to the fact that the southern part of the central clay plains with their poor water supplies were unattractive to settlement. But it is also due to the historical influence of the slave trade which caused some of the more northerly of the southern tribes, such as the Dinka and the Shilluk, to retreat farther to the south. Slave-raiding in Bahr-el-Ghazal Province seems to have resulted in severe depopulation.

This lack of contact was accentuated during the period of Condominium rule. For most of the time the entry of northerners into the south was restricted and Arab influences were discouraged. Conversely, few southerners were permitted to go north. Independent cultural development continued in the south; indigenous traditions were encouraged; and the entry of Christian missionaries was facilitated, whereas in the north their activities were strictly circumscribed. English became the *lingua franca* of the south, while Arabic was the normal means of communication in the north. This policy of separate cultural development, abandoned only towards the end of Condominium rule, has now been replaced by a positive attempt to achieve national unity through Arabization of the south.

Yet unity of any kind must remain difficult to achieve while the south remains so backward an area economically and socially. There are few educated southerners and the capacity of southern peoples to participate in the life of the modern Sudan is thereby limited. The centres of economic growth have always lain in the north. This is illustrated today by the migration of young southern men to provide low-grade, unskilled labour in the cities of the north. This imbalance between the size of the southern population and the lack of economic opportunities is likely to increase. Compared with most of northern Sudan the population of the south has a high rate of natural increase; and, when the south receives its full share of medical facilities and these have had their impact on the high death rates of the region, the rate of population growth there is likely to be dangerously accelerated.

This contrast between north and south is the most acute manifestation of a more general problem. In the near future the main differences in development between the various regions of Sudan are likely to be accentuated rather than diminished. The central Sudan – in particular the under-utilized southern parts – will benefit from the expansion of mechanized agriculture and gravity irrigation. Adjacent areas may profit as well. Thus agriculture and animal husbandry in the nearer parts of the west may expand and pump schemes are already extending southwards from Central Sudan into neighbouring parts of Upper Nile Province. But generally in the north, far west and south the situation is not so promising, despite plans for minor improvements in transport. Projects such as the establishment of agricultural processing plants often seem to be put forward for social reasons rather than with any real hope of engendering economic development. Throughout the country the prospect is that regional discrepancies are likely to become more, not less, apparent.

The Horn of Africa

Physical Features

In the Horn of Africa the striking contrast between the highland massif of Ethiopia and the surrounding lowlands is clearly reflected both in the distribution of rainfall and in the cultural history and ways of life of the people. Thus the highlands are moist, have a high density of agricultural population and retain an ancient Christian (Coptic) culture, whereas the lowlands are arid and have a scant nomadic population which is mainly Moslem.

Uplifted in a zone of tectonic instability, the highland is divided in two by an extension of the East African rift. The western part, the Ethiopian Highlands and Plateaus, has a rolling surface at about 7000 ft (2100 m). It is deeply dissected by gorges and interrupted by mountains which rise to over 13,000 ft (4000 m). The depression, which runs from southwest to northeast, contains a series of lakes in the south, and is drained by the funnel-shaped valley of the Awash river in the north. The south side of the rift is edged by another mountainous area, often called the Eastern Highlands, the northeast extension of which swings round to form the maritime ranges of Somalia. Southwards the mountains merge into the Somali-Galla or Eastern Plateau which eventually drops down to the lowlands bordering the Indian Ocean (Fig. 12). While ancient crystalline rocks edge parts of the massif, particularly in the north and west, much of the higher land is composed of great masses of lava and other extrusive igneous rocks. These are mainly of Tertiary age, although, especially in the rift where recent rocks predominate, vulcanism has continued to the present. In contrast, most of the lowlands together with the Eastern Plateau are composed of sedimentary, generally Mesozoic rocks. The lavas weather to provide extensive areas of fertile soil in the highlands, but soils derived from the crystalline rocks in the north tend to be stony, rather poor in nutrients and easily eroded. In the south laterites, steppe and immature desert soils alternate according to climatic conditions.

The Horn of Africa has a complex rainfall pattern. The west and the highlands have a tropical rainfall régime. The main rains fall in the summer but there is also an atypical minor wet period in early spring. Southeast Ethiopia and Somalia are influenced by the monsoonal system of the Indian Ocean. The main rains occur in March–May, and there are subsidiary falls in October and November. The coastlands of the Red Sea have a little rain in winter, while along the Gulf of Aden occasional showers occur between September and May. In general, rainfall increases with altitude and also towards the south (Fig. 13). Thus while the annual total in the highlands of southwest Ethiopia locally exceeds 80 in (2000 mm), that of the northern coastal plains is less than 8 in (200 mm).

The rivers draining the highlands are of great importance to the arid lowlands, despite the fact that many fail to reach the sea. Most of the rivers of the Ethiopian Highlands flow west towards the Nile basin, but an exception is the Omo which flows south to Lake Rudolph. Those of the Eastern Highlands flow towards the Indian Ocean, the Juba and Shibeli being the most important. The narrow northern coast has numerous short streams descending from the steep escarpment, but the Awash is the only river of any appreciable size.

Both rainfall and temperature affect the vegetation pattern, but in the hot lowlands rainfall is the more important. The arid coastlands support ephemeral grasses, scrub and salt-tolerant plants which are used for seasonal grazing. Better pasture is found in the open acacia parkland of the Somali-Galla Plateau. Thickets line watercourses and xerophytic shrubs edge the scarps, but true forest is found only in the western lowlands. In the massif, vegetation shows an altitudinal zonation corresponding to decreasing temperatures, with the highest areas exhibiting a distinct Afro-Alpine flora. The Ethiopians themselves, recognizing the connection between altitude and climate, divide their country into four zones:

	Approximate Altitude	Mean Annual Temperature
Kolla	0–6000 ft (0–1800 m)	79°F (26°C)
Wayna Daga (Woina Dega)	6–8000 ft (1800–2400 m)	72°F (22°C)
Daga (Dega)	8–11,000 ft (2400–3400 m)	61°F (16°C)
Urec (Wirch)	over 11,000 ft (3400 m)	under 61°F (16°C)

Except for the deciduous forests of the southwest, one of the most striking characteristics of the rolling highland surface is the absence of trees. Centuries of activity by man, and, in the north, the long dry seasons, have checked the growth of natural woodland. Indeed, in many areas the most common trees are not the remaining stands of indigenous juniper but eucalyptus, which was introduced at the end of the nineteenth century and widely planted to compensate for the scarcity of wood.

Historical Background

The contrasts and similarities of Ethiopian and Somali development become clearer when the history of the two countries is considered together. Ethiopian history is impressive in its continuity: the modern state of Ethiopia has behind it many centuries of barely interrupted independence. On the other hand the Somali Republic is a post-colonial creation, and the history of the area it embraces shows little political continuity. Physical factors partly account for this contrast. The steep scarps of the Western Highlands provided a considerable measure of protection for the Christian kingdom, while the lowlands, most of which are now in Somalia, lay open to the incursions both of Moslems and, later, of European invaders.

Both countries have been influenced by their proximity to Arabia. The Strait of Bab-el-Mandeb, the shortest crossing between Arabia and Africa, is a mere twenty miles (32 km) wide. From the tenth to the fourth centuries B.C. a series of Semitic migrations took place from South Arabia to the north of what is now Ethiopia; and the fusion between these Semitic

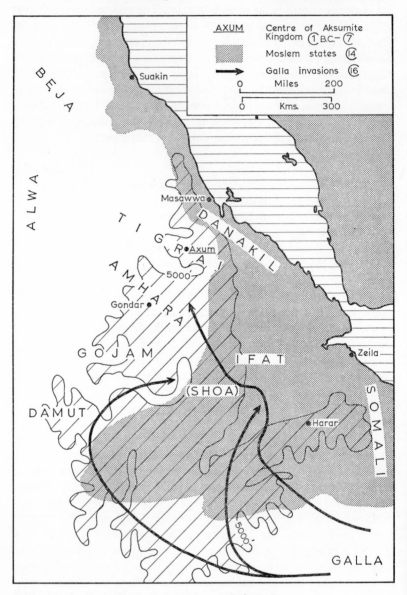

Fig. 17a. The Historical Development of Ethiopia
(a) Early Ethiopia (after Jesman, 1960 and Trimingham, 1952).

immigrants and the existing Cushitic population produced the race which was to dominate Ethiopia. The immigrants themselves came from a mountainous region and settled in the northern part of the Ethiopian

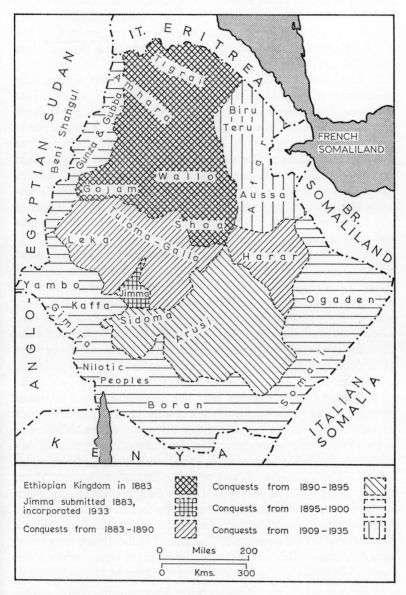

Fig. 17b. (Redrawn from Trimingham, 1952).

Highlands. They brought with them the traditions of a well-developed civilization and introduced advanced systems of irrigation and agriculture. Semitic influences were formative in the development of the Ethiopian kingdom of Axum, which was the principal power in the area from the first to the seventh centuries A.D. Under its patronage Christianity was introduced from Egypt in the fourth century; and this provided the last of the main cultural influences that have gone to make up Ethiopia's own distinctive civilization.

In the centuries that followed, Ethiopia's dominance was challenged by the spread of Islam, the first effect of which was to close the traditional sea routes and thus to impose isolation on the country (Fig. 17a). The lowlands were virtually abandoned to the Moslems and the centre of Ethiopian rule gradually moved south along the spine of the country into the heart of the Western Highlands. The Moslems rapidly established trading settlements along the coast. From there they moved inland to found states in the eastern part of the massif, and even penetrated the fringes of the Ethiopian Highlands. Not until the sixteenth century were the Moslem armies decisively beaten. But by then Islam had taken a firm hold on the coastal regions as well as on the Eastern Plateau and Highlands.

The main theme of Somalia's history has been the gradual expansion of Hamitic Somali from the shores of the Gulf of Aden towards northern Kenya. While the precise reasons for this expansion are not clear, some of the impetus was probably due to the immigration of Arab settlers, who, while generally absorbed by the existing Cushitic population, introduced Islam to the area and seem to have provided some of the leaders for the expansionist movement. The northeastern part of the Horn is in any event particularly susceptible to population pressure on its limited land resources, and this has caused a migratory drift to the more fertile south, which has continued intermittently to this day. The first major Somali migration seems to have taken place in the eleventh century A.D. This and subsequent migrations, following in the main either the course of the Shibeli river or the chain of wells along the coast of the Indian Ocean, gradually disestablished the Galla who were the most numerous of the Cushitic peoples and who in turn moved south and west to overrun Bantu country. Then, drawn forward by the vacuum created by the collapse of the Moslem states of Ethiopia, the Galla began to ascend the Eastern Plateau and penetrate the Ethiopian kingdom (Fig. 17a). Weakened by regional division, Ethiopia offered them ineffective resistance. The lines of Galla advance accentuated these divisions – which were already inherent in the broken nature of the country – by separating the provinces from each other and from the capital.

In the mid-nineteenth century Ethiopia was still a grouping of largely independent political units, but by the middle of the twentieth century the

Ethiopian Empire had become a unitary state (Fig. 17b). This process involved both the reduction of regional divisions in the highlands and the extension of central authority, first over the eastern massif and then down into the lowlands. This political unification under indigenous rule took place at a time when the foundations of other modern African states were being created by European colonial policies.

But Ethiopia did not secure control of the whole of the Horn. This was largely due to the fact that in the 1880's and 1890's European colonial powers became interested in the coastal areas, particularly because of their strategic importance in relation to the Suez Canal. The French acquired the transit trade of Ethiopia by establishing a colony around the port of Djibouti and by running a railway up to Addis Ababa in 1903. The British, who required a steady supply of meat for their Aden garrison, secured the nearest part of Somaliland with its pastoral population and large numbers of livestock. The Italians, who wanted a colony of the classical type which would provide Italy with raw materials and receive some of the country's surplus population, took the more fertile lands to the south and also Eritrea. From 1942 to 1948 this whole fragmented area acquired a certain measure of unity under the British Military Administration, which governed the British and Italian colonies together with Ethiopia's province of Ogaden. Thereafter, the former boundaries were restored, the Italians receiving back the administration of her former territory as trustees for the United Nations. In 1960 the former British and Italian territories were united to form the independent Somali Republic, or Somalia.

The new country inherited certain problems from the colonial era. The natural differences between the north and south had been accentuated by the colonial powers, making unity more difficult to achieve. While the British administration in the arid north was content to maintain order, the economy of the better-watered south received a definite stimulus from the Italian colonists, who established plantations and small processing industries. The arbitrary colonial boundaries ignored the distribution of the indigenous people and their way of life. While the aim of many other newly independent African states is to create national awareness among their diverse peoples, the preoccupation of the ethnically uniform Somali Republic is to attain unity with the other Somalis who live outside the present national territory. This fact, which has acquired increasing significance with the growth of the Pan-Somali movement, has seriously embittered relations with neighbouring countries, particularly Ethiopia, whose possession of Ogaden province is, perhaps, the primary source of discontent. Furthermore, the people of the northern region can only maintain their customary way of life if they are able to migrate to the green plains of Ethiopia's Haud for part of the year. Although the migratory rights of Somalia's tribesmen are upheld by treaty, incidents have occurred with increasing frequency in the area since independence. The future status of the Northwest Frontier Province of Kenya after independence was also a source of bitter disagreement between Somalia and Britain, and the legacy of this dispute has strained Somalia's relations with independent Kenya ever since. The existence of these various manifestations of the Pan-Somali problem is indeed the main factor making for political instability in the area at present.

Ethiopia

The Ethnic Pattern

Ethiopia has been described as a museum of peoples (Fig. 18). The ethnic diversity of the country, which contrasts strongly with the ethnic homogeneity of Somalia, is largely explained by the historical events already described. The bearers of Ethiopia's characteristic civilization – the Amhara and similar groups of mixed Hamitic and Semitic origin – form only about a third of the population. They are dominant in the Western Highlands, the traditional heart of the country. The immigrant Galla, who are rather more numerous, predominate in the south, especially in the highlands where they have adopted an agricultural system virtually identical with that of the Amhara, while the lowland minority retain their former nomadic way of life.

Some of the Cushitic peoples of the massif escaped the influence of the early Semitic immigrants and have largely retained their cultural identity. The Sidamo form the largest group of these, comprising about 9 per cent of the country's population. They are isolated in the far southwest, confined on three sides by the Galla and, like many other people in the south, show evidence of Negroid as well as Hamitic origin. In the north there are remnant groups of Agow stock. Their numbers are declining because, except in the remotest areas, they are becoming assimilated with the Amhara. Other ethnic minorities have more uncertain racial origins. Throughout the Horn of Africa there are small bands of hunters who form endogamous castes, as also do smiths and leatherworkers on occasion. While some groups seem to be of Hamitic origin, others appear to be descended from Negroid or Bushmanoid peoples who probably inhabited much of the area in former times. There are also the Falasha: old-established communities of Jews who live in the west of the Ethiopian Highlands. Religious differences further complicate the cultural map. Although the Semitized-Hamites are predominantly Christian, the Jabouti, most of whom are descendants of early converts to Islam, form 10 per cent of the population of the Ethiopian Highlands and carry on much of the commerce and crafts of the area. The Galla, for their part, while often

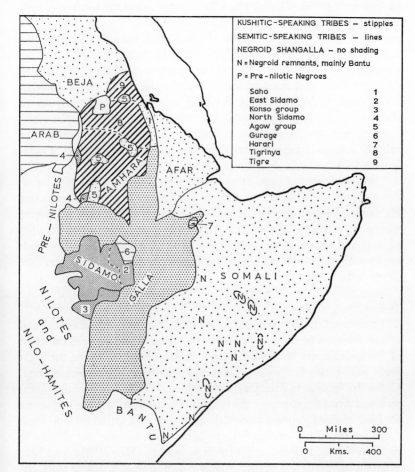

KUSHITIC-SPEAKING TRIBES — stipples
SEMITIC-SPEAKING TRIBES — lines
NEGROID SHANGALLA — no shading
N = Negroid remnants, mainly Bantu
P = Pre-nilotic Negroes

Saho	1
East Sidamo	2
Konso group	3
North Sidamo	4
Agow group	5
Gurage	6
Harari	7
Tigrinya	8
Tigre	9

Fig. 18. Peoples of the Horn of Africa (after Cerulli, 1956; Huntingford, 1955; Lewis, 1955, 1965; Murdock, 1959; Sommer, 1965; and Trimingham, 1952)

Moslem, include pagans and Christians. In Ethiopia, both Christian and Islamic influences are increasing, so that paganism is now largely confined to remote areas particularly the southwest.

In general the culture of the Amharic groups is spreading in the massif. This is partly the result of government policy. But it is also due to the fact that, since the unification of the country in the nineteenth century, peoples from the north have settled in the Eastern Plateau and Highlands.

In Ethiopia ethnic and topographic boundaries often coincide. In particular the Amharic peoples have been reluctant to leave the congenial environment of the plateau. The hilly country below the western escarpment has a population of 'Shangalla' or Negroid peoples. The north is a retreat for the pre-Nilotic group of Negroes, while the south is peopled by Nilotes, including Nilo-Hamites. The eastern lowlands, in contrast, contain nomadic peoples of Cushitic origin: from north to south they include some Beja, the Saho, and the Afar (or Danakil) of the coastal plains, together with Somali and Galla. These low-lying areas are comparatively recent additions to the Ethiopian state and for the most part their peoples retain their distinct traditions. Only in Eritrea, the area which received the original Semitic immigrants, has there been appreciable mingling of highland and lowland cultures.

The distribution of population relates closely to the physical environment. Most of Ethiopia's 22 million inhabitants live in the temperate highlands, although at very high altitudes low temperatures and the rugged nature of the terrain limit settlement. In the highlands population densities often exceed 130 per square mile (50 per km²), whereas the 'Kolla' lowlands are sparsely populated, with – except in the west – densities of less than 13 per square mile (5 per km²).

Indigenous Agriculture

The peoples of the Ethiopian massif are settled farmers with an agricultural system which is in many ways unique in Africa. While many of the crops of the Sudanic and Southwest Asian complexes are found here, the highlands were themselves an important minor centre of plant domestication. Coffee, indigenous to Ethiopia, is still gathered in the forests of the southwest and forms the country's chief export. The cultivation of teff and ensete for food has hardly spread beyond the highlands, but within Ethiopia these crops are important staples. Perhaps because the country was already so rich in cultivated plants, only two crops from the New World have been generally adopted. Red pepper, widely grown in small irrigated plots, has come to form the basic condiment, and maize is admirably suited to the warmer and moister parts of the country.

The distribution of individual cultivated plants shows an altitudinal zonation (Fig. 19). Of the major crops by far the greatest variety is to be found between 5000 and 10,000 ft (1500–3000 m). It is indeed on the rolling surface of the plateau, in the temperate lands of the 'Wayna Daga' and lower part of the 'Daga', that agriculture is best developed. Higher up, grain crops gradually give way to high mountain pastures used for sheep-rearing. In most of the lower areas, aridity restricts agriculture to the drought-tolerant millets. As temperatures are fairly uniform throughout the year, it is the availability of moisture that determines the length of the growing season. Thus, in the higher and therefore wetter parts of the massif

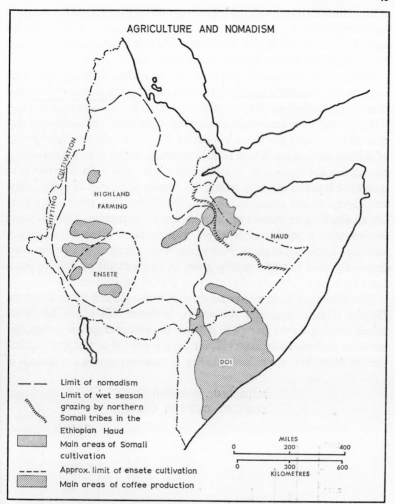

Fig. 19. The Indigenous Agricultural Economy of the Horn of Africa (after Lewis, 1955, 1965; Mariam, 1962; and Sommer, 1965)

two crops a year are usual, while in the drier parts of the uplands agriculture is confined to the main rainy season.

Field crops predominate in the highlands. Grains are the most important but large quantities of pulses and various oilseeds enter the rotation. Teff, the traditional grain of the Amharic Christians, has a high status value and is cultivated with exceptional care wherever possible. Despite this, however, barley with its tolerance of poor conditions is more widespread. It is found at high altitudes where soils are infertile or rainfall is erratic, and, because it matures quickly, it is the crop most commonly grown outside the chief rainy season. Wheat is also important, and the legumes grown include broad beans, chick peas, haricots and lentils.

Although there is now some concern about erosion, land-use techniques are generally successful and the fertility of much of the highlands has been maintained throughout the centuries. The value of legumes in maintaining soil fertility is known and regular fallowing is practised. Land is cleared and cleaned by burning and the ash is left on the soil: a technique reminiscent of shifting cultivation. There is little terracing, which is rather surprising considering the heritage of South Arabian immigrants. Such terracing as does exist is found not only among the Semitized peoples of Harar, Shoa and Tigre, but also among the Sidamo. On sloping land, stones are simply left on the field or thrown up in piles along the contour, thus reducing erosion with a minimum of effort. Nor is there extensive irrigation, although some is found in association with terraces, and streams are frequently used to water nearby plots. In much of the massif, however, drainage is more important, particularly for the cultivation of teff.

The Ethiopian farmer uses an ox-drawn plough and keeps livestock. Despite certain superficial similarities, however, this is not temperate mixed farming on the European pattern. No fodder crops are grown, nor are fields systematically manured, for dung is needed as fuel and building plaster. Moreover, the animal complex so common among the nomads of

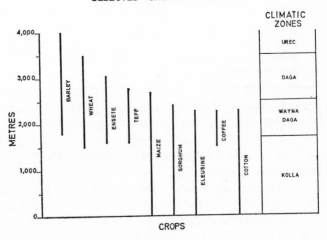

ALTITUDINAL DISTRIBUTION OF
SELECTED CROPS IN ETHIOPIA

Northeast Africa exists here only in a modified form. Cattle confer status. They are milked but seldom killed for meat, although smaller livestock are eaten. Altitudinal transhumance exists but is not universal, perhaps because in much of the area sufficient natural pasture can be found locally to supplement the grazing available on fallow or stubble fields. During the rains, high well-drained land is used for livestock, while, particularly in the wetter areas during the dry seasons, shallow clayey depressions, too waterlogged for crops, provide green grass. More extensive movements do take place, especially along the eastern edge of the massif. Cattle from highland farms spend part of the year at lower altitudes, often in the care of nomads who themselves may make seasonal use of the grazing provided on the slopes of the scarp.

In the warm wet uplands of the southwest, a greater variety of crops is raised. Root crops, typical of tropical Africa rather than the Middle East, predominate. Unique among them is the ensete or false banana, the staple of the Sidamo (Fig. 19). Like the true banana of Uganda this plant has created a landscape of its own. Elsewhere in highland Ethiopia, except in a few of the Galla areas, rural communities live in hamlets; but here in the southwest there are dispersed farms, each surrounded and protected by a thicket of ensete. Furthermore, as one small ensete garden can support a whole family, the density of population is significantly higher here than in the grain-growing regions. Although the use of the ox-drawn plough is spreading, traditionally cultivation is by the hoe. Cattle are, however, important because in contrast to the rest of the highlands, fields are often regularly manured. The ensete is a perennial plant which takes six to eighteen years to mature, depending on temperature. It is the leaf sheath that is eaten, and the fibre, which is a by-product, has a wide variety of uses. Indeed, excess fibre and surplus dairy products are the main export items of the area. However, ensete cultivation appears to be declining, partly as a result of the spread of grain production within the region. Moreover, where the ensete is found outside the southwest it is often half wild, utilized sporadically and then only for fibre, which suggests that this plant may once have been much more widely cultivated.

Both these highland systems of settled agriculture contrast with rural ways of life in the lowlands. The 'Shangalla' of the western foothills are typical shifting-field cultivators. Honey, which they obtain as a result of subsidiary hunting and gathering, is one of their few products that reaches highland markets. Elsewhere below 5000 ft (1500 m) pastoralism is more important than agriculture. In the south the Borana Galla combine cattle-herding with some hoe agriculture, while farther east aridity hinders the dry-farming activities of both the Galla and the Somali. In the northern and coastal lowlands cultivation is confined to *wadi* beds where primitive

6

flush irrigation is practised. The nomads of these areas supplement their meagre income by selling salt or fish. Like the Somali, they also obtain incenses, gums and charcoal from the thorn scrub vegetation.

Contemporary Development

Ethiopia's greatest resource is probably her agricultural potential. A recent survey suggests that less than a fifth of the cultivable area is at present being cropped. Ample land is available for both pasture and cultivation, even in the highlands with its concentrations of population. The moist, warm lands, too, hitherto unattractive and sparsely peopled, offer opportunities for future development.

It is perhaps the very stability of Ethiopian traditions, combined with centuries of isolation, that makes the task of modernizing agriculture particularly difficult. Because the country maintained its independence for so long, the economy never became orientated towards western markets: as it did in the case of many African countries which experienced colonial rule. The Italians appreciated the commercial potential of the country, but their rule was too brief to effect many permanent changes. Indigenous farming is still primarily on a subsistence basis. Individual holdings are small and seldom exceed 10 acres (4 hectares). Conservation and inertia frequently result in local overcrowding and the fragmentation of family farms. Medieval systems of land tenure and taxation still smother peasant initiative, although government land grants have recently increased the number of peasant proprietors and attempts have been made to improve the lot of tenants. The big landowners, the Church and the feudal lords, have rarely been agricultural innovators in Ethiopia.

The development of commercial agriculture is seriously hindered by poor communications. In the massif the river gorges serve only to divide the country. The steep scarps and broken ranges edging the highlands make the lowlands difficult of access. Only from Addis Ababa and Asmara do roads and rather out-of-date railways carry exports to the coast. The highlands themselves have a rudimentary network of all-weather roads, but the west and south of the plateaus are ill-provided for. Moreover, there are virtually no feeder roads – merely trails for pack animals – so that, with a few exceptions, commercial agriculture is only possible close to the main highways.

Coffee is a traditional product in Ethiopia, but unfortunately centuries-old methods of exploitation have proved inadequate in the face of modern competition. Over 80 per cent of the coffee comes from trees that grow wild or semi-wild in the forests of the southwest. Such natural bounty has its drawbacks. Despite ideal physical conditions, yields are inevitably low because most trees regenerate naturally and receive little, if any, attention.

Moreover, careless picking and drying, together with rough handling and poor transport, result in much of the crop being damaged before it reaches the market. The second most important centre of production is in the highlands around Harar. Here the trees are cultivated and indeed often irrigated on terraced plots. A Coffee Board has been set up to improve the quality of this crop and more new plantations are being encouraged. Ethiopia's coffee production has doubled since the second world war, and it now accounts for over half by value of the country's exports. Yet Ethiopia still contributes only 1·5 per cent of the world's coffee and so has little influence in a world market subject to over-production and falling prices. There is therefore a pressing need to diversify the country's exports.

Surplus agricultural produce – oilseeds, pulses and some cereals – are already marketed abroad. However, the utilization of livestock in particular could be improved and this would enable both the nomads and the population of the northern highlands to play a fuller part in the modern economy. The southern plateau with its traditional Moslem crops – coffee, tobacco and the stimulant chat – has for long been an area of cash crop production. Pioneering activity, partially sponsored by the government, is resulting in the extension of agriculture to the lower southern areas, which previously have been under-utilized by pastoralists. In general there is a tendency for commercial cultivation to be extended into the hotter parts of Ethiopia. For here a different range of crops can be produced which are capable of supplementing the temperate products of the highlands.

Cotton provides a striking example of this process. Because it was the country's chief import, stringent attempts have been made to grow it locally over the last few years. Large areas of black cotton soil are available in the western lowlands, but they cannot be used at present because communications with the rest of the country are so inadequate. Considerable quantities are, however, being grown in the lowest parts of the massif where road or rail transport is available. Moreover the *wadis* of the northern and eastern lowlands are being utilized for cotton, and there are large irrigated concessions on the rivers Gash and Awash, while another company supervises cultivation by nomads in the smaller *wadi* beds.

This concession agriculture is an important feature of the modern Ethiopian economy. The first concessions were developed in Eritrea during the colonial period. Faced with the limited prospects offered by the dry, rather infertile and already well-used soils of the uplands, the Italians developed irrigation agriculture in the foothills. The largest concession on the Gash, like its counterpart at Kassala in the Sudan, produces sorghum and cotton. Farther upstream first bananas and then citrus become important. But in Ethiopia proper, concessions are of more recent development.

While there are some in the southern plateau, the main area is again in a lowland valley. Since 1960 irrigation has been provided on the Awash. About 990,000 acres (400,000 hectares) of land are said to be cultivable, but inadequate water resources will undoubtedly limit development to a smaller area. Large commercial enterprises have been established in the valley to produce a variety of crops, especially sugar, which was until recently wholly imported, and cotton. Processing industries based on hydro-electric power are also growing up along the upper part of the valley. Population is moving down the slope and squatter farmers are cultivating lowlands previously left to the nomads. With these recent developments, Ethiopian agriculture has abandoned its traditional highland fastness and has descended to the plain to make fuller use of the country's varied environments. So far, however, it is the accessible eastern lowlands with their admittedly limited potential that have received attention. The wetter, western lands remain undeveloped because they – together with neighbouring areas in Sudan and Kenya – have some of the poorest communications in the whole of Africa.

In this account of Ethiopia attention has been focused on the highlands because their 'temperate equatorial' environment is unique in Africa. Indeed, in some ways Ethiopia has more in common with the Andean states of South American than with other countries in its own continent. In both cases temperate plateau lands have nurtured ancient cultures and sustained high densities of population on the basis of settled agricultural systems, while the surrounding lowlands have remained sparsely peopled and relatively backward. In both regions, however, the drier coastlands have recently developed more than the inaccessible forests of the interior plains.

French Somaliland

It is perhaps more appropriate to consider French Somaliland with Ethiopia than with Somalia because, although the federation of Eritrea with Ethiopia in 1950 gave the ancient kingdom a sea coast and two ports – Massawa and Assab – Ethiopia's chief outlet remains Djibuti in French Somaliland at the terminus of the railway which was built inland to Addis Ababa as early as 1903. Djibuti contains rather over half the 90,000 population of French Somaliland. The territory, most of which is desert and semi-desert, comprises the last French Colonial possession in Africa. Recent claims for independence have revived speculation as to its future. While economic realities might be held to favour federation or integration with Ethiopia, the Pan-Somali movement in the Horn of Africa deeply affects French Somaliland where about half the population are Somalis.

Somalia

Population and Economy

Unlike most African countries the Somali Republic is largely populated by a single ethnic group (Fig. 18). The Somali people, moreover, extend into the adjacent territories of northern Kenya, the Ogaden province of Ethiopia and the southern half of French Somaliland (Table VI). In Kenya the Somali comprise about 60 per cent of the population of the Northern Frontier District, the other inhabitants being Bantu and Galla, some at least of whom have adopted Islam and other Somali cultural traits. In French Somaliland, the Somali slightly outnumber the Afar, the other main ethnic group, but there is also a large Arab commercial community. In Ethiopia 10 per cent of the population are Somali.[1] The existence of these Somali minorities in neighbouring territories has created numerous boundary problems during the present century and it has acquired particular significance since Somalia became independent in 1960 and began to foster Pan-Somali nationalism. The Somali Republic is in fact one of the few countries of Africa where ex-colonial boundaries have not been tacitly accepted since independence.

The Somali are divided into two sections. The Somali proper are composed of four main clan families, the Dir, Isaq, Hawiye and Darod. They comprise over four-fifths of all Somalis and are found throughout the country. The Sab people, with their two branches – the Rahanwein and Digil – are much less numerous and are confined to the area between the Juba and Shibeli rivers. The Somali proper are primarily pastoral nomads, while the Sab have a strong bias towards cultivation. Furthermore, while the tribal structure of the Somali is based on lineage, Sab society has been modified so that tribes embrace immigrant groups of different genealogical descent. Moreover the Sab show evidence of mixture with the Galla and pre-Galla Negroes who previously lived in the area. Some of the earlier inhabitants of the country still form distinctive remnant groups in southern Somalia, and their numbers have been swollen by bands of ex-slaves. Most are Bantu agriculturalists but a few are hunters, possibly of even earlier Bushmanoid stock. Generally they cluster beside the rivers, but a minority are found in the inter-riverine area. Their survival may be due to the fact that the immigrants were not originally cultivators and therefore did not covet their agricultural lands. Indeed, the Somali actively avoid parts of the river banks where tsetse flies abound. Most of these Negro groups are attached to Sab tribes, although normally they have inferior status, and they are gradually being absorbed into Somali society.

[1] There are also Somali commercial communities in ports along the neighbouring seaboard of Africa and the Middle East, the largest being in Aden where the Somali number 20,000.

Other ethnic minorities live along the coast. One of these, in the south, represents an extension of East Africa's Swahili people. The mercantile ports have a high proportion of Arabs, including recent immigrants, as well as small Indian communities. These old and often decaying towns have a cultural life of their own, quite different from that of the rest of the country, and their numbers swell and ebb with the seasonal movement of dhow traffic up and down the coast.

Somalia is one of the few countries in the world with a nomad majority, and as such warrants more attention than its small population would otherwise suggest. Nomadism certainly poses its own special problems for the modern state. Despite Somalia's ethnic homogeneity, the tribal structure of pastoral society is seen as a threat to national unity; and the migration pattern implicit in nomadic life tends to ignore political boundaries. Furthermore, the nomadic section of the community is usually the last to experience modern development, both because the very raison d'être of nomadic life is an extremely limited environment, and because it is notoriously difficult for a government to bring modern services to a nomadic population. But Somalia cannot afford to allow its nomads to remain economically backward, for that would be to inhibit severely the development of Somalia itself.

Altogether about 73 per cent of Somalia's population is nomadic. There are, however, major differences in ways of life between the north and south of the country. In the main these are the result of variations in the physical environment. In the generally arid Northern Region (former British Somaliland), the proportion of nomads rises to 85 per cent and agriculture has only recently been adopted by a small minority. The most important subsidiary occupation in this area of limited opportunity is the gathering of incense, of which Somalia is the world's main supplier. Southward the climate becomes wetter, nomadism shades into transhumance and cultivation becomes more common. Here, too, river water is available for irrigation. In the Southern Region (formerly Italian Somalia), about 35 per cent of the population are already permanently settled, and almost 50 per cent are engaged in some agriculture, although the majority of these combine cultivation with animal husbandry. The population density for the country as a whole is only 8 per square mile (3 per km²), but in the fertile agricultural area between the rivers Shibeli and Juba the figure is doubled.

Pastoralism

The main factors influencing nomadic movements are the supply of water and of grazing land, but minor considerations include the animals' need for salt (or salt pasture), and the avoidance both of areas infected with human or animal diseases, and of especially high temperatures which debilitate stock. In general, nomadic movements follow a fairly regular seasonal cycle which varies in response to rainfall. The grazing territory of a clan is not rigidly fixed but rather defined by usage and maintained by effective occupancy. Where water is plentiful it is freely available to all, but where supplies are difficult to obtain the group constructing and maintaining a water point has exclusive rights to its use. Rights to grazing and even to water are ultimately defended by force. Quarrels are most frequent in the dry season of scarcity. The grazing grounds of clans frequently overlap, particularly, it seems, if the area is comparatively overcrowded. A strong clan, moreover, may gradually encroach on the territory of a weaker clan, thereby adjusting the balance of power between nomadic groups.

Both in their choice of livestock and in their methods of animal husbandry the Somali nomads strive to make full use of the limited environment. The distribution of animals is essentially similar to that found in the Sudan. Camels are used in the driest parts, since they require infrequent watering and can subsist on scrubby browse plants. Sheep and goats, which are usually herded together, are most widespread. Cattle are confined to wetter regions where better grassland pastures are available and frequent watering is possible.

Camels assume great importance in the north where they are a source of milk as well as being essential as beasts of burden. But they are more: a man's wealth and status are measured by the size of his camel herd. In contrast, sheep and goats are kept primarily for subsistence, supplying milk and meat and being sold if ready money is needed. In the south and in the best watered parts of the north herds of cattle may replace camels, while donkeys are substituted for baggage purposes. Commercial exploitation of the pastoral industry is handicapped by the tendency to accumulate livestock. Large numbers of animals are an insurance against dry years when some will die and others be killed for food as milk yields decline. It is also essential that sufficient breeding stock remain. At such a time drought-resistant camels are particularly valuable.

Because of their different water requirements camels and flocks are usually herded separately, and in this way the best use is made of the available grazing. During the rains, when fresh grass is available and animals require little or no water, the differences between the grazing patterns of the livestock are minimal as all the animals fan out over the countryside. In the dry season, however, flocks move close to home wells and overgrazing becomes a problem; only camels with their wider range are able to feed further away. Women and children accompany the slowly moving flocks, while the youths go off to herd and camp with the camels. Although large hamlets may spring up in favoured localities, especially in the dry season, the basic nomadic group is nevertheless small. It consists of several families and its composition is always changing. This facilitates mobility and allows maximum flexibility in the use of pasture.

In the north there are two main areas of home wells. The most important is in the well-watered maritime ranges, but the beds of the numerous streams which drain the highland scarps also provide permanent water. The rocky, dune-strewn coastal strip is, however, very arid. As elsewhere along this seaboard, the nomads use the grazing provided by the scanty winter rains and then ascend the highlands such as the Haud plateau in the southwest, where they benefit from early summer storms. Despite good rainfall, however, the Haud plateau lacks permament wells and can only be used on a seasonal basis. If the first rains are heavy it can be occupied continuously until after the autumn rains, but if not a retreat home must be made in the summer. Recently, lined *hafirs* have been dug which, together with the sale of water from trucks, prolong the period during which families and flocks can stay in the Haud.

In the south, too, nomadic movements frequently take place in a south-western direction from the wells of the coast into the interior, and the pastures of the Doi exert an attraction similar to those of the Haud. Because of generally better water supplies, particularly in the area between the rivers Shibeli and Juba, nomadic movements are often reduced. However, transhumant pastoralists make extensive use of the rivers in the dry season.

Indigenous Agriculture

Agriculture is increasing in Somalia, but only about 10 per cent of the area with dry-farming potential is as yet cultivated. There are in fact consider-able reserves of agricultural land, some of which is irrigable. Nomads are slow to overcome prejudice against agriculture, and in an area of uncertain rainfall animal husbandry seems to offer greater security against drought and famine. Even in the south, where cultivation is most widespread (Fig. 19), only 19 per cent of the population rely solely upon agriculture, and this percentage includes Negro cultivators and all those living in irrigated areas.

In the south, rain cultivation occurs in the area of relatively high rainfall between the Juba and Shibeli rivers and in places along the dune-lined coast. The waters of these rivers are also used for flood irrigation. Water from the Juba is led off into natural depressions, while in the case of the Shibeli, which flows above the level of the land, flooding is achieved by simply breaking its banks. In areas of rain cultivation, farmers concentrate runoff on to their fields by means of channels and bunds. There is in fact no sharp distinction between the two types of agriculture. The crops grown are similar, although their relative proportions vary, and yields are generally

higher on the flood lands. In non-irrigated areas drought-resistant sorghums occupy most of the land, while along the rivers maize may replace
them as the chief cereal, and minor crops such as cotton, beans, sesame,
gourds and manioc can be grown more widely. There are two floods and
two rainy seasons each year, so that, theoretically at least, two crops can be
grown. The area harvested and the yields achieved are very variable,
particularly in the non-irrigated areas. While inadequate rains are the most
common hazard faced by the dry-farming cultivator, the land of the
riverine agriculturalists frequently suffers from uncontrolled flooding and
consequent waterlogging.

In the north, cultivation is confined to the well-watered western highlands and the adjoining parts of Ethiopia, apart from a few places where
flush irrigation is practised (Fig. 19). Some features of the agricultural
system, such as the use of water conservation techniques and heavy reliance
upon sorghum, are similar to those of the southern areas of dry-farming,
but because of poor autumn rains only one crop a year is grown. There
are, however, other major differences between the cultivators of the north
and those of the south. In the south, the Somali have practised agriculture
for several hundred years: in the north it was introduced only during the
twentieth century. In the south agriculture was learnt from the Bantu,
among whom immigrant Somali came as conquerors, while in the north
agriculture spread to the nomads as a result of contact with the neighbouring Galla. The Somali of the south are apt to relegate their cultivation to
Negro vassals, although this practice is less common among the Sab,
many of whom, like the northerners, perform their own agricultural tasks.
From the Negroes the southerners learnt hoe cultivation, from the Galla
the northerners adopted the ox-drawn Ethiopian plough, Thus, although
both groups of agriculturalists keep cattle, in the north these animals are
more fully integrated into the farming economy. There they graze locally
throughout the year, while in the south the cattle are sent off to distant
pastures, at least during the spring rains when most cultivation takes place.
In the south, long periods of settled cultivation have modified nomadic
attitudes. The village is the basic social unit, permanent houses of Negro
types are built, and there is a trend towards individual land ownership. In
the north few changes have occurred as yet. Clans cultivate the lands that
their livestock formerly grazed and hamlets consist of groups of nomadic
huts. The size of the hamlet often varies with the seasons. Kinsmen who
are still nomadic join the villagers in autumn and winter, while in the rainy
season part of a villager's family may still migrate with the flocks. For all
those who have recently taken up cultivation, whether northerners or new
immigrants to the south, livestock continue to play an important part in the
rural economy.

6*

Plantations and Commercial Development

Although plantation cash crops occupy a mere 25,000–35,000 acres (10,000–14,000 hectares) they are of paramount importance in the economy of Somalia. Bananas, which have replaced cotton as the chief crop, provide over three-quarters by value of the Southern Region's exports, and the country is virtually self-supporting in sugar. Yet plantation agriculture only survives because it is protected from foreign competition and because the bananas have a monopoly in the Italian market. Skilled and patient Italian enterprise developed the plantations in the face of heavy odds. But labour is scarce, and irrigation along the Shibeli is hampered, both because the river dries up for two months each year and because, except during flood periods, the water along its lower course is brackish. Furthermore, costs of exporting to European markets are high and neighbouring countries generally lack purchasing power. Thus, compared with many other African countries, Somalia remains capable of only small-scale production of commercial crops.

Yet the area under irrigation in Somalia could be extended to perhaps 500,000 acres (200,000 hectares). Although the Juba river provides more favourable conditions for irrigation than the Shibeli, its riverine lands have been developed less because, until 1925, it formed the border with Kenya. Recently irrigation has been extended among local Somali farmers, better water supplies have been provided for rainland cultivators, and mixed farming has been encouraged. Yet because of the limitations of the environment it is likely that in the long run the livestock sector of the economy will offer the best prospect for development. Despite low levels of commercialization, meat and hides (especially goatskins) have long been the chief export of the Northern Region and the main non-plantation product of the south. New wells are encouraging more efficient use of the generally adequate grazing resources and the indications are that, as supplies are improved and the nomad's life made more secure, surplus stock will be more willingly sold.

It must be emphasized that, mainly because of its aridity, Somalia is a very poor country. Its few known resources cannot readily be developed and its economy remains heavily dependent on foreign aid. This economic weakness is in fact the country's cardinal problem. But its other problems are prodigious: the awkward shape of the country wrapped round the coast of the Horn of Africa; the sharp contrast between the resources and ways of life of the northern and southern regions, which has been accentuated by their differing colonial associations with Britain and Italy; the eccentric position of the only large town, chief port and capital of Mogadishu; the political implications of the Pan-Somali movement; and the problem of nomadic pastoralists crossing the frontiers of the country, particularly in the Haud-Ogaden border zone. Somalia is indeed one of the many examples of new nations in Africa that have inherited a legacy of difficult problems as a result of arbitrary colonial partitioning.

TABLE II.I *Land and Population in Egypt*

Date	Area Cultivated (million feddans)	Area Cropped (million feddans)	Agricultural Labour Force (millions)	Total Population (millions)
1897	5·0	6·7	—	9·7
1907	5·4	7·7	2·4	11·3
1917	5·3	7·7	2·8	12·8
1927	5·5	8·6	3·5	14·2
1937	5·3	8·4	4·3	15·9
1947	5·7	9·2	4·2	19·0
1960	5·9	10·4	4·3	26·1
Percentage increase of 1960 over 1897	12%	55%	80%	170%

Sources: Statistical Handbooks of Egypt and *Statistical Handbooks of the United Arab Republic*, Cairo.

TABLE II.II *Land Ownership in Egypt*

Area (feddans) Owned	1952 (before land reform) % total owners	1952 (before land reform) % total land	1964 % total owners	1964 % total land
less than 5	94·3	35·5	94·3	54·8
5–49	5·3	30·4	5·4	31·9
50–99	0·2	7·2	0·2	6·4
100–199	0·1	7·3	0·1	6·9
over 200	0·1	19·7	—	—

Source: Central Agency for Public Mobilisation and Statistics, 1965.
Statistical Handbook of the United Arab Republic, Cairo.

TABLE II.III   *The Expansion of Irrigation in Sudan*

Type of Irrigation	Area Commanded in 1965	Possible Future Expansion
Basin	*Northern Sudan.* Average 80,000 feddans. The area flooded varies from 10,000 to over 100,000 feddans	—
Flush	*Gash.* The area flooded varies from 40,000 to 70,000 feddans.	—
	Tokar (on River Baraka). The area flooded varies from 30,000 to 150,000 feddans	—
Gravity	*Gezira.* 1,000,000 feddans	*Khashm el Girba.* 319,000 feddans.
	Managil. 800,000 feddans	*Kenana.* 1,200,000 feddans.
	Khasm el Girba (phase 1). 179,000 feddans	*Rahad.* 500,000 feddans. *Jonglei.* 500,000 feddans.
Pumps	Government and Private. Area flooded 1,195,000 feddans	Government and Private 1,310,000 feddans

Note. The *Kenana* and *Rahad* schemes await further surveys and the completion of the Roseires Dam.

The *Jonglei* canal project, which would by-pass the *sudd* and would affect the fishing and seasonal grazing of about a million Nilotes, has been shelved indefinitely. There is therefore no immediate prospect of extra water for irrigation from this source.

Sources include Ministry of Irrigation and Hydro-Electric Power, 1957 and Central Office of Information, The Republic of Sudan, 1966.

TABLE II.IV   *The Khashm el Girba Scheme*

Total irrigable area	—	500,000 feddans
Area irrigated under phase 1	—	179,000 feddans
Size of tenancies	—	15 feddans[1]
Crops grown on tenancies	—	5 feddans of cotton
	—	5 feddans of wheat
		5 feddans of groundnuts

[1] In addition, all Nubian tenants have received one feddan of land freehold, on which they may grow what they wish. This is in compensation for any privately owned riverine land which they may have held in northern Sudan.

TABLE II.V   *The Distribution of the Somali People*

Somali Republic	2,250,000
Ethiopia	c.1,000,000
Kenya	200,000
French Somaliland	37,000

Source: Lewis, I. M. 1965. *The Modern History of Somaliland,* Weidenfeld and Nicolson, London.

References and Select Bibliography

AWAD, M. 1954. The assimilation of nomads in Egypt. *Geographical Review*, Vol. 44: 240–252.

BARBOUR, K. M. 1959. Irrigation in the Sudan: its growth, distribution and potential extension. *Transactions and Papers, Institute of British Geographers*, Vol. 26: 243–263.

    1961. *The Republic of the Sudan: A Regional Geography*, University of London Press, London.

    1961. Population, land and water in central Sudan. 137–156 in Barbour, K. M. and R. M. Prothero (eds.), *Essays on African Population*, Routledge and Kegan Paul, London.

    1964. North and south in Sudan, a study in human contrasts. *Annals of the Association of American Geographers*, Vol. 54: 209–226.

BEDDIS, R. A. 1963. The Aswan High Dam and the resettlement of the trasts. *Annals of the Association of American Geographers*, Vol. 54: 209–226.

BEDDIS, R. A. 1963. The Aswan High Dam and the resettlement of the Nubian people. *Geography*, Vol. 48: 77–80.

BESANÇON, J. 1957. *L'homme et le Nil*, Gallimard, Paris.

BROOKE, C. 1959. The rural village in the Ethiopian Highlands. *Geographical Review*, Vol. 49: 58–75.

BUXTON, D. R. 1948. The Shoan plateau and its people: an essay in local geography. *Geographical Journal*, Vol. 114: 157–172.

CERULLI, I. 1956. *Peoples of South West Ethiopia and its Borderland*, International African Institute, London.

DAVIES, H. R. J. 1964. An agricultural revolution in the African tropics: the development of mechanised agriculture on the clay plains of the Republic of Sudan. *Tidjschrift voor Economische en Sociale Geografie*, Vol. 55: 101–108.

GAITSKELL, A. 1959. *Gezira: A Story of Development in the Sudan*, Faber, London.

HAMDAN, G. 1961. Evolution of irrigation agriculture in Egypt. 119–142 in Stamp, L. D. (ed), *A History of Land Use in Arid Regions*, Unesco, Paris.

HANCE, W. A. 1954. The Gezira: an example in development. *Geographical Review*, Vol. 44: 253–270.

HANSEN, B. and MARZOUK, G. A. 1965. *Development and Economic Policy*, North-Holland Publishing Co., Amsterdam.

HUFFNAGEL, H. P. (ed.), 1961. *Agriculture in Ethiopia*, F.A.O., Rome.

HUNT, J. A. 1951. *A General Survey of the Somaliland Protectorate, 1944–1950*, Crown Agents for the Colonies, London.

HUNTINGFORD, G. W. B. 1955. *The Galla of Ethiopia; the Kingdoms of Kaffa and Janjero*, International African Institute, London.

HURST, H. E. 1952. *The Nile: A General Account of the River and the Utilization of Its Waters*, Constable, London.

INTERNATIONAL BANK FOR RECONSTRUCTION AND DEVELOPMENT·
1957. *The Economy of the Trust Territory of Somalia*, Washington.

ISSAWI, C. 1963. *Egypt in Revolution: An Economic Analysis*, Oxford University Press, London.

JACKSON, S. P. 1961. *Climatological Atlas of Africa*, The African Climatological Unit, University of Witwatersrand, Johannesburg.

JESMAN, C. 1960. *The Ethiopian Paradox*, The Institute for Race Relations, Oxford University Press, London.

KARP, M. 1960. *The Economics of Trusteeship in Somalia*, Boston University Press, Boston.

LAST, G. C. 1962. Introductory notes on the geography of Ethiopia. *Ethiopian Observer*, Vol. 6: 82–134.

LEBON, J. H. G. 1960. On the human geography of the Nile Basin. *Geography*, Vol. 45: 16–26.

    1965. *Land Use in Sudan*, Geographical Publications, Bude, Cornwall.

LEWIS, I. M. 1955. *Peoples of the Horn of Africa: Somali, Afar and Saho*, International African Institute, London.

    1961. *A Pastoral Democracy: A Study of Pastoralism and Politics among the Northern Somali of the Horn of Africa*, Oxford University Press, London.

    1965. *The Modern History of Somaliland from Nation to State*, Weidenfeld and Nicolson, London.

LITTLE, T. 1965. *High Dam at Aswan: The Subjugation of the Nile*, Methuen, London.

MARIAM, M. W. 1962. *A Preliminary Atlas of Ethiopia*, Addis Ababa.

    1964. The Awash valley, trends and prospect. *The Ethiopian Geographical Journal*, Vol. 2: 18–24.

    1964. The background of the Ethio-Somalian boundary dispute. *Journal of Modern African Studies*, Vol. 2: 189–219.

MINISTRY OF IRRIGATION AND HYDRO-ELECTRIC POWER. 1957. *Sudan Irrigation*, The Government of Sudan, Khartoum.

MOUNTJOY, A. B. 1952. Egypt's population problem. *Transactions and Papers, Institute of British Geographers*, Vol. 19: 121–134.

MURDOCK, G. P. 1959. *Africa, its Peoples and their Culture History*. McGraw-Hill, New York.

SIMOONS, F. J. 1960. *Northwest Ethiopia: Peoples and Economy*, University of Wisconsin Press, Madison.

SMEDS, H. 1955. The Ensete planting culture of eastern Sidamo, Ethiopia. *Acta Geographica*, Vol. 13: 1–39.

SOMMER, J. W. 1965. Ethiopia, *Focus*, Vol. 15, The American Geographical Society, New York.

TOTHILL, J. D. (ed.). 1948. *Agriculture in the Sudan*, Oxford University Press, London.

TRIMINGHAM, J. S. 1952. *Islam in Ethiopia*, Oxford University Press, London.

ULLENDORFF, E. 1960. *The Ethiopians: An Introduction to Country and People*, Oxford University Press, London.

3 East Africa

3 East Africa

By A. WARREN

The problems that confront the people of East Africa in planning their future development stem largely from the fragmentation and variety of the region's geography. In the first place there are strongly contrasting physical landscapes: glaciers fill the valleys of the higher peaks; temperate downlands cover highlands on the equator; broad bush-covered plains stretch for immense distances in the lowlands; dense forests and barren deserts complement each other; and the eastern margin is bordered by a tropical coral coast. This physical diversity is reflected in the variety of East Africa's 32 million people; in close proximity live primitive hunters and nomadic pastoralists, peasant cultivators and large-scale commercial farmers, industrial workers and the office staffs of the large cities. These elements form a large number of competing pressure groups, and the political systems within which they operate vary almost as widely, from ancient indigenous institutions to the political patterns of the twentieth century.

This physical and cultural diversity has made East Africa an area of great interest to a large number of specialists, whose interests are as varied as the material with which they work, for studies of East African environments and people can illustrate a whole range of scientific problems. But the most pressing need is for such studies to be directed towards a fuller under-standing of the difficulties facing societies that lack both capital and educated manpower and yet are trying to build modern and productive nation states. The main purpose of this essay is to present what seems to the author to be the necessary background to such an understanding.

The pattern of East African society is perhaps best seen as a number of superimposed and to some extent interwoven strands. Its various human groups have seen different opportunities and limitations in their environ-ment, so that each incoming group has had to adjust to a unique situation in relation both to its predecessors and to its own particular demands. East Africa has witnessed a succession of invasions by different peoples and ideas, and it is with these and the patterns and problems that they have created that the principal section of this essay will be concerned. But it is necessary first to examine the broad environmental framework of the region, the potentialities and restrictions of which have affected all the groups who inhabit it today. The main features of this environmental framework are indicated in Figures 20, 21 and 22, but some of its details need further elucidation.

The Physical and Ecological Framework

Much of East Africa consists of wide, monotonous plains which have, for the most part, been formed on the hardened, mainly Pre-Cambrian rocks of the Basement Complex. These rocks have been subjected to intense and protracted weathering in the past so that the sound rock is now frequently buried beneath a deep mantle of friable and decomposed material. In places water movements within this mantle have concentrated iron and aluminium which, when cemented together, form a very hard and durable lateritic crust within the soil.

If they are undisturbed the plains are gently undulating, with here and there higher areas where harder rocks have resisted weathering more successfully. But for a variety of reasons streams have cut down into the plains. This may have been due partly to the rise of the continent as a whole in relation to sea level; partly, and perhaps more importantly, it may have been caused by earth movements which lifted or depressed different parts of East Africa; and partly it may have been the result of repeated changes in climate over the last million years or more. The rise of the continent us a whole appears to have taken place in a number of stages, because the streams seem to have cut extensive plains at a number of (not always distinct) levels. As erosion cut into the old weathered surface at each new phase it uncovered hard cores of more resistant or less well-jointed rock which were still unweathered. These now stand up above the new level as steep-sided 'inselbergs' which vary in size from a mere pile of boulders to extensive hill masses. Where laterite was well developed, particularly in parts of southern Uganda, erosion has cut valleys between hills which are flat-topped because of the protection afforded by their hard caps. The site of Kampala extends over a number of such flat-topped hills (Fig. 20).

This landscape of wide plains, isolated steep-sided hills and laterite-capped zones is typical of much of Africa. What distinguishes East Africa from most of the rest of the continent and, incidentally, makes it scenically one of the most beautiful parts of the world, is that its surface has been drastically modified along restricted belts by a series of earth movements, with spectacular uplift in some parts and deep depression in others. The first of these movements probably began at a very remote period, but a new phase of movement started in the Miocene and culminated in the Pleistocene. Much of the present rift scenery, in fact, has appeared during the human period. During this long history of earth movements, some areas were affected at one time, others at another, and the precise details of the sequence of rifting is to some extent still speculative. It is clear, however, that the most important expression of the movements was the creation of two major rift valleys: the Eastern and Western. In each case an elongated arch of country was lifted up, while at the apex of the arch there was slight depression and parallel faulting, with the sinking between the faults of long trough-like valleys. This pattern is best developed in central Kenya and along the western border of East Africa from Lake Albert to the southern end of Lake Tanganyika, but even within these zones there is considerable variation. The height to which the shoulders of the rifts rise differs considerably, for whereas in some places there is today very little surface expression of the rift, in others mountain blocks rise steeply above the valley floors: Ruwenzori, for instance, rises to 16,795 ft (5120 m) above sea level and the Aberdare mountains in central Kenya rise to 13,113 ft (3994 m). The pattern of the rifting itself has been complex. Sometimes it has left a simple scarp slope, whilst elsewhere – just to the west of Nairobi, for instance – it is expressed in a series of stepped blocks. Associated with the main valleys are a number of branches, such as the Kavirondo valley in western Kenya and the valleys around Ruwenzori, while at the southern end of the Eastern Rift there is a fanning out of minor branching valleys and rift highlands, and elsewhere there are parallel rift valleys like the Lake Rukwa trough. Another kind of major earth movement produced broad tilted blocks and single scarps such as the Iringa highlands in central Tanzania. Away from the elongated belts of intense movement there were gentler warpings. The Lake Victoria basin sank, flooded, and was later tilted, while a series of similar basins in central Tanzania were filled with sediments.

The uplift and rifting were accompanied both within the rift zones and in nearby areas by extensive vulcanicity. Along much of the Eastern Rift, in particular, and to a lesser extent in the central and southern parts of the Western Rift, fluid lavas flowed out from faults, flowing over the scarps into the rift valley and away from the scarps over the surrounding countryside. In places these lavas have masked the faults, and elsewhere they themselves have been fractured by later movements. In the desert plains of northeast Kenya lava fields of this kind cover vast areas. Associated with the lavas, but often farther from the actual rift zones, high cones of lava and ash were piled up into peaks thousands of metres high. Some of these, in northern Uganda for instance, have since been eroded to mere stumps, but others remain to form Africa's highest peaks: Kilimanjaro, Kenya, Elgon, Karisimbi and Rungwe. Both within the rift and away from it there are numerous smaller cones and flows, some of very recent formation and some still active. Parts of the Eastern rift valley in Tanzania, for instance, still experience ash showers from cones, and in 1938 Karisimbi gave off an extensive lava flow which reached Lake Kivu. Some areas, for example parts of the Serengeti plains and the southern highlands of Tanzania, have been covered in the recent past by ash showers, and these have usually added a fertile upper layer to the soil.

Uplift of the rift highlands gave increased erosive power to the streams on their slopes. The Aberdare block was cut into on its eastern side by a series of deep parallel valleys which are very typical of Kikuyuland, while in Ankole in southwestern Uganda the streams etched out basins of deeply weathered granite from between margins of harder rock to give a landscape of wide 'arenas'. The deep valleys in the highlands cut up the country into numerous hills whose isolation has had a significant effect on the lives of their inhabitants.

The earth movements had an important secondary effect in that they disrupted parts of the drainage system which formerly drained the plains. In the west the primeval rivers are thought to have drained westward into the Congo; these were cut across at various times and the main drainage is now to the Nile. Uplift also meant that many rivers were ponded back in their old valleys to form lakes like Lake Kioga, while others had their courses reversed, either gently, so that there is now only an ill-defined and swampy watershed between their eastward and westward flowing portions, or more drastically, so that the water spilled eastward over former watersheds and cut deep gorges in the process. Some rivers, especially in Rwanda and Burundi, were dammed by lava flows to form long branching lakes like Lake Kivu.

The sinking and later tilting of Lake Victoria flooded valley systems around its shores to form a branching system of swamps, bays, estuaries and islands. This complex pattern has since been modified by the growth, at various levels, of a series of barrier beaches and spits, which have been swept round by the circulation of the lake waves. The zone of these bars reaches 2 miles (3·2 km) in width and in many places they pond up large lakes on their landward sides.

In much of the Western Rift closed basins came into existence which, when flooded, formed more lakes, some of them very deep: Lake Tanganyika, for instance, is over 4600 ft (1400 m) deep. In the Eastern Rift, Lake Rudolf is analogous to this, but most of the lakes in the east and some in the west are much shallower, having been formed by lava-damming, and in the drier climate of the rift valley floors they are often saline. The deeper lakes are often relatively poor in fish, but the shallower ones – and in particular Lake George and Lake Kioga – are among some of the world's richest fishing grounds. Some parts of the rifts have filled with a deep series of unconsolidated sediments eroded from the surrounding highlands and

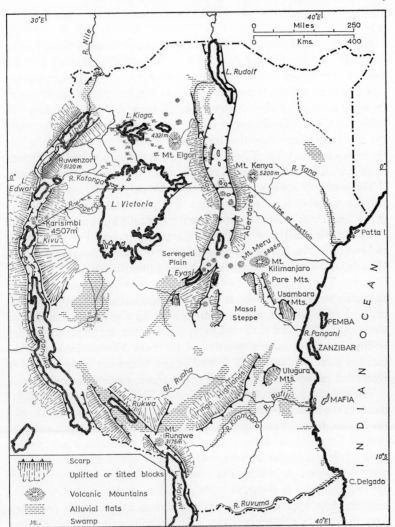

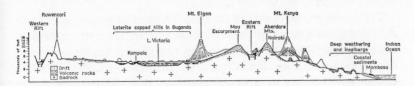

Fig. 20. East Africa: Relief and Drainage

scarps. These sediments are often coarse, unstable and very liable to erosion.

Along the Indian Ocean coast is a strip of country which differs in many ways from the rest of East Africa. Here the sea has, at various periods, covered the margins of the continent on which marine sediments (mostly limestones) have been deposited as well as detritus (usually sandstones) from the eroding interior. Following uplift these deposits have been left behind as a series of sedimentary rocks, the most recent of which constitute the raised coral limestones that form many of the offshore islands, such as the barren eastern plain of Zanzibar, as well as the immediate East African hinterland. The modern coast is lined for much of its length by coral reefs.

The pattern of uplift and rifting has added variety not only to the scenery but also to the climate of East Africa. The plains are in general areas in which large zones of similar climate merge gradually into one another. The climate here is mostly semiarid, with extreme desert conditions in the north and east of Kenya, less extreme conditions in central Tanzania and eastern Uganda, and increasing humidity westward towards the Congo borders. (Fig. 21.) The highland areas of East Africa, however, intercept more rain and suffer much lower moisture losses by evaporation. The highest mountains are snow-covered, and there are glaciers on Kenya, Kilimanjaro and Ruwenzori. The floors of the rift valleys, in contrast, are areas of abnormal aridity, but the gentler depression of the Lake Victoria basin and the creation there of the world's second largest freshwater body has led to significant increases in rainfall around its margins, particularly in the north.

The seasonal pattern of rainfall in East Africa is the result of the movements of the rather ill-defined rainbelt or 'convergence zone'. In December this lies in southern Tanzania, but during the year it moves northward through East Africa and into Sudan. Then from September it moves south again. This means that over most of Tanzania and in the extreme north there is only one main season of rain, whereas in the central areas there are two, although in the most lands around the northern shores of Lake Victoria these appear only as slight variations in an almost seasonless climate. A second convergence zone in the west between the moist air from the Congo and the drier air from the east sometimes has an effect on the climate of western East Africa; its movement eastward can bring much moister weather to the western highlands.

The northward movement of the main intertropical convergence draws in behind it rain-bearing winds off the Indian Ocean. Where these come up against the highlands they bring heavy precipitation on the windward slopes: on Kilimanjaro, for instance, the southeastern slopes are much moister and therefore more heavily populated than the northwest-facing slopes. These winds also bring moisture to the coast, which north of

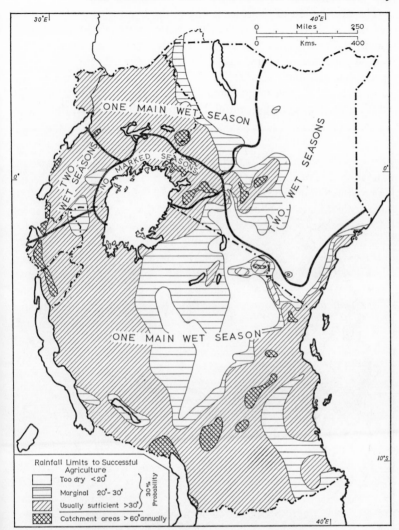

Fig. 21. East Africa: Rainfall Patterns (after Kenworthy, 1964)

Dar-es-Salaam is much wetter than the hinterland. They do not affect the southern coast of Tanzania, where the coastal climate is not markedly different from that of the interior. The contrast between the favourable northern coast and the dryness of its immediate hinterland – the 'Nyika' – was one of the reasons for the isolation of the interior until the end of the last century.

The distribution of moisture is one of the two major controls of the vegetation pattern in East Africa. The wetter areas can support closed-canopy forest, while the driest areas can only carry sparse scrub. In their natural state the remaining areas are largely wooded, although, under special soil conditions or where flooding is frequent, woodland gives way to open bush or even to grassland (Fig. 22). However, human activity, which is the second major control, has substantially modified the original

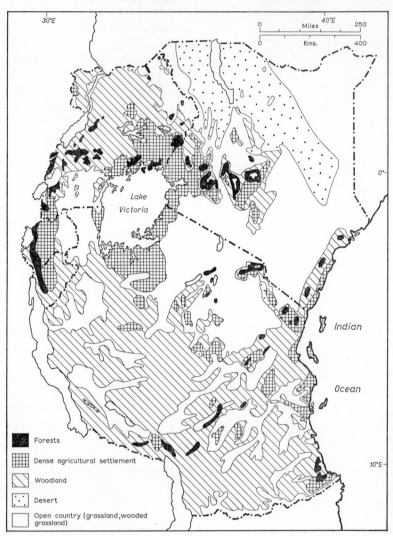

Fig. 22. East Africa: Vegetation Cover

vegetative cover. Except in the most inaccessible mountain areas, closed-canopy forests cannot be found today outside Forest Reserves and timber set aside either for reserves of firewood (as around Kilimanjaro) or for the protection of water catchments and timber (as in the Aberdare mountains). There are also, in western Uganda in particular, some commercial plantations of introduced conifers. Most of what must formerly have been forest along the Lake Victoria shores of Uganda now carries only tall grass and occasional trees, while the high forests of Rwanda, Burundi and the Aberdare mountains have been fast falling to the axes of cultivators. Many areas formerly wooded have been opened up by cultivation, fire, and the grazing, browsing and trampling of domestic animals to become virtually grasslands, and many areas of thinner woodland in Northern Kenya have reverted nearly to desert. The rate of deforestation has been accelerated in the present century by the increase in human population. For instance, the vegetation in northwest Uganda, southwest Uganda and neighbouring Rwanda and Burundi, Sukumuland around the southern shore of Lake Victoria, and the southern highlands of Tanzania, can now all be described as 'steppe'. The changes, however, have not all been towards deforestation. It seems likely, for instance, that in Tanzania many areas formerly kept open by cultivation and grazing have reverted to woodland since abandonment. The same is true of parts of western Uganda. There has, in fact, been both advance and retreat of the woodland edge.

In planning policy vegetation cannot be treated as a static resource because of the delicacy of its adjustment to the physical environment and the way in which it can be modified by human activities. In this sense it is more important to understand the dynamics of the vegetation pattern than the details of its morphology; and the importance of recognizing the ecosystem in which solar energy, climate, soil, plants, vertebrate and invertebrate animals and man are all involved, has recently won more widespread recognition in East Africa.

One example of the importance of this ecological approach to East African administration concerns the inter-relationship of woodland and the trypanosomiasis disease which affects both domestic cattle and men. It also helps to explain the fluctuations in the vegetation pattern. Trypanosomiasis may be fatal, and, being endemic in large parts of East Africa, particularly Tanzania, effectively closes the land to cattle production. Smaller areas are closed to human settlement. The main varieties of the disease which affect East Africa are carried by species of tsetse fly which normally inhabit woodland and transmit the disease from game animals which do not themselves suffer any ill-effects. The disease is carried in a cycle which involves the flies and their favourite habitat (the woodland), game and domestic stock or human beings. These constitute an ecosystem in which a change in any one element leads to changes in the whole system. One such chain reaction was started by the introduction of a new factor towards the end of the last century. In the 1880's and 1890's a series of rinderpest epidemics swept Africa from Eritrea to the Cape, killing millions of cattle and in consequence many of their herders: the Karamojong tribe in northern Uganda, for instance, was decimated. Before this time cattle grazing and grass burning had kept as open grassland areas which if undisturbed would have been wooded, and after the epidemic these areas did in fact revert to woodland. The Kagera valley in northern Tanzania formerly carried a fairly high density of pastoral population, but it had to be abandoned and it remains an empty area to this day. Game animals moved into the abandoned areas taking the disease with them, and the incidence of the human disease reached alarming proportions. In Uganda between 1900 and 1906 perhaps 200,000 people or one-tenth of the Baganda died, and by the 1920's the fly belt was advancing menacingly on Kampala. The situation was further aggravated by ivory hunting and the consequent decrease in the numbers of elephants who had kept the bush thin. In 1947–1948 the Government attempted to attack the problem by bush clearance and game eradication. People in the newly-infected areas around Lake Edward and in southern Busoga were resettled in fly-free areas, and similar resettlement schemes were undertaken in parts of southern Tanzania. By 1963 the Uganda Government could claim that 7,000 square miles (18,000 km²) of the country had been cleared of tsetse, but this resulted in further disturbance of the ecosystem which brought new dangers, such as intensified soil erosion in the cleared areas and a consequent increase in habitats suitable for the mosquitoes that act as carriers of the malarial diseases.

Trypanosomiasis is not the only disease with a complex ecology and wide significance to the economy. East Coast fever also limits cattle production in many areas, especially in southern Tanzania, and its introduction to new areas may lead – as it did among the Karamojong in 1934 – to extensive movements of cattle and their owners and eventually to litigation and conflict between tribal groups. Thus changes in ecosystems can have direct repercussions in the political sphere.

The ecosystem in the Lake Victoria area has recently attracted attention, again because of its economic significance. Schemes were being proposed in which some of the papyrus swamps in southern Uganda were to be drained for agriculture to make use of their nitrogen-rich soils. It was found, however, that the swamps were spawning grounds for the *Tilapia* – a fish upon which the lake fisheries largely depend – and that draining would endanger this rich source of protein. It was clear, too, that draining would have other repercussions. Malarial mosquitoes in this part of Uganda inhabit the swamp margins rather than the swamps, and draining would therefore increase the habitats available to these insects; drainage in parts of southwestern Uganda had in fact already led to an increased incidence of malaria among the local inhabitants. Moreover, draining kills the papyrus, which not only supplies the rich organic layer in the marshes and shelters it from the decomposing effects of the sun, but also gives shelter to snails which mix the humus with the mineral soil. The best use of these swamp soils seems, in fact, to have been achieved in parts of Rwanda. There they are not drained but the earth is heaped into mounds and crops similar in form to papyrus are grown. The creation of fish ponds in these swamps has also been successful.

The importance of the ecological approach to planning and development is not confined to the rural economy. It has been found, for instance, that an urban environment provides the most favourable habitat for a number of diseases, notably yellow fever and bilharzia, because they can spread more easily among dense populations; and in East Africa urban congestion brings in its train a number of serious health hazards. Furthermore, urban water supplies depend on an understanding of the ecology of catchment areas. The Nairobi supply, for instance, was endangered when it was proposed to replace bamboo on the Aberdare mountains by introduced conifers. It was already known that replanting with tea had increased storm flow by 300 per cent in some areas, and that complete cutting of the bamboo could lead to a further increase. The change to conifer plantations was therefore preceded by careful experimentation, and although it was found that the conifers protected the soil as effectively as bamboos, it was also shown that the conifers were slightly more wasteful in that they used more water in transpiration.

Perhaps the most serious disregard of the ecosystem in areas of marginal rainfall over the last seventy years has been overcropping and the shortening of periods of bush fallow by subsistence cultivators. A common agricultural method in East Africa is to crop the land until yields tail off and certain indicator weeds appear. The land is then left to revert to bush for up to thirty years, during which time it recovers much of its lost fertility. The establishment of peaceful conditions and the resultant increase in population has meant that methods suited to better environments are applied to marginal land (among the Kamba and Chagga for instance) and, more importantly, that the length of the fallow period is reduced, sometimes to dangerously low levels; thus soil structure deteriorates and the soil becomes liable to severe erosion. Increases in cattle populations because of disease control also lead to erosion as a result of overgrazing and trampling. Direct runoff tends to replace slow percolation into the soil and stream flow becomes erratic. Streams that were formerly perennial may begin to dry up for part of the year and the hippopotamus, crocodile and fish populations begin to suffer. Many areas have already been irretrievably lost to cultivation because of soil erosion, and the problem remains acute in many other areas despite extensive governmental anti-erosion programmes.

Against the background of this broad physical framework, and as a dominant element in the ecological complex, the human population of East Africa presents a pattern of intricate variety. It is important to consider the ways of life and attitudes of the various human groups from two points of view. In the first place East Africa has seen a succession of cultures which is reflected in the present distribution of people and in their levels of development and ideals. Secondly, one must consider the various groups as producers in the modern economy. To do this, it is convenient to treat separately the various economic tiers of East African society – hunting and collecting; subsistence farming; pastoralism; cash crop production; mining, manufacturing and distribution; and the superstructure of administrators, teachers and the like. In each case it is necessary to consider the relationship of the way of life to its resource base and to examine the distribution of its population within the region.

Hunting and Collecting

At a not very remote period East Africa was inhabited only by a sparse population of hunters, whose numbers had probably remained fairly static for thousands of years. Although they ranged widely in search of game, they always favoured the margins of the moist highland blocks; and around the margins of the Great Lakes they may have achieved a settled and moderately productive way of life where fish were abundant. Fishermen lived on the shores of Lake Edward as long ago as 6000 B.C., and other non-agricultural fisherfolk can still be found on the shores of the East African lakes. As the idea of agriculture spread and as agricultural peoples gradually moved into the better lands, hunting as a way of life became more and more restricted to the remote, difficult or poor areas (Fig. 23). Most of the hunting peoples, perhaps after periods when they co-existed and traded with the agriculturalists, gradually took up agriculture. Many of them remained in their old homelands and it is probable that many cultivators in southern Tanzania are descended from hunting groups, because fossil evidence suggests that the agriculturalists intermarried extensively with the aboriginal people. Some cultivating groups still rely partly on the older methods of hunting and collecting, reverting to them particularly in times of famine or at the lean end of the dry season. Several groups, in fact, have only recently taken to agriculture.

Very few hunters and collectors still exist in East Africa. The only real survivors are the Kindiga (Fig. 24), of whom there are only about 600 left.

They live near Lake Eyasi in Tanzania and still lead a nomadic life. The men collect honey and hunt game and birds with large bows and poisoned arrows, while the women collect vegetable material such as baobab fruits. Their only domesticated animal is the dog. There are five bands whose size varies between 20 and 100 depending on the optimum number for a hunting group.

Other non-agricultural groups are in the stage of trading with more

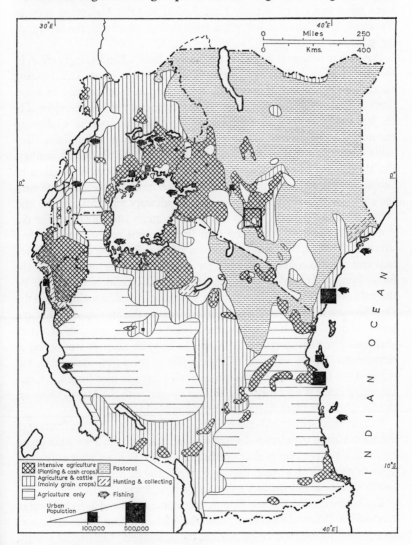

Fig. 23. East Africa: Ways of Life

advanced agricultural peoples. The Dorobo, for instance, who have recently retreated from many of the highland forests in Kenya and northern Tanzania to the forests of the Mau escarpment, are expert hunters, bee-keepers and sorcerers. Yet they have also learned to trade with the Nandi cultivators and with the Masai pastoralists. A similar group, the Twa in Rwanda and Burundi, have become further integrated into the economy of their neighbours, acting as potters and serfs for the Tutsi aristocracy. On some lakes and rivers, notably Lake Rudolf and the Malagarasi river in Tanzania, small bands of fishermen trade their produce with the surrounding peasants.

Pressure to change is strong on the hunters today. Land-hungry tribes in the surrounding country are cutting into Kindiga territory. One hunting band has already settled and taken to herding and cultivation. In other parts of East Africa the changeover is in progress or has been completed in the last few years. Not far from the Kindiga the Sandawe have taken up the new ways while still retaining some hunting habits. In southern Tanzania the Safwa and the Kinga were still hunters in the nineteenth century. On the fringes of the moist Kenya coastlands the Boni have taken to simple tillage, although they are still semi-nomadic. Intermarriage with the surrounding tribes and general loss of identity will soon see the end of the Boni and perhaps of the Dorobo as hunters and collectors. On the slopes of Ruwenzori the Amba men hunted until recently, while their women cultivated, but the men have now taken to intensive banana cultivation and even to coffee production for cash. In Rwanda and Burundi the forest hunting grounds of the Twa are being increasingly taken over by the cultivating Hutu people, a process which has practically eliminated the Dorobo from the eastern Kenya highlands near to the overcrowded Kikuyu lands. Many administrations too restrict hunting in the interests of watershed and game conservation. In Kenya in 1937 an attempt was begun to settle some Dorobo on smallholdings. Some of these have succeeded, but many of the new settlers have given up their plots and now form a landless labouring class. Where they have been in contact with the Masai, however, the Dorobo have more willingly taken up cattle herding.

Even in their strongholds the hunters now form only a minute fraction of the East African population. In Rwanda and Burundi the Twa make up no more than 1·3 per cent of the population, and the Boni number only some 3000 to 3500. With a rapid decline in their way of life these people may totally disappear as a distinct group in the next decade.

Yet hunting, collecting and fishing have not disappeared as techniques in East Africa. Where supplies are particularly good, fishing forms an important part of the food source for many of the peasant and subsistence groups, for instance the Luo around the Kavirondo Gulf in western Kenya and the

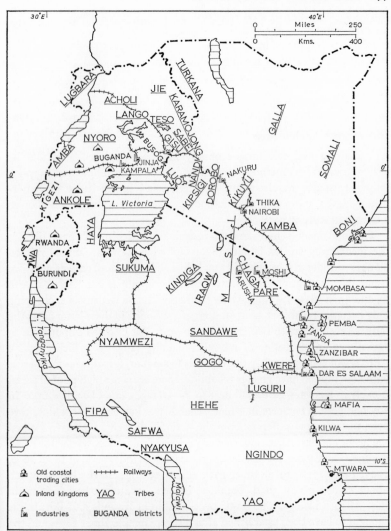

Fig. 24. East Africa: Tribal Groups and Economic Development

Kenyi on the eastern shores of Lake Kioga. On the coast, too, the Swahili and Arab peasantries often consume large quantities of fish. Hunting is still practised by many tribes as a subsidiary method of obtaining food, or as a ritual activity. It was also the basis of an important barter trade towards the end of the nineteenth century. The East African interior was then the source of large amounts of ivory and other hunting products which were traded by Arab and Swahili middlemen on the coast and sold in the Far East and Europe. In the twentieth century hunting and game-watching by tourists has become an important source of foreign revenue in all the East African territories. Very recently culling from over-stocked game reserves has begun to yield large amounts of game meat which is being canned for export.

Indigenous Agriculture

The hunting and collecting economy has been replaced gradually by agriculture. At first methods of cultivation were very simple and supplied only subsistence requirements, but later, and in particular in better-watered areas, more complex methods produced a surplus which allowed a change in cultural outlook.

The fundamental environmental restraint on agriculture in East Africa is the inadequacy and variability of precipitation. If mean annual rainfall alone is considered it can be said that below 20 in (500 mm) only pastoralism is possible; in areas of single-season rainfall cropping is unreliable between 25 and 35 in (625–875 mm); while in areas with two wet seasons, cropping only becomes reliable at 40 in (1000 mm), although in these latter areas the farmer can often raise two crops in the year. But of equal importance to agriculture are measures of rainfall reliability (Fig. 21) which shows a pattern which only roughly corresponds to amount, for whereas most areas with high rainfall have greater reliability, there are some high rainfall areas, notably in Kenya, where a fall near to the average cannot be relied upon in any one year. The areas in which reliability is low are those which have been the principal sufferers from the periodic droughts that have marred the history of East Africa and started periods of migration, warfare or tribal decline. There were, for instance, serious famines in Rwanda in 1890, 1900, 1905, 1906, 1916, 1918, 1925, 1928 and 1933–1944, in the last of which about 50,000 people died. Famines, indeed, have often been critical in East Africa's history. The Tutsi overlordship of Rwanda and Burundi is thought to have been established after a severe famine about 1675, and the easy European penetration of Kenya followed two devastating droughts in 1887 and 1892.

The East African Royal Commission of 1954–1955 chose the figure of 30 per cent probability that an area would get less than 30 in (750 mm) of rainfall in any one year as the limit of dependable agriculture; while the 30 per cent probability that an area would receive between 20 and 30 in (500–750 mm) was thought to indicate marginal conditions (Fig. 21). In these areas severe famines, which endanger the livelihood of the primitive cultivator, may occur more than once in twenty years.

Another characteristic of rainfall as it affects the East African cultivator is that it often falls with great force and intensity. Heavy rains over a wide area, particularly if they fall on drought-hardened soil, can lead to very destructive floods. Rainfall fluctuations on a vast scale are reflected in the levels of the Great Lakes. In 1963 the steamer services of Lake Albert had to be withdrawn prematurely because of the flooding of harbour installations; and around the Kavirondo Gulf in Kenya agricultural land has recently been extensively flooded. On a smaller scale rain showers are often intense, and this has been given as a justification for the fragmentation and wide separation of agricultural plots in the Kavirondo area and the Kamba country. If one plot is levelled by an intense shower of rain or hail, then the peasant still has others to fall back on. In Sukumuland the peasant may select the erratic pattern of wetter areas each year for his crops.

Within the areas in which agriculture is possible other environmental restraints are on a local rather than a regional scale. East African soils are not generally fertile. In the areas underlain by Basement Complex rocks a common sequence of soils can be recognized. Bare rock and very thin soils are found on the upstanding inselbergs; these give way to dry, coarse, reddish soils on the upper slopes around the edges of the hills, and sometimes to soils with a hardpan where the slope evens out; and in the bottoms, near the streams, and over wide plains in northern Uganda and Kenya there are dark clay soils. Where there are laterite caps the surface soil is often grey and thin.

There are certain enduring patterns in the rural economy that show close adjustment to these environmental possibilities. In the drier areas and the grasslands pastoralism alone is successful; in the areas of marginal moisture, and in the drier parts of the areas of reliable rainfall, shifting cultivation and grain crops, often combined with pastoralism, have been the best ecological response; and in the wetter areas where perennial crops, particularly the banana, can be grown there are more stable and prosperous purely peasant societies. But cutting across these environmental patterns are cultural patterns that derive from the history of the region.

Techniques of food production such as implements, crops and stock types are important cultural attributes from this point of view and they have been introduced to East Africa from three main directions. From the west came the methods of tillage that are the basis of most surviving forms of cultivation and which were accompanied by the Bantu language. In southern Tanzania they survived relatively unchanged until the end of the nineteenth century but in the north and northeast they came into contact with and were modified by a second set of cultural influences spreading from the Nile Valley and Ethiopia. Among the latter was one early agricultural tradition that included such techniques as the stall-feeding of

7

cattle, manuring, irrigation and terracing, and which survives in isolated pockets to this day. But most of the peoples who came from the north and who now practise tillage, such as the Luo, probably adopted their present techniques from the Bantu-speakers. A more enduring feature of the northern culture, and one which has had more far-reaching effects, has been the cattle economy, which is still found in its purest forms in the drier parts of East Africa and which has affected agriculturalists wherever cattle-keeping is possible. As the Bantu culture spread from the west into Uganda and northern Tanzania, and from the southwest into southern Tanzania and so northward to the Kenya coast and the eastern highlands it crossed paths with the Nilotic and Hamitic peoples reaching southward around both sides of Lake Victoria. Although agriculture may first have been introduced to East Africa as long ago as 2500 B.C. and spread more widely at the beginning of the Christian era, many of these movements are fairly recent. The pastoral kingdoms in Rwanda and Burundi were established only in the seventeenth century, and the Luo are still moving southward down the eastern shore of Lake Victoria. Some observers have even seen the recent (1966) disturbances in Uganda as another expression of these southward migrations of intrusive northerners. As for the Bantu, they too have been involved in movements over the last few centuries: the Kikuyu, for instance, have been penetrating the eastern Kenya highlands since about the fourteenth century. The third source of agricultural techniques in East Africa was the Indian Ocean coast, through which in early times came crops and farming systems from Arabia, India and Indonesia, and this has been the chief direction from which European and American crops and methods have penetrated in the twentieth century.

In early agriculture the absence of individual ownership and market exchange meant the close integration of cultivation and non-material aspects of culture and the three sources of food-producing techniques were in this way also sources of three different attitudes to group organization. These attitudes have had important effects on the map of East Africa, both through their influence on early development and by affecting the enthusiasm and ability with which the opportunities of the present century have been taken up. The Bantu tribes were for the most part organized around simple family groups and lineage systems; land was held by the tribe; and there was little tradition of communal activity. The amorphous political system of these people has hindered their acceptance of European ideas of centralization and individual ownership. In particular the Lugardian concept of indirect rule did not succeed because few of the Bantu tribes had established leaders. Some of the northerners had a society equally alien to European forms. They, too, lacked chiefs and their main system of organization was the grouping of people into age sets which were convenient for war. This has been one of the main causes of conservatism among some of these tribes, for instance the Masai, amongst whom the age set of men educated in the new ideas and aspirations is only now coming to power. Co-operative societies have however been easier to organize among some of these groups. A separate northern influence in certain areas was the idea of chiefs and kingship. Whatever its source – and this is very uncertain – it produced the advanced kingdoms of southern Uganda and of Rwanda and Burundi which readily embraced European ideas and have been more successfully integrated into a cash economy than most East African peoples.

Subsistence Farming

True subsistence agriculture, like hunting and collecting, is disappearing in East Africa. Like its predecessor it survives only as a remnant way of life in the poorer areas where population density is very low (Fig. 23). In addition to a few remnant subsistence groups, however, there are people for whom the change over to an elementary cash economy has been recent and who retain many of their old attitudes.

The main stronghold of the subsistence way of life is in Tanzania south of the latitude of Dar es Salaam, although some of the more densely populated areas here have recently been introduced to cash cropping. Everywhere outside the highlands in this zone trypanosomiasis and East Coast fever prevent the keeping of all but small domestic stock, such as poultry. Indeed, some people – for instance the Ngindo – are almost completely vegetarian. Only in the wetter areas does the number of crops cultivated exceed the minimum of two staple grains – sorghums and millets – together with a few others such as yams and the bambara groundnut, although more recently exotic crops like maize, cassava and sweet potatoes have become popular.

Early subsistence agriculture probably achieved only a small advance on hunting and collecting in terms of the number of people it could support. Life was still semi-nomadic, fields being cleared, worked to exhaustion and then abandoned. In the Luguru hills, not far west of Dar es Salaam, iron for agricultural implements was not known till the end of the nineteenth century. Land was held according to lineage, and the basic social unit was the family living on its own land in isolated hamlets of 20–50 huts. Livestock was of minor importance and included only goats and chickens. In the central and southern highlands, where cattle can be kept, they were not integrated into the farming system. Pastoralism was simply tacked onto primitive subsistence agriculture, perhaps because of the relatively recent introduction of cattle, which seem to have reached the Gogo and the Hehe only in the seventeenth century. In some of the drier parts, however, cattle almost replaced cultivation as the main source of subsistence, although they are fewer in number now than they were a century ago before disease and tribal disturbances cut down their numbers.

Many factors restricted the development of these peoples in southern Tanzania. Marginal moisture conditions and poor soils are common; on many of the wide plains it is difficult to get water in the dry season; and both trypanosomiasis and East Coast fever are at their most severe in this part of East Africa. In a number of areas, however, tillage would certainly be possible, and some resettlement schemes have already proved this to be so, but cultural restrictions have been as important as the limitations of the physical environment. It was among the tribal groups of the south that the Arab slavers had their main source of supply. In 1790 some 4000 slaves a year were being exported from Kilwa alone, many of them from the southern Tanzanian hinterland, for the Yao, the Ngindo and the Nyanja were especially favoured as slaves. Slaving reached its peak in the nineteenth century when guns became available, and tribal raiding and warfare, too, began to cut down the population. A rebellion in the 1890's was met with severe punitive repression by the German authorities; and during the Maji-maji rebellion of 1905–7 similar repression and famine killed perhaps half a million people. All these disturbances had two main effects. Depopulated land tended to be invaded by game, woodland and trypanosomiasis, which further discouraged human settlement; and people were driven from the plains into the remoter and poorer highlands, where there were fewer possibilities for development. Only in the present century are people such as the Luguru beginning to move out again from their hills. To this day enormous areas of southern Tanzania are completely uninhabited.

In the north of East Africa there are fewer surviving groups of purely subsistence cultivators. Some groups, however, have been slower than others to take up the new ideas, and in fact for many the change did not really come until recently. Those that still survive or have only recently adopted some cash crops are found in areas remote from the lines of European penetration. Thus the fact that the Acholi and Lugbara in northwestern Uganda have only very recently taken up cash crops is due largely to their distance from the railhead. There is also a general correspondence of subsistence agriculture with drier areas where only a limited range of poor crops can be grown. An interesting example is that of the Kamba near Nairobi who occupy two different ecological zones. In the moist rich lands they grow coffee as a cash crop, and their assimilation of the cash economy there is far advanced; but out on the dry plains they still practise shifting-field subsistence cultivation. Similarly the Sukuma practise quite profitable cash-crop agriculture on the moist lake shores but in the drier interior they cultivate meagre grain crops for subsistence.

However, there are instances when cultural factors have been the principal hindrance to advance. The Nandi and the Kipsigi live in moist areas of rich soils almost astride the Uganda railway (opened in 1901) and yet they did not adopt cash crops and new methods such as terracing and hedging until the second world war. Hostility to the new crops and methods and a failure on the part of the administration to convince the peasant of the value of cash seem to have been the restricting factors here. Attitudes to land tenure have also hindered development. Communal land rights among many tribes restricted the scope for individual initiative, while among the Kikuyu land could be owned but was subject to fragmentation on inheritance.

Nevertheless the north is not subject to such severe physical and historical restraints as those under which the south labours. Although trypanosomiasis occurs it is much more limited. Large areas of the north are favoured by rainfall and soils; and although there was formerly much tribal raiding – the Sebei were under continual attack from the Karamojong, the Masai raided their agricultural neighbours, the Nandi attacked the less well organized Bantu tribes of the Kavirondo area, and the Acholi had fought a series of chronic internal wars for generations – slaving had a much less severe impact. Furthermore, the raids and punitive measures of the colonial powers – such as the attacks of Egyptian Sudanese troops on the Acholi and Lugbara and the British punitive expedition into Mt Elgon – were nowhere as severe in their effects as the Maji-maji rebellion in the south. Finally the hills to which the people could retreat were much more fertile in the north than in the south, particularly Mt Elgon and the Eastern Highlands of Kenya which have rich volcanic soils. The combination of all these more favoured conditions has meant that many northern groups have now taken up cash crop farming.

Pastoralism

In the north of East Africa it is only some isolated pastoral groups who still maintain a subsistence way of life.

Some of the limitations on cattle-keeping in East Africa have already been referred to; tsetse infestation means that most of Tanzania outside the southern highlands and the southern shore of Lake Victoria, and some areas in the west of Uganda and coastal Kenya cannot profitably support herds of cattle; dense forest in parts of southern Uganda is another restriction; while in limited areas of northern Uganda unpalatable tall grass is a discouragement; and in the northeast of Kenya extreme aridity is a further deterrent. But outside these areas cattle are kept almost everywhere on pastures of *Themeda* grasses which are among the richest in Africa, and in fact support the highest cattle densities on the continent. The pastures are grazed by a variety of livestock, although cattle are the most numerous; these cattle are not as good producers of milk or meat as European cattle but they are better adapted to the harder conditions and the incidence of disease. In the north, in the drier areas of Kenya, cattle are supplemented by camels and sheep which tend to browse rather different parts of the vegetative cover.

Patterns of pastoralism in East Africa are due both to cultural and ecological controls. Culturally pastoralism is a relatively recent introduction, having been brought into the region by people who were still migrating at the end of the nineteenth century. The idea spread out ahead of the pastoralists themselves to Bantu people farther south.

True pastoralist groups today are composed almost entirely of these northern people, who still inhabit the drier parts of the region where only cattle-keeping is possible. There are two major groupings: in the north and east of Kenya the culturally distinct Somali who are Moslem, and Galla who are Pagan, are true pastoralists, living a nomadic life moving from water point to water point in search of the best pasture for their herds. In northern and central Kenya and in the east of Uganda, other pagan groups, generally called Nilo-Hamites, are also largely pastoral. Chief among these are the Masai, the Turkana and the Karamojong who are also nomadic, moving their herds up into the wetter highlands in the dry season and down into the plains in the wetter months of the year.

Where the ideas and people associated with pastoralism spread westward or southward into better-watered areas, pastoralism tended to become more and more subsidiary to cultivation. In many tribes, such as the Nilo-Hamitic Pokot or the Bantu Kamba, there are sections of the same group subsisting mainly on pastoralism in the drier parts of their territory, and mainly on tillage in the better-watered parts. The adaptation is fairly exact, since movements into one zone or another by a tribe seem to lead to a change in their method of subsistence; there are examples in recent years of tribes which have become pastoral on moving to a drier area and of tribes taking up tillage on moving to a wetter area. But the cultural distinctiveness of the cattle people remains: cattle-keeping is seldom really integrated with tillage, and remains in many tribes an important part of their ritual and cultural values. Nevertheless it is in the areas where tillage is also important – for instance among the Kamba, Luyia, Kikuyu, Luo, Sukuma, Lango and Teso–that the highest densities of cattle are to be found.

Farther west again the pastoralists moved in as a culturally distinct aristocracy among Bantu cultivators. Here they have retained their purely pastoral way of life, but have relied on a lower caste of tillers for agricultural products. It is interested to speculate that the cultivators may have prepared the ground for the herders by felling the woodland and thus clearing the area of tsetse. In Ankole, Bunyoro, Rwanda and Burundi the aristocracy have had supreme political power until recently, moving their temporary capital *kraals* in slow circuit through their kingdoms. They have now been replaced by Bantu republican régimes in Rwanda and Burundi where they were formerly particularly powerful, but they have been absorbed by the Bantu in the other kingdoms.

The pastoral way of life and the cultural patterns associated with it have meant that many of the pastoral groups have been held back in this century by conservatism, and by the fact that they live in remote or unattractive areas. The Karamojong, for instance, were only brought under effective political control in 1926. The pastoralists, indeed, have often actively resisted development: in Burundi, for instance, the Belgian colonial administration latterly regarded the Tutsi aristocracy as a brake on any advance towards a cash economy. Today the herders are often poor and backward when compared with the rest of the population. In Kenya they have a life expectancy of twenty-five years as against forty-two years for the population as a whole. Their growth rate, too, is relatively very low.

The suppression of tribal warfare brought about by European administration, as well as later governmental attempts to halt cattle disease, have sometimes been unwitting agents of other changes in the pastoral societies of East Africa. By allowing cattle numbers to increase they have resulted in overstocking of the land, deterioration of pastures, and soil erosion. It has become obvious that numbers will have to be reduced and both voluntary and compulsory reduction schemes have been started. Even in 1929 it was estimated that there were 200 per cent too many cattle on Kamba land, while later destocking schemes in Iraqw country aimed at reductions of 52 per cent. Many schemes have met with at least limited success, even though reductions in the numbers of cattle directly offend the cultural values of the herders: but there are still many areas carrying too many cattle, and in some areas (Rwanda and Burundi for instance) destocking has not succeeded. On overstocked land even small disturbances can precipitate real hardship, as did the droughts of 1961–1962 among the Masai when so many cattle were lost that many Masai gave up herding altogether. At present 60–70 beasts are needed to keep one family at a subsistence level, but if the Masai can be persuaded to sell cattle and buy grain the number could be reduced to 30–35 and the capacity of the land to support people might well increase. Interest in the drier areas has intensified in recent years, for it is an economic rationalization to use the wetter lands primarily for vegetable-production and the drier lands for animal-production. The Karamojong have been encouraged since 1936 to sell cattle in southern Uganda where higher incomes from cash crops have meant an increased demand for luxury foods such as meat; and the Kenya

Government has set up, in the dry east at Archers Post, a factory for hides, bone meal and meat. The Rwanda and Burundi authorities have also been trying to develop the marketing of meat, hides and milk, and to improve the quality of local stock. Where such rationalization fails, resettlement into agricultural plots may be the answer. The Jie in northern Uganda have been to some extent forcibly resettled, and the Kenya Government is encouraging the Masai to settle and take up cash cropping in the better-watered parts of their tribal lands.

A recent development in East Africa has been large-scale investment in animal production. At first large private European-owned ranches were established in Kenya and Tanzania and more recently the Tanzanian Government has begun to invest in ranching, while in Uganda advisory services are encouraging better quality cattle on Buganda mixed farms. Both Kenya and Tanzania now export meat and in 1964 animal products made up 4½ per cent by value of exports from the East African common market area (of course little of this is produced by the purely pastoral groups).

Numerically, however, pastoralists do not comprise a very important element in the population of East Africa. In Rwanda and Burundi the Tutsi pastoral aristocracy made up about 15 per cent of the total population before the recent disturbances, during which many fled. In Kenya the pastoral tribes number about 550,000 people or only about 8 per cent of the population; in Uganda and in Tanzania, where the division between the herder and non-herder is less clear, their numbers cannot be easily estimated, but they are smaller than in Kenya. Yet, although few in number, the pastoralists occupy more than a quarter of the area of East Africa.

The Development of Early Peasant Farming

Before the end of the nineteenth century several groups in East Africa had progressed from a shifting subsistence to a settled peasant way of life. The release of people from whole-time food production had enabled some of them to develop more materially and politically elaborate societies, and it is these groups that have changed most markedly under the impact of new ideas and technology in the twentieth century. Nevertheless to see their present problems in perspective it is necessary to look briefly at the environmental and cultural background against which they evolved.

If the areas in which cultivation can be practised in East Africa are limited, the areas in which settled agriculture can flourish are even more so (Fig. 23). In Kenya it has been found that crop yields and soil fertility rise continuously as mean annual rainfall increases from 30 in (750 mm) to a peak fertility in areas with 40–50 in (1000–1250 mm), while increased soil leaching depresses yields again in areas with more than 50 in (1250 mm). At the lower ranges only grain and other seed crops do well, and above 50 in (1250 mm) only tree crops prosper; but in the middle range of rainfall totals planting crops – on which most early permanent cultivation in East Africa depended – are the best choice, Rainfall reliability, and especially reliability of the onset of the wet season, is important as well. In Buganda, where the rainfall régime is nearly seasonless, climatic conditions are almost ideal for cropping. In contrast, in the moist Kavirondo Gulf lands, agricultural officers complain that rainfall conditions seldom ever suit cotton or coffee. Temperature and cloudiness can also be limitations, for whereas it has been estimated that in Buganda about 4 acres (1·6 hectares) are necessary to support a family, in the higher wet parts of Kigezi the estimate rises to 7 acres (2·8 hectares). Some resettlement schemes in the higher parts of Kenya have had to be abandoned because of low temperatures and drizzly weather. Seasonality is also significant. In areas with two seasons and two crops a family can be supported on about half the area needed in zones with a single season. Where technology permits irrigation, as on the slopes of Kilimanjaro, the availability of perennial streams has given some added advantages.

Soils have been a further limitation on permanent agriculture. In many of the moist areas slopes are steep and soils thin and when these soils are over-used they are very liable to erosion. This is especially true of south-western Uganda and of Rwanda and Burundi. Elsewhere the soils on the top of laterite caps are usually too grey and thin for tillage, and it is only where the cap has been cut into by erosion that there are more fertile soils on the valley sides. These are the sites of intensive agriculture in the north-western highlands of Uganda and in Buganda, where the thick cover of elephant grass gives added fertility in the form of a rich humic layer. In the Kenya highlands, especially the southern slopes of the Aberdare mountains and in parts of the Nandi and Kipsigi lands, and on the northern and southern volcanic hills of Tanzania, volcanic deposits give a deep very fertile red soil. When all these factors have been taken into account it can be seen that the favoured areas are small and widely distributed.

Where natural advantages have been combined with certain crops and techniques, peasant groups have achieved high levels of productivity. The most important agricultural advantage of most tropical lands is that they can support planting crops such as the banana which is one of East Africa's two most important food crops (along with maize). In Uganda alone the banana is the chief staple of some 2·5 million people. It supports population densities of 200 to 500 per square mile (75–200 per km²) in Buganda and of up to 1000 per square mile (400 per km²) on the slopes of Mt Elgon. The banana is a garden crop grown near the house and once the land has been cleared and planted by the men the plot requires only rudimentary

7*

cultivation by the women to yield crops for at least a generation; the men are then free for warfare, politics, or the cultivation of cash crops. The banana is seldom the only food crop, and is sometimes replaced as a staple by maize, sorghum or millets.

Banana cultivation, however, depends on social stability: where society was being continually interrupted by warfare and raiding or where the population was still in movement it could not flourish. Since the imposition of peace in the present century banana cultivation has spread much more widely than before; the Amba, the Nyoro, the people of southwestern Uganda and of Mt Elgon, and many of the highland tribes of Kenya have now adopted the banana as a staple. Today it has become a major subsistence crop in most of the moist areas from Lugbara in the northwest and Nyakusa in the southern highlands of Tanzania to the lands of the Chagga in the east.

Other techniques conferred less important advantages on certain groups. Irrigation is often combined among the Chagga and Tieta with terracing, and with stall-feeding of cattle and manuring of the 'in-field'. In the far south some tribes have developed remarkably advanced techniques. The Nyakyusa have an elaborate method of ridging their fields and of digging in weeds as manure. Some of their neighbours have developed pits or mounds to counteract soil loss on some steep slopes. Where it is possible, the use of two environments to complement each other has made for more efficient land use. The Chagga, for instance, use the higher moist lands for bananas and other crops often under irrigation, and the drier lands downslope for grain crops and cattle; and the Kamba of the moist highlands often keep their cattle out on the dry plains. In Rwanda and Burundi the Tutsi overlords can graze their cattle on unused fields and open country (sometimes by employing Hutu peasants) and their cattle products can be made use of to complement the crops of the cultivators. In some areas, for instance on the northern and eastern shores of Lake Victoria and among the Fipa on the shores of Lake Tanganyika, fish can supplement the diet and help support a more stable population.

On the coast, peasant cultivators have been providing food to the small trading cities for centuries. This has been especially true of the moister coast north of Dar es Salaam, which had the added advantage of exotic crops from an early date. Rice, mangoes and maize were in early use here, and fishing added to the food resources. On the southern coast East Coast fever and trypanosomiasis precluded cattle and the more arid conditions meant that people here, such as the Kwere, could become little more than subsistence farmers. On the islands – particularly Zanzibar – on the other hand, crop production progressed beyond the peasant stage to plantation agriculture.

Cultural restrictions, it is true, kept many groups at the subsistence level in environments which, even with simple techniques, could have yielded surpluses, but in other groups cultural traits conferred positive advantages. The Ganda, in particular, who developed an elaborate bureaucratic system, were at the end of the nineteenth century expanding territorially and seeking contacts with the outside world. Their organization for warfare gave them not only the internal advantages of organized labour for public works such as roads, but also meant that booty gained by raiding other tribes could be used to oil the wheels of patronage and exchange. The Chagga on Kilimanjaro, although frequently driven into their large stone fortresses by Masai raids, evolved a form of centralized political control with an elaborate hierarchy of slaves, peasants and feudal overlords. The organization of the kingdoms of Rwanda and Burundi also resulted in remarkably high concentrations of rural population at the time of European penetration.

By the end of the nineteenth century peasant society had reached a level beyond which there could not, with some drastic readjustment, be any considerable increase in population. Higher densities of population were being supported than ever before, but they were still held in check by war, famine and disease. Commercial exchange had only just started; and although specialization of function, for instance in iron working and pottery, was long-standing, it was not well developed. It is true that political organization was often advanced, although only among a few of the inter-lacustrine kingdoms of the northwest. But these societies represented enormous human potential on the verge of real economic and social advance, and many of them took to the new ways with enthusiasm.

Modern Commercial Patterns

Peasant Cash Crop Farming

Development of the indigenous pattern in the present century has depended more on cultural than environmental factors. Most of the better-watered areas have the potentiality to produce something of value in the cash economy, but the attitude of the peasant or subsistence farmer, the distance from lines of communication, and the policies of the colonial administrations and the newly independent African governments have been of paramount importance in twentieth century advance.

In the north the people of the interior who most interested the European capitalists and evangelists were the Ganda, whose sophistication had amazed early travellers and the European reading public. Buganda offered opportunities for trade and became the object of early European penetration. But so much attention was concentrated on the Ganda that it was only after the second world war that the frontier of development really spread out farther north or west. But in Kenya, through which the Uganda railway passed, the course of development was rather different. The route of early porterage lines and later the railway passed through what was at first seen as valueless territory, and the purpose of the first developments here were merely to try to get more trade for the line. Cotton was tried, not very successfully, among the Kavirondo tribes; and (a more important venture) Europeans were invited to settle on apparently empty lands. But the Kikuyu and the Luo could be said to have had no European contacts before 1900, whereas many Ganda were by then already literate. Later development in Kenya continued to be very much influenced by proximity to the railway. Here change has been more erratic and drastic, in contrast to the relative stability that was maintained in Buganda.

In Tanzania the fertile Kilimanjaro highlands represented a more limited goal and European penetration did not lead to such far-reaching results, although the Chagga themselves quickly took to commercial coffee production. The British-German agreement had cut across the former porterage routes which once led northward from Kilimanjaro and those which had reached Buganda by the western shores of Lake Victoria. The line of the central railway was dictated mostly by the lure of trade from the eastern Congo and, via steamer traffic, with the Rwanda and Burundi highlands. In most of Tanzania, in fact, the European impact was more diffuse. Cash cropping was neither encouraged to the same extent as in the north nor taken up with so much enthusiasm by the few tribal groups who had access to the railway. The country was poorer and very thinly populated and the few advanced groups, such as the Nyakyusa, lived far from the new transport lines and markets. Nevertheless these lines have left their mark on the economic geography of Tanzania. A belt of commercial and cash crop development extends west of Dar es Salaam along the railway-line, and the most economically advanced parts of the country are along the Kilimanjaro line in the north.

Other important controls of development were the administrative policies of the colonial governments. In Buganda the introduction of cotton as a cash crop had early support from the government, intensive research and extension services were officially encouraged, and it soon became the declared aim of the government to make Uganda primarily a country of peasant farmers. In many parts of Kenya, on the other hand, the government restricted the growth of certain cash crops and aroused the hostility of many tribes. However, during the second world war the Kenya government encouraged grain production among the Kavirondo tribes and the Kipsigis, and this form of cultivation has endured as a source of cash income. In Rwanda and Burundi, the early forced labour policies of the Belgian government frightened many people over the border into south-western Uganda; while in Tanzania inter-war uncertainty about the territory's political future meant less investment and slower development.

Along the lines of European penetration and administration came a whole new complex of opportunities and ideas. After a period of major upheaval in places such as Buganda, the first major force for change was the imposition of peace, for many of the old political and economic patterns, both internal and external, had been dictated by war. The reaction to peace was very frequently a redirection of energy into agriculture. New crops such as manioc (cassava), which acted as a famine standby, and old crops such as the banana, the cultivation of which had been inhibited by instability, allowed the population on the land to increase.

Following the suppression of warfare – often at a remove of several years – came the cash economy. In the more highly organized indigenous states, such as Buganda, the whole machinery of government was re-focused from warfare on to cash crop production. In many areas the cash incentive arose from the imposition of taxes. In Busoga and in northwestern Uganda, for instance, this was what prompted the first demands for money. Gradually cash and the foreign goods which it could buy began to replace the exchange values, such as cattle, of the old societies. The passports to the cash economy, when it came, were either crop-production or the sale of labour.

The crops which can be grown for profit in East Africa are restricted by both environmental and historical factors. The two most popular peasant cash crops have been coffee and cotton. The primary stimulus was partly philanthropic, in that missionaries introduced coffee to Kilimanjaro and missionary capital was behind the introduction of cotton to Uganda; and partly a response to overseas demand, for instance in the cotton mills of Lancashire.

The first shipment of cotton left Uganda in 1904. Its cultivation was enthusiastically taken up, first in Buganda by a new class of land-owners, and later even more profitably in Busoga and Teso. By the 1920's the Baganda were already employing immigrant labour from Rwanda and Ankole on their farms and a prosperous land-owning class was emerging. Cotton production increased despite world economic depressions and it surged ahead in the war years. Although perhaps not ideally suited to the climate of southern Uganda, cotton gives high yields here and there have been very few crop failures. It is best suited, however, to slightly drier areas and it has been a popular crop with which to introduce the peasant to cash crop production. It can be harvested at seasons which are different from those at which subsistence crops are harvested and, with reasonable precautions, can be kept free from disease. It was introduced, in spite of some apathy, to the tribes of the Kavirondo area in western Kenya to help make the new Uganda railway pay; but here its cultivation was not an unqualified success because rainfall is not so reliable, and there have been difficulties in supervising the quality of the crop. In fact cotton still does not figure prominently among Kenyan exports. In Tanzania cotton was introduced among the Sukuma as an alternative to further land exhaustion and by 1957 they were producing 80 per cent of the country's cotton. Cotton has also been introduced into the lower-lying areas of Rwanda and Burundi although neither country produces much for export. In 1964 cotton accounted for 15 per cent by value of East African exports (excluding Rwanda and Burundi).

Coffee has generally been a later introduction than cotton, perhaps because, being a more permanent crop, its commercial cultivation can only be successful in stable societies. It has now, however, become much more important. In Buganda it has slowly replaced cotton as the chief cash crop. High quality arabica coffee has been successful on Mt Elgon, while the less demanding varieties are grown elsewhere in Uganda, and it is now spreading to the moister lands in the southwest. Coffee was the first cash crop among the Chagga, and has been highly successful, helping to bring into being a prosperous landowning class and, from 1925, a powerful co-operative which is now branching out into other fields such as technical education and research. In Kenya coffee was restricted to European farmers until 1935, after which time only a few licensed African growers were permitted, so that even in 1956 only very small amounts were African-grown. But after the Mau Mau rebellion it was used to introduce the Kikuyu to cash cropping, and, in spite of fears to the contrary, African-grown coffee has maintained a high standard of quality. Excluding Rwanda and Burundi, coffee comprised nearly 36 per cent by value of East Africa's exports in 1964, and only about 15 per cent of this is produced by large-scale farmers. In Rwanda and Burundi coffee was introduced to alleviate chronic poverty and it now makes up 40 per cent of the export income.

Other cash crops are of less importance in East Africa. Pyrethrum, which was introduced during the second world war, was at first grown only by European farmers in the upland areas in Kenya, Tanzania and Rwanda, but its cultivation has since been taken up by peasants in these areas. Kenya now produces two-thirds of the world's pyrethrum, although in 1962 only about 30 per cent of this was peasant-grown. In all it forms 17 per cent by value of exports from the East African common market area. Tea is a more demanding crop which needs high rainfall with an even distribution and considerable investment in processing plant near the fields. Consequently it is still mainly grown as a plantation crop, in Buganda, on the Ruwenzori slopes in western Uganda and in Kenya. However, many of the tea factories in western Uganda are now encouraging peasant outgrowers in the neighbourhood to grow tea under supervision. Sugar is another crop, the cultivation of which is being extended from plantations by outgrowing methods, for instance in southern Buganda and Busoga and in the Kavirondo area, and in the new Kilombero Valley Scheme in Tanzania, where newly established peasant holdings are growing sugar. Cocoa has also been tried as a cash crop, not very successfully in Buganda, but with more success in the Usambara mountains of northern Tanzania, while a variety of less important cash crops are also grown by peasant farmers, particularly tobacco, and, near the coast, cashew nuts and copra.

Some of the maize which is produced around the Kavirondo Gulf is exported and many of the food crops are now widely involved in the local cash economy. Rice is grown in the wetter areas, for instance between the beach ridges in coastal Sukumuland, in the Kavirondo area, by the Nyakyusa in southern Tanzania, and on the lower slopes of the Pare Mountains. On many of the new peasant holdings near Nairobi, especially the smaller ones, the Kikuyu have taken up market gardening and the growing of pineapples for canning, while some market garden produce, such as winter strawberries, is even reaching the British market from Kenya.

Another important economic consequence of European administration, in addition to the rise of cash cropping, was the spread of paid employment. By 1959 about one-third of all males in East Africa had at one time been in paid employment. As with cash cropping, this development was stimulated by the release of young men from warfare, and in some areas – for instance in central and northwestern Uganda – by tax demands. The most drastic effects of labour migration have been felt by the remoter peasant communities who, because of the expense of transport, have until recently not been able to produce cash crops. The mobility which labour-seeking introduced is not a new feature of East African culture – almost all groups have traditions of high mobility – but from an early date on the coast, and from about 1900 in the interior, individual mobility has largely replaced tribal movement. Migration is now largely confined to men, who therefore preponderate in the areas which attract labour, while the women are left behind to mind the farms. Migration rates are very high among the Nyakyusa, the people of Rwanda, Burundi and Ankole, and among the Acholi and the Lugbara. In 1958 it was estimated that among the latter two tribes one-fifth of the adult men were absent, and in 1954 one-third of the Nyakyusa were away. Huge numbers of Rwanda and Burundi men work as labourers for prosperous Uganda landowners. There were 345,000 immigrant labourers in Buganda in 1948, most of them from the two small kingdoms. More went eastward to the mines of Katanga; in 1950 about 15,000 men were leaving each year. The Nyakyusa prefer to go south to the mines of the Zambia copper belt, or to the Rand, while the Lugbara and the Acholi work in the sugar plantations and industries of southern Uganda. The Nyamwezi of central Tanzania, who have a long tradition of movement as porters, are another group with a high migration rate, particularly to the sisal estates near the coast. One of the peculiarities of these migrations in the west and south is that they are temporary. Their main motivation is the accumulation of sufficient capital to set up home. Most people therefore make only about three year-long visits away and perhaps only 40 per cent of migrants stay away permanently. Raising wages often means that a labourer simply remains for a shorter time; and it is one of East Africa's chronic problems that it cannot easily or quickly build up a class of trained and skilled industrial workers.

In Kenya there are high migration rates among the Masai, the Kikuyu and the Luo, but here the character of the movement is rather different. These migrations result chiefly from overcrowding at home and they often involve the movement of whole families. The Masai and the Kikuyu formerly lived near European farms to which they migrated as squatters to settle in small plots in return for employment. Now many of the squatter settlements have been rationalized into permanent holdings. The Luo and Kamba, however, followed a pattern of migration more like that in western East Africa and acted as Kenya's main non-agricultural labour force (along with the universal Kikuyu).

The introduction of private land ownership and cash cropping seems to cut down the rate of migration. It has already done so among the Nyakyusa and may do the same among the Acholi. This could have serious effects on the East African economy through shortage of labour. But some agricultural consolidation schemes, notably in Kikuyuland, have created a landless class who migrate to the towns and, in Nairobi, cause a serious unemployment problem. On the other hand some peasant farmers, particularly among the Baganda, the richer Kikuyu and the Chagga, are now themselves able to employ agricultural labourers and herders.

Until 1950 cash cropping and labour migration had resulted in little change in the domestic economy and agricultural systems of most peasants. A large part of the new income went towards taxes. But improvements had made themselves felt in certain areas. One stimulus was the threat of serious soil erosion. Administrative pressure for soil conservation was sometimes so strong that, for instance in the Luguru Hills, it nearly resulted in rebellion. Terracing was adopted on many of the steeper farmlands, and today it is one of the most conspicuous features in the landscape of south-western Uganda, Rwanda and Burundi, Kikuyuland and the Pare and Usambara mountains. Where it was successful it produced a close pattern of fields enclosed by hedges, as in the Kipsigi country in Kenya, but progress was often slow and many terraces in Kenya have recently been abandoned.

After the second world war it was realized that real progress would need to be made in improving the areas already farmed rather than in moving population to new areas with only marginal moisture conditions. Ox-ploughing had replaced the hoe in Teso and other parts of central Uganda at an early date, and its use has been slowly spreading. In some areas it has been replaced already by the tractor plough. By 1960 there were about 2000 tractors in Tanzania, which were being used not only on their owners' farms but were also being extensively hired out. Tractors are also being adopted by other communities, for instance the Kipsigi in western Kenya. Furthermore, government agricultural extension work and the release of high quality cattle from European farms in Kenya has made possible improved methods of integrated mixed farming in Uganda.

The food resources in the peasant economy have also been improved. Maize had been introduced to many areas in the south before the colonial period and it has now become one of the main standby crops for peasant and subsistence farmers, especially the new varieties of hybrid maize which can better withstand marginal moisture conditions. Manioc (cassava) is another American crop which has become widely popular, mainly because it can grow on almost exhausted soil and withstand drought conditions. Where fishing is possible productivity is being improved by the provision of better boats with engines, by government marketing schemes, and, notably in Lake Victoria, by the introduction of new fish species, although over-fishing is already becoming a problem. In southern Uganda, wet sites have been used for fish ponds and these are adding welcome protein to the diet.

Because of the close bond between agriculture and the culture of the peasant society, the new ideas were bound to have an effect on the whole way of life. The main change has probably been the disruption of this relationship of culture and food production, and the creation of groups who are not tied so closely to the soil. This has been linked with a whole new attitude to land tenure. The greatest changes have come in Buganda and Kikuyuland where both a new landowning class and a class of landless people have appeared. In Buganda the agreement of 1900 gave freehold tenure to only 3700 landlords. The remaining 99 per cent of the population found themselves tenants on land to which they had formerly had some rights. In spite of the misunderstandings and later regrets about this agreement it did, in a complex way, stimulate cash-crop production among the new landowners. In the long run, the agreement has produced a land-owning class of cash crop producers, who value land as a resource, a situation which is new to East Africa.

In Kikuyuland pressures on the old system and governmental action have produced a very sudden change in the land-use pattern. Before the

Mau Mau rebellion the Kikuyu population had been increasing steadily since the coming of the Europeans. Restricted by European land apportionment, pressure on the land had become unbearable (Fig. 25), and Kikuyu customs of land inheritance aggravated the situation. There is a record of one man having twenty-nine different plots (one of which was 14 miles (23 km) from his homestead) which added up to only 9 acres (3·5 hectares) in all. With the Emergency and the enquiries that followed it came revolutionary government action. The scattered homesteads were gathered into regimented villages, and later the land was reapportioned into consolidated holdings with homesteads on which people were encouraged to grow cash crops such as coffee, tea, pyrethrum and even sugar; and legislation prevented further subdivision. Although the effects have been most spectacular among the Kikuyu, land replanning has also started among other tribes in Kenya. In areas which had formerly been occupied by European farmers and which were close to areas of peasant overcrowding, land has been bought by the government and sold freehold to peasant farmers in lots of various sizes depending on the owner's capital. Most of the farms were of a size thought to be able to yield a family income of about £25 a year. Eventually a favoured few will have larger farms (up to 200 acres, 80 hectares) with an income of perhaps £100 a year. These sudden changes have brought into existence a landowning class, while the landless must find work either on the new farms or in the cities.

In most of Tanzania and in Rwanda and Burundi the administration has played a less active part in changing attitudes to land tenure, although the younger progressive element in society has pressed for individual ownership against the entrenched conservative element adhering to the old ways of communal ownership or tribal apportionment. Among the pastoralists cattle were regarded as more valuable than land, and this has been another hindrance to reform of land tenure. A landowning class of cultivators is slowly emerging and prospering through individual initiative and investment. In Zanzibar, on the other hand, it has needed a revolution to change the old system of tenure which held back initiative and reform.

A variety of other social and economic changes have also resulted from the imposition of colonial rule. The establishment of peace halted many tribal movements and allowed populations to increase more quickly. Latterly this trend was encouraged by improved control of epidemics, by the adoption of new food crops and, in some areas, by money earned through wage labour. Overpopulation in some areas created dangerous situations and became a hazard to the maintenance of soil fertility and political stability (Fig. 25). Settlement was pushing out from wetter to drier areas and intensive methods of cultivation in the poorer areas were producing soil erosion, for instance among the Arusha, the Kamba and the

Chagga. To avoid trouble, administrations have had recourse to two plans. One is to introduce cash cropping, which gives additional income that can be used to augment local food supplies. The other involves resettlement schemes, a device which has been widely popular in the past. By 1962 two thousand refugees from Rwanda who had crowded into already over-populated parts of southwestern Uganda were resettled on new land and encouraged to grow groundnuts as a cash crop. The Belgian government moved many peasants from overcrowded parts of Rwanda and Burundi to new homes in similar highland areas in the eastern Congo. In Burundi ten thousand families have been resettled in the low-lying Ruzizi Valley in 25-acre (10-hectare) farms. In Kenya the 1951 Swynnerton Plan, which followed the Mau Mau rebellion, envisaged two irrigation schemes to resettle peasants from the overcrowded Kikuyu lands. Some very large schemes are still on the drawing-boards. In Kenya a large-scale irrigation scheme is planned in the Tana valley, and in Tanzania lack of capital is holding back what is intended to be a very large scheme in the Kilombero valley. The ill-considered Groundnut Scheme has been succeeded by a corporation whose main interest is in planning resettlement in Tanzania. It is unfortunate, however, that one of East Africa's peculiarities is an absence of extensive areas of alluvial valley lands, which are the mainstay of most large-scale agricultural schemes elsewhere in Africa and Asia.

In other areas soil exhaustion has resulted in migration without administrative interference and usually within tribal lands. The Sukuma have been abandoning the exhausted drier areas and colonizing the Lake Victoria shore, and the Pare have moved out on to the plains from their eroded hill lands.

Other changes are less tangible: Christianity, literacy, consumer goods, trading, lorry transport, and the vote have all had their effects on the social structure and geography of East African peasant communities.

Dispersed huts and hamlets are now the rule among these communities. Although this has always been true of some communities, for instance in Rwanda, many villages were more nucleated in the past, mainly for defence. This was the case in Kigezi, in the southern parts of Tanzania around Songea, in Sukumaland, and in Kikuyuland where some villages were even fortified. Peace has allowed these settlements to become dispersed, but there are also new nucleating influences. Churches, mission schools and hospitals, small stores often run by Asian traders, and road junctions tend to form new central places for village growth. The commonest pattern is still of dispersed huts, each with an intensively cultivated and often manured plot of subsistence crops, such as bananas, near the house or on richer soils, such as those of the valley bottom. Farther away are the cash crops or the more extensively cultivated food crops which are planted on a

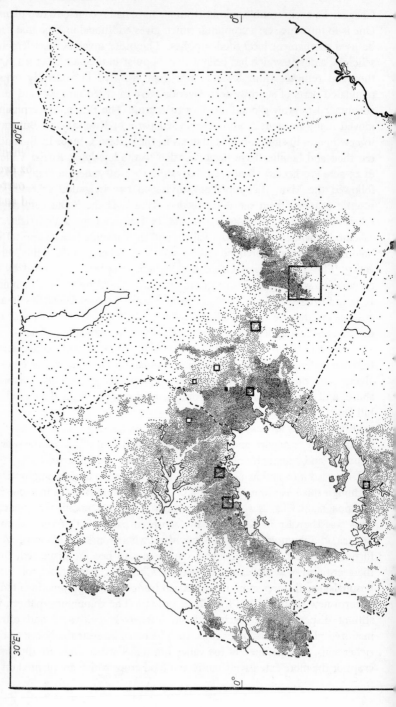

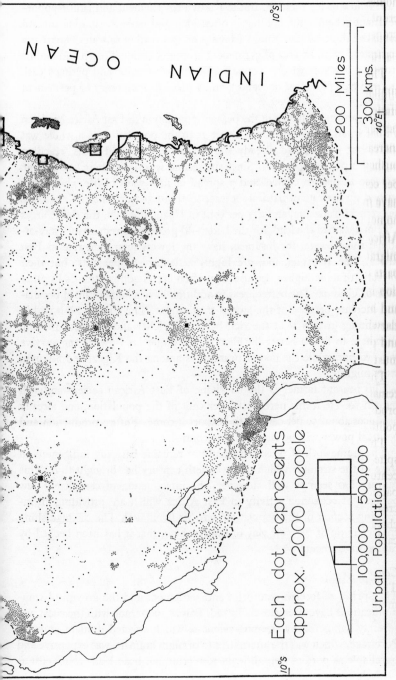

Fig. 25. East Africa: Population Distribution, 1962 (after Porter, 1966)

bush fallow or ley rotation. In the Kikuyu resettlement and land reapportionment schemes the holding is often long and narrow, running up and down the slope, so that it has a frontage on to a road or to water. There is a homestead, with an area of permanent cropping beside it (cash and famine crops); a less intensively cropped area for subsistence and perhaps cash crops; a tree plot (fuel or wattle); and a piece of temporary or permanent pasture.

The pattern of change in the peasant population in East Africa has been similar in all territories. Until about 1939 the population as a whole was static, but growth had already started in the better-off areas, reaching perhaps 1 per cent per year. Since the second world war there has been an increase in disease control and a spread of new ways of life which have pushed up the rate of natural increase to about 30 per cent in Kenya, 1·8 per cent in Tanzania, and 2·5 per cent in Uganda. Again, the richer areas have maintained the lead, for the better-off groups are remarkably stay-at-home; the Chagga, for instance, have the lowest migration rate in East Africa. The Baganda, too, are highly sedentary as peasants; but their migration rate is higher because they often act as administrators in other parts of Uganda. The better areas in addition have a higher rate of population increase because of the labour they attract. The pattern both within and among groups is of the rich becoming richer and the poor moving elsewhere to find a better livelihood. The larger land-owner can survive and prosper, while the poorer peasant, as among the Kigezi and Kikuyu, must migrate.

The peasant farmer is the backbone of East African society and will remain so. He forms perhaps 88 per cent of the population, and already produces about 50 per cent of the export income. Future production and political power will be largely in his control.

The framework of peasant agriculture remains basically indigenous in spite of the stimulus which the twentieth century has brought to it. This century has seen as well, however, the introduction of completely new patterns of economic activity to East Africa which are providing an increasing section of the population with its livelihood. The distinguishing characteristic of the new way of life has been that it has been backed by capital investment.

Communications

The spread of foreign enterprise and settlement and the growth of communications have been closely linked. Before 1900 trade with the coast was severely hampered by sleeping-sickness, which affected draught animals. Porterage, which was the alternative to draught animals, was expensive and unreliable as porters were difficult to recruit and head loads could cost as much as £500 a ton to carry from Uganda to Mombasa. Indeed the spread of cities along the coast reflected the ease of the coastal dhow travel compared with the difficulty of inland movement.

The early Europeans who interested themselves in East Africa realized that the railway would be the only answer to these problems. But development could not start immediately, as the failure of premature attempts to build tramways around Mombasa showed. Capital had first to be raised in Europe and labour had to be imported from India. In 1901 the railway from Mombasa reached Lake Victoria and in 1904 the export of cotton started from Buganda. The line from Tanga reached Moshi in 1911, and the link from Dar es Salaam reached Lake Tanganyika in 1914 and Lake Victoria in 1928. The early railways linked up with steamers on the Great Lakes, but many of these have now been superseded either by rail loops or by the growing volume of road traffic (Fig. 24). Only the Lake Tanganyika trade from Burundi, and the Lake Victoria trade from Bukoba to the railheads at Mwanza and Kisumu, remain as important steamer links.

Until recently the railways have been seen as the main avenues of development in East Africa. Population has flocked to them and the cash economy and other innovations have spread out from the towns which they serve. But in East Africa, as in the rest of the world, the railway era seems now to have passed. New lines built since the last war have not brought the hoped-for development, and one or two lines, notably the southern line which led inland from Mtwara, have had to be abandoned. The reason for this is a great increase in the importance of road transport. Motor buses and lorries have been serving more and more of the region using an increasing ramification of roads. It was due primarily to the competition of trucks that the Lake Albert and Lake Kioga steamer services were withdrawn, and the projected railway to Zambia from Mtwara or the Kilombero Valley may never materialize if the roads in the area are improved. In East Africa as in West Africa 'The Road' is playing an essential part in the life of modern Africans. Mobility is very much the sign of the new society, whether it be only movement to the local market by women or the lengthy migrations by men looking for paid employment. New roads bring in visitors and new ideas to the remoter areas; they act as foci for settlement and development; and they help to increase exchange of goods and so to alleviate the hazards of famine and drought.

The prime purpose of the railways was to bring goods to the coast, and they have left their mark in the coastward orientation that characterizes much of the East African economy. However, the ports themselves have often proved to be bottlenecks to trade. Until 1956 only Mombasa of the major ports had deep-water berths, and in the immediate post-war years there were long queues of goods awaiting shipment at all the main ports.

Since that time Mombasa itself has enlarged its berthing capacity and it remains East Africa's major port, handling 72 per cent of East African trade in 1961, but Dar es Salaam can now berth ocean-going ships, and the old groundnut port of Mtwara can also deal with deep-drawing craft although it is no longer fully used. The rest of the coast, including important ports such as Tanga and Zanzibar, is only served by lighters. Ever since the first steamer reached Zanzibar in 1872 there has been a steady decline in the old coastal dhow trade. It now survives only for local traffic in bulky domestic products such as firewood.

Large-Scale Commercial Agriculture

Once the railway had been built the field was open for the introduction of new ways of life. The first foreign enterprises to be established were cotton ginneries in Uganda. These have now been absorbed by a more complex web of East African industry. A second introduction, which has had important and lasting effects in certain districts, was European settler and plantation agriculture.

European settlers were first attracted and later encouraged to stay by several factors. The many highland areas over 5000 ft (1525 m) seemed attractive and healthy; the government needed settlers for colonial consolidation and to bring in revenue for the administration and the railway; and the land appeared empty partly because of the disease, famine and war which had preceded the Europeans and, in some marginal areas, because of a basic misunderstanding of indigenous methods of shifting cultivation in which a plot of land might be left idle in bush fallow for up to thirty years. Once established, the European farmer could tide himself over bad years better than the African because of his superior credit facilities, and although droughts and disease did lead to fluctuating fortunes at first, this meant that the European could work areas which had too unreliable a rainfall for the African peasant. Latterly, too, new crop and animal varieties suited to the East African environment became available, and these were taken up more eagerly by the better-educated European farmer than by his African counterpart.

Kenya has the largest proportion of highland in East Africa; through its territory ran the Uganda railway which needed revenue; it did not have an advanced cash crop-producing peasantry such as had developed in Buganda; and at the beginning of this century large parts of the Kenya Highlands appeared to be empty. They therefore attracted the major group of European settlers. Although, since political independence in 1962, the settlers have been eclipsed in their role as the country's major political pressure group, they are still very important to the country's economy. Nevertheless, since 1960 there has been a steady decline in the number of

Europeans in Kenya, so that in 1964 a total of only about 49,000 remained, some 40 per cent of whom were urban rather than rural dwellers.

The number of settlers in the other territories has always been very much fewer than in Kenya. In Tanzania large plots of land for settler agriculture had been bought in the early days in the northern highland areas, notably around Kilimanjaro and Meru, and later there was some interest in the southern and central highlands around Mbeya and Iringa. In Tanzania more than half of the Europeans are urban and there has been a slower decline in their numbers; in 1964 there was a total of about 20,000 in the country. In Uganda there has never been a settler community of any size, since most foreign agricultural investment has been in plantation agriculture. The number of Europeans is therefore much fewer, and yet here, too, there has been a steady decline since 1961; in 1964 some 9,000 remained in the country. In spite of official discouragement there was a little settlement of Europeans in Rwanda and Burundi, mainly in the higher northern parts of Rwanda and around the shores of Lake Kivu.

The 'homestead' type of European settlement based on mixed agriculture has become rare since the second world war as many farmers have gone over to small-scale plantation crops such as coffee and tea. The European farms vary in size from smallholdings to vast ranches, but in 1961 41 per cent of them were in the category of 500 to 2000 acres (200–800 hectares). In contrast to the African holdings the European farms are widely dispersed between neat fields with hedges and rows of trees. The non-plantation crops grown are wheat, barley, maize and oats, together with cattle, sheep, pigs and poultry, depending on the local climate. Labour comes from African squatters who have moved with their families from their tribal lands, and who settle and cultivate small subsistence plots on the European land in return for a set number of days work per year on the farm. This squatter population became a major element of the population of the 'White Highlands' and in 1961 they numbered about 1 million; many have since been resettled on land purchased by the government from departing settlers.

Although the products from these mixed farms are important internally to East Africa, not many of them contribute a major part of the export income. The main export crops of European farms are coffee, tea and pyrethrum, and European farmers contribute the major part of these crops in Kenya. Even in 1964 European farmers still controlled the production of more than four-fifths by value of Kenya's agricultural exports although they comprised hardly 0·1 per cent of the population. In Tanganyika, too, a significant proportion of the exported cash crops came from European farms.

With political independence the situation of the European farms has become more precarious. In Kenya perhaps half of the farmers will remain and continue to contribute to the economy. The other half will probably eventually be bought out by the government and their farms reapportioned to African peasant farmers. This is particularly true of the farms which border the areas of high density African population, such as the tribal lands of the Nandi, the Kipsigi, the Luyia and the Kikuyu. Overall there will be a net increase in population in the former 'White Highlands' where the programme of resettlement should be completed in 1967. In Tanzania there has been similar pressure on the government to repurchase European-held land in the northern highland areas.

Perhaps in some areas the European settler will be replaced by a more highly capitalized African farmer. In Kenya a limited number of Africans are to be settled on farms which it is hoped will yield an income of as much as £250 a year. But in Uganda there is already emerging a small number of large-scale farmers, some growing coffee or tea and some becoming prosperous mixed farmers. In Tanzania the Agricultural Corporation is trying to establish some larger African-owned farms in parts of the area of the former Groundnut Scheme. But it will be many decades before the peasant is effectively replaced as the backbone of the rural life of East Africa.

Foreign agricultural investment in plantations is an older and more economically important feature of the East African scene. Plantations of a sort were established by the Omani dynasty in Zanzibar in the mid-nineteenth century for the production of cloves. As with the later plantations on the mainland, these were owned by absentee landlords (who lived in Zanzibar town), and they were worked by imported labour, in this case slaves imported from the mainland who formed about three-quarters of the total population of Zanzibar. Latterly there developed a tenant system in which the land was rented out by the old plantation owners to peasant farmers. This tended to stifle initiative, and there was continuing bitterness, which erupted in the recent revolution and takeover of the whole system by a left-wing government.

In planning future development, the early European administrators and capitalists thought at first mainly in terms of plantation agriculture, since even in Uganda they could not envisage a major economic contribution from the local peasants. In Uganda a few investors tried several tropical crops such as cocoa and rubber, but mostly with very little success. The only plantation crops which survived here were sugar and tea. Sugar in particular needs a heavy capital investment in processing plant and careful organization of production so that there is little idle time at the mill. Its production is concentrated today in three major plantations, two in Uganda and the other in the neighbouring moist lands of the Nyanza province of Kenya. All are controlled by large Asian companies and they act as powerful magnets for paid labour. The Uganda plantations draw from the western highlands rather than from the nearer, more prosperous Baganda.

In Tanzania the search for a paying plantation crop was more systematic and eventually sisal was chosen. The crop later spread to the parts of the Kenya Highlands and the Kenya coast. Sisal cannot be economically produced except on large plantations, since it needs very heavy capital investment in light railways, water supplies and processing works. In 1962 the sisal plantations in Tanzania employed 28,000 men, and although there has been a slight recession since, they are still a large employer of labour. Tanzania and Kenya produce about 60 per cent of the world's sisal and it makes up 16 per cent by value of the export income of East Africa (excluding Rwanda and Burundi). The pattern of this plantation industry is slowly changing. Instead of employing a large, always changing, labour force of men, the companies have deliberately been recruiting whole families and adjusting their wages accordingly; this has meant some sudden increases in the cost of labour, but it is tending to normalize life around the estates and in the neighbouring villages. Here, too, there is a move to increase the proportion of sisal grown by peasant out-growers.

In all the territories, including Rwanda and Burundi, there has been an increased interest in tea, for it can be grown in high wet areas which are not suited to any of the other main plantation crops. Although it needs quite heavy capital investment in processing plant, the units are usually much smaller than those for either sugar or sisal, and it is being more successfully cultivated by peasant out-growers. Tea comes fourth on the list of East African exports, earning about 5·5 per cent of the export income.

An important change in the pattern of plantation agriculture in recent years has resulted from its official encouragement by the newly independent East African governments. In Tanzania the major governmental venture has been the Kilombero Valley sugar plantations which, although they will not export, will save Tanzania substantial amounts of foreign currency. It is deliberate government policy here that an increasing share of the sugar crop should come from peasant out-growers who are being settled in the area. In Tanzania, too, government agencies are branching out into a variety of large-scale agricultural enterprises, such as the cattle ranching and meat canning venture in the Rufiji Delta. Similarly, the government-backed Uganda Development Corporation has shown an interest in tea growing in the moist western highlands of the country. This form of large-scale government investment in agriculture is likely to become progressively more important in East Africa.

Mining and Industry
Another interest for the foreign investor and latterly for government

corporations has been mineral exploitation. East Africa is not yet fully explored for minerals, but discoveries, with a few exceptions, have not been as encouraging as those farther south in the continent. A knowledge of metal-working may go back to the beginning of the Christian era in northern East Africa, but the local smiths used only low-grade ores which they often mined from laterites. In this century, on the other hand, long and costly lines of communication have meant that it is only economic to mine high-grade ores.

The main mineral export from East Africa is diamonds. These were discovered in a very rich volcanic pipe in northern Tanzania as recently as 1940, and by 1964 they were earning £8 million or 4·5 per cent of the income of the territories (excluding Rwanda and Burundi). Diamonds are followed closely in importance by copper, most of which comes from the government-supported mine at Kilembe in western Uganda. The copper is partly refined at the mine and then sent by rail to an electric smelter near the hydro-electric station at Jinja. In 1964 copper brought in £6·5 million or another 4 per cent of East African exports. Rwanda and Burundi earn 38 per cent of their export income from tin, wolfram, titanium and columbite. Although minerals are important as sources of foreign currency they are not large employers of labour. The diamond mines employ about 3000, while the Uganda copper enterprises employ only some 4500 men at Kilembe and Jinja. In 1963 mining and quarrying employed a total of 156,000: only a minute fraction of the employed population of East Africa.

Before the second world war most industrial activity in East Africa was concerned with the primary processing of agricultural products and such products still comprise the main contribution of industry to exports. Cotton ginneries have for half a century been a part of the southern Uganda scene, but this type of first stage bulk reduction is being added to now by more sophisticated 'agricultural' industries. In Jinja the Uganda Development Corporation has invested in a textile factory, and in Dar es Salaam a mill for producing baler twine using the produce of the local sisal plantations has been opened. Canning factories have also opened up a market for local meat produce and for the pineapple growers of Kenya.

Before the war the local market for manufactured goods was small enough to be met by imported goods from Europe. During the war supplies from Europe were reduced, and this, together with growing prosperity among certain groups, increased the demand for locally produced goods. To meet this demand consumer goods industries have been established, mainly in and around Nairobi, but also in other major cities, notably Dar es Salaam, Jinja, and Mombasa. Industrial growth has not been smooth, but in general it has been progressive.

Industrial development in East Africa has met with two main problems, apart from the slow growth of the consumer market. In the first place, capital has been difficult to attract, partly because of the lack of a developed infrastructure. This problem is, however, being slowly overcome. One major project was the building of the huge Owen Falls dam across the Nile at Jinja. Its primary purpose was to attract industry with cheap power. At first the response was slow, but more recently there has been renewed growth, not only of several industries in Jinja itself but also in nearby areas to which the power can be transmitted cheaply. In a similar way, power stations on the Pangani river in northern Tanzania are now supplying power to local sisal-processing plants and to new industries in Dar es Salaam. Where capital from private sources cannot be attracted, the government itself often steps in. It is one of the purposes of the Uganda Development Corporation, for instance, to promote and encourage new industries.

The second major problem in East African industry is that labour productivity is very low. Labour has been a problem since the beginning of the twentieth century. It was because of the expense, unreliability and scarcity of local labour that Indians had to be imported to build the Uganda railway. Today the character of the industrial labourer, drawn as he is by the attraction of earning enough cash to set up with a wife and a farm in the homeland, has meant that few skills have developed. Even a rise in wages often brings a 'reverse' response, since it means that the required capital is more quickly accumulated by the labourer and he can return home sooner. It has been estimated that Tanzanian labour is 25 per cent less efficient than labour in Europe, partly because of the lack of experience, and partly because of poor nutrition and health. But the problem is not the same throughout East Africa. In Kenya there is an unemployment problem in Nairobi, which is due in part to consolidation of holdings and the displacement of landless peasants. There might here be the nucleus of a permanent industrial labour force.

Despite the problems of industry in East Africa it has been employing a slowly increasing number of people. There appears to have been a slight recession in Kenya following independence, but in general the trend has been upwards. In 1963 a total of about 96,300 people were employed in manufacturing and repair in East Africa (excluding Rwanda and Burundi); nearly half of these were in Kenya and a third in Uganda. This growing importance is being reflected in a small but significant export of manufactured goods. For example, shoes from the Limuru factory near Nairobi are now being sold in the United States.

In addition to manufacturing a larger number of people are employed in public service and other non-agricultural work. In 1963 there were altogether 1,098,300 people in paid employment in East Africa (about 4 per cent of the population), of whom 418,700 were employed in agriculture, forestry and fishing, and 679,500 (or 2·5 per cent of the population) were employed in all forms of non-primary production.

Trade and Urban Life

Trade has had a long history on the East African coast but has only recently been developed on a considerable scale in the interior. Before the time of Christ there were small traders on the East African coast trading with Romans and Greeks, and later with Persians, Indians, and even Chinese merchants. The trade centres were small towns which were connected commercially and sometimes even politically with the Hadramauti and Omani sections of the Arabian coast. The fortunes of individual towns varied, but towards the end of the last century Zanzibar controlled more of the coast than had any other city since the period of loose Portuguese rule between the fifteenth and the eighteenth centuries. The trade which supported Zanzibar, as it had supported its predecessors, was in high value goods such as ivory, and slaves which were of increasing importance from the end of the eighteenth century.

The population on the coast was largely indigenous, with a slight mixture of Arab and perhaps some Persian blood. There grew up, however, a largely Arab aristocracy of landowners and governors, and a middle class of mainly Indian traders and moneylenders. At this time ways of life were developing among the coastal communities which were to become familiar over much of East Africa in the twentieth century. The coastal peoples were more or less detribalized, and had a high degree of individual mobility. Their common language, Swahili, and their common faith, Islam, meant that they achieved a broad cultural homogeneity. Swahili has become the lingua franca of much of East Africa, and especially of Tanzania.

For centuries the coastal merchants relied on people from the interior to supply them with trade, and only in the nineteenth century did they begin to venture inland themselves. The policies of Sultan Sayed Said in the middle of the century in particular were expansionist, and in 1843 Arab traders reached the court of Buganda, and small stockaded forts began to appear along the main trade routes. Some of the Swahilis and Arabs moved inland themselves, but much of the increasing volume of trade fell into the hands of some of the more vigorous inland groups such as the Nyamwezi in Tanganyika and the Kamba in Kenya.

The transfer of political power to the Europeans in the late nineteenth century, and later the building of the railway, meant that much of this ancient network has been replaced and commerce is now largely in the hands of new immigrant groups. Many of the larger commercial concerns and some of the more specialized skilled workers are European, but, increasingly, Asian enterprise has been injecting capital into commerce. Already in the later nineteenth century most of the Swahili and Arab trading expeditions were financed by Indian capital, but in this century 'Asian' interest has extended to the farthest corners of the region where in almost every village there is a small shop owned by an Indian family selling essential consumer goods. Indian enterprise has reached out to the sugar estates of Kenya and Uganda, to sisal processing, to cotton ginning, to timber sawmilling and to many other commercial activities.

The chief characteristic of most of the commercial population is that it is urban. Like commerce, towns were unknown in the interior before 1900, for although the *Kibugas* or capitals of the Kabakas of Buganda may sometimes have extended over 20 square miles (52 km²) and housed between 19,000 and 30,000 people, they were not towns in the strict sense. Until latterly the *Kibuga* was moved at the death of each monarch, so that even the huge ceremonial grass buildings were only regarded as temporary; at the same time, although the court was surrounded by thousands of officials and people seeking influence, each lived in his own compound and was fed very largely by the produce of his own garden. These *Kibugas* were not commercial but political centres, comparable to the *kraals* of the pastoral kings to the west which were moved in slow circuit around their domains.

The first of the new towns in this century were purely administrative centres and many remain so to this day. Most of them consist of little more than a sparse network of carefully laid-out streets, a courthouse, a few government offices, a small market with Asian shops and the houses of the administrators. The rural African finds little to attract him to such places.

The bigger East African towns, however, are acquiring a more truly urban character, in which the familiar signs of urban life, such as overcrowding, class structure, industry, trade unionism and political parties are appearing. Although each East African city has its own distinctive character and problems, there are certain features common to them all. One is that Africans seldom form more than 60 per cent of the population (Nairobi 59 per cent, Dar es Salaam 60 per cent, Kampala 45 per cent in 1958). The urban African, coming as he does to work in industry, does not usually come for a lengthy stay; nor does he bring his wife or family (in 1958 the man–woman ratio in Nairobi was 4–1). This has meant that most Africans live in boarding-houses and have little time to develop true urban life. Tribal groups – and there are usually very many in African cities – tend to cherish their tribal loyalties for the sake of security. But there is now emerging in greater numbers what may be called the truly urban African. Nairobi, for instance, has seen in the last few years a great influx of people displaced from the land who will probably become permanent residents, and in Dar es Salaam there is now a tradition of local music halls and an urban slang. Other signs of truly urban life, such as increased delinquency, mental disorder and disease, and decreased fertility, are also appearing. Although urbanization is increasing it is still rudimentary – at the latest census only 6 per cent of Kenyans, 3 per cent of Tanzanians, and 1·5 per cent of Ugandans could be described as urban (although this does not include many 'peri-urban' areas).

A corollary to the low percentage of Africans is another conspicuous feature of all the main East African cities: their Asian character. This is partly because most of the immigrants from India were small traders and therefore town dwellers, but it is also a result of ordinances which forbid these immigrants, particularly in Kenya, from owning land. Being far from homogeneous – they include Ismaili Moslems, Gujeratis, Goans and many others – the Asians tend to be clannish and they have not become fully integrated into East African life. In spite of a very high birth-rate their numbers have tended to decline slowly by emigration since 1963, although there was a slight increase in Kenya in 1965. The decline is due in part to hostility from the Africans, who see the Asian monopoly of commerce as unhealthy. In Kenya the government has repeatedly urged the Asians to introduce Africans into their firms, and in Uganda there has been a deliberate policy of encouraging the African trader, with the result that one-third of the country's trade is already in African hands.

Europeans tend to be mainly urban and they include a few remaining administrators as well as commercial employees and technicians. British political and commercial control over the last half-century has meant that most of the European population is British, but it also includes Greek, Italian and German elements. Between 1948 and 1957 there was a steady growth in the number of Europeans emigrating to East Africa, the newcomers being mostly technicians and technical experts, and many of these went to live in the towns. Since that time, however, there has been a slow but steady decline in European numbers.

In physical appearance and layout the towns display their newness. Until the post-war period most buildings were temporary in character and they have been easily removed to make way for modern layouts and tall office blocks. Planning control has a long history in East Africa, the interest being due in no small measure to concern for public health. Adopting many of the functions of the *Kibuga*, Kampala continued its tradition of a careful layout and since 1912 has had a coherent town development plan. Dar es Salaam was planned by a scientific officer of the German administration. Nairobi was laid out as a railway camp but has outgrown its early simple plan. Planning has not prevented slums and disease, but many of the poorer quarters are made of such flimsy materials that they are easily removed to make way for municipal housing.

The towns are also the main centres for the growing educated and articulate sections of the East African population. In the region as a whole education has from an early date been closely connected with missionary activity, and it is against this background that many of the educated men have grown up. Uganda, for instance, is to a large extent a Christian country, part Catholic, part Protestant, and here, as elsewhere in East Africa, the local church or school is often the chief focus of the scattered rural community; but gradually in all the territories education is coming more under the control of state and secular organizations such as the Chagga Co-Operative and the Kikuyu Independent Schools Association. A literate community has long existed – in the 1890's for example there were already many educated Baganda – but its growth is slow. In 1962 East Africa (excluding Rwanda and Burundi) had an educated reading population of about 2 million who were served by 11 local newspapers and 300,000 radio receivers. Most of them live in the towns, where their cultural life often centres around the university colleges and training colleges, and distinct élite groups are beginning to form. As yet, however, the educated and moneyed classes have tended to remain distinct.

The Political Framework and Prospect

The five nation states into which East Africa is now divided have rather different political attitudes and histories. In many ways Tanzania can be regarded as a senior partner. Until this century Zanzibar (which is now a part of Tanzania), together with its loose confederation of small states on the mainland, was the only part of the region in contact with the rest of the world, and its Swahili language and culture, and to some extent its Moslem faith, have added a degree of cohesion to the modern state of Tanzania. However, since the revolt on the islands of Zanzibar and Pemba in 1964 the Arab aristocracy has lost its former political power. The mainland territory of the former Sultans was incorporated at a much earlier date partly into the British colony of Kenya and partly into the German colony of East Africa. On the southern mainland German capital laid the basis of the sisal industry and the territorial infrastructure of communications and administration before the first world war, after which 'Tanganyika' became a League of Nations mandate under British control. Its peculiar position as a mandated territory gave Tanganyika some advantages, such as United Nations supervision, but because of uncertainty about its future it suffered some disadvantages as well. However, in 1961 it became the first of the East African territories to attain independence. In 1964, after the revolt of the African and Shirazi elements of the population, Zanzibar united with Tanganyika to form the United Republic of Tanzania.

Tanzania has perhaps the poorest resource base of the new nations of

8

East Africa. Much of its area is almost uninhabited because of tsetse or East Coast fever, because of poor soils or meagre water supplies, or because of the raids of slavers at the beginning of the nineteenth century. It is a very large country with a population of only 10 million, in which the few environmentally-favoured areas are widely separated. But if its cultural history means that its people are divided into many small uncentralized groups in the northwest such as the Bahaya have strong cultural affinity the mid-twentieth century. The rich peoples are neither sufficiently numerous nor sufficiently centralized to form competing pressure groups, which has meant that a fairly unified single party has been able to control most of the government. In spite of their internal diversity most of the Tanzanian (mainland) peoples are Bantu-speakers which means that there are few separatist movements. Only the Masai in the north and small groups in the northwest such as the Bahaya have strong cultural affinity with peoples in the neighbouring states. Tanzania's internal unity has been perhaps the main reason why it has been the chief supporter of plans for an East African political union.

The second senior partner in East Africa is Uganda although it is the smallest and least populous of the three principal territories, with only 7·5 million people. The southern kingdom of Buganda had a highly centralized organization by the end of the nineteenth century, and in Buganda and neighbouring Busoga the new ideas and patterns of the twentieth century took an early and very thorough hold. An educated and wealthy class of Baganda administrators, landowners and churchmen was quick to emerge, whose economic support was the cultivation of coffee and cotton and whose status was protected by agreements and by government policy. However, the prosperity of the south did not spread until very recent times to the north or to the west, and the south has grown to some extent at the expense of these other areas, drawing in labour and concentrating capital and energy. The distinctiveness of Buganda was encouraged by the practices of the colonial administration, and entrenched in the constitution prior to independence in 1962. Ugandan politics became a conflict between the rest of the country and the Baganda, and this division came to a head in the fighting in Kampala in 1966 and the alteration of the constitution in favour of a more centralized structure. Uganda, like Tanzania, has few separatist problems in its border areas. Only on the northeastern frontier which cuts between related tribes of pastoralists has there been trouble and some cattle raiding.

If Tanzania and Uganda are the senior partners, Kenya – with nearly 9·5 million people – is perhaps the richest of the East African nations. Before independence Kenyan politics were in the hands largely of a vociferous European minority. Proximity to the areas of European farming in the Highlands and to the main industrial and commercial developments along the railway line gave advantages to certain indigenous groups, however, and when the nation became independent in 1963 political control fell largely into the hands of two groups: the 'Nilotic' Luo from the west and the 'Bantu' Kikuyu from the central highlands. Independent Kenya was a nation born with many new problems. In the north and east the ethnically and culturally distinct Somali tribes refused to co-operate in the new state, claiming affinity with their cousins in the Somali Republic. Among the pastoral tribes, such as the Masai, independence came at a time when conservatism was beginning to break down as a new 'age-set' came into control, and these people began demanding a greater voice in the government of the country. Just prior to independence there had been a massive reorientation of the land policy of the colonial administration which created a whole new class of small peasant farmers together with a class of landless labourers. The problem which these new groups were to create had no precedent. Independence saw a loss of confidence in the country among some European and Asian settlers in whose hands were the main sources of export income, commercial control and capital. The upheaval has meant the creation of an entirely new pattern of human geography, the details of which have still to stabilize and be fully appreciated.

The two small states of Rwanda and Burundi on the western border of East Africa are in many ways quite distinct. At the time of German penetration they, like Buganda, had centralized aristocratic organizations. They were therefore a distinct part of German East Africa and after the first world war were separated from the rest of German East Africa and mandated to Belgium. Their development has therefore been oriented westward and the methods of colonial administration were rather different from those of the rest of the region. Their linkage to the Congo had many effects: emigrant labour, for instance, was attracted to the Katanga mines; overpopulation was relieved by resettlement in areas in the Congo; and Belgian settlers spread from the Congo into the Highlands of Rwanda. Following the break-up of Belgium's African empire the two states became independent kingdoms in 1962. However, by then a revolt by the Bantu-speaking Hutu had unseated the Tutsi aristocracy in Rwanda and replaced it with a republican régime. In the less centralized kingdom of Burundi the royal house continued with reduced power until it was ousted in 1966 by another Hutu revolt. Both Rwanda and Burundi had a high density of population even before they came into contact with the European powers and this high density continues to be the central problem facing the two countries today. They are in fact among the most densely peopled agricultural countries in the world. Burundi has a population of over 2·5 million and an overall density of 246 per square mile (95 per km²), and Rwanda a population of nearly 3 million and an overall density of 280 per square mile (108 per km.²). There are also the problems of distance from major lines of communication and inadequate markets for industrial produce. Exports from these two land-locked nations must go through two transhipments before they reach the coast at Dar es Salaam, and there is only very limited opportunity to relieve rural overcrowding by urbanization or by extensive cash crop production.

Among the former British colonies in East Africa there has been, for many years, co-operative control of monetary, postal, transport, medical and agricultural services and research through the medium of the East African Common Services Organization (EACSO). It was the hope of many East Africans that this would be strengthened on independence and perhaps extended to political unity which might include peripheral states such as Rwanda, Burundi, Malawi and even Mauritius. Internal politics in the three principal states have, however, tended to postpone if not permanently preclude any political cooperation. In Uganda in particular the Baganda have been lukewarm in their support for East African unity. Technical co-operation through EACSO continues, however, and may even be enlarged. And the East African states as a whole have recently (1966) been negotiating as a group with the European Economic Community. It is at least possible that extended economic cooperation in East Africa may eventually bring political unity in its train.

References and Select Bibliography

BAKER, S. J. K. 1956. Buganda: a geographical appraisal. *Transactions and Papers, Institute of British Geographers,* Vol. 22: 171–180.

BECK, A. D. 1964. The Kilombero valley of south central Tanzania. *East African Geographical Review,* Vol. 2: 37–43.

BELLIS, E. 1964. Soil Surveys in Kenya. *Sols Africains,* Vol. 9: 137–144.

BELSHAW, D. G. R. 1964. Agricultural settlement schemes in the Kenya Highlands. *East African Geographical Review,* Vol. 2: 30–36.

BHARATI, A. 1964. The Indians in East Africa: a survey of problems of transition and adaptation. *Sociologicus,* Vol. 2: 169–177.

BLACKER, J. G. C. 1965. Population growth in Kenya. *Bulletin of the Inter-African Labour Institute,* Vol. 12: 246–266.

BLACKIE, J. R. 1964. Hydrology and deforestation in the Aberdares. *East African Geographical Review,* Vol. 2: 17–22.

BROWN, L. H. 1964. An assessment of some development schemes in Africa in the light of human needs and the environment. *International Union for the Conservation of Nature and Natural Resources, 9th Technical Meeting, Nairobi:* 280–287.

BULLOCK, R. A. 1965. Landscape changes in Kiambu. *East African Geographical Review,* Vol. 3: 37–45.

DIXEY, F. 1956. *The East African Rift System,* Supplement No. 1, Colonial Geology and Mineral Resources Bulletin, H.M.S.O., London.

OORNKAMP, J. C. 1966. Surface, drainage, and tectonic instability in part of southe   Uganda. *Geographical Journal,* Vol. 132: 238–252.

ELKAN, W. 1964. Some social implications of industrial development in East Africa. *International Social Science Journal,* Vol. 16: 390–399.

ETHERINGTON, D. M. 1963. Land resettlement in Kenya: policy and practice. *East African Economic Review,* Vol. 10: 22–34.

FEARN, H. 1955. The diverse pattern of African Agriculture in the Nyanza Province of Kenya. 21–28 in Stamp, L. D. (ed.), *Natural Resources, Food and Population in Inter-Tropical Africa, International Geographical Union Symposium, Makerere,* Geographical Publications, Bude, Cornwall.

FOSBROOKE, H. A. 1964. Pastoralist. *International Union for the Conservation of Nature and Natural Resources, 9th Technical Meeting, Nairobi:* 60–65.

FUGGLES-COUCHMAN, N. R. 1964. *Agricultural Change in Tanganyika,* Food Research Institute, Stanford, California.

GILLMAN, C. 1949. A vegetation type map of Tanganyika Territory. *Geographical Review,* Vol. 39: 7–37.

GOLDSCHMIDT, W. et al. 1965. Variation and adaptability of culture: a symposium. *American Anthropologist,* Vol. 67: 400–408.

GULLIVER, P. H. 1955. *The family herds: A study of two pastoral tribes*, Routledge and Kegan Paul, London.
       1960. Incentives to labour migration. *Human Organisation*, Vol. 19: 159–163.

GUTKIND, P. C. W. 1960. Congestion and overcrowding: an African urban problem. *Human Organisation*, Vol. 19: 129–134.

HARPUM, J. R. 1963. The evolution of granite scenery in Tanganyika. *Records of the Geological Survey of Tanganyika*, Vol. 10: 39–46.

HUNTINGFORD, G. W. B. 1955. The economic life of the Dorobo. *Anthropos*, Vol. 50: 602–634.

KENWORTHY, J. M. 1964. Rainfall and the water resources of East Africa. 111–137 in Steel, R. W. and R. M. Prothero (eds.), *Geographers and the Tropics: Liverpool Essays*, Longmans, London.

LARNAUDE, M. 1950. Un haut pays d'Afrique: le Ruanda-Urundi. *Revue de géographie alpine*, Vol. 38: 443–473.

LEWIS, I. M. 1963. The problem of the Northern Frontier Province of Kenya. *Race*, Vol. 6: 48–60.

LEYS, C. and P. ROBSON (eds.), 1966. *Federation in East Africa*, Oxford University Press, London.

MCMASTER, D. N. 1960. Change of regional balance in the Bukoba District of Tanganyika. *Geographical Review*, Vol. 50: 73–88.
       1962. *A Subsistence Crop Geography of Uganda*, Geographical Publications, Bude, Cornwall.

MALCOLM, D. W. 1953. *Sukumaland*, Oxford University Press, London.

MIDDLETON, J. F. M. and D. J. GREENLAND. 1954. Land and population in West Nile District, Uganda. *Geographical Journal*, Vol. 120: 446–457.

MORGAN, W. T. W. 1963. The 'White Highlands' of Kenya. *Geographical Journal*, Vol. 129: 140–155.

O'CONNOR, A. M. 1966. *An Economic Geography of East Africa*, Bell, London.

OLIVER, R. and G. MATHEW. 1963. *History of East Africa*, Vol. 1. Oxford University Press, London.

PEETERS, L. 1962. Le rôle du milieu géographique dans l'occupation humaine du Ruanda-Urundi. *Bulletin de la Société royale de géographie, Anvers*. Vol. 74: 29–47.

PERIERA, H. C. 1961. Land use hydrology in Africa. *Commission for Technical Co-operation in Africa, Inter-African Conference of Hydrology, Nairobi*: 45–50.

POLLOCK, G. 1960. Industrial development in East Africa. *Economic Geography*, Vol. 36: 344–354.

PORTER, P. W. 1965. Environmental potentials and economic opportunities – a background for cultural adaptation. *American Anthropologist*, Vol. 67: 409–420.
       1966. East Africa – Population distribution: Map Supplement No. 6. *Annals of the Association of American Geographers*, Vol. 56: 180 and map.

PRINS, A. H. J. 1963. The didemic, diarchic Boni. *Journal of the Royal Anthropological Institute*, Vol. 93: 174–185.

ROBERTSON, A. G. 1963. Tse-tse control in Uganda. *East African Geographical Review*, Vol. 1: 21–32.

SOPER, T. 1959. Labour migration in Africa. *Journal of African Administration*, Vol. 11: 93–99.

SOUTHALL, A. W. 1961. Population movements in East Africa. 157–192 in Barbour, K. M. and R. M. Prothero (eds.), *Essays on African Population*, Routledge and Kegan Paul, London.

TURYAGYENDA, J. D. 1964. Overpopulation and its effects in the gombolola of Buhara, Kigezi. *Uganda Journal*, Vol. 28: 127–133.

VESEY-FITZGERALD, L. D. E. 1964. Grasslands. *International Union for the Conservation of Nature and Natural Resources, 9th Technical Meeting*, Nairobi: 111–115.

WASAWO, D. P. S. 1964. Some problems of Uganda swamps. *International Union for the Conservation of Nature and Natural Resources, 9th Technical Meeting, Nairobi*: 196–204.

WOODBURN, J. 1962. The future of the Tindiga: a short account of the present position and the possibilities for the future of a hunting tribe. *Tanganyika Notes and Records*, Vol. 58–59: 269–273.

WRIGLEY, C. C. 1959. *Crops and Wealth in Uganda*, East African Institute for Sociological Research, Kampala.

Further information on East Africa relevant to this essay can be found in the national atlases of Kenya, Uganda, and the former territories of Tanganyika, Belgian Congo and Ruanda-Urundi; in the publications of the East African geological, agricultural and forestry services; and in the following locally-published journals: *The East African Agricultural Journal, The East African Economic Review, The East African Geographical Review, The Proceedings of the East African Academy, Tanganyika Notes and Records, Uganda Journal*, and (from the former Belgian Congo) *Zaïre*.

4 West Africa

4 West Africa

By B. W. HODDER

North and South in West Africa

West Africa exhibits a greater degree of political diversity than any other major region in Africa. Here are no less than fourteen states, containing about one-third of the total population of the continent, and having been subjected at varying times to the differing policies of the major colonizing powers: France, Britain, Portugal and Germany. Environmentally, too, there is great diversity, both within and between the various countries of the region. The present patchwork of state units in West Africa cuts across a succession of physical environments, ranging from the Guinea coast forests of the south to the arid lands of the Sahara in the north. These east-west trending environmental zones are determined very little by relief, most of the region comprising plains and low plateaus under 1500 ft (460 m) high. West Africa is in fact an area of few surface barriers and so with a general ease of overland movement. Only in a few areas do substantial uplands occur: the Fouta Jalon and Guinea highlands in the west, rising to over 6000 feet (1830 m); the Jos plateau, averaging over 4000 ft (1220 m) in northern Nigeria; and, highest of all, the Cameroon-Adamawa highlands, extending over the southern portion of the boundary between West and Equatorial Africa and rising to over 13,000 ft (4000 m) in Mt Cameroon. Compared with other parts of tropical Africa, West Africa is thus an area of low average elevation, and to this fact is largely due the unimportance of European settlement in the region.

Relatively little affected by variations of relief or by irregularities of coastal alignment, climate is the main determinant of environmental differences within West Africa. The heaviest (over 1500 mm per annum) and least seasonal rainfall is in the south. Farther to the north rainfall decreases to under 250 mm per annum and becomes much more seasonal and unreliable. These facts offset to a large extent the peculiar natural advantages of the north in terms of its rather better, less heavily leached soils and relative freedom from the tsetse fly. In the south there are still large forested areas, although much of the forest has either been cleared or changed from tropical rain forest into various types of secondary forest. Farther north, however, savanna woodland gives way to savanna grassland, which thins first into xerophytic scrub and finally into desert. While the present transition from the southern forests to the northern savannas is neither regular nor easily distinguishable on the ground, recent work on the forest-savanna boundary suggests that in historical times it was more distinct than it is now.

This environmental contrast between north and south in West Africa is matched by the pattern of population distribution, in which it is possible to distinguish two parallel if discontinuous east-west belts of greater density in the north and south separated by a 'Middle Belt' of relatively low population density. The southern, wetter belt includes a number of population nodes of very high densities – over 2500 per square mile (1000 per km²) in some cases – notably in Iboland (Eastern Nigeria), the highly urbanized Yorubaland (Western Region of Nigeria), southern Ghana and south-eastern Ivory Coast. The northern belt of high population density includes the great Hausa emirates of Maiduguri, Kano, Katsina and Sokoto; northern Ghana; the Mossi country around Ouagadougou in Upper Volta; the Fouta Jalon; and Senegambia. It was in these northern parts of West Africa that the great medieval empires of West Africa arose.

The 95 million people of West Africa can also be divided very broadly into northern and southern clusters: the northern Sudanic, usually Islamic, groups like the Hausa, Fulani, Mossi and Bambari; and the southern Guinea, usually pagan or Christianized peoples like the Ibo, Yoruba, Akan and Mende. The southern peoples are generally more literate than their northern counterparts, educational facilities being more developed in the south, and the Islamic code of the north tends to perpetuate the rigid political and social hierarchy of the northern emirates. The south, too, is more urbanized, is more directly in touch with external contacts through the ports, has a better network of communications, and is more highly developed economically.

The agricultural economies further emphasize the fundamental contrast between north and south in West Africa. The basis of the northern agricultural economy is grain, especially sorghum and millet, together with the main export cash crops of groundnuts and cotton, both of which are normally grown as part of the normal rotation of field crops. Floodland cultivation for maize, rice and sorghum is another distinctive feature of the northern agricultural economy. Livestock, too, is especially characteristic of the north in West Africa; although the south has longer and more reliable rainy seasons, the natural grasses there tend to be too coarse for good pasture and the dangers of disease, notably from the tsetse fly, are greatest. The long dry season in the north allows Fulani pastoralists to graze their cattle on the stubble and crop litter after harvest, and this helps to manure the land.

In the southern parts of West Africa the basis of the agricultural economy is either rice, rotated with groundnuts and *fonio*, which are crops particularly characteristic of the southwestern parts of the region; or root crops, especially cassava and yams, in the eastern half of the area. Maize and guinea corn are also frequently grown in this rice-root crop zone of West Africa, as are bananas and plantains, cocoyams, melons, pepper and tomatoes. Export crops in the south are chiefly perennials, and include the oil-palm, cocoa (chiefly in Ghana, southwestern Nigeria and the Ivory Coast), and coffee (chiefly in the Ivory Coast).

However, in the pattern of agricultural production, as in the physical environment and population distribution of West Africa, it would be misleading to exaggerate the sharpness of the transition from north to south. Agriculturally, for instance, quite a large part of West Africa – perhaps rather under one-quarter of the total area – lies in neither the northern 'grain' economy nor in the southern 'rice-root' economy, but represents a transitional pattern of mixed grain and root crops. Yet this 'north-south' or 'savanna-forest' dichotomy in West Africa, while admittedly only the very broadest of generalizations, is a valid and useful concept in practice and is certainly fundamental to any understanding of the history of the region

Pre-Colonial West Africa

The Growth of Indigenous States

Though Europeans did not make any direct contacts with West Africa until the fifteenth century, and their political control of the region did not really begin until the latter half of the nineteenth century, West Africa has probably the longest record in sub-Saharan Africa of contacts with the civilized world. Certainly the region had contacts with northern and northeastern Africa, and so indirectly with Europe and the Mediterranean, long before the Portuguese voyages.

Before the fifteenth century, however, outside contacts meant for the most part trading links across the Sahara. How these contacts between the savanna lands of West Africa and the centres of Mediterranean civilization arose is conjectural; but during the fifth and fourth millennia B.C., when a moister 'subpluvial' climate seems to have prevailed over the Sahara, the limits of settlement in West Africa were probably located much farther north than they are today. Ancient cart tracks across the Sahara suggest the existence of definite lines of contact and trade which continued despite the subsequent desiccation of the Sahara and retreat southward of the West African negro. Gold, slaves, ivory, ostrich feathers and hides moved northward across the Sahara in return for salt and luxury items (Oliver and Fage, 1962: ch. 5).

Furthermore, the introduction of the camel to the Sahara by the fourth century A.D. allowed a more extensive and frequently-used series of caravan or long-distance trade routes to develop. It was now possible to link in a more regular and reliable way the trade centres of North Africa with the savanna lands of West Africa, and in these savannas there arose a number

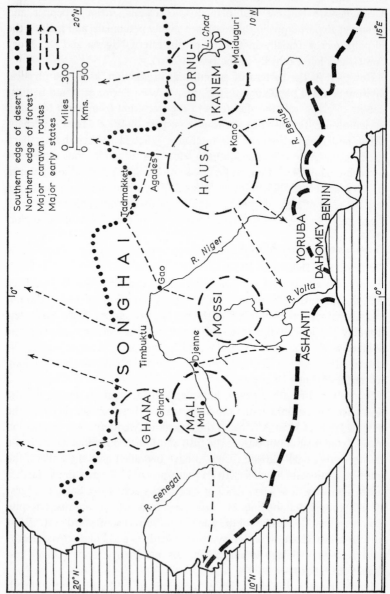

Fig. 26. Major States and Trade Routes of Pre-European West Africa. The location of the states is

of powerful states whose cavalry could operate freely on the open plains. Along the southern fringe of the Sahara arose such great commercial empires as Ghana and Mali, and trade flowed along the trans-Saharan routes from the north, together with a number of broader cultural influences, notably the Islamic religion (Fig. 26). Initially, most of these major savanna or 'sudanic' states developed in the western parts of the region, but from the eleventh century onwards the western routes were disrupted by northern invasions, and interest shifted eastward to those routes that linked North Africa with the rising West African sudanic states of Mossi, Songhai, Hausa and Bornu-Kanem through the centres of Gao, Tadmakket and Agades.

All these West African states were alike in being oriented northward to the Sahara; and not until the thirteenth century, when the northern routes were firmly established, was there any substantial movement to make contacts with the southern parts of West Africa. Yet here in the forest lands of Guinea were areas ecologically very different and with obvious possibilities for trade in forest goods. The peoples of the south, too, were now organizing themselves into definite, often powerful, state units with which trading connections could be established. It is true that most of the so-called 'forest-states' like Ashanti, Dahomey and Yoruba originated in the country fringing the northern edge of the forest; that much of their ritual and political organization seems to have derived from contacts with earlier savanna states to the north; and that the forest itself was barely penetrated for direct trading activities until the fifteenth century. Yet the products of the southern forest lands – ivory, kola nuts and gold – were soon being traded between the forest states and their older neighbours in the savannas; and southwards in return came not only the products of the savanna lands but also beads, trinkets and cowrie shells which had already been traded across the Sahara. In this sense the new southern-oriented trade which took place in West Africa from the thirteenth century can be looked upon simply as a southward extension of the long-established trans-Saharan caravan trade.

Thus when the Portuguese first reached the West African coast in the mid-fifteenth century, they found there a highly developed system of long-distance trade moving generally in a north-south direction between North Africa and the Guinea coast and passing through the Saharan, savanna and forest belts of West Africa. West Africa, in fact, offered a fertile field for European trading enterprise. Long-distance trading contacts with the interior could be tapped at the coast, and contemporary reports indicate both that regional and labour specialization of production was already well advanced and that there was already in existence an indigenous money economy. But the economy of West African peoples was still essentially self-sufficient. With the one exception of salt, the articles being traded over long distances were luxury items. It could hardly be otherwise while the costliest form of land transport – head porterage – had to be used in and through the tsetse-infested and fodderless country of the forest belt (Oliver and Fage, 1962: 108).

European Coastal Contacts

Direct European contacts with the West African coast began in the fifteenth century with the Portuguese, who founded a number of bases, notably at Arguin and Elmina (Gold Coast). These contacts and bases were, however, for trade rather than colonization; and each section of the coastline became known for some special trade: the Grain Coast (from the malagueta pepper, or 'grain'), the Ivory Coast, the Gold Coast and the Slave Coast. By 1500 Portugal had established a trading complex in West Africa extending eastwards to the lands of the Niger delta.

A number of changes were to take place over the next two hundred years. After about 1530 the Portuguese had to face competition from other Europeans, and by the seventeenth century the Portuguese had been almost completely ousted by Spanish, Dutch, French and British traders. At about this time, too, the rising demand for labour in the West Indies and Central America gave a new impetus to the West African slave trade. Previously, West Africa had really very little except ivory, gold, spices and gum arabic to offer European traders; but from the middle of the seventeenth century slaves began to dominate European interests along the West African coast. In the earlier stages of the West African coastal trade the main focus of interest and activity was at the Gold Coast, where access to gold was easiest; but the focus of interest now began to shift farther east to the Slave Coast itself.

A number of reasons have been advanced to explain the almost exclusively coastal location of European interests in West Africa before the late nineteenth century: an unindented coastline with few natural harbours, offshore winds, coastal currents setting strongly eastward, a difficult surf barrier, cataracts in the lower courses of the few navigable rivers, the tropical rain forest, and diseases of all kinds. For much of its history, in fact, the interior of West Africa has been less accessible from the sea than from the north across the Sahara. But even if all the above difficulties had not existed, it is doubtful whether European traders would have been allowed to penetrate inland. The most important single reason why Europeans remained at the coast was probably that the Africans in the coastal states 'were already well enough organized . . . to keep the overland trade in their own hands' (Oliver and Fage, 1962: 14). A number of early attempts to penetrate were made by Europeans: at first, unsuccessfully, by the Portuguese, and later by the French, who succeeded in advancing well up the Senegal river to trade for gold. On the whole, however, European traders were content to remain at the coast where they were conveniently provided with slaves and other trading items by African middlemen.

These opportunities for trade with Europeans at the coast led to an increasing emphasis in West African economic life on the southern parts of the region. Furthermore, the northern savanna states were at this time being disrupted by a series of wars to establish wider military and political empires and, with the principal exception of the trade in slaves to North Africa, trans-Saharan routes were becoming less significant as major arteries of international commerce. Thus the focus of trade in West Africa – both in slaves and, later, in 'legitimate' commerce – moved southward towards the coast and away from the savanna lands of the interior.

The change from slaving to legitimate trade in West Africa was by no means so straightforward or simple as is often supposed. The abolition of the slave trade by Britain in 1807 had no immediate effect on the amount of slaving: other countries simply rushed into the vacuum left by the British prohibition, and later in the nineteenth century an increased demand for slaves in the sugar plantations of Cuba helped to give the slave trade a further boost. Then there were several motives in most attempts to suppress slaving. Broadly speaking these motives were humanitarian, economic, or both, it being recognized that slaving and legitimate trade were connected in such a way that an increase in one led to a decrease in the other. While some authorities supported the suppression of slaving as a means of encouraging legitimate trade, others encouraged legitimate trade chiefly as a means of suppressing the slave trade. Thus legitimate trade and slaving existed side by side well into the first half of the nineteenth century.

By the end of the eighteenth century, however, Europe was already beginning to search for new products in exchange for her own rapidly expanding exports to West Africa of such items as textiles, salt, hatchets, and muskets. There now seemed to be little hope of expanding traditional exports from West Africa – ivory, gold-dust, furniture woods and gum opal: the supply of ivory was falling, the prices of woods were depressed, and gold production was falling. By the closing years of the eighteenth century, traders along the West African coast were already looking out for a new basis for their trade, and they were fortunate to find in West Africa an indigenous tree crop – the oil palm – which was capable of providing a solid basis for the growth of legitimate trade in West Africa throughout the nineteenth century. Europe, 'restless and innovating in the throes of the industrial revolution' (Hancock, 1940: 158–160), provided a ready market for the oil, which was used in the manufacture of soap and margarine, in the tinplate industry, and as a general lubricant. In 1799, only 2579 cwt of West African palm oil was imported into Liverpool, but this product was soon to form the basis of a new and massive export trade.

The growth of the palm-oil trade and the industrial revolution in Europe led to much closer and more direct associations between West Africa and Europe than had ever occurred during the days of the slave trade. In Britain there now developed close links between West African trading firms and British manufacturers. During the nineteenth century Manchester cottons captured the West African cotton trade, and other British products were successful in competing against similar products from other European countries and even against those of West Africa itself. Thus in the Niger delta (Oil Rivers) the growth of legitimate trade in palm oil was accompanied by the import of salt from Cheshire with which local salt could not compete in quality, volume or price; tools and weapons produced in the hinterland were unable to compete with equivalent articles imported from Birmingham; and Norwegian dried cod (stockfish) competed successfully with local dried fish (Jones, 1963: 88-9).

But one feature changed very little during the first three-quarters of the nineteenth century: trade continued to focus on the southern, coastal parts of West Africa. This was natural enough in that the whole basis of the new legitimate trade – the oil palm – was for reasons of climate concentrated in the Guinea coastlands, and more particularly in the wetter portions around the Niger delta. In the drier parts of West Africa, as in the Senegal valley, crops like the groundnut were introduced. On the other hand, this period did see some isolated and often locally important attempts at penetration by European traders and missionaries; and these attempts were stimulated by European exploration of the West African interior in the years between 1780 and 1860, beginning with the travels of Mungo Park and ending with the journeys of Barth in the northern savanna lands. Most of the early efforts to develop trading contacts of a more direct kind from the coast into the northern interior failed, however, often because of the very high sickness and mortality rates; and even after Baillie's 1854 expedition up the Niger, when the medicinal value of quinine was demonstrated and up-river trade became feasible, the remaining problems of isolation and lack of security still seemed too formidable for any merchant to solve without government backing.

A few traders and officials, nevertheless, continued to interest themselves in the vast savanna hinterland of the Guinea coast and were fully aware of the importance of these northern areas to future trading life in West Africa. Goldie, in particular, insisted upon looking at the whole trading problem of West Africa from the north, fixing his attention upon the large populations lying between the Sahara and the Guinea forests. He realized that here was a great potential market for British traders and that if the British left the whole of it to France they would find themselves crowded out even from the coastal markets which they had already earned (Hancock, 1940: 165). International rivalry for the hinterland was clearly an important consideration, and the interdependence of commercial trading interests and political control was fully recognized, it being appreciated that trade could not flourish without a *pax*, and that this *pax* could not be guaranteed without some form of political control. In the mid-nineteenth century, especially, physical security became increasingly difficult to maintain as a number of the savanna groups, notably the Fulani, pushed southward, forcing many of the forest peoples back before them. From the 1860's European powers in West Africa found themselves obliged to protect their own trading stations, posts and missions by active intervention. Governments realized that they would have to assume direct responsibility for maintaining peace if legitimate trade was to flourish and the slave trade to be finally eradicated. The interdependence of economic and political factors was now very evident. By the early 1880's, sections along much of the West African coast were being claimed by the traders and administrators of one or other European power (Fig. 27); missionary, trading, military and administrative contacts were developing in the hinterland from some of these coastal footholds; and the stage was set for the European scramble, finally to be set in motion by the 1884–1885 Conference and Treaty of Berlin, which laid down that European colonial claim to territory could only be secured by 'effective occupation'.

The European Impact

The scramble among European powers for territory in West Africa took place so rapidly after the Berlin Conference of 1884–1885 that within a decade the main lines of the future states of West Africa had been laid down. France gained most of the area, but her territories included large tracts of desert and semi-desert, and it was the British who acquired the largest share of the population and much of the natural wealth of the region. The British territories, however, had the disadvantage of being separated from one another by large stretches of French territory. By this time, too, the Germans had laid claims to Togoland, the Portuguese had registered their rights to Portuguese Guinea, and Liberia's independence, originally granted in 1847, was confirmed.

Economic Effects

In trying to assess the economic effects of the European colonial impact it must be remembered that in spite of the growth of the West African oil-palm trade, late nineteenth and early twentieth century Europe was not in

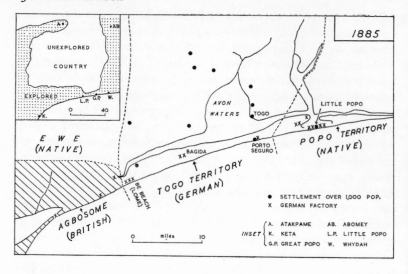

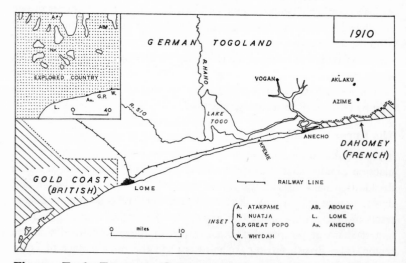

Fig. 27. Early European Contact and Control along the Western Coast of the Bight of Benin (after Langhans, 1910)

need of a greatly increased supply of West African products. West African markets accounted for a negligible proportion of European exports, and the motivation for the 'scramble' was certainly not primarily the need for tropical raw materials and foodstuffs in West European countries. The ideal colony was not so much one that could provide much-needed raw materials as one that could be self-supporting financially; and this meant that taxes had to be paid and imposed, or at least that adequate customs dues had to be collected. This was impossible, however, before people had something to grow and sell, so that the problem was essentially one of creating opportunities to earn cash incomes which could then be taxed. Whichever way this was done – by peasant growing of cash crops, by plantations, or by mining – the incentive was the imposition of direct taxation; but cash incomes, and consequently taxation, could not be increased until governments had provided the necessary background of law and order by establishing the basic structure of civil administration (Oliver and Fage, 1962: 204–5).

One important economic effect of the European impact was the construction of new lines of transportation. These were, in fact, an important corollary of the new general peace, many of the earliest lines being built partly to facilitate control over the expanding hinterlands of the coastal protectorates or colonies, although this was bound up with the desire to facilitate internal and external trading and a general increase of production. In some areas, river, lagoon and tidal creeks dominated the early pattern of transport. The Oil Rivers, Niger, Benue, Senegal and Gambia were all waterways of importance. But in most other cases, as in that of the Volta, rivers were found to be of much less value as commercial waterways, impeded as they so often are by shallows and rapids and by sandbars across their mouths. Until the 1920's roads were more often built or improved for military and strategic than for economic reasons: an attitude which was wholly understandable in that the chief means of moving goods of all kinds on land, at least in the southern forest areas, was by head loading. From the commercial point of view, then, it was necessary only to keep clear a path or track wide enough for a single file of head porters. By the time motor transport became more common in the 1920's, however, one of the most powerful incentives for the building of motorable roads had become the relatively high cost of head porterage and the difficulty of getting porters.

But the European impact on lines of transport is perhaps best illustrated by the building of railways in West Africa. Unlike East Africa, the more productive (moister) areas were here found to be in the south near the coast, and they were divided between the several competing colonial powers. Both the British and the French built railways inland from the coast, but the French, with their large contiguous areas in West Africa, planned their lines to supplement the navigable sections of the Senegal and Niger rivers. The one common desire in all railway building in West Africa, however, was to secure effective political control of the interior and to develop and retain within a particular colony as much trade as possible.

A second important economic effect of the European colonial impact is suggested by the fact that, with the exception of oil palm, most of the cash crops in West Africa today were introduced or developed by Europeans in the colonial period. In addition to the early introduction of food crops such as manioc and maize by the Portuguese along the coast, a large number of other new crops were introduced later. Particularly important were the major cash crops – cocoa, coffee and rubber – the economic success of which depended heavily upon the building of new lines of communication, notably the railways, to the ports of West Africa. In Nigeria the correlation between export crops and railway building was especially close: groundnuts, for instance, did not figure significantly in exports from Lagos until after the completion of the Lagos–Kano railway in 1912; and the same is true of cotton and hides and skins, all of which originated in the northern savanna lands. Cocoa, on the other hand, only developed as a large-scale export crop in Nigeria during the 1920's when road transportation improved so rapidly (Hodder, 1959).

Thirdly, while European agricultural settlement of the kind and extent found in parts of northern, eastern and southern Africa was never a feature of the colonial period in West Africa, there was some European settlement, especially in French West Africa. In British West Africa plantations were not normally allowed. The planter's frontier failed to secure lodgement (Hancock, 1940: 189) in West Africa, despite the fact that on health grounds plantations had become practicable by the early twentieth century. In French West Africa, on the other hand, freehold plantations were freely granted to non-Africans so that those crops that were best grown on plantations, such as coffee, rubber and bananas, could more easily be established. Coffee and bananas were also much encouraged in the former French territories by guaranteed markets in France at prices higher than world prices. Similarly, in French Guinea and the Ivory Coast coffee and bananas assumed great importance, whereas across the boundary into Ghana cocoa became more important. A contrast, too, may be drawn between, on the one hand, the efforts of the local German Togo administration in 1913 to encourage the raising of a variety of cash crops and, on the other, the intense monoculture practised in Dahomey. In sum, the pattern of export production in West Africa reflected the affiliations of the colonies and the differing policies of the various administering powers.

The British were most successful in the Gold Coast and Nigeria. The economic development of British West Africa as a whole, moreover, was greater and rather more rapid than that of French West Africa. In general, British areas were more attractive to the European trader and investor; and the parts of West Africa occupied by Britain were those in which European, particularly British, trade was already well established before the twentieth century. In addition, Britain had more money available for investment overseas, and her territories in West Africa possessed a number of natural economic advantages: compared with the French territories, the British areas were small and thickly populated, mineral as well as agricultural resources were richer, and Africans had already begun to develop these resources before the colonial period.

Finally, the economies of the separate states of West Africa were very much the creation of the colonial powers controlling them; and each of these economies was in some degree a classical economy with a limited range of products, limited capital and markets, and emphasis on agricultural production which in West African countries was mostly in the hands of peasant farmers. But the degree and nature of economic development varied significantly from country to country within each of the major colonial areas. For example, the French had most success in Senegal and Ivory Coast: Senegal always retained a privileged position within the French empire in tropical Africa; and Dakar, as the seat of government for French West Africa, developed as a great urban centre, containing within it over 10 per cent of Senegal's three million people.

Thus the economic and related social changes brought about in West Africa by the European colonial impact thrust its peoples into modern economic life. Economic development, and in particular the rise of export tree crop production, further encouraged the southward movement of people and radically affected the pattern of population distribution in West Africa. Urbanization was a corollary of this development and the growth of towns was to play an increasingly important part in the rise of economic and social institutions and in the emergence of indigenous political activity in West Africa.

Political Effects

The most significant political effect of the European colonial impact was the creation of new systems of administration, although these varied from country to country according to the colonial power responsible for introducing them. In the British areas a system of indirect rule was established. This began with Lugard in northern Nigeria, was later extended to southern Nigeria, and was eventually introduced into the other territories of British West Africa: the Gold Coast, Sierra Leone and Gambia. Indirect rule was adopted in these territories on the grounds that the African was illiterate, that he was too remote from Western ways, and that not for some time would he be able to operate the machinery of parliamentary government. Preserving and working through existing traditional institutions, indirect rule was most successful where it began – in northern Nigeria – for here the indigenous political institutions were of a kind to encourage it. There were large, tribally homogeneous areas with hierarchical chiefdoms through which the British could administer their territory; a single district might be over 30,000 square miles (78,000 km²) in extent and have a population of up to 2 million.

When extended to southern Nigeria and to other parts of British West Africa, however, indirect rule met with varying degrees of success, depending largely on the nature of the existing indigenous institutions through which it had to operate. In southern Nigeria and throughout most of the forest areas of British West Africa it proved generally less successful. For here were numerous small tribes, each with its own language, gods and institutions. British rule could operate less successfully through the numerous elective chiefdoms of southern Nigeria than through the few very large hierarchical chiefdoms of the north. Many of the southern chiefdoms, too, had little centralized authority or administrative machinery, few constituted judicial institutions, and no sharp divisions of rank, status and wealth. This is not to suggest that all West African peoples fell neatly into one of the two West African political systems: it is more accurate to consider these two types as extremes rather than as exclusive categories. Nevertheless, in a great many cases indirect rule was clearly not suited to the indigenous tribal structure and existing institutions.

Indirect rule was also to some extent incompatible with modern economic development in West Africa. This system of government was very much dependent upon the authority of the chief, but modern economic forces worked against such traditional powers. This was most clearly seen in the towns of British West Africa where polyglot, detribalized populations arose. In these towns, traditional tribal ties tended to be overridden by loyalties of a more modern kind: to trade unions, market associations, youth societies and political parties; and very soon the cocoa-farming groups of the countryside were drawn into their orbit.

A corollary of the system of indirect rule in British West African territories was that land belonged to Africans and so could not be bought by Europeans; for this reason, as well as for reasons of climate, European agricultural settlement was not encouraged. In the French territories, on the other hand, all land was recognized as being French, it being an essential element of French colonial policy that their territories in West Africa were simply Overseas Territories of France. It was further assumed that all Africans would eventually become Frenchmen. Consequently, large European concessions were allowed in French West Africa, although the unattractive equatorial lowland climate inhibited any considerable growth of European settlement in the region. With its larger area (some three times greater than British West Africa) and system of direct rule, French West Africa required a higher percentage of administrators within the European population than was needed in the British territories.

More French women and children were brought out from France and a greater number of Europeans were in technical and clerical occupations.

There was a further contrast in the form of law enforcement by police and army. In French West Africa there was a large army cantonment in every important town; and not only officers, but also non-commissioned officers, were European. Furthermore, whereas the British were encouraged to speak local African languages, the French were not encouraged to do so. It would be unfair to suggest, as some commentators do, that French interest in creating a native army for use outside West Africa was the sole reason why France practised direct administration in their West African territories. It was rather a method of control which happened to fit the character and traditions of the French, and especially their desire for logical systems of order.

Thus whereas France considered her French West African territories to be part of France, in British West Africa the colonies were distinct and largely autonomous units. There the principle of ultimate independence was accepted, but in French West Africa it was never entertained. In French eyes there were no peoples in their West African territories awaiting liberation and there was no racial discrimination to abolish: there were simply populations who felt themselves to be French and who wished to take – and to whom France wished to give – an increasing part in the life and democratic institutions of the French community. Herein lay perhaps the most important difference between British and French colonial policy, at least until the second world war. Before then 'the political history of French West Africa was essentially administrative history – the history of the impact of metropolitan ideas and interests on the practical day-to-day problems of administration in a poor, thinly populated and undeveloped country' (Robinson, 1955: 140). During and after the second world war, however, a number of changes took place, and many of the distinctions between British and French colonial policy in West Africa began to blur. Indirect and direct rule moved closer to each other; and in both British and French territories individual land tenure began to supplement collective ownership, either African or European. By the 1950's, too – largely as a result of unrest in North Africa, the Indochinese war, and the work of the *Rassemblement Démocratique Africain* (*RDA*) – the principle of ultimate independence became accepted in the French as in the British territories.

Important differences remained, however. Britain was trying to develop political systems in its West African colonies which would evolve parliamentary types of government, including even opposition parties. France, on the other hand, tried to create strong political ties between her contiguous territories in West Africa. British policy in the four enclaves of

British West Africa was thus pragmatic and differed from country to country, whereas French policy was more doctrinaire and attempted to treat its possessions in West Africa as a whole.

Some comment should also be made here on the two states in West Africa which have never come within the direct influence of British or French colonial policy: Portuguese Guinea (the only remaining colonial territory in the region) and Liberia (the earliest independent state). Portugal's impact on Guinea was very similar to that of French administration in West Africa. Portugal considered Guinea to be part of her Overseas Territories and governed by direct rule. Unlike France, however, Portugal was not prepared and is still not prepared to allow independence to her West African territory. By way of contrast, Liberia is a particularly interesting case because it illustrates very clearly how independence and close ties with the United States have excluded the country from the material advantages of colonial rule. Furthermore, an important factor in the country's political evolution has been the attitude of many of the returned American Liberians: they were often almost as foreign to Africa as were European colonists elsewhere, and they kept apart from the local inhabitants. This division between the settlers and local people came to be expressed politico-geographically, the Liberian government ruling a coastal strip to a depth of about forty miles inland, but being ignored or having little impact in the interior. Since 1954, admittedly, real attempts have been made to involve the indigenous population in the political affairs of the country, and differences between the two groups are decreasing. But the division between the 'country' and the 'province' and its implications 'are indicative of the problems of forging a nation state out of the varied population of Liberia, which has not seen the advantages of enlightened colonialism nor the unifying effect of the nationalist response to European rule' (Blij, 1962: 373).

One final political effect of colonial rule in West Africa has been the evolution of élites in all countries of the region. The concept of an élite is of great importance in West Africa, for it is a familiar one within the context of traditional African life, and élites are now in control of most of the newly independent governments. But there is a significant contrast between the élites of the southern parts of West Africa and those in the north (notably in northern Nigeria, Niger, Mali, Guinea and Senegal), where Islam has profoundly affected the processes of élite formation produced by the social changes of colonial rule. Post (1964: 54), in fact, places all West African states into a spectrum ranging from those countries which the traditional élite remains relatively powerful to those states in which it has failed to play any significant role.

The present pattern of political states in West Africa is solely the creation of European colonial rule. The territorial framework of almost every state dates back only to the 1880's or later, and no modern state is in any way coincident territorially with the limits of any of the earliest indigenous states of West Africa. Within this superimposed state pattern of wholly European origin the intensity of the European cultural and political, as well as economic, impact is evident in very many ways. In particular, the modern political institutions of most West African states are still patently based upon British and French models.

Independent West Africa

Liberia has been independent since 1847, but the modern race to independence in West Africa began with Ghana in 1957 and finished with Gambia in 1965; only Portuguese Guinea remains dependent. All West African countries, however, face contemporary problems – particularly those of an economic and political nature – of great severity and complexity.

Economic Problems

Implicit or explicit in much of the literature on West African affairs today is the view that the resource base of most of the states of the region is inadequate and must always constitute a barrier to substantial economic progress and so to political development and stability. Yet in no other part of the continent is it so misleading as in West Africa to generalize about the natural resource base for economic development. In the first place, West African states cover a wide range of environmental types and can perhaps most usefully be considered in three main groups.

The northern, landlocked nations of Mali, Niger and Upper Volta suffer from being desert and sudanic (savanna) areas, so that their physical resources and agricultural land use are dominated by lack of moisture, and the northern Saharan sections of Mali and Niger are quite undeveloped. In these three northern states, too, physical resources, notably water supply, vegetation and soils, are severely limited in range and variety. Consequently agriculture is similarly restricted except where, as in the inland Niger delta, water control and irrigation works have allowed more sophisticated economic systems to develop. The second group of western, coastal states stretches from Liberia in the south to Senegal in the north, and varies widely from mountainous, wet and heavily forested states like Liberia and Guinea to the largely savanna states of Senegal and Gambia. These western states, however, are like the northern savanna states in that each country is characterized by little diversity in its physical environment. While Senegal and Liberia have sharply contrasting environments, each has little internal variety of natural resources. The third group – the Guinea coastal states – stretches from Ivory Coast to Nigeria and includes the most prosperous states of West Africa. To some extent this relative prosperity appears to be the direct result of the diversity of physical environments and natural resources existing in each country; and this diversity is itself due largely to the way in which these Guinea coastal states cut at right angles across the successive east-west environmental zones referred to earlier.

In considering West African mineral resources the national context is especially important. The significant point about minerals in West Africa is not their geographical distribution over the region as a whole but rather their location and importance in relation to the size, population and existing economy of each state. Thus, whereas phosphate production in Togo is slight by regional and even more by world standards, the importance of phosphates in the economy of Togo is perhaps greater than in any other country in the world. Oil in Nigeria and iron in Guinea are similar instances of the potentially great significance of mineral resources to individual West African states.

In human resources, too, it is impossible to generalize usefully about West African states. A country like Nigeria with a population of some 56 million can hardly be compared in this sense with the 324,000 of Gambia. A number of West African states – Gambia, Portuguese Guinea, Liberia and Togo – have populations of under two million, and many observers suggest that such populations make economic and political viability impossible. Perhaps even more significant, however, is the range of population densities – from about 3 per square km in Niger to over 60 per square km in Nigeria. Quantitatively speaking it is probably true to say that all West African states suffer economically from insufficient populations; and qualitatively, too, all suffer from the general low level of education and from the widespread lack of technical skills.

The financial resources for economic development in West African countries are also very inadequate, whether from domestic savings and investment or from foreign investment. All West African countries continue to depend heavily upon overseas sources for capital, and most of them are still closely tied in this way to their former metropolitan countries. Ivory Coast, for instance, continues to depend very heavily upon French investment and loans.

Realistic examination of the physical, human and financial resource base of any country in West Africa seems, however, to suggest that there are no absolute barriers to economic development; and that all the difficulties revealed by resource analyses can be overcome, if the need to do so is sufficiently urgent. The pattern of agricultural and industrial development in any one West African country is the result of a complex of many historical, political and economic as well as physical and social circumstances rather than a direct causal effect of a given resource base. The Volta, Niger and Konkouré hydro-electric dams; the aluminium industry of Ghana; the building of great new ports like Cotonou and Tema; the construction of new railways such as the Bornu railway of Nigeria; the *Office du Niger* scheme; the Richard Troll scheme in Senegal: these are but a few examples of attempts – which have met with varying degrees of success – to speed the processes of economic development in the various countries of West Africa.

One of the most fundamental economic problems in West Africa today concerns the composition of the export/import trade. This is typical of tropical, developing, former colonial, countries in that exports are dominated by a very few products (primarily agricultural and mineral raw materials) and that imports are dominated by manufactured goods.

Although all West African countries are over-dependent on a few export products, their number and importance varies significantly from country to country. Both Senegal and Gambia, for instance, depend on groundnuts for over 80 per cent by value of their exports, while at the other extreme Nigeria has 60 per cent of the value of her exports accounted for by as many as three items – cocoa, palm-produce and groundnuts – in roughly equal proportions. In one country at least, minerals are the most valuable item of export, Sierra Leone having about 80 per cent of her export earnings provided by mining; and iron in Liberia, bauxite in Guinea, phosphates in Togo and oil in Nigeria are earning increasing proportions of export revenues.

Much has been written on this tendency to depend on a small number of export commodities in West African countries. Some of the difficulties are related to repercussions on the production side of the economy as well as on labour market policy, soil deterioration, crop pests, crop diseases, and dietary levels. But the economic instability resulting from over-dependence on one or two export products, and so on a very narrow range of world market prices, is commonly given the most attention: in the period 1948–1958, for instance, the purchasing power of exports in Ghana fluctuated by about 13 per cent and in Nigeria by over 20 per cent. In some commodities price drops have been particularly striking over the past few years, the average price of Ghanaian cocoa falling by over 32 per cent and of Nigerian palm kernels by 29 per cent in the period 1959–1961. In some cases demand, world prices and production are fairly successfully balanced from year to year, as with the mining of tin in Nigeria, which is regulated by the International Tin Council; and the scope for this kind of organization is great in a situation where substitutes and alternatives in world demand are growing. All substantial fluctuations in world market prices, and so inevitably in the value of exports, not only affect export earnings and balance of payment situations, but also result in changes in the customs duties received by governments. This last point is of particular importance in countries where export/import duties still make up over half the total government revenues (over 60 per cent in both Ghana and Nigeria).

A study of the most recent trends in West African exports reveals an increasing tendency towards the diversification of export commodities. A number of new export crops, such as ginger in Sierra Leone, beniseed in Nigeria, and karite seeds in Upper Volta, are now being rapidly expanded. This trend, however, is perhaps most clearly seen in Ivory Coast where great efforts are being made to lessen the dependence on coffee and cocoa and to reduce imports of such items as sugar, rice and cotton. To this end an intensive programme of cash diversification is being carried out, notably with cotton, rice, sugar, tobacco, rubber, coconuts and jute. In Togo, efforts are being made to increase the value of exports by further processing before export, notably in the case of tapioca manufacture from manioc.

The fact that imports into West Africa are dominated by manufactured products provides a powerful argument for industrialization in the region. Such industrialization has among its major objectives both the earning of more foreign exchange, by increasing the value of raw material exports through further processing, and the saving of foreign currency by substituting domestically produced items for imported manufactured goods. Some success has been achieved in this direction with the rapid increase over the past few years of such import-reducing industries as flour-milling, beer, tile, ceramic and cheap textile industries; meat-canning and fish-canning; and car assembly plants, especially in Nigeria, Ghana and Ivory Coast. On the whole, however, import-replacing industrialization has so far shown little sign of changing the traditional West African pattern of foreign trade by reducing the imports of manufactured items. In Ghana, for instance, exports continue to be dominated by agricultural raw materials and imports by manufactured goods despite such industrialization. What has changed is the ratio of manufactured consumer goods to manufactured capital goods in her imports (Cantor, 1964).

A third and closely related economic problem in West Africa concerns internal and external market opportunities; and there is much to be said for the view that all agricultural and industrial development in West African countries is more seriously limited by lack of market opportunities than by any other single factor. Within all territories – even in Nigeria with some 56 million people – the domestic market is limited by low purchasing power; and in many West African states the population is so small that even if the per capita purchasing power were to rise sharply, the domestic market would still be too small to support industrial production on any economic scale. It is for this last reason, in fact, that the economic viability of many West African states – especially those with under three million people – has been questioned.

Concerning market opportunities between states in the region, it is at first sight rather surprising that the amount of inter-state trade in West Africa is so small, for example about 1 per cent of Nigeria's recorded external trade and just over 4 per cent of Ghana's. West Africa is a veritable patchwork of states, containing between them a population of about 95 million, and it might reasonably be expected that inter-state trade under such circumstances would be more significant than it is. While the published figures are certainly too low, failing to take account of a probably substantial unrecorded movement across frontiers, they do indicate the relatively unimportant role that inter-state trading has in West Africa today.

One of the reasons for this relative lack of inter-state trade is undoubtedly the present pattern of land communications which tends to channel all the trade of a state through its main port. In West Africa generally, the main lines of communication drain towards the coast. The transport system was designed primarily to serve the overseas export/import trade and paid little attention to the domestic, particularly inter-state market potential in the region. East-west communication is especially difficult. Inter-state trade is also discouraged because there is a notable lack of goods suitable for this kind of trading: with broadly similar environmental patterns and colonial economic histories, neighbouring states in West Africa frequently have very similar economies. Finally, the variety of currencies tends to militate against easy trading relations. West African countries fall into two main groups – franc and sterling zones – although Liberia is attached to the United States dollar and Guinea and Mali have their own currencies. This whole problem is made even more difficult because the economies of the states in the franc zone, together with the Portuguese colony, are far more closely integrated with France and Portugal respectively than are the sterling countries with Britain.

As far as overseas markets are concerned, reference has already been made to the way in which all West African economies depend upon only a few raw material exports and so are at the mercy of fluctuations in world prices and demand. As the Geneva Conference on Trade and Development has concluded, countries in areas like West Africa urgently need to find a larger and more secure place in the immensely complicated channels of world trade. Present international trading policies still underpin the old traditional circuit of Western manufactures in return for raw materials. Western tariffs still discriminate against processed goods from West Africa. For West Africa, as for other parts of the continent, 'it should surely not be beyond our wisdom to devise trading policies which have the opposite effect – that of stimulating local advance, stimulating local manufacture, building up export incomes, and in fact avoiding the situation . . . in which every penny of aid that has been given has been nullified by the collapse of raw material prices and by the unbroken increase in the cost of Western manufactures' (Ward, 1964: 43).

Political Problems

The overriding political aim of creating within the separate states of West Africa a real sense of national unity has not so far met with any great success. This is not surprising. The centrifugal forces working within each of the states of the region are complex and formidable. The north-south dichotomy, tribalism, the existing 'Creole' élite groups in the coastal towns, the present pattern of international boundaries, railways and roads: these and other divisive forces produce tensions and polarities which make the creation of genuine national sentiment a most difficult operation. Historically, West African nationalism has always been essentially negative – anti-colonial – and could never be expressed as a desire to win back freedom and independence by former nation states. In large measure it has been left to the European colonial powers to create the basis or framework for true nationalism, even at the tribal level. Although a number of writers use the terms 'nation', 'state' and 'country' interchangeably, it is important to emphasize that a true nation, in the sense of one with a common culture, language and historical experience, is most closely approximated in West Africa by the tribe. Nations as such do not exist in West Africa and must be consciously constructed in the post-independence era (Post, 1964). The need to develop true nationality – a 'nation myth', or a 'state idea' – is indeed one of the most intractable problems in West Africa today.

The difficulties of achieving this are to some extent common to all countries in the region, but each state also has its own special problems. Nigeria's special difficulties arise from her great size and diversity, which until 1966 was expressed politically through tribally dominated regional governments: the Yoruba in the West, the Ibo in the East, and the Hausa in the North. Only in the Mid-West region was there no single dominant tribe, although this fourth region was formed largely as a result of dissatisfaction by the Edo-speaking groups with the Yoruba-dominated Western Region of which the Mid-West was formerly a part. From as far back as 1951 the main support for the major party within each Nigerian region had come from the majority ethnic group of that region, and regional minorities – such as the Tiv of the 'Middle Belt' – had grown increasingly apprehensive about their future in an independent Nigeria. It remains to be seen whether the present (1967) avowedly anti-regional and anti-tribal military régime can impose a sense of nationhood upon the seething undercurrents of tribal antagonism which are so characteristic of this vast and most populous of African countries. The first military government of 1966 tried to foster a sense of national unity by imposing a unitary form of government upon this vast territory. But the most recent military régime has attempted to suppress regional, tribal and party allegiances by following the procedure adopted in Congo Kinshasa: so increasing the number of administrative units that the size and power of each unit is reduced to manageable proportions. In mid-1967 the country was divided into twelve 'states'; and this act helped to precipitate the Biafra secession war which, if successful, could result in the complete disintegration of Nigeria.

Very different special problems of creating national unity are illustrated by Togo. One of the major difficulties there is the small size and population of the country which, according to some writers, has no economic or political viability. The north-south problem is also particularly acute, for, although the territory extends for some 375 miles (600 km) inland from the coast, it is nowhere more than 75 miles (120 km) wide; and communications between the southern and northern areas are confined to the railway, which reaches inland only to Blitta in the relatively empty lands of central Togo, and to the one road which continues into the heavily populated northern districts. A further and commonly cited divisive force in Togo is the fact that the largest ethnic group – the Ewe – extends over the boundary into southeastern Ghana (Fig. 28). This particular problem is examined later in this essay.

A final instance of the special difficulties each country in West Africa has to face in trying to bring about national unity is that of Sierra Leone where one of the main forces working against national unity – the complex of social and political problems created by the presence in the Freetown area of 120,000 Creoles – was largely responsible for the fact that Sierra Leone did not gain its independence until 1961. These Creoles, who are descendants of freed slaves, have a strong Yoruba element and a composite language (*Krio*) of their own. But they now constitute a primarily English-speaking, Christian and relatively well-educated élite. Voting in the 1951 election was largely an expression of reaction against former Creole predominance over the major tribal groups, notably the Mende and Temne; and the successful party – the People's Party – had been founded by a Mende, Sir Milton Margai. Not until 1961 was he able to create a broad coalition government, opposed by only a fairly small radical element in Freetown, which lasted until the military coup of 1967.

Another group of political problems arises from the form of administration in the several territories of West Africa. It has already been noted that

9

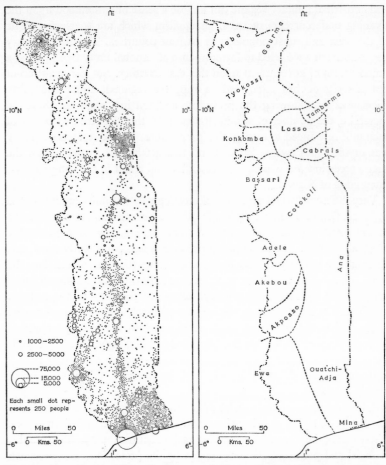

Fig. 28. Population Distribution and Main Tribal Groups in Togo
(1961 Census of Population, Lome; and Carte Ethnographique de l'Afrique
Ouest, Dakar, 1957)

the European powers provided Africans – in different ways and to differing
extents – with training in political life and so left contrasted legacies in
the form and ideals of governmental institutions. There has been much
change and adaptation since independence, but it already seems apparent
that 'Western' democracy, and especially the Westminster model of
parliamentary government, is unlikely to prove adaptable to West Africa.
There has been an increasing emphasis on the one-party system; and this
trend has now been confirmed by the failure of Nigeria to make 'Western'
democratic federalism work.

The emergence of one-party states and the suppression of the parliamentary opposition, which has been so characteristic a feature of West African politics since independence, has been the subject of much discussion. According to one authority, the tendency for the opposition to disappear is due to the absence of social divisions forming a basis for rival parties; to the lack of any real ideological divisions; and to the lack of dispute in the West African context over the ends of good government (Post, 1964: ch. 3). It is also true that the experience of party government in a central assembly chosen by secret ballot and on the basis of complete adult suffrage is still sufficiently novel in West Africa to raise doubts about its relevance to local conditions (Austin, 1963). Yet, although the one-party system need not exclude the essentials of democratic government nor involve the assumption by one man of dictatorial powers, it was in West Africa that the outstanding example of such a development did in fact take place. Until his overthrow in 1966 Nkrumah dominated and controlled not only his own party – the *Convention People's Party* (*CPP*) – but also the whole of Ghana.

A third outstanding political problem is the continued existence in the region of West Africa's last colonial territory: Portuguese Guinea. On most counts this is a country of little importance. It is small, with a heavily indented, mangrove-forested coastal plain, merging inland to tropical rain forest and finally to savanna country in the interior. The capital is the old slave port of Bissau (population 10,000) and the total population of the colony is only 525,000. This is one of Africa's least developed countries, exporting only very small amounts of palm products, rice, groundnuts, hides and skins.

As a small northern outlier of Portuguese territory in southern Africa, however, Portuguese Guinea has great political significance. It represents the last stronghold of colonialism in this most politically aware and diverse region of Africa. Although its European population has never been very great, and today amounts to no more than about 0·1 per cent of the total population of West Africa, Portuguese Guinea is an ever-present reminder of European colonialism in West Africa. Opposition to Portuguese rule here is more considerable and active than in any other of Portugal's African territories. But whether Portugal would be prepared to defend this small isolated West African enclave against internal or external attack remains to be seen. Strategic considerations suggest that she would. Portuguese Guinea clearly has importance as a staging point by sea and air between Portugal and her southern African territories; and as such this small West African colony is seen as essential to the maintenance of Portugal's African empire.

A fourth set of political problems in West Africa concerns the present pattern of state units and boundaries in the region. Greatest attention is normally focused on the fact that most West African boundaries cut through tribal territories. West Africa, indeed, contains what are now regarded as classic examples of this phenomenon. Perhaps the best known case is that of the Ewe, now divided by the Ghana-Togo boundary. Today the Ewe problem is believed by many observers to be the main cause of strained relations between Ghana and Togo. Constant friction arises along the international boundary between them, especially where it passes through Eweland. The frontier interrupts trade, leads to accusations and counter-accusations about the smuggling of arms and subversive elements, and imposes hardship on those communities, some of whose members normally cross the border for seasonal labour or other temporary visits.

The main historical facts about the Ewe problem have been widely discussed and require only the briefest mention here. Living between the Volta and Mono rivers in an area that stretches inland from the coast for over 80 miles (130 km) in places, the Ewe have been divided between the British, Germans and French in varying ways since the end of the nineteenth century. First, as a result of negotiations between the British and German colonial powers, about four-fifths of Eweland was incorporated into German Togo and one-fifth into the British Gold Coast. Secondly, after the conquest of German Togo by British and French forces in 1914, Eweland was redistributed so that some three-fifths was in British territory and two-fifths in French territory. Thirdly, after the 1914–1918 war, yet another adjustment was made, the French area being extended westward to include the entire coastline of former German Togo. As a result of the formal mandate agreements of 1919, Eweland was divided into three political elements: two of them under the British (in the Gold Coast and in British-mandated Togo) and one under the French (in the French-mandated area). After the second world war, the two mandated areas continued to be administered by the British and French respectively as trusteeship territories of the United Nations. Fourthly, and finally, the British trusteeship territory was incorporated into the new independent state of Ghana in 1957, while former French Togo became, in 1960, an independent republic. The Ewe, then, after a most complicated and chequered political history, are today divided between the two independent republics of Ghana and Togo (Hodder, 1967).

Faced with a record of similar, if less kaleidoscopic, political changes elsewhere in West Africa, it is difficult to avoid the conclusion that any solution to the problems they create lies not in the manipulation of the boundary, nor in the annexation of one country by another, but in the development of social and economic, if not political, cooperation between neighbouring states. Between Ghana and Togo the possibilities of some such form of cooperation are obvious: much closer trading links, the joint regulation of tariffs, the reduction of visa and travel requirements, and the improvement of all forms of communication between the two countries. Furthermore, Ghana's Volta Scheme at Akosombo could then develop as the natural power centre for the whole Volta valley, and the abolition of the boundary as a social and economic barrier would re-establish the traditional mobility of labour across it (Austin, 1963).

There does indeed seem to be an urgent need for much closer practical cooperation between states whose boundaries cut through apparently homogeneous tribal lands. To achieve this it may be necessary to question two sets of assumptions: first, those held about the nature of the tribe or ethnic community in terms of its extent, numbers, composition, coherence and sense of unity; and secondly, those held about the significance of such boundaries. It is perhaps too often assumed that effective national unity is the necessary precondition for international cooperation, so that the Ewe problem, for instance, is viewed solely as having a centrifugal influence which works against the growth of national unity and so, inevitably, is a source of contention between Ghana and Togo.

Yet there are a number of cases in West Africa where the geographically arbitrary nature of a political boundary matters little to the people living on either side of it. Certainly this appears true of the Ewe, most of whom seem content to leave the boundary where it is, and have no strong desire for Ewe unity as such. The Ghanaian Ewe think of themselves first as Ghanaian and secondly as Ewe; the Togolese Ewe think of themselves first as Togolese. What these people object to is not that they live in one country rather than another but that they are cut off from their farms, their kinsmen and their sources of seasonal labour every time the boundary is closed by one of the two governments concerned. The need here, as in most parts of Africa, is to concentrate attention, not on the geographical analysis of former colonial or present state boundaries, nor on how to redraw the political boundaries more in accordance with 'geographical realities', but rather to study ways of ensuring that boundaries function solely as the territorial limits of administrations and not as barriers to all movement and contact between states. While the realities of the Ewe and similar problems in West Africa support the argument for leaving the international boundaries as they are, they do at the same time indicate some of the opportunities for creating larger regional groupings for the purposes of social and economic development (Hodder, 1967).

The same conclusion seems to hold in considering the wider issues of arbitrary colonial partitioning in West Africa. The European colonial powers were themselves fully aware of the arbitrary and logically unsatisfactory nature of the pattern of states they had created, and they tried on a number of occasions to amend the political map more in accordance with the realities of natural features, trade, population, administration and communications. But on the whole there has been very little change in the pattern of states since the early years of the twentieth century. In West Africa, at least, 'political units once created tended to defy their creator's attempts to terminate their existence' (Hargreaves, 1963: 17). Gambia was an outstanding example of this. With an area of only about 11,000 km², it extends for just over 180 miles (320 km) along the Gambia river but nowhere reaches the natural margins of the river basin; nor does it reach the river's source, which lies in Guinea. Gambia, in fact, is never wider than 22 miles (34 km). The boundary between Gambia and Senegal cuts across natural features and settlement patterns. It also largely isolates the southern region of Senegal (Casamance) from the rest of the country; and French and British statesmen had in fact long been agreed on the desirability of incorporating Gambia into its French-held hinterland, as well as on the compensation to be received by Britain. Gut Gambia, once created, 'clung to its precarious existence as if it were a living being and not an artificially contrived colony' (Hargreaves, 1963: 367). Local interests – especially European commercial interests and those of the educated Africans – refused to countenance any change. The continued subjection of Gambia and Senegal to quite different colonial systems had created wide divergencies in administrative, cultural and economic patterns between the two countries; and this glaring example of political, economic and social incongruity has now been perpetuated in the contemporary pattern of independent states.

However unsatisfactory on academic or practical grounds the present pattern of states in West Africa may be, there is in the region a general acceptance of these old colonial boundaries as frameworks for the nation states of today. It is generally appreciated that the indigenous, pre-colonial political pattern – a multi-cellular tribal pattern of great complexity and fluidity – could never provide an adequate basis for independence in the modern world. Furthermore, the fact that the colonial governments were only prepared to hand over power on a territorial basis and at differing times, formalized and perpetuated the old, colonial divisions of West Africa. Also, the political élites in all West African countries naturally enough set out to establish their influence within existing territorial areas; their approach was inevitably pragmatic, and they have subsequently found it easier to work within the framework inherited from the colonial powers.

There is indeed much to be said for maintaining the existing pattern of political states in West Africa. The fact that existing boundaries cut across 'geographical regions' or areas with 'similar physical, social or economic conditions' is often interpreted as an obstacle to national development. But, as shown earlier, the colonial practice of setting up territories reaching from the coast into the hinterland gives to the separate states – at least along the Guinea coast – the advantages of environmental diversity. It is significant that those states with the most homogeneous physical environments – Liberia, Sierra Leone, Mali and Niger – seem also to possess the least potential for development.

Regional Groupings and Unity in West Africa

There would seem to be strong, even compelling reasons for some form of regional economic if not political cooperation in West Africa. In no other part of the world, except perhaps Central America, is there such a large number of very small states, many of which have similar economies and appear to lack sufficient economic basis for independent political existence. Furthermore, three of these states – Mali, Upper Volta and Niger – are landlocked and so have to use trade routes through, and port facilities in, one or more of their neighbours. Even coastal states may also depend on ports other than their own: in Guinea, for instance, cattle are exported and consumer goods imported through Sierra Leone's port of Freetown, which serves a large part of Guinea more directly than can her own port of Conakry. In other cases, transit trade is necessary because of inadequate facilities for specialized goods: until the new port of Cotonou was opened in 1964, for example, Dahomey could not handle large imports of oil, which had to be imported through Lagos and brought into Dahomey along the coastal lagoon system of waterways.

The need for inter-state cooperation, however, is more clearly shown in the case of the landlocked territories. Thus the Republic of Niger is closely linked to Dahomey in a number of ways; and as a result of *Opération Hirondelle*, begun in 1953, exports were expected to pass through the similarly French-speaking country of Dahomey to Cotonou rather than go by the shorter route across English-speaking Nigeria to Lagos. Since 1963, however, the tonnage sent to Cotonou by road and rail from Niger has declined, partly because of recent strained relations between the two countries. There is now some use of the long route through Upper Volta (Ouagadougou) and Ivory Coast (Abidjan); but even more important, there has also been a conscious decision on the part of the Niger government to route at least half of its trade through Nigeria. To this end new roads are being constructed in eastern rather than in western Niger. Transit trade from Niger through Nigerian ports did in fact increase from some 44,000 tons in 1964 to over 62,000 tons – mostly groundnut products, ginned cotton, and hides and skins – in 1965 (Harrison Church, 1965). Data of this kind are little more than estimates, and to the figures given above another 25 per cent should perhaps be added for clandestine trade through the Niger centres of Maradi and Zinder to Nigeria. It is also impossible to calculate exactly to what extent this trade is true transit trade or simply inter-state trade. While it is true that the Nigerian (Lagos) route for Niger groundnuts is shorter and better-equipped than the routes through Cotonou or Abidjan, and that overseas marketing facilities through Nigeria are often superior for hides, skins and cotton as well as for groundnuts, it is also true that the huge population of Nigeria provides an attractive market for livestock from the Niger Republic and that imported goods are much cheaper and more varied in Nigeria than in Niger (*ibid*).

Another reason for encouraging some form of cooperation between states in West Africa is to facilitate inter-state trade beyond that demonstrated by the needs of the landlocked states. It has been argued that economic cooperation of this kind in West Africa is undesirable, particularly where it implies the establishing of customs unions; for the simultaneous existence in West Africa of several dovetailing and superimposed customs unions may lead to serious technical complications. Furthermore, the economic value of customs unions that embrace isolated countries remote from their centres of gravity has been legitimately questioned. Yet inter-state trade could conceivably be an important means of widening the domestic market because, with the possible exception of Nigeria, all West African states suffer from the fact that their domestic markets for their products are inadequate. It is true that this question of widening the domestic market in West Africa is not solely a matter of reducing the economic barriers set up by the present patchwork of political units: it is also related to the improvement and extension of transport facilities and to an increase in the size and purchasing power of the local population. Nevertheless, there is little doubt that the present pattern of international boundaries still works against the expansion of local markets, encourages the building of high tariff walls, and in general helps to perpetuate the divisive tendencies in West African economic life.

Other factors suggesting the need for cooperation between West African states can only receive the briefest mention here. Some remarks have already been made about the need to reduce tariff barriers and about the opportunities for cooperation presented by the existence of tribal lands spreading across two or more adjacent political units. In economic development, cooperation is required also to facilitate large-scale planning, to avoid unnecessary duplication in research, and to solve the practical problems of developing the major West African rivers – particularly the Niger – for hydro-electric power, irrigation and navigation. Politically, too, cooperation may be necessary to increase West Africa's potential for effective defence and – both economically and politically – to increase the bargaining power of the region in continental and world affairs.

On the other hand, the difficulties lying in the way of achieving any kind of regional cooperation, either in economic or political matters, are many and formidable. The fundamental dichotomy between north and south, in terms of environment, population, religion and economy; the complicated pattern of tribes and tribal languages; the different colonial associations, reflected in official languages, educational and legal systems, and in administrative frameworks; the different currencies and trading relations; the different levels of wealth and development; and the poor communications between neighbouring states: all these factors combine to hinder cooperation at any level. Then there are the extreme inequalities in size and population among the states of West Africa, which result in the smaller nations fearing domination by the larger. Indeed, there appears to exist no articulate desire for regional cooperation at any level. The concept of West Africa as a distinctive region is at best vague; and the exact form of any federation, confederation or customs union is no more agreed upon than is the method by which might be achieved.

A number of attempts to form regional groupings have, however, taken place within West Africa since the late 1950's. One of the more important of these was the Benin-Sahel Entente, established in 1959, involving loose links between Ivory Coast, Upper Volta, Niger and Dahomey. A solidarity fund for mutual assistance into which each state paid 10 per cent of its revenue was set up; and from this Niger, Dahomey, and Upper Volta each received five-sixteenths annually, while Ivory Coast received only one-sixteenth. There was close coordination of development plans, taxation policies, public administration, labour legislation, public works, transportation and communications. The entente was aimed primarily at economic cooperation between the member states, although it had some political significance as an experiment in parallelism: a counterweight to the richer Ghana that it surrounded and to Nigeria that it partly adjoined (Harrison Church, 1963:97–8).

The economic basis for the entente is sound. As a group of contiguous states it comprises a market of over twelve million people. Its member countries had comparable administrative experience under the French, their constitutions are similar, and they have the same official language and currency. There has for long been considerable movement of peoples and goods between these states – labourers from Upper Volta working on the coffee and cocoa farms of the Ivory Coast, and Niger labourers working in Dahomey – and the Ivory Coast railway and port of Abidjan have long been vital to the overseas trade of Upper Volta, as it is now also to that of Niger. The economic basis of the entente, too, is well diversified, ranging from the coffee, cocoa, bananas, timber and diamonds of Ivory Coast – easily the most prosperous French-speaking state in West Africa – to the oil palm of Dahomey and groundnuts and cattle products of Upper Volta and Niger.

9*

The Benin-Sahel Entente has met a number of difficulties, but the most important is one which has resulted in the failure of other similar attempts in Africa over the past decade: the great differences in wealth and levels of development of the member states. Thus the Ivory Coast, while contributing so much more than any of the other members, receives relatively little and quite understandably has begun to resent what amounts to subsidizing her poorer neighbours. This is not a new development. In the 1950's the Ivory Coast had been most anxious for independence and had opposed federalism between the French-speaking states for essentially the same reason. The Ivory Coast was then providing some 40 per cent of the annual exports and nearly 90 per cent of the dollar earnings of French West Africa, but federal taxes levied from Dakar resulted in price increases of up to one-half in the Ivory Coast.

Among the French-speaking states of West Africa, perhaps the greatest force for regional cooperation has been the adherence of most of these states to the concept of the French Community. In 1958 all the former French states were given the option of autonomy within the French Community or of complete independence. Only Guinea opted for the latter, and joined with Ghana in the Ghana-Guinea Union. The French Community, however, soon changed radically in character and this led to other attempts at cooperation, as with the abortive Mali Federation between Senegal and Mali (then called Soudan), which broke up in 1960.

The Union of African States (*U.A.S.*), established in 1961 and lasting until 1964, was a later development of the Ghana-Guinea Union but included also Mali. Regarded by its member states as a nucleus for a future United States of Africa, it was open to any other state or federation accepting its aims: the pooling of resources, the liquidation of all forms of colonialism, a common planning directive, the harmonizing of foreign policies, a joint defence policy, and the rehabilitation of African culture. This *U.A.S.* was an interesting experiment in that it had to grapple with a number of important problems – partial non-contiguity of the member states, two official languages, three different currencies, varying relations with former colonial rulers, poor communications between states, and widely differing levels of development. On the other hand, the *U.A.S.* embraced a market of over fourteen million people and possessed largely non-competitive exports: Ghana's cocoa, manganese, gold, diamonds and timber; Mali's groundnuts, cotton, rice, cattle and river fish; and Guinea's coffee, bananas, iron, bauxite, alumina and diamonds. While economic cooperation between the three states was less than had been hoped for, politically it was of major importance as a first attempt to bridge the gap between the French-speaking and English-speaking territories of West Africa. (*ibid*: 95–7.)

Another example of attempted economic integration in West Africa is the (French) West African Monetary Union. This currently involves Ivory Coast, Dahomey, Upper Volta, Niger, Senegal and Mauritania. Its currency is the *C.F.A.* franc (*Communauté financière africaine*) which is freely convertible into French francs. Several other examples of economic integration being discussed include the West African Free Trade Area, which would cover Sierra Leone, Guinea, Liberia and Ivory Coast, and the attempt to bring about some form of association between Senegal and Gambia, sometimes referred to as Senegambia.

At the heart of all attempts at establishing regional cooperation or unity in West Africa lies a controversy over the best means to achieve this end: whether first and foremost by political action or by economic integration. The first method was advocated by Nkrumah and assumes that only political union can overcome 'balkanization' and that it must precede other forms of cooperation. The second method rests on the assumption that economic integration is the first necessary step, out of which political union might eventually grow. It is sometimes argued that the first, political, approach is simply the expression of a new African form of colonialism. But it is fair to point out that Ghana has in fact been the pioneer in a number of movements for closer cooperation between states since 1957; and Ghana's willingness to surrender its political sovereignty to a wider grouping of West African states was in fact formally written into the constitution.

Whatever the merits of these two radically opposed approaches to regional unity in West Africa, the difficulty is to find solid links upon which regional cooperation can be based. It is only too easy to state the arguments for cooperation and to detail the difficulties of bringing such cooperation to fruition: the same exercise can be carried out for every part of the African continent today. Perhaps the problem is one of interpretation: the Ewe problem, for instance, can be interpreted as divisive or as a link and basis for cooperation. Perhaps, too, it is false to assume that national unity is the essential prerequisite for effective international cooperation: might it not rather be an obstacle to cooperative endeavour? Throughout West Africa, certainly, there is a need for detailed studies of the practical difficulties and likely advantages involved in schemes of closer association between independent states, and of the different forms such association can take.

References and Select Bibliography

AUSTIN, D. 1957. *West Africa and the Commonwealth*, Penguin, London.
1963. The uncertain frontier: Ghana and Togo. *Journal of Modern African Studies*, Vol. 1: 139–145.

BAUER, P. T. 1954. *West African Trade*, Cambridge University Press.

BOVILL, E. W. 1958. *The Golden Trade of the Moors*, Oxford University Press, London.

CANTOR, D. J. 1964. Effects of import-replacing industrialization on the foreign trade of Ghana. *Nigerian Journal of Economic and Social Studies*, Vol. 6: 231–238.

CROWDER, M. 1962. *Senegal*, Oxford University Press, London.

De BLIJ, H. J. 1962. *Africa South*, Evanston.

FAGE, J. D. 1964. *An Introduction to the History of West Africa*, Cambridge University Press, 3rd ed.
1963. *An Atlas of African History*, London.

HANCOCK, W. K. 1940. *Survey of British Commonwealth Affairs, 1918–1939*, Vol. 2, Part 2, Oxford University Press, London.

HARGREAVES, J. 1963. *Prelude to the Partition of West Africa*, Macmillan, London.

HARRISON-CHURCH, R. J. 1963. *West Africa*, Longmans, London. 3rd ed.
1963. *Environment and Policies in West Africa*, Van Nostrand, Princeton.
1965. The Niger Republic, *Focus*, Vol. 16.

HODGKIN, T. and SCHACHTER, R. 1960. *French-Speaking Africa in Transition*, Praeger, New York.

HODDER, B. W. 1959. The Growth of Trade at Lagos. *Tijdschrift voor Economische en Sociale Geografie*, Vol. 50: 197–202.
1967. The Ewe Problem: A Reassessment, in C. A. Fisher (ed.) 1967. *Essays in Political Geography*, London.

HODDER, B. W. and C. W. NEWBURY. 1961. Some geographical changes along the slave-coast of West Africa. *Tijdschrift voor Economische en Sociale Geografie*, Vol. 52: 77–84.

JONES, G. I. 1963. *Trading States of the Oil Rivers*, Oxford University Press, London.

LANGHANS, P. 1910. Die Deutsche Togoküste 1885 und 1910. *Petermanns Geographische Mitteilungen*, Vol. 56.

MORGAN, W. B. and R. MOSS. 1965. Savanna and forest in Western Nigeria. *Africa*, Vol. 35: 286–294.

MORGAN, W. B. and PUGH, J. C. 1967. *West Africa*, Methuen, London.

OLIVER, R. and FAGE, J. D. 1962. *A Short History of Africa*, Penguin, London.

POST, K. W. J. 1964, *The New States of West Africa*, Penguin, London.

POUQUET, J. 1954. *L'Afrique Occidentale Française*, Hachette, Paris.

PRESCOTT, J. R. V. 1958. Nigeria's regional boundary problems. *Geographical Review*, Vol. 48: 485–504.

ROBINSON, K. 1955. Political development in French West Africa. In Stillman, C. W. (ed.). 1955. *Africa in the Modern World*, Chicago.

THOMPSON, V. and R. ADLOFF. 1958. *French West Africa*, Constable, London.

UNITED NATIONS. 1964. *Conference on Trade and Development*, Geneva.

WARD, B. 1964. *Towards a World of Plenty*, Toronto.

West Africa, London.

WHEARE, K. 1949. *The Nigerian Legislative Council*, Oxford University Press, London.

ZARTMAN, W. I. 1965. The politics of boundaries in North and West Africa. *Journal of Modern African Studies*, Vol. 3: 155–163.

5 Equatorial Africa

5 Equatorial Africa

By B. W. HODDER

Introduction

Many of the contemporary problems of Equatorial Africa stem from one simple positional fact – that the land boundaries of the area touch upon all the other major divisions of the continent. Equatorial Africa cuts a broad swathe down the centre of the continent, reaching from the depths of the Sahara in the north down to the upland plateau of Southern Africa. Eastward it abuts on to the edge of the East African highlands, while to the west it borders the Cameroon Mountains and the lands of the Niger. Far to the north and northeast the problems of Equatorial Africa are akin to those of North Africa and the Sudan; to the east and south they resemble those of East and Southern Africa respectively; while the northwestern fringes have problems similar in many ways to those of West Africa. Most of the centrifugal forces at work within Equatorial Africa originate outside its borders and are thus rather different, both in degree and in kind, from those operating in other major areas of the continent.

Indeed, there might appear to be little justification for grouping together the countries of Equatorial Africa. In a sense the area is little more than a collection of the peripheries of neighbouring regions and it has perhaps least claim to any kind of homogeneity. Yet it is convenient to treat its constituent countries together, not least because they include the former territories of the Belgian Congo and French Equatorial Africa and so make it possible to draw comparisons between Belgian and French colonial policies and to indicate how they have affected social, economic and political life in the various states since independence.

The Physical Setting

Equatorial Africa embraces perhaps a wider range of physical environments than is to be found within any of the other major divisions of the continent (Fig. 29). Stretching almost from the Tropic of Cancer to 13°S, and from the Atlantic to the East African highlands, Equatorial Africa is a patchwork of contrasting environments, ranging from desert to tropical rain forest, and from swampy lowlands to upland plateaus and high mountain peaks.

Structurally the most important feature of the region is the Congo basin:

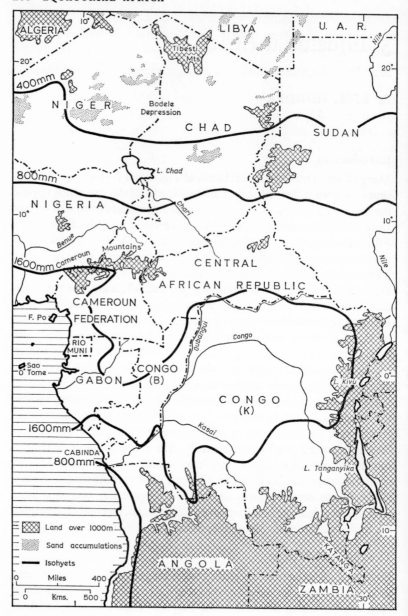

Fig. 29. Equatorial Africa. The isohyets indicate mean annual rainfall.

a shallow alluvial depression, rising gradually from about 1000 ft (305 m) in its centre to rather over 3000 ft (915 m) on much of the surrounding plateau rim. In the centre of this vast basin there are extensive level tracts, intersected by ill-defined drainage channels, sluggish streams, scattered lakes and swamplands, yet it also contains one of Africa's greatest rivers – the Congo – which curves across it for some 3000 miles (4830 km).

The surface deposits in the centre of the basin are largely Quaternary alluvials, and towards the edges Tertiary and Secondary sedimentaries appear. But much of the upland rim itself consists of continuous outcrops of ancient Basement Complex rocks, some of which, notably in the south-east, are highly mineralized. Volcanic rocks are significant in two main areas: one related to the São Tomé–Cameroon fault line, the other associated with the Kivu outpourings on the western edge of the East African plateau. The soils of the Congo, most of which are of ferralitic type, are by no means so uniformly poor as is often suggested. Work in the former Belgian Congo, especially, has shown how strikingly soil type and fertility can vary over only very short distances.

Lying athwart the equator, the Congo basin has a characteristically equatorial climatic régime but much of it is somewhat sheltered by its surrounding rim and so has a rather lower rainfall than does the Atlantic coast. The average annual rainfall in the basin itself is rather over 60 in (1500 mm) and is fairly well distributed throughout the year, although the occurrence of double maxima and minima frequently results in perceptible if brief dry seasons. During these latter periods diurnal ranges of temperature increase sharply and there may even be occasional spells of exceptionally low relative humidities, when fog, mist and haze obscure the view for days at a time. Under the prevailing equatorial climate the natural vegetation – now largely degraded – is a luxuriant layered tropical rain forest, with a continuous canopy and a rich variety of lianas and epiphytes, which extends as 'gallery forest' along the stream courses penetrating into the grassland savanna country of the upland rim.

To the north the Congo basin merges almost imperceptibly into the Chad basin. While of similar structure to its southern neighbour, the Chad basin has far fewer natural advantages. Here is no extensive outcropping of ancient, highly mineralized rocks around the periphery; and no major system of perennial waterways passes through it. In fact it forms one of the great internal drainage basins of the African continent and over much of it rainfall is low, seasonal and very unreliable. The vegetation is savanna grassland, merging northwards into scrub and finally the barren desert country of the Sahara.

No homogeneity of physical environment or resources can be distinguished within Equatorial Africa; nor does any one of its states have a distinct physical basis for its identity. But from an economic point of view two features stand out: the existence of minerals in the ancient fringing uplands of the south, notably in Katanga; and the utilization of the Congo river system for transport and hydro-electric power. The fairly even régime of the Congo and its major tributaries, notably the Kasai and Oubangui, reflects the fact that large areas of the Congo basin have a relatively high and regular rainfall. But the existence of falls and gorges along the rivers' courses severely limits their use for transport in places, although it greatly increases their value for hydro-electric development. This is particularly true where the Congo gathers its tributaries together and breaks out through the western rim of uplands to reach the Atlantic Ocean in a series of impressive but unnavigable gorges and rapids which have perhaps the greatest hydro-electric potential in Africa.

Early European Contacts

At the time of European penetration, Equatorial Africa was the least-known part of the continent, but it is not true that it remained wholly isolated from the outside world until the Portuguese coastal contacts of the late fifteenth century. The northern parts of Equatorial Africa – at least in the savanna lands lying between the deserts of the north and the Congo forests of the south – shared in the ancient caravan-trade that linked the Mediterranean with the savanna or sudanic states stretching across the continent in a belt from the Atlantic coast of West Africa to the Upper Nile valley. To the east of Lake Chad these early states flourished for a time, but they never made trading contacts through the forest barrier to the south similar to those established by the savanna states of West Africa. For here in northern Equatorial Africa there was no promise of trading contacts with Europeans southwards. Wadai, perhaps the most famous of the ancient savanna states of Equatorial Africa, had external relations across the desert to the north and along the sudanic belt itself: westwards to the powerful states of West Africa and eastward to the kingdoms of Darfur, Kordofan and Upper Nile (Fig. 30). This sudanic belt – the 'Broadway' or 'Bush Lane' of Africa – formed in fact the major avenue of mobility across the continent from west to east. But to the south of Wadai the forest remained a barrier to movement.

In the southern forest lands of Equatorial Africa the first outside contacts with Europeans were coastal in origin. Diego Cão discovered the mouth of the Congo (Zaïre) river in 1482, and so put the Portuguese immediately in contact with one of the great indigenous African states – that of the Bakongo – whose capital was at the site of the modern São Salvador do Congo in Angola. This state of Bakongo was then of fairly recent origin, having been in existence for less than one hundred years. By the late fifteenth century, however, it was already clearly defined territorially, being bounded in the west by the sea, in the north by the Congo river, in the east

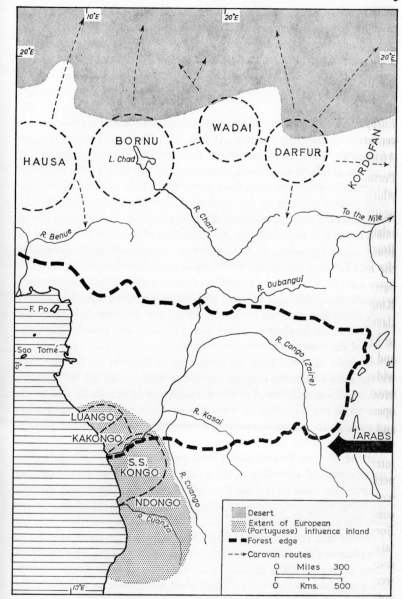

Fig. 30. Early States and Portuguese Contacts in Equatorial Africa (after Fage, 1963). The sudanic states are shown diagrammatically.

by the Cuango, and in the south by the Cuanza river. Across the Congo to the north lay the outlying areas of Luango, Kakongo and Ngoyo, while to the south and southeast lay Ndongo and Matamba. The Bakongo were great hunters and warriors; they knew how to make iron weapons and tools; they were skilled in pottery and weaving; they kept livestock and cultivated millets and sorghums; and they used cowries and cloth for money. Although they were illiterate, their economic, social and political organization was efficient enough to give them control over some two million Africans.

Until 1575, Portuguese efforts in the Congo were largely confined within the limits of Bakongo country. At first, too, Portuguese and Capuchin missionaries were more important than traders as representatives of European civilization in the Congo. But, by the end of the sixteenth century, European interests throughout the whole of western tropical Africa were beginning to be dominated by slaving. Certainly for the Portuguese, the chief attraction of the Congo coast lay in the cheap labour which it was able to provide for the plantations of the New World; and for nearly three centuries, in fact, the west coast slave trade dominated relations between Europeans and Congolese. As the demand for slaves in Brazil increased, so native slave traders extended their activities deeper into the hinterland, although Ndongo and Ngola remained the chief supply bases. According to some estimates, during the seventeenth century the Kingdom of Congo alone provided some 15,000 slaves a year for European slavers at the coast; and altogether over thirteen million slaves are believed to have been imported from the Congo region between the late sixteenth and the early nineteenth century. Slaving on such a scale led not only to a widespread fear and hatred of the Portuguese, but eventually also to the break-up of the Kingdom of Bakongo; for European agents and traders operating in the Congo hinterland commonly undermined the prestige and authority of the Bakongo king by encouraging his subjects to revolt.

Yet the effective limit of direct Portuguese penetration into the Congo interior remained the valley of the Cuango river. Beyond this immediate perimeter there was no real motive for Europeans to move inland, for they were being adequately provided with slaves by African middlemen at the coast. Up to as late as 1877 the only substantial direct contacts between Europeans and the peoples of Equatorial Africa were those which had taken place at the coast or around the mouth of the Congo. There were, of course, indirect trading contacts with the interior; but direct contacts were negligible, and even the Congo river was known to Europeans for only about 100 miles (160 km) upstream.

In West Africa the main motives for direct European penetration in the latter half of the nineteenth century were to protect trade and to prevent competing European powers from laying claim to the hinterlands of their coastal footholds. These motives were not entirely absent in Equatorial

Africa. But an additional and perhaps even more important factor here lay in the work of two men – Livingstone and Stanley. It was Livingstone's explorations in the east of the Congo basin, and Stanley's first epic journey across Africa from Zanzibar to the mouth of the Congo in 1874, that really opened up the Congo to European influence; an influence which, it was hoped, would 'open a path for commerce and Christianity and . . . destroy the evils of African tribal society and the Arab slave trade' (Slade, 1962: 20). The Arabs had in fact first crossed to the western shore of Lake Tanganyika in about 1840 and in the next forty years they extended their authority over the whole country up to the Lomami River.

In 1879 Stanley took service under King Leopold II of Belgium who was soon persuaded of the Congo's potentialities and founded the commercial and exploratory *Association Internationale du Congo*. Until 1884 Stanley was engaged in trying to establish a practicable land and water system of transport from the mouth of the Congo to what was soon to become the town of Stanleyville, over 1000 miles (1610 km) upstream. By this means Leopold prepared the way for international recognition of his rule over the whole Congo area and persuaded most European powers that it would be better to leave the Congo basin as a free-trade area under his 'international régime' than to let it fall into the hands of any one nation. The Congo Independent State was finally recognized by America, France, Britain and Germany at the Berlin Conference of 1884; and limitations were placed on the level of import duties that might be levied on goods entering the Congo Free Trade Area, which stretched from coast to coast, took in the greater part of central Africa, and so was considerably more extensive than the Congo State itself.

While Leopold was preoccupied with his Congo lands in the late 1870's and early 1880's, France was becoming increasingly interested in those areas lying immediately to the north of the Congo river. French interest here had begun earlier in the century in 1839 when Bouët-Guillaume obtained the right of residence at two small places on the left bank of the Gabon estuary; and in 1843 similar rights were obtained on the other bank. During the next few years arrangements of this kind were made up and down the coast, and in 1849 the French followed the British example at Freetown in Sierra Leone by settling a number of freed slaves at a place to which they gave the name Libreville. Yet it was not for some years that the French made any attempt to spread inland from the coast. In 1875, however, De Brazza travelled up the Ogooué river and then moved southward to plant the French flag on the bank of the Congo opposite the site of Leopoldville. In the course of a second expedition in 1880, De Brazza founded Brazzaville and from there made a number of treaties which placed under French protection large areas immediately to the north of the

Congo river. At about the same time, Germany was laying claim to the coast and immediate hinterland of the country around the 'hinge of Africa' in what was to become known as German Kamerun.

By the 1880's, then, Germany, France and King Leopold II of the Belgians had laid claim to most of Equatorial Africa and for some time they continued to dominate the history of this part of the continent. The Portuguese and Spanish were now confined to small offshore islands and tiny mainland enclaves. Long excluded from Africa by treaty and by her own preoccupations in the Americas, Spain had obtained Fernando Po and Annobón in 1778, when the Portuguese ceded the islands for use in the slave trade. In 1879 Fernando Po had become a Cuban penal settlement, and Rio Muni, which had become Spanish in 1610, owed its survival as a Spanish colony largely to the fact that it was wedged between German and French spheres of influence.

By the close of the Berlin Conference in 1885, Equatorial Africa had been carved up into European colonies, although vast stretches had yet to be explored and boundaries drawn beyond the often very narrow coastal settlements; this was particularly true of the French lands of Equatorial Africa and of German Kamerun. Leopold, with his early attempts to explore and provide communications within his territory, was already in a position to claim the bulk of the Congo basin and much of its immediate periphery, even though he possessed only a narrow coastal outlet at the mouth of the Congo. His was a large and diverse colony, but even more varied was the territory claimed by the French. Stretching northward from the Congo river, the French-controlled lands reached through the Gabon rain forests into the northern savannas, eventually penetrating deep into the Sahara desert beyond the Bodele depression and the Tibesti mountains. Between 1886 and 1891 the French secured most of Gabon and Middle Congo (now Congo Brazzaville) and then proceeded to expand east and northeast through the country lying between the Chari and Oubangui rivers towards the Nile, and north towards French North Africa. De Brazza became the first governor of French Equatorial Africa in 1886, although at that early date the northern territories had not yet been secured, and indeed the final conquest of the French Congo was to take a further twenty years. It had originally been the hope of the French to carve out an empire for themselves which would join French Somaliland on the Red Sea with a huge tract of Central Africa reaching westward to Senegal and southward to the Congo river; but this project was frustrated by the encounter between Kitchener and Marchand at Fashoda in 1889. The French, however, did complete their conquest of the countries to the south of Fashoda and joined French West Africa to French Equatorial Africa by way of Lake Chad, thereby creating a continuous French area from the Mediterranean to the Congo. The Chari-Chad district was now seen to be of vital importance, for it was in this critical area where their different territories converged that the conflicting aims of the colonial powers were brought into sharpest focus. The Islamized country of Chad, however, presented the French with many difficulties, and the territory was not transferred from military to civil administration until 1920. After several experiments, the whole French Congo was divided into four colonies, joined together in the federation of French Equatorial Africa – *L'Afrique Equatoriale Française* (*A.E.F.*) – whose headquarters was set up at Brazzaville in the extreme south.

In German Kamerun the southern boundary of the colony was fixed against Rio Muni and French Congo as early as 1884, but the northwestern and eastern boundaries could not be defined until after the German advance inland, which took place towards the upper Benue and northwest and east from Douala. The northwestern boundary with British Nigeria was defined in 1893, and the eastern boundary with French Congo in 1894. Another major change occurred in 1911–1912 when the area of German Kamerun was extended east and south, leaving Rio Muni as an enclave within the German territory and giving Kamerun access to the Oubangui and Congo rivers through a narrow southern corridor. The latter was ceded by France to Germany in exchange for agreeing to a French protectorate over Morocco, even though the new Kamerun corridor cut French territory in Equatorial Africa in two.

However, after the capitulation in 1914 of the German troops in Kamerun to French and British forces, the boundaries of Kamerun were restored to their pre-1912 position, and the whole territory was divided between the French and British in such a way that the French secured the larger, eastern part and the British received two elongated sections adjacent to their own territory in Nigeria. Under the mandate system, and later under the trusteeship system, the Cameroons were now administered in three different units, two of which were British and one French.

Colonial Rule

Belgian Colonial Policy

It is perhaps more true of Congo Kinshasa (formerly Congo Leopoldville) than of any other African country that there can be no real understanding of its contemporary social, economic, and political life without some appreciation of its colonial history; and it is now almost a truism that many of its present problems have their origin in the Belgian colonial period.

The Belgian Congo was unique in the history of African colonization in that it began, and continued until 1908, not as a government colony, but as the personal possession of King Leopold II. It was owned and directed by him from Brussels. On his second journey in 1879 Stanley had been instructed to set up 'a republican confederation of free Negroes ... not a Belgian Colony, but a powerful Negro state' (Slade, 1962: 20). With the international recognition of the Congo Independent State in 1884, Leopold became owner of all 'vacant' or 'unoccupied' lands, which were then parcelled out into concessions. Both here and farther north, the concession system in some form or another seemed necessary if export commodities were to be produced in such a sparsely populated equatorial country.

The years of Leopold's Congo Independent State (1884–1908) were years of considerable achievement when the upper Congo was explored, Christian missions multiplied, attempts were made to establish the Congo State on the Upper Nile, and a vigorous campaign was waged from 1892 to 1895 against the Arab slave trade. During these years, too, European administration began to penetrate to distant parts of the country, even to Katanga in the extreme southeast. In the Katanga, transport links and at least a skeletal administration had to be set up in order to claim 'effective occupation', to reserve the mineral wealth for future exploitation, and to keep out Rhodes and the British South African Company.

Leopold was eventually defeated by the difficulties and expense of running this private estate: a territory of over 900,000 square miles (2,340,000 km²), or more than seventy times the size of Belgium. Although he spent his own considerable private fortune on the Free State, it was not nearly sufficient even to deal with the one crucial problem of transport. Leopold was fully aware of the need for transport in his state: he it is who is credited with the now famous dictum 'coloniser c'est transporter'. A good deal had already been achieved by Stanley in integrating land and water transport before 1884; and here, as in much of Africa, an important stimulus to railway construction was the Berlin Conference decision that a title to territory could be sustained only by effective occupation. But the continual loading and reloading involved in the Congo's river-rail transport system proved to be uneconomic. Improvements were urgently needed, and as King Leopold could not provide the necessary capital himself, he compelled his concessionaires to fulfil specific annual production quotas. As a result, labourers were mishandled, 'conscript law' allowing chain-gang flogging was introduced, and an 'ill-controlled and barbarous native soldiery' was employed 'to levy arbitrary amounts of tribute on rubber and ivory for the benefit of the state and the concessionaire companies in which it held interests' (Oliver and Fage, 1962: 199).

Not only did these measures fail in an economic sense, but when news of the alleged atrocities leaked out, international opinion, culminating in the British-organized Congo Reform Campaign, forced Leopold to give up his private empire and hand it over to the Belgian Government. This he did in 1908. The Congo was not the only part of Africa where European government abused its power, but in the Congo the scale of the abuse was exceptional (Slade, 1962). After 1908 colonial rule in the Belgian Congo, while certainly very much less repressive than during the Leopold period, continued to be highly centralized and directed from Europe. All orders came from the *Ministère des Colonies* in Brussels, so that Belgians on the spot, even in areas of European settlement, had little or no influence on colonial policy. During the Belgian colonial period, however, a number of important changes in social and economic life took place.

In the first place, the Belgians carried out a rapid development of their colony's mineral resources. In 1891 copper had been discovered in the Katanga, associated with the Palaeozoic dolomitic rocks of the Kambove series; and in 1900 Tanganyika Concessions had obtained a grant of prospecting rights in Sud-Katanga. The major operating company – *the Union Minière du Haut Katanga* – was formed in 1906 to exploit an area of 20,000 square kilometres and to hold rights until 1990. Production of copper began in 1911, 2,500 tons being produced in 1912. Tin, manganese, zinc, cadmium, uranium, radium and coal were also mined and, together with copper, were eventually to provide two-thirds of the value of the colony's exports. In 1928 *La Société Internationale Forestière et Minière du Congo (Forminière)* was given similar exclusive rights to parts of Kasai and certain other areas. For many years, in fact, mineral development, notably in the Katanga – an undulating plateau lying at about 3500 ft (1100 m) in the extreme southeast of the country – remained the chief objective of Belgian economic policy.

Throughout the colonial period the mining industry in the Congo enjoyed a rapid rise in prosperity. During and after the second world war there was a boom in mineral production when the loss to the Western allies of Southeast Asian sources of copper and tin gave a great impetus to local mineral development and imparted considerable economic and strategic significance to the colony as a whole. By 1953 the value of Congo's mineral exports had increased fourteen-fold over the figure for 1939.

Mineral development in the Belgian Congo, confined as it very largely was to the southeastern plateau fringe of the country, depended to a very great extent upon the availability of adequate transport facilities; and indeed minerals largely determined the direction taken by railways in the Congo. By 1928 the Bukama–Port Francqui rail link had been completed and large areas of the Lomami, Sankuru and Kasai country opened up. This railway – the *Chemin de fer du Bas-Congo au Katanga (B.C.K.)* – enabled a rail and river route between the Lower Congo, Leopoldville and Katanga to be established which connected Katanga with the rest of the Congo. Hitherto Katanga's only link with the outside world had been via the Rhodesia railways and Beira. In all, some 1530 miles (2450 km) of new railways were built between 1920 and 1932. They were the 'great harbingers of change' in the Congo (Nicolai and Jacques, 1954: 29).

Mining in the Congo also had important effects on other aspects of Congolese life, for mining in the southeast supplied the major avenue for the investment of Belgian capital in the country. Although it was located on the margin of the colony, Katanga received the greater part of Belgian capital and enterprise and represented in industry and commerce the 'centre of gravity' of the country. Smelting furnaces were set up at Elisabethville and Jadotville and copper was subsequently exported as crude copper rather than as ore. Coal for these smelters was being produced in the Congo by 1925, and hydro-electric power was made available from the Cornet falls on the upper Lufira river.

Mining also influenced labour policy. In the Belgian Katanga – and in strong contrast to what was happening in the Rhodesian and South African mining areas – the mining companies after 1925 pursued a policy of labour stabilization, encouraging all employees to bring their families and settle down in the mining settlements (cités des travailleurs) as a permanently urbanized class. An essential element of this policy was the renewable three-year contract. Rejecting as far as possible a policy of seasonal or semi-permanent migratory wage-labour, the Belgians aimed at creating settled populations of whole-time industrial workers. To this end they laid great emphasis on African advance in the field of technology so that every form of skilled work was open to Africans. There was no industrial colour bar, and the African became increasingly absorbed into the industrial life of the country. Furthermore, the Belgian mining companies provided attractive living conditions, especially in the copper belt, where planned settlements with good water supply, sanitation, schools, hospitals and trading centres were laid out. Their labour system was also designed to regulate the flow of labour from rural to mining and urban centres, with the double object of avoiding excessive depletion of manpower in the rural areas and of creating a permanent skilled labour force in the industrial centres. The example of Union Minière in Katanga was followed by Forminière, the Kilo-Moto mines, and by the Huileries du Congo Belge. For a number of years the Belgians recorded the number of Congolese living outside their customary tribal lands, and these figures provide a useful indicator of the extent of migration – much of it to the industrial towns – within the Congo: 6 per cent in 1935, 9·8 per cent in 1945, and 23 per cent in 1957 were classified as non-coutoumière (Smith and Blacker, 1963).

Secondly, the Belgians had an equally dramatic impact on agricultural life and development in the Congo. The discredited concessionary system established by Leopold was not entirely abolished – the need to produce agricultural commodities for export and the problem of labour shortage still existed – and the 'conscript law' was not immediately terminated; but the Belgians removed the worst excesses of the system. There was no alienation of the African's land as such: concessions referred exclusively to 'vacant' land and were made subject to the reserved rights of the Congolese. Furthermore, the worst abuses of the Free State had always been associated with the collection of wild rubber, which at one time had represented 80 per cent by value of the Congo's exports; but during the second decade of the present century wild rubber production declined drastically as a result of competition from plantation rubber. European-owned rubber plantations were established on a small scale in the Congo; coffee production, too, was developed by European farmers; and African-grown cotton was sold and processed largely through European companies. But it was above all to the oil palm that the Belgians turned when plantation rubber from the Far East began to supplant local wild rubber which had hitherto been the mainstay of the Congolese economy. The indigenous oil palm proved to be of poor quality, and in 1911–1912 the Belgian Government accepted a British offer to assist in the organization of the oil palm industry in their colony. British Leverhulme interests were represented by the *Huileries du Congo Belge*, and other concessions were later granted to plantation or oil-processing companies.

Much has been written on peasant farming in the Congo, and in particular on the *paysannat indigène* programme, which was launched by the Belgians in 1942 with the dual aim of developing a settled and prosperous peasantry and of checking the drift to the towns. Realizing the great significance of soil fertility to peasant agriculture, the Belgians undertook a systematic and intensive programme of soil mapping. By independence, some 15 million acres (about 6 million hectares) had been surveyed; approximately 200,000 tracts of land, covering over 3·5 million acres (1·4 million hectares) had been divided into plots; and over 200,000 farmers with their families (about 8 per cent of the total rural population) had been settled under the *paysannat* scheme, while many others had independently made the transition from subsistence to peasant cash farming. Most *paysannats* were given advice about the crops and farming techniques best suited to their particular locality, they were provided with social services, and marketing facilities were guaranteed (Staner, 1955).

Thirdly, together with these major developments in mining and agriculture went two changes of considerable political significance. During the Belgian colonial period there was a marked increase in the number of Europeans – from about 3000 (of whom 1700 were Belgians) in 1908 to over 75,000 in 1952 – although only about 10 per cent of the total European population could be regarded as permanently settled in the country. This fact is important because it helped the Belgians to resist the creation of political institutions involving the granting of the franchise either to Europeans or to Africans. The other change was a great increase in the urban population: from 8.3 per cent in 1938 to 15 per cent in 1946, and to over 21 per cent by independence in 1960.

In assessing the colonial period in the Congo it is important not to underrate the Belgian achievement. The economic advance they brought about in their colony was impressive. Vast mineral and agricultural enterprises such as *Union Minière, Forminière* (Kasai), *Forescom* and *Huilever* created large communities within the exchange or cash economy. By 1960 the Belgian Congo had one of the highest per capita incomes in Africa, Africans living standards were high, the country had the best literacy rate in the continent, and primary education was both extensive and efficient. Medical services were excellent and African housing probably the best in tropical Africa. One of the central aims of Belgian colonial policy was in fact the social and economic betterment of the African.

It is true that the Belgian colonial system was essentially exploitative: in 1930, for instance, 30–40 per cent of the nominal value of the exports from the colony were absorbed in Belgium; and in 1928, when a ton of copper from Katanga sold for 1080 fr. on export, only 640 fr. remained in the Congo. It is also true that the Belgian colonial system was rigidly paternalistic and made no provision for African development beyond the lowest levels of responsibility. There was little secondary education and no university until Louvanium was opened at Leopoldville in 1955. Furthermore, it was not Belgian policy to encourage promising young Congolese to go to Belgium for higher education. In 1955 there were no Congolese graduates outside the Church; and at independence there were only thirteen African graduates in the country. Nevertheless, economically and socially the Belgians achieved a great deal in the Congo.

Politically, however, Belgian policy was wholly negative. No political rights of any kind were allowed either to African or to European until 1958, the Governor-General having previously reported direct to Brussels. This is not to say that there was no process of élite-formation or indigenous political activity: at an early period the pressures of the European impact gave rise to messianic movements; and at a later period economic growth, urbanization and primary education gave rise to a self-conscious élite, and to *évolué*-led political movements in the late 1950's (Anstey, 1966: 263). But it needs to be emphasized that one of the tenets of Belgian policy was that political advancement should not be promoted actively: it should be allowed to develop simply as a by-product of social and economic progress. By first promoting social and economic betterment, it was argued, 'we are forging the weapons with which the natives will conquer their political freedom, if we do not have the wisdom to grant it gracefully when the time is ripe' (Ryckmans, 1955: 77). During 1955, in fact, the Belgians were examining the feasibility of a thirty-year time limit for independence in the Congo. Yet while philosophically their policy may have had much to commend it, it was clearly unrealistic and in particular it was out of touch with the speed of political change in Africa during the 1950's. The Belgian colonial policy was conceived and operated on far too long a time-scale and remained essentially theoretical rather than urgent and pragmatic.

French Colonial Policy

The French form of colonialism in Equatorial Africa differed in a number of ways from the colonial policy of the Belgians. In social and political matters the French system was less paternalistic and more realistic. French educational policy eschewed any attempt at universal primary education but laid some emphasis on secondary and higher education for the chosen élite. Africans were allowed to gather political experience in their own electoral colleges, which, while they may have emphasized the inequality of status between Africans and Europeans and so to some extent have exacerbated racial rivalries, did at least enable the African to express himself politically.

In the economic development of their territories in Equatorial Africa, however, the French adopted policies which resulted in substantially less progress than occurred in the Belgian colony. Like Leopold, 'the French first sought to develop their equatorial territories by means of concessions which gave to the grantees monopolistic control over forest produce with a guarantee of an ultimate freehold over selected areas of land' (Hailey, 1957: 743). The first rush of concessions in 1899 involved about two-thirds of the whole of French Congo and thus seriously affected the use by Africans of their own land. But with the French, as with the Belgians, public feeling in Europe led to a drastic revision of the concession system. Long negotiations ended in the abandonment by some companies of their concessions in return for compensation in various forms, including the granting of freehold rights over considerable areas of the country. In 1951, however, there were still some 330,000 acres (134,880 hectares) covered by concessions.

The French also established European-owned plantations, especially for oil palm and rubber, although on a much smaller scale than in the Belgian Congo. The French *paysannat* schemes, too, were very similar to those of the Belgian Congo, and were equally well adapted to local conditions, no single formula being accepted. The technical and financial resources devoted to the French *paysannats* were, however, much less than those provided in the Belgian Congo.

As for mineral and industrial development, French Equatorial Africa never yielded any economic catalyst such as the Katanga–Kasai area provided for the Belgian territory. Not that there were no minerals. Gold, industrial diamonds, lead, zinc, copper and manganese: all were known to exist, and some were exploited. But preliminary survey work was sketchy and production remained at a low level; little capital was forthcoming; and no integrated system of transport and communications was developed. At independence the only railway lines were very short sections running inland from the coast, the most important being the 300-mile (480 km) Congo–Ocean railway from Pointe Noire to Brazzaville, completed as early as 1934.

In sum, the economic development of French Equatorial Africa was never remarkable and remained very much less impressive than that of the Belgian Congo. Furthermore, the French achieved relatively little in the way of social improvement. Unlike the Belgians, the French both encouraged and depended upon seasonal or temporary migrations for many of their agricultural, mineral and industrial enterprises. While from an economic and social point of view the Belgian Congo was by the 1950's one of the most advanced countries in Africa, French Equatorial Africa remained one of the most backward parts of the continent. The reasons for this very striking difference lay very little, if at all, in the natural and human resource base of the two areas. Partly it was accounted for by the contrasted policies of the European powers. But more important was the fact that, while the Belgian Congo was Belgium's only overseas responsibility, Equatorial Africa was just one – and perhaps the least prized – of France's overseas possessions: compared with her territories in North and West Africa, for instance, France paid Equatorial Africa scant attention. Physical and social surveys, capital investment, agricultural, mining and industrial development were all pursued with greater enthusiasm and energy in those parts of the French empire – elsewhere in Africa and in Southeast Asia – which ranked higher in the French colonial hierarchy. Politically, however, French Equatorial Africa was far more ready for independence in 1960 than was the Belgian Congo. In spite of their generally low economic and social standards, the new countries that emerged from French Equatorial Africa did have the great advantage of possessing an élite of highly educated Africans who had already acquired some political experience.

The Population Problem

The outstanding demographic fact about Equatorial Africa is the low average density of population. This part of Africa, indeed, is often cited as a classic example of a large region whose human resources are insufficient for successful social and economic development; and this same fact has a number of important political implications.

The essential facts about the numbers and geographical distribution of population in the region are summarized in Table 1.1. In Congo Kinshasa the average density is 17 per square mile (7 per km²), the highest densities occurring in the eastern highlands and lower Congo, the lowest densities in the former provinces of Katanga, Orientale and Equateur. Elsewhere in Equatorial Africa the average density is even lower – about 6 per square mile (2·5 per km²) – although in Cameroun the figure rises to 29 per square mile (11 per km²) and in some of the islands it is well over 100 per square mile (39 per km²). In Congo Brazzaville about 70 per cent of the population lives in the southern half of the country, the Brazzaville area itself having about 44 per square mile (17 per km²), followed by the coastal regions with 15 per square mile (5·5 per km²), while the forested zones of the north and the Bateke plateau have average densities of under one per square mile. Gabon has a rather more evenly distributed population, but the Central African Republic has its highest densities along the Oubangui river and the Chad border, the eastern three-eighths of the country having only about one-sixteenth of the total population. Finally, in Chad, the population density is highest in the south, especially in the Chari-Logone basin; while north of the 15° parallel there is an average of only one person to every four or five square miles (Fig. 2).

In trying to explain this generally low density and uneven distribution of population in Equatorial Africa, reference is commonly made to such factors as climate, disease, forest vegetation, and the history of slave-raiding in the area. In Congo Kinshasa, Gourou (1951) distinguishes two parallel east-west bands of above-average density – one to the north and one to the south of the equator. Local diseases, particularly malaria and sleeping sickness, are found to help in explaining the central band of low population density. Gourou explains the southern belt of above-average density, however, by reference to vegetation types: here, he notes, is a belt where the equatorial forest is sufficiently dry in some years to be burnt, but where fires are not so intense as to damage the soil.

Population data for the former Belgian Congo are very much better than for the rest of Equatorial Africa or indeed for most other parts of tropical Africa. Running their country more like a large business concern and able to devote all their attention and resources to the Congo, the Belgians collected a great deal of often very detailed and reliable demographic information, including records of urban-rural distributions and population growth rates. Available data show that the urban population of the Congo had risen to over 21 per cent of the total by 1960, but even more striking was the increase in the population of the largest urban centres. In 1923,

10

Leopoldville (now Kinshasa) had a population of only 17,825, but by 1958 it had risen to some 368,000 and today (1967) it is over half a million. The four largest cities in Katanga, all mining centres, had a total population of 325,644 in 1958, whereas none of them existed in 1900. Official Belgian policy, encouraging permanent settlement of whole families in the towns, resulted in sex ratios which were better balanced than in most African cities, but even so there were until recently about 70–80 women to every 100 men in Congolese towns.

Data for the urban population of all other states in Equatorial Africa are very much less reliable and complete. Congo Brazzaville has an urban population of 19 per cent of the total, and no less than 14 per cent live in the capital city of Brazzaville alone. All other states in Equatorial Africa, however, have only a few small and isolated urban centres: Libreville and Port Gentil in Gabon, Douala in Cameroun, and Bangui in Central African Republic. Chad has the lowest urban population (3·5 per cent) of all countries in the region.

There is little definite information about early rates of population growth in the Belgian Congo. In 1885 Stanley made a purely speculative estimate of 43 million for the total population of the Congo Basin, appreciably more than was found to inhabit the country in the inter-war years. This and similar early subjective estimates contributed to the belief that population in the 1920's was declining, thereby threatening the whole basis for economic development in the Belgian Congo. It is true that the death-rate was probably very high, especially during the Leopold period when there were few restrictions on the use of labour, when men were frequently removed from their communities for long periods, and when the incidence of disease was heightened by migrations and by the introduction of new diseases by Europeans. But most authorities now suggest that the population in the Congo was only about 9 million in 1900 and approximately the same in 1925. The rate of growth of population is estimated to have been about 0·6 per cent per annum from 1925–1940, 1 per cent per annum in the decade 1940–1950, and 1.9 per cent per annum from 1950–1957. Today the rate has risen to 3 per cent in some parts of the Congo, notably in Katanga, although in a few areas there are signs of declining populations. In one of the demographic sample surveys taken in 1956–7 it was shown that those areas with excessively low crude birth-rates seem to be associated with high rates of syphilis and so with a large proportion of childless women. Among the Azande, too, the net reproduction rate was found to be only 0·63 per cent in 1959, and this was apparently also due to low fertility.

The generally low density of population in Equatorial Africa has often presented problems of development for agriculture, mining, and industry – especially for plantation interests in the rain forest zone and for mining companies in Katanga. The literature on French Equatorial Africa reveals how often the French were concerned at the shortage of manpower for economic development in their territories, more particularly in Gabon and Congo Brazzaville. In the Belgian Congo, too, strong measures were taken to correct the labour shortage, a number of protective laws being promulgated and positive programmes designed to promote population growth being introduced. It was hoped to increase the population of the Belgian Congo to 25 million by 1980. On the other hand, the low population density has had a number of beneficial effects, both social and economic. In the former Belgian Congo, the shortage of labour led to limitations being placed on the number of workers that could be recruited from any tribal area; workers were encouraged to settle permanently in employment areas; and recruitment was often carried out on a family basis. The large compounds for bachelor migrants so characteristic of South African mining and industrial areas were not to be found in Katanga. Employers were also obliged to maintain certain standards of rations, medical facilities, housing and sanitation in all non-tribal areas. On the economic side, the population shortage stimulated the introduction of labour-saving machinery, which led to the training of more technicians and also stimulated the desire to upgrade agricultural methods.

The other most important facet of the population problem in Equatorial Africa concerns the tribal composition of the population (Fig. 31). The divisive forces of tribalism have been particularly apparent among such tribes as the Bakongo, Lulua, Lunda and Fang which represent strong centrifugal forces in the various countries. Indeed, a great mosaic of tribes characterizes Equatorial Africa, although most of them may be classified as Bantu. Of the seventy most important tribes in Congo Kinshasa, 49 are Bantu, 16 are located along the northern border and are classified as Sudanese, one is Nilotic and one Hamitic. In his study of culture clusters in Congo Kinshasa, Merriam (1959) distinguishes six major ethnic groups – the Bakongo, Baluba, Mongo, Kuba, Mangbeti-Azande and Warega – the groups varying in size from 2 million (Mongo) to 75,000 (Kuba), and each group being made up of a number of distinct tribes. There are also several hundred dialects, although four African languages – Kokongo, Kiluba, Lingala and Kiswahili – are spoken or understood by most Africans, and French is used as a *lingua franca* throughout the country.

In the rest of Equatorial Africa the tribal pattern is even more complicated than in Congo Kinshasa. Cameroun has some 140 tribal groups, while there are about forty tribes in Congo Brazzaville and about the same number in Gabon. Ethnic groups range from Negrillos in the rain forest to groups of Bantu and Hamitic peoples. They often differ widely in degree of development and in degree of contact with modern influences, and these contrasts tend to accentuate tribal differences and help to explain some of the major contemporary political issues. In Congo Brazzaville, for instance, the Bakongo assume a position of dominance resented by the others; in Gabon the Fang are prominent; and Chad is beset by tribal differences and antagonisms of often acute proportions. Only Central African Republic appears to have no dominant group and, significantly, no overt problem of tribalism.

Congo Kinshasa: Problems of Unity

Many circumstances have combined to produce in Congo Kinshasa a complex of tensions and polarities which impede the development of a stable, unified state. According to some writers, the most important of these has been the legacy of Belgian colonial rule. It has already been noted that perhaps the most valid criticism of Belgian colonial policy is that it miscalculated the force and speed of political change in mid-twentieth-century Africa. Little or no political progress was made until 1958, with the result that at independence in 1960 there was no nucleus of Congolese with any considerable political experience. Furthermore, Belgian administrative institutions did not appear to have great relevance in the independent state. Although the Belgians had attempted a nominal form of indirect rule, their severely centralized system of administration had tended in practice to undermine the authority of the traditional chiefs, whose cooperation formed the basis of effective indirect rule in British Africa. Belgian missionary groups, too, had a divisive effect because they encouraged the vernacular tribal languages. Finally, the great haste with which the Belgians finally handed over power to the Congolese was a crucial factor in precipitating the Congo crisis.

Yet it is possible to exaggerate the part played in the Congo crisis by the Belgian colonial legacy. Perhaps the rapid handover from Belgian to Congolese power was inevitable, and could not have been anticipated. Nationalist assertion developed with exceptional speed in most parts of Africa during the late 1950's; pressures from anti-colonial world powers and agencies, notably the United States and United Nations, were reinforced by the events of the Leopoldville riots of 1959; and from the Belgian point of view there was the desire to protect and secure Belgian economic investments, especially in the Katanga. Furthermore, while Belgian policy had made its own contribution to the forces of disintegration in the Congo, it had also created some basis for unity: a common language and culture, a common currency, a good system of universal primary education, and sound social and economic foundations.

While it is impossible to discount altogether the centrifugal effects of Belgian colonial rule, there is some justification for the suggestion that many of the present problems of Congolese unity derive more from a combination of physical and cultural circumstances.

In the first place, Congo Kinshasa suffers from its great size and almost completely landlocked nature. Then the very fact that much of the Congo is structurally a basin has, in these equatorial conditions, tended to push settlement and economic life outwards towards the higher, healthier and mineralized rims and away from the relatively inhospitable centre. The population, too – its low density, uneven distribution and highly complicated tribal pattern – has had a divisive effect. Indeed, as far as ethnic and linguistic complexity are concerned, Nigeria is the only other African country which compares with the Congo.

The uneven pattern of economic development in the country also makes integration difficult. The two major economic core areas, around which the processes of social mobilization have been most intensive, are Kinshasa (Leopoldville) and Lubumbashi (Elisabethville); but these two towns occupy eccentric positions. The remarkable integrated system of rail and river communications in the Congo has been something of a unifying factor: from the time of Leopold it has been intended not only to facilitate economic exploitation but also to knit together the several widely dispersed regions that offered the best economic prospects. But even this integrated system of communications has been unable to unite the widely separated and often highly discrete communities of a country the size of the Congo; and the two major axes of communication – the Congo River and the *B.C.K.* railway line, which link the capital at Kinshasa to the interior – have by their very pattern tended to limit social and economic development to the 'rimland' and make it difficult for the population of the central basin to mix with the peoples of the periphery.

Congo Kinshasa displays, in fact, 'the problem left to Africa by the uneven and unequal apportioning of Europe's share-out – perhaps the most damaging legacy left by the white man' (Perham, 1964: 113). This vast area taken over from the Belgians by the Congolese has no physical or cultural unity. It does not even have that 'fragile basis for the future cooperation of disparate tribes' provided in British territories by 'a Western-educated élite, native representation at the centre, and the freedom to create a native press' and political parties (*ibid*: 113). The six regions formerly comprising the provinces of the Belgian Congo expressed not only administrative convenience but also the great diversity of this vast country. Leopoldville Province, controlling the single narrow outlet to the sea, was the commercial and administrative province. Equateur was backward and isolated, although with important European-owned plantations of rubber and oil palm. Orientale was very much less remote, and from Stanleyville (now Kisangani) this province had connections downstream to the coast as well as by road northeastward and eastward to Sudan. In Orientale Province, too, Africans were much more involved in cash agriculture: oil palm, rubber, cotton and coffee. Kasai produced not only diamonds but also basic foodstuffs – notably manioc, maize and vegetables – for the main towns and industrial centres of Leopoldville and the Katanga. Kivu Province, on the edge of the East African plateau, possessed many of the most valuable cash crop plantations. Finally, there was Katanga, which was in many ways more closely linked to Central African countries than to the Congo and contained the bulk of the mining and industrial activity of the country.

The divisive effects of all these circumstances – physical, social and economic as well as the more narrowly historical – have continued into independence. Congo Kinshasa remains a territorial framework with little basis for national strength, unity or independence. This has expressed itself since independence in a number of secession movements, of which the principal has been in Katanga. Indeed, the civil war in the Congo in 1960 was provoked by the secession of its richest province.

The Katanga problem has never been a simple issue of tribal separatism. Unlike most secession movements in Africa, the secession of Katanga in 1960 was not so much the result of the fear of domination of one tribe by another as the result of the convergence of a combination of historical, economic and social factors; and to this extent Katanga epitomizes the whole Congo problem.

Although the frontier between Katanga and Zambia follows for several hundred miles the divide between the Congo headstreams (notably the Lualaba and Lufira) and the upper Zambezi, this watershed is hardly perceptible on the ground. In its topography as in its geology and mineral resources, Katanga is part of the Central African copper belt; in fact the economic history of the Katanga is closely tied with that of its southern neighbours, and it was from the south that the railway first penetrated into the Katanga mining area. Climatically, Katanga is well suited to European occupation, and at independence about half of the Belgians in the Congo lived along the railway line between the Zambian border and Bukama. The settler population in Katanga had affinities with that of Zambia and Rhodesia, and white settlers in Katanga made the idea of secession economically attractive and politically meaningful both to European settlers and to Katanga Africans. Many of the African labourers in the Katanga mining and industrial area came originally not from the Congo at all, but from the heavily populated mandate, trusteeship, and now independent territories of Rwanda and Burundi over 1000 miles (1600 km) to the north.

Geographical realities, then, made and continue to make the movement for Katanga secession entirely logical, but, from the point of view of Congo

Kinshasa, secession could only have harmful effects. For without Katanga, Congo Kinshasa loses much of its justification as a political unit. Katanga provides so much of the country's wealth – estimates vary from 45 per cent to 85 per cent – that without its most southerly province Congo Kinshasa could only continue with difficulty as an economically viable unit. On the other hand, it is to be questioned whether Congo Kinshasa can afford to endure for long what has been called 'Katanganization': the acceptance by the Congolese of the argument that the vital economic resources of Katanga must necessarily entitle its political leaders to a dominant position in the government of the country.

The case of Katanga is the most obvious and significant case of secessionist tendencies in the Congo, although there are others. One of these – Kasai – is more clearly a simple expression of tribalism. In Kasai, where the *Forminière* Company mines diamonds and gold, the tribal issue is the basis of a complex north-south problem, emphasized here by the location of the two provincial capitals of Luluabourg and Bakwaya lying close together on the main railway line. On independence, the Luba peoples (Baluba) were driven south by the Lulua majority. As a result, the population of southern Kasai rose from 332,620 in 1958 to 1,348,030 in 1963, and the population of Bakwaya itself increased from 40,000 to 200,000 in the same period. Kalonji rallied the Baluba tribe into his break-away state, known as Kalonji's 'Diamond State'; but such was the rate of immigration from the north that food production and distribution proved quite inadequate. Many died from starvation, labour problems intensified, and the movement eventually collapsed.

Another secessionist problem in Congo Kinshasa is that of the Bakongo in lower Congo. This again is primarily tribal in origin, but it is greatly exacerbated by the fact that the boundaries between Congo Kinshasa, Congo Brazzaville and Angola cut through Bakongo tribal lands. Since 1960, other attempts at secession have also taken place in the former Kivu and Orientale provinces.

The problem of achieving unity in Congo Kinshasa is clearly a formidable one. According to some Congolese, it demands the creation of some form of federal constitution which would allow the greatest degree of regional autonomy within the framework of a national state covering the whole of the former Belgian Congo. Other Congolese, however, believe that a strongly centralized, unitarian approach is needed. At independence in 1960 the unitarians had 71 seats, the federalists 66, an evenly balanced situation; but the largest single party was Lumumba's *M.N.C.* unitarian party which therefore formed the government in the critical opening months of independence. Since independence, however, and in particular since the assassination of Lumumba, federalism has gained more ground, although the clash between unitarians and federalists continues to be the focus of Congolese politics.

Partly with the aim of reducing the power of large regional groupings, the former six provinces of the Congo were divided in 1963 into twenty-one administrative units, Katanga alone being divided into three new provinces. With the federal territory of Kinshasa there was a total of twenty-two divisions. This redrawing of provincial boundaries was, however, criticized as a reversal to tribalism. The Bakongo, for instance, now had their own province in the Congo. But in fact only six of the twenty-one provinces were recognizable ethnic entities, and several other factors, including distance from a provincial capital, were taken into account. The twenty-two administrative divisions proved too unwieldy, however, and were later regrouped into eleven.

Apart from the need to achieve political stability and a sense of national unity, two other urgent requirements in Congo Kinshasa are physical security within the state and substantial economic aid from outside. The need for peace and order has been accentuated by the civil war, by rebellion and by the activities of the United Nations in the country since independence: 'the story of the Congo's independence, is in its own context, as bloodstained and involved as that of its creation under King Leopold II' (Perham, 1963: 115). The economic effects of the disorders and the United Nations action were disastrous, most agricultural and much industrial production being affected. In 1965 production was still only about 80 per cent of what it was in 1960, living standards had deteriorated, and the essential interdependence of political progress and economic and social prosperity had been more than adequately demonstrated. Fully restored, and given access to expanding world markets, the agricultural areas of the Congo have great potential in a number of export products, especially in animal and vegetable oils, timber, cotton, coffee, tea, spices, rubber and fruits. Petroleum has been discovered near the Congo estuary, there is still a great potential for diamond mining in Kasai and for copper and other mining in Katanga, and the potential hydro-electric resources of the Congo are among the greatest of any country in the world. The Inga hydro-electric project on the lower Congo now seems likely to go ahead, the first stage being scheduled for 1967. Studies for this project began as long ago as 1929 and were completed before independence. Providing for sixteen stages altogether, the completed plant would produce 28,000 MW, compared with 750 MW for the Volta scheme and 880 MW for the Niger project. Furthermore, a rapid programme of industrialization in the Congo has been planned for the years 1965–1970, and a large steel mill is planned for Kimpoko near Kinshasa in 1972. Given peace and security, the economic potential of Congo Kinshasa is impressive. But a second and related need is for outside help, both to maintain peace and security and to support the country's economic growth: 'the Congo illustrates in extremest form the need of Africa for outside help . . . For all UNO's unstable foundations and poverty of resources, only its services, financed in large measure by America . . . saved Congo from an even deeper collapse into barbarism' (*ibid*: 115).

The Congo crisis has had an important impact on the rest of Africa. In the white settler country to the south, the Congo crisis has been interpreted as further justification for withholding majority rule from the African. In black Africa, however, it has in the long run drawn African nations more closely together, reaffirmed and strengthened African faith in the United Nations, and confirmed African anti-colonial sentiments. The recent history of the Congo, in fact, has been 'a happy hunting ground both for those who seek evidence of the iniquity of colonial powers, and for those who argue the unreadiness of African states for independence' (Anstey, 1966: 261). The most recent (1967) crisis confirms this view.

With Congo Kinshasa it is still too early to conclude that the lessons of the past few years have been learned, or that the burdens of independence are as yet fully appreciated. Like most African states, it is not yet a nation, and the difficulties of creating a sense of national unity in such a large, sparsely populated, diverse and tribally conscious country have already been indicated. Today Congo Kinshasa is 'a region enclosed within the broken framework of a colonial state within which, given time and much sustained help, the peoples may grow through cooperation into national unity, and into the prosperity for which Belgium laid some promising foundations' (Perham, 1963: 115).

Northern Equatorial Africa: Problems of Cooperation

The five independent states lying to the north of the Congo – Congo Brazzaville, Gabon, Central African Republic, Chad and Cameroun – today share three related characteristics: poverty, very low density of population and poor transport facilities. All these countries compare unfavourably with the former Belgian Congo in terms of social and economic development, and some reasons for this contrast have already been suggested. In particular, French Equatorial Africa was always regarded by the French as the poor relation of French West Africa: 'the economic and social backwardness of the French equatorial countries, their jealousy of their West African cousins and consequent reaction against them, together with the much stronger hold of the French concessionary companies and the French administration in French Equatorial Africa, often produced sharp contrasts between the two regions' (Thompson and Adloff, 1961: 271). Secondly, northern Equatorial Africa has a remarkably low density of population, there being barely 10 million people in the whole area and, finally, all states have poor transport facilities and two of them – Chad and Central African Republic – are entirely land-locked.

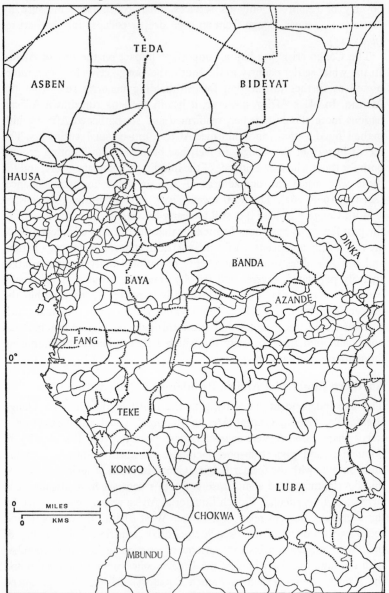

Fig. 31 The Pattern of Tribes in Equatorial Africa. Only a few of the larger tribal areas are named (after Murdock, 1959).

The most southerly of the five states – Congo Brazzaville – has always suffered by comparison with Congo Kinshasa across the river to the south and east, although, with the Congo forming the main line of communication for both states, the relations between them have often been close. Yet Congo Brazzaville has always seemed poorer and less sophisticated, a contrast emphasized by even the most superficial comparison of the two capital cities facing each other across the Congo. In an economic sense the relationship between the two Congos is clearly lopsided. Congo Kinshasa, too, has traditionally provided employment for workers from the Brazzaville area; and at least until independence, the deficit in French Equatorial Africa's trade with the Belgian Congo was so substantial that each year the Paris *Office des Changes* had to allocate 130 million Congo francs to finance trans-frontier commerce.

On the other hand, developments in the two adjacent territories have sometimes been wastefully competitive. Parallel rail lines run along opposite sides of the Congo, river ports have been built on opposite shores of Stanley Pool, two large airfields have grown up on the outskirts of the opposing capitals, and now the two countries have their own plans to build large and costly hydro-electric plants – at Inga and Kouilou – each of which will be capable of producing more than enough power for the present needs of both countries.

Congo Brazzaville is one of the poorest of the five northern states. Apart from timber, only groundnuts, sugar cane and palm products earn any significant foreign exchange. Copper and iron resources, however, are likely to be exploited soon, and an important current development is the hydro-electric dam on the Kouilou river behind Pointe Noire. Here an aluminium smelter is being built with capital from France, Germany and the United States. There have also been many attempts to increase local food supplies and to improve the livestock industry, notably in the fertile Niari valley which runs due west towards the coast from the inland river capital of Brazzaville.

But apart from poverty, the two most important facts about the political geography of Congo Brazzaville are, first, its strategic position at the mouth of the Congo and, secondly, the tribal basis of political life. The first is clearly reflected in the pattern of communications. The country has an important port at Pointe Noire and a railway system reaching inland upstream from there to Brazzaville (the Congo–Ocean railway); another line reaches northward to the Gabon border to facilitate the export of Gabon's manganese. Entrepôt trade with Gabon, as well as with the landlocked states of Central African Republic and Chad, is indeed very important to Congo Brazzaville. Above Brazzaville the river is navigable up to Bangui in Central African Republic, but Congo Brazzaville also has an extensive road system, including an all-weather road through to Cameroun. The tribal basis of politics is evident from the fact that the Bakongo tribe is dominant in this country of less than a million people and that they also spread out over the international boundaries into Congo Kinshasa and Angola. The importance of this fact in the political geography of Congo Kinshasa has already been indicated. Within Congo Brazzaville each of the three main political parties represents one of the three major tribal groups – Bakongo, M'Bochi and Vili – and each of these is also supported by one or more of the many religious sects which flourish in the area.

Gabon lies immediately to the north of Congo Brazzaville and is notable for having a higher standard of living than any of its neighbours. The country has good mineral and forest resources, is self-sufficient in food, and at Port Gentil has an important and growing industrial complex based largely on the processing of crop products. Oil, uranium and manganese are exported and the country is unique in Equatorial Africa in maintaining a favourable balance of trade. Indeed, with the aid of foreign capital from the United States, Germany and France, Gabon looks forward to a bright economic future. It has already received very large loans from the World Bank for transport and communications. The road system is now fair, and at present the manganese at Moanda is exploited by *Comilog* and taken by cable railway across the Congo Brazzaville border to M'Binda from where it travels by the new railway line to join the Congo–Ocean railway to Pointe Noire. A new railway, however, might enable the manganese to leave Gabon through its own port at Port Gentil, and another railway is planned to connect the Gabon estuary opposite Libreville with the north-western corner of Gabon in order to tap the rich iron ores of Belinga, where exploitation is due to begin in 1970 (Hilling, 1963).

This relative wealth gives Gabon great political and economic significance in Equatorial Africa, although at the same time it perhaps makes Gabon less inclined to cooperate with its poorer neighbours. In spite of its relative wealth in the context of Equatorial Africa, however, Gabon is still a poor country. It has a population of only half a million, much of the country is still under tropical rain forest, and most eastern parts of Gabon remain quite undeveloped because they are exceedingly difficult to reach. Politically, too, tribalism is rampant. In particular the Fang, who are the dominant tribe and spread over into Rio Muni and Cameroun, constitute a major divisive element in the country today.

Central African Republic is perhaps the poorest of all the former territories of French Equatorial Africa and its economy is precariously dependent upon external aid. Wholly landlocked and contained between the Oubangui and Chari rivers – hence the country's former name of Oubangui-Chari – Central African Republic is understandably preoccupied with the need to improve communications with its outlets. At present the main outlet for its exports is by river, down the Oubangui from the head of navigation at Bangui to join the river Congo through to Brazzaville, and from there to join the Congo–Ocean railway to Pointe Noire. Central African Republic has no railway, but its road system connects with both Chad and Cameroun. With a population of under one and a half million and a very low level of economic development, landlocked Central African Republic's approach to the political problems of independence has been regionalist and internationalist. Politically, as well as economically, its very identity depends upon cooperation between states. Significantly enough, it was in the Central African Republic that President Boganda first proposed the idea of a United States of Latin Africa, to include at least the former states of French West Africa, French Equatorial Africa, Cameroun, Congo Kinshasa and Angola, and so to create a Latin bloc large and powerful enough to act as a counterbalance to the leadership of Ghana in West Africa and of Egypt among the Arab States. Although this grand concept died with Boganda, Central African Republic is still in the vanguard of regional movements for inter-state cooperation.

Similarly landlocked, Chad is also preoccupied with the need for inter-state cooperation, and with plans for developing its outlets to the sea. At present it is a poor country, exporting some groundnuts, rice, sorghums and cattle, but it possesses a considerable agricultural potential west of the Chari river, where the land is more densely populated and where moisture and soil conditions are believed to be less restricting. Once again, communications are the key to development. The Chari is navigable seasonally – from Fort Lamy to Fort Archambault between August and December – as is the Logone; and Chad is linked with Central African Republic by a good road from Fort Lamy to Bangui, from where the river-rail route to Pointe Noire begins. This export route, however, is both long and expensive. There is a much shorter route through Cameroun – by road to Yaounde, thence by rail to Douala – and 'the existence of this comparatively short route is one of the reasons why France hoped to retain the Cameroun within the framework of France Outre Mer after 1960' (Thompson and Adloff, 1961: 271). Nevertheless, if inducements were not offered to Chad to ship through former French territory, an even cheaper route would be through Nigeria to the port of Lagos. Two major projects now being considered in Chad are a rail link with either Cameroun or Central African Republic, and a trans-Saharan road to North Africa.

One of the most important political issues in Chad today – the north-south dichotomy – is characteristic of many West African territories. And indeed Chad's physical environment is much more reminiscent of Niger and Mali than of Gabon and Congo Brazzaville. A large part of Chad is semi-desert, which merges into true desert and the Tibesti mountains, whereas the southern parts of the country are savanna lands. The south, which has a population of about the same size as the north, is much more developed and provides some 80 per cent of the country's revenue. In the north, the Muslim influence is very strong, and since independence a number of unsuccessful attempts have been made to re-establish the traditional systems of Islamic authority and administration.

An equally important political issue, however, is Chad's external relations. The country has important contacts not only with its immediate southern neighbours in Equatorial Africa – Cameroun and Central African Republic – but also with the West African state of Niger to the west and, perhaps even more importantly, with the Arab countries of Sudan and Libya to the east and north. Because the population of Chad includes the largest group of Moslems in Equatorial Africa and lies athwart the traditional overland routes of pilgrimage from West Africa to Mecca, the country has been longest in contact with the holy cities of Arabia and with Al Hazhar University in Cairo. Many thousands of the poorer pilgrims still cross Chad on foot on their way to Khartoum and the Red Sea ports. A number of boundary problems, however, have originated between Chad and Sudan, largely because of banditry and the incursion of refugees from Sudan. To the north, Chad's external relations are chiefly with the Libyan Fezzan, which from ancient times has been one of the keys to the heart of Africa, acting as an avenue of overland communication between the Mediterranean and Negro worlds and between Egypt and the Sahara. The strategic and political significance of the Fezzan is still great and some African leaders hope that Libya will turn away from the Arab world towards Black Africa.

Although Cameroun is not landlocked, one of its most urgent needs is certainly for better communications, both with its neighbours and within its own borders. At the moment there is a railway running eastward from Douala to Yaounde and northward from Douala to Nkongsamba. The road connection from Yaounde through to Fort Lamy in Chad is one of the few good roads in Cameroun, although even this is not an all-weather road. A number of rail and road projects exist, including extending the railway to Chad from Yaounde, and the Cameroun and Nigerian governments are jointly interested in improving the navigation of the Benue; at the moment it is navigable from July to October when it carries northern traffic between Garoua and Burutu (Nigeria).

Given good communications, Cameroun's economic potential is considerable. The country is already self-sufficient in most foodstuffs, and it has a wide range of export crops, including bananas, cocoa, coffee, pineapples, raw cotton, palm products, rice, groundnuts, sugar cane, and cattle products. There is also some tin and bauxite, and a major hydro-electric station with an aluminium smelter has already been set up at Edéa.

Like Chad, Cameroun has the north-south problem which is so characteristic a feature of West African countries: the better-developed south having generally more favourable physical conditions for agriculture and settlement; and the north being drier, poorer, more isolated from export points, feudal, less educated and strongly Moslem. But Cameroun also has a troublesome east-west problem, and this is to some extent the legacy of the different colonial or trusteeship associations of East Cameroun (with the French) and West Cameroun (with the British). West Cameroun, as the former British Southern Cameroons, was far more fully integrated into the Nigerian administration than was East Cameroun into that of French Equatorial Africa. France always treated its trusteeship territory as a separate unit; and this has made it easier, perhaps, for East Cameroun to face independence. Differences between east and west in language, education, administrative organizations, trading patterns and associations have all posed problems for Cameroun unity, and there still exists a customs barrier between the two parts of the country. This east-west problem continues in spite of the fact that the Bamileke people, formerly split by the Franco-British trusteeship boundary, have been reunited by the inclusion of the former Southern British Cameroons in the new state of Cameroun. Ethnic ties between east and west Cameroun are strong; and there were also compelling economic grounds for unification, the German-planned communication network of East Cameroun, for instance, providing direct export routes for West Cameroun products. The fact that an east-west problem exists today within Cameroun is eloquent testimony to the powerful legacy of differing colonial impacts on the two former trusteeship territories.

One of the two outstanding characteristics of the political geography of Equatorial Africa north of the Congo is the strength of tribal allegiances. This is a common feature of most African states, but perhaps nowhere in the continent are politics so clearly based on tribalism as they are in the countries of northern Equatorial Africa. Tribal reactions to political events are the rule and a number of serious clashes between tribes have taken place since independence. The independent states of former French Equatorial Africa and Cameroun provide perhaps the best evidence for the view that territories without a well-defined nationalist movement are particularly susceptible to tribal divisions; and that in the absence of an established élite and a widespread nationalist sentiment, political organization inevitably comes to depend on tribal allegiance.

The reason for the political importance of tribalism in these territories is not so much the actual fragmentation of tribal communities – which is, after all, common to most of Africa – as the generally very low level of economic development and the lack of contact between the various parts of the region. This is one of the most backward areas of Africa, characterized by great poverty, illiteracy, very low population densities, little urbanization, and a serious lack of communications both within and between the constituent states. Furthermore, there were in northern Equatorial Africa only weak foundations for the growth of political movements – no substantial trade union movement and no considerable educated community or élite. Politics in the various states remain largely attached to local feeling based on tribal and, to some extent, on religious foundations.

On the other hand, while tribalism has for long been a difficult problem in the area, these states did have considerable experience of politics before independence, even though it was local tribal politics rather than national politics. While the former Belgian Congo may be said to have suffered from lack of political experience, the former states of northern Equatorial Africa may be said to have suffered from a surfeit of it.

The other important point to emphasize about these territories is that they became independent without there being any strong indigenous pressure for self-government. French Equatorial Africa is a clear example of an area that became independent as a result of external pressures rather than by its own intent. Even as late as 1956, most of the African leaders in the area would have preferred to retain strong links with France rather than take the path to complete independence. Each of the four territories of French Equatorial Africa was to a greater or lesser degree aware of its economic weakness and anxious to retain French economic, technical and military support.

To strengthen their economies and to counter further balkanization, several economic and political links have been proposed between the states of northern Equatorial Africa. One of the difficulties of association has been the opposition of Gabon – as the richest of the states – and another has been the centrifugal forces represented in Congo Brazzaville by the powerful Bakongo looking across the river to their fellow tribesmen in Congo Kinshasa and in Angola, and in Gabon by the Fang looking northward to their kinsmen in Cameroun and Spanish Rio Muni. Some agreement, especially on customs matters has, however, proved possible, partly because Gabon still needs to export its manganese through Congo Brazzaville and because Chad can threaten its southern neighbours by proposing to use Nigerian rail and port facilities. A customs union between the four former countries of French Equatorial Africa – the *Equatorial Customs Union* (*U.D.E.*) – was set up in 1959, and this was joined by Cameroun in 1961.

A more recent development has been the setting up of the *Economic Customs Union of Central and Equatorial Africa* (*U.D.E.A.C.*). This came into operation in January, 1966, and is designed to facilitate a variety of connecting links between its member states, which comprise the former territories of French Equatorial Africa and Cameroun. The aim is to strengthen inter-state solidarity in economic and political matters and it is based on the belief that the best way to achieve African cooperation and unity is through regional economic groupings.

The aims of *U.D.E.A.C.* include the provision of communications to the sea for the landlocked states of Equatorial Africa. According to one proposal, railways will link Fort Archambault in Chad and Bangui in the Central African Republic with the port and growing industrial centre of Douala. There are, however, two major problems associated with *U.D.E.A.C.* The first is the continued reluctance of Gabon to remain a member of a union from which it will apparently gain little while being expected to contribute a great deal. To some extent this also now applies to Cameroun and Congo Brazzaville, which have direct access to the coast and are more industrialized than either Chad or Central African Republic. The second problem relates to the location of economic, and especially industrial, projects. The cotton textile industry is a case in point. Most of the cotton is produced in Chad, Cameroun and Central African Republic; yet there are plans to build textile mills not only in Chad and Central African Republic but also in Congo Brazzaville and in Gabon (at Libreville), although neither of these two latter countries grows any cotton.

Conclusion

The central location of Equatorial Africa makes it a bridge between many different parts of the continent, and so endows the region with unusual significance. The political stability and economic development of the countries of Equatorial Africa are of crucial importance for the whole continent, and the success or failure of such a state as Congo Kinshasa in achieving effective national unity and economic prosperity is an issue about which all African countries are necessarily deeply concerned.

The difficulties of achieving economic development and political stability, let alone national unity, are, however, very great. Equatorial Africa, including as it does within its large and varied framework the characteristics of so many neighbouring regions, is environmentally the most diverse of the major regions discussed in this book. Physically the contrasts are extreme, the tribal pattern of the population is immensely complicated, and there are the most striking disparities in levels of social and economic development. With long land frontiers, very low population densities and poor communications, the newly independent states of Equatorial Africa appear to have a very inadequate basis either for creating national unity or for sustaining economic and social progress.

References and Select Bibliography

ANSTEY, R. 1962. *Great Britain and the Congo*, Clarendon, Oxford.
⎯⎯⎯ 1966. *King Leopold's Legacy*, Oxford University Press, London.
BIEBUYCK, D. and M. DOUGLAS. 1961. *Congo Tribes and Parties*, R.A.I., London.
GOUROU, P. 1951. Notice de la carte de la densité de la population au Congo Belge et au Ruanda-Urundi, *Atlas Général du Congo*, Brussels.
HAILEY, Lord. 1957. *Africa Survey, Revised 1956*, Oxford University Press, London.
HATCH, J. 1962. *Africa Today – and Tomorrow*, Praeger, New York.
HILLING, D. 1963. The changing economy of Gabon. *Geography*, Vol. 48: 155–165.
LERAT, S. 1961. Une région industrielle au coeur de l'Afrique: le Katanga meridional. *Cahiers d'Outre Mer*, Vol. 14: 435–442.
MERRIAM, A. 1961. *Congo: Background of Conflict*, Evanston.
NICOLAI, M. and J. JACQUES. 1954. *La Transformation des Paysages Congolais par le Chemin de Fer: L'Exemple du B.C.K.*, Brussels.
OLIVER, R. and J. D. FAGE. 1962. *A Short History of Africa*, Penguin, London.
ROBERT, M. 1946. *Le Congo Physique*, Liège.
RYCKMANS, P. 1955. Belgian 'colonialism', in Quigg, 1964: 71–83.
SLADE, R. 1962. *King Leopold's Congo*, Oxford University Press, London.
SMITH, T. E. and J. G. BLACKER. 1963. *Population Characteristics of the Commonwealth Countries of Tropical Africa*, London.
STANER, P. 1955. Le paysannat indigènes du Congo belge et Ruandi-Urundi. *Bulletin Agricole du Congo Belge*, Vol. 46: 468–549.
STANLEY, H. M. 1885. *The Congo and the Founding of its Free State*, London.
THOMPSON, V. and R. ADLOFF. 1961. *The Emerging States of French Equatorial Africa*, Constable, London.
Union Minière du Haut-Katanga, 1906–1956, Brussels.

6 Southern Africa

6 Southern Africa

By C. BOARD

'It would be almost possible to take a piece of chalk, and on the face of the continent [Africa] to map out spatially the areas of each type: predominantly European, genuinely African, and those covered by the processes of change.'

BRONISLAW MALINOWSKI (1938)

Introduction

Although Malinowski intended this statement to apply to anthropological studies of culture contact it is equally applicable to the geographical study of the continent. As a statement made with reference to work in areas of Africa where contact with Europeans was significant, it is particularly appropriate to the southern tip of the continent, where this contact is over three centuries old. Although the processes of change worked earlier and faster in the south, they are at present working more slowly there as governmental policies attempt to preserve the differentiation brought about by the colonization of Southern Africa.

The changing map of Southern Africa is here regarded as the record of the operation of spatial processes involved in culture contact over a length of time extending further back even than the first settlement of the Cape by the Dutch East India Company in 1652. The results of contact are most striking when they occur between peoples of widely different character-istics, whether in numerical strength, wealth, technical achievement or culture. Southern Africa differs from the rest of the continent south of the Sahara chiefly because the process of contact has spread farther in space and has extended over a longer period of time than elsewhere. In the interpretation of the geography of the area, such contact has to be con-sidered as fundamental, along with the physical and biological environment. At the same time it would be both foolish and unconvincing to interpret the changing geography of Southern Africa in isolation from the rest of the continent; and clearly reference must be made to external forces in Europe and the wider world. This essay will attempt briefly to sketch in the web of interconnection that has resulted in one of the modern world's most complex political and social problems: a problem as unique as its solution appears to be incapable of peaceful solution.

By regarding Southern Africa as a system within the world-system in which the present state of dynamic equilibrium is maintained by a com-plexity of mutually interacting forces – physical, economic and political – one is less tempted to ignore factors which may conventionally be considered irrelevant. Today's situation does not result merely from the actions of a handful of farmers who, when forced by the hostile environment to seek new pastures, took themselves off into a land occupied by weaker brethren whom they proceeded to place under permanent subjection. It is equally not the place of this essay to suggest solutions, even if this were possible. It is, however, important to realize how the situation arose and what its main features are at present, because opinions are no substitute for an understanding based on the facts of geography. In so far as the map is a record of the geography of an area, the changing map provides the way to an understanding of the processes underlying that geography.

In summary, the creation of the modern pattern of Southern Africa is best seen as the gradual evolution of a complex environmental system in a unique geographical position. A sparsely settled, largely semi-arid plateau with narrow margins and inhospitable coasts stood in the way of the early Portuguese and Dutch traders voyaging to the Indies. Its discovery and use resulted in a permanent farming settlement in the extreme southwest which quickly outpaced any restraints placed on it. The trekker pastoralists would have dominated all the sub-continent south of 15°S latitude had it not been for equally influential forces opposing them. Well organized Bantu-speaking peoples with an Iron Age culture awaited them in the tropics and southeastern coastal belt as well as in the mountainous interior. Events in Europe at the end of the eighteenth century, alterations in the balance of power, and the industrial revolution gave Britain an interest in the Cape on the route to India. The superior power of Britain was more successful in restraining the diaspora of trekkers, although control was not achieved for over a century and then only through a combination of capital investment and immigration from Europe, diplomacy and the force of arms, the race for colonial territories undertaken by Germany, Portugal and Britain, and the inherent wealth of the sub-continent in diamonds, gold and cheap labour. Once the process was begun, given events in Britain and Europe in the nineteenth century, the pattern of the twentieth century is seen as an almost inevitable result. The contribution of the African environment is by no means negligible, but is not of itself sufficient to explain the creation of a major part of the world where differentiation and segregation of peoples, by race, colour or social class is the norm rather than the exception. Indeed, such characteristics also apply in some measure to political developments and to language, religion and culture, in spite of very powerful world forces at work to reduce the number of such distinctions. Attempts to alter the pattern of progress by the introduction of peoples (from India, Germany, Britain) or by the imposition of policies designed to divert the course of events in the situations which had developed, seem only to have been absorbed by the powerful momentum of the forces they were meant to control. English settlers in the Eastern Cape colony became as conscious of their superiority as were the Afrikaners; the anglicization of the Boer republics after 1900 failed to take root. The liberal franchise of the Cape Colony which made no distinctions in race and creed has disappeared, having received the first blows from within the Cape Colony itself. At the same time the pastoral trekkers and the cattle-loving Bantu tribes have become prisoners of their own systems; both required limitless land and both have been forced to change their way of life: in the first instance to one working for others, and in the second to become manual workers in mines and factories. Social changes have followed hard on such economic changes, but political distinctions created at a time when there was room for all have largely remained. Britain, although an unwilling participant in the colonial problems of the region, ultimately became so involved as to attempt an imperial grand design in order both to keep control of the mines and to look after the interests of all the peoples of South Africa. The German protectorate and colonists in the west were absorbed into the same system, with British aid and encouragement, but the Portuguese provinces remain, flanking the three territories which until 1963 comprised the Federation of Rhodesia and Nyasaland. None of these lands has quite the distinctive pattern of the Republic of South Africa or South West Africa. In the Portuguese coastal territories the writ of a European power continues to run. In the interior, British influence is now separated from the best lines of communication (the sea) by independent, unstable or mildly hostile countries. With former lines of communication with the south having been disrupted by the unilateral declaration of independence in Rhodesia in 1965, both Zambia and Malawi may look northward for inspiration and assistance rather than to Britain. In Zambia and in Angola and Moçambique remnants of plural societies survive as legacies from their colonial associations. Malawi shares many characteristics with Botswana and Lesotho in that their land-locked positions make them hostages to more powerful neighbours. None of them has to any great extent harboured settlers of European extraction who would have made inordinate demands on their limited land resources. Swaziland, often grouped with Lesotho and Botswana as the former 'High Commission Territories', contains a significant proportion of white settlers and has a moderately good resource base. Although once administered by the Transvaal (South African Republic), it never formed part of the Union of South Africa. Malagasy is in many ways an Africa in miniature, with high plateau, rough coasts, great climatic contrasts, and a mixture of peoples. Its French colonial past, too, provides a contrast with that of other territories in Southern Africa.

Rather than adopting a general chronological framework in order to show how the forces at work in Southern Africa have brought about its present spatial structure, this essay seizes upon a number of important themes which characterize the distinctiveness of this part of the continent. In the discussion of these themes time is important as one of the dimensions in which the forces are operating, but the spatial dimension is treated as its equal. The two dimensions merge in the changing map.

The Peopling of Southern Africa

Pre-European Movements

The movements of peoples form a theme which is central to the understanding of the forces that have created Southern Africa's present geography. It would be a mistake to assume that the only important movements are those in historical times or that those of the European colonizers are necessarily the most significant. Although the latter may have had far-reaching effects, much of the character and indeed many of the present problems of this great region are closely connected with movements of indigenous and other non-European peoples.

There is little doubt that the ancestors of the present-day Bushmen were among the earliest inhabitants of Southern Africa. They were formerly scattered over a wide area between the Zambesi and the Cape Coast and possessed what can be termed a later Stone Age culture (Fagan, 1965: 33). Three distinct sub-cultures have been recognized by archaeologists, depending on the broad pattern of variation in the physical environment. The *Nachikufan* culture developed in the savanna woodland country between Lake Nyasa and the Katanga area, in Zambia and the Congo. Their stone artefacts (arrow-heads, cutting tools and drills) suggest that they made use of the woodland, preparing vegetable foods as well as hunting wild game. These people lived on into Iron Age times. Evidence of the *Wilton* culture is widespread in lightly wooded grassland country from the middle Zambesi across the northern Kalahari into the Kaokoveld of South West Africa and down the west coast and along the south coast of the Cape. Their tools are lighter stone and bone implements and it is known that they dug up roots and tubers as well as hunted animals as large as elephant and rhinoceros. This culture spans the period from the sixth millennium B.C. to well into the first millennium A.D. and there is evidence that the Wilton people eventually adopted an Iron Age cattle-keeping economy, presumably through contact with Iron Age immigrants. *Smithfield* man's cultural area coincides with outcrops of indurated shale in the interior of present-day South Africa and centres on the Vaal and upper Orange River basins. This shale was very suitable for scrapers and other light tools. Wooden implements, among them digging sticks which were weighted for gathering roots and tubers, are also found. The last two groups left a graphic record of their existence in the form of skilful coloured paintings of hunting on the walls of caves and rock shelters in which they lived. They were all skilful hunters who moved about after game and *veldkos* (bush fruits). The later Stone Age folk left no vessels and the occurrence of stone bowls in northeast Zambia and in South West Africa has been ascribed to a migration of Neolithic pastoralists with 'Hamitic' racial features from East Africa.

The Iron Age came to Zambia about the beginnings of the Christian era and is represented by sites along the Zambesi where pottery and iron slag have been found. At another site near the Tanzanian border, stones for grinding cereals testify to agricultural activities. In the course of the next four or five centuries Iron Age farmers became established in Mashonaland (Rhodesia) and later pushed across the Limpopo into the Transvaal which provided good, tsetse-free cattle country. Finds near Inyanga in eastern Rhodesia show that a proportion of Iron Age peoples there had Negroid racial features, suggesting that immigrants intermarried with local people of 'Bush' type. Such people probably kept cattle as well as hunted game and lived side by side with Stone Age peoples who imitated their economy. On the ridge between the Kafue and Zambesi rivers and centred on Kalomo and Choma are found the remains of Iron Age farmers who grew sorghum and millet on enlarged anthill mounds. They also kept cattle and small livestock which were slaughtered for meat. Burials indicate that these people possessed some Negroid characteristics. They lived in relatively permanent villages unlike similar people farther north near Mazabuka who cultivated lower mounds and then moved away when the soil was exhausted. There is some evidence for trade in copper objects between villages, but contact with coastal traders seems to have been rare. Farther south in Matabeleland (Rhodesia), the Limpopo valley and Botswana, new waves of migrants brought new cultures to Iron Age people. It was they who controlled gold and copper mining in Rhodesia and although they did not make much use of the metals themselves they seem to have traded them with their neighbours. The latter included the Karanga (or Shona) peoples, whose ancient stone constructions are today found in three main areas: in Mashonaland, in the Inyanga mountain area and over a wide area in Matabeleland between the Shashi and Sabi rivers. The exfoliating granite of these areas is ideal for dry stone walling and ruins like those at Zimbabwe do not occur farther south. The stone buildings are associated with villages of pole and *daga* (mud and grass) huts. Iron tools and jewellery of copper and gold are associated with these settlements. The Karanga immigrants had entered Zambia from the Lake Tanganyika area in the ninth century A.D. and by the fifteenth century they had established themselves in the area as far south as the Limpopo river. They learnt iron working from the pre-existing Iron Age peoples and were able to settle amongst them and gradually gain control of large areas of country by virtue of their superior organization. Chiefs apparently controlled the intermediaries through which the people approached *Mwari*, a supreme being. In the period between the middle of the fifteenth and the eighteenth centuries an even more powerful group of people appear to have gained control of the Rhodesian settlements, probably backed by Arab traders from the East Coast who thus extended and shielded their market. The fortunes of the powerful Mashonaland empire of *Monomotapa* depended on the influence of the rulers and their vassals in the southern part of Rhodesia, the kingdom of *Changamire*, formerly Butua. In the sixteenth century, after Vasco da Gama had reported on the wealth of the East Coast, the Portuguese effected economic penetration, displacing Arab traders. They were able to establish trading posts such as at Masapa in the Mazoe valley north of the present Salisbury. Such trading ventures did not lead to political control, however, which remained in the hands of the Iron Age peoples of the plateaus. Indeed, after a campaign against the Portuguese at the end of the seventeenth century the latter continued to control only a puppet Monomotapa in the Tete and Sena region of the Zambesi valley. It is considered by Fagan (1965: 125) that the imperial activities of the Rozwi overlords were probably the result of overpopulation in their homeland. The relatively infertile Inyanga highlands in eastern Rhodesia were settled in later Iron Age times by immigrants from the north who intermarried with local Shona people. They built fortified settlements, but it is their skill in building cultivation terraces often faced with stone walls as well as stone pit-enclosures for livestock which distinguishes them from their neighbours on the plateaus to the west. Although they were there in the sixteenth to eighteenth centuries A.D. their material remains suggest an impoverished and rather isolated society.

In the second millennium A.D., as more Iron Age peoples migrated southward from central Africa, the pressure on land grew and warfare became more common. The cattle-owning Ila/Tonga-speaking peoples reached what is now Zambia from the north possibly in the twelfth century. Later, but mostly in the seventeenth and eighteenth centuries, came offshoots of the powerful Luba/Lunda empire which had developed between Lake Tanganyika and the Central Angola highlands. Of these groups the Bemba, and the Lunda who followed them across the Luapula into northern Zambia, are the most important. They both had strong political organizations and the latter were able to dominate the people among whom they settled because they obtained firearms by trading ivory and slaves with the Portuguese on the west coast. The Lozi of the upper Zambesi flood plains in Barotseland may also have a similar origin.

In South Africa later Iron Age peoples fall into two groups known by their material cultures *Uitkomst* and *Buispoort*. The Uitkomst people post-date the ninth century A.D. Iron Age settlement of the Soutpansberg south of the Limpopo, and probably survived until the coming of Europeans to the Transvaal. Buispoort settlements are known in the Rustenburg area northwest of the Magaliesberg as well as from a wider region stretching from Lydenburg in the eastern Transvaal to the Kalahari in the west. Both groups built stone enclosures, kept cattle and cultivated with iron implements. It is thought possible that their descendants are the Sotho-speaking peoples of the present-day Transvaal whose pottery resembles theirs. Much of Natal was also probably settled by Sotho peoples moving in from the north. To the east the coastal belt has been settled by the Nguni group of Bantu-speaking peoples who are known from the records of shipwrecked Europeans to have occupied the coastal area of the Transkei at least as early as the sixteenth century. They were nomadic cattle herders and left few permanent traces of settlement.

The other major group of peoples living in Southern Africa at the time of European settlement in the Cape were Hottentots. It is likely that they owe their physical characteristics to intermarriage between Bushmen and early Iron Age Negroid immigrants. At all events their language possesses distinctive clicks as does Bushman speech. Schapera (1963: 37) suggests that the Nguni tribes were in the Transvaal much earlier than is usually supposed because even the Transvaal Ndebele have clicks in their language derived from contact with the Hottentots, who may therefore have been more widespread on the High Veld than is commonly believed. One of the Hottentot cultures is found along the coasts of the Cape where middens testify to subsistence from seafoods and *veldkos*. The other culture belonged to Hottentot pastoralists who kept long-horned cattle and fat-tailed, hairy sheep and who lived in small nomadic bands supplementing their diet with game which they shot with bows and arrows.

Bantu-speaking peoples with tribal names which have often survived to the present occupied the coastal belt of Moçambique at least three centuries ago. In the west the Bantu-speaking Ambo and Herero are thought to have migrated from central southern Africa and to have followed the rather dry, but habitable grasslands along the highlands away from the arid coast until the Herero met and clashed with the Nama Hottentot.

The development of empires or native states in northern areas during the sixteenth and seventeenth centuries was to be the dominant factor in migrations in the south in the nineteenth century. The Zulu leader, Shaka, continued the process of welding together many of the hundred or so tribes who lived in the area of modern Natal. By virtue of his ambition, ruthless-ness, and military prowess, he was able to create a Zulu empire which extended from the coast to the Kalahari. Minor chieftains originally under

Shaka's sway or who challenged him were driven out of Zulu country and found refuge to the west, north or south. The Basuto under Moshesh successfully avoided open clashes with Shaka as did the Swazi under Sobuza. Both nations had been able to organize and develop a nucleus in a weakly held area: the first in the mountains and foothills beyond the Drakensberg, the second below the escarpment but inland from the Lebombo ranges. Other Nguni hordes created havoc where they went, conquering or driving out those already in occupation of large areas. Chief Mzilikazi was one of these, who settled first in the central Transvaal (1825), and then was driven out by Boers and Zulu *impis* into Rhodesia in 1840 where he settled among the Rozwi whose power he broke. The Matabele, as they were called from the way they disappeared behind their huge cow-hide shields, became the overlords until the Europeans arrived in 1890. Yet another horde of Nguni, under the control of Zwangendaba, was driven out of Zulu country across the Limpopo, laid waste the Karanga empire in the Sabi valley, destroying Zimbabwe in 1830, and crossing the lower Zambesi to harry the tribes east of the Luangwa. Eventually some of them settled in southern Malawi and the rest moved on to the Lake Victoria region.

As a result of the chaos, instability and migrations connected with the rise of the Zulu empire, the Bantu-speaking peoples were not able to resist the incursions of European settlers, traders and missionaries. The Portuguese and Arabs had shown the way in Zambia and Angola where they were aided by the Bemba. Other tribes sought the expertise and firepower of Europeans to protect them from the Zulus or other groups. Land concessions were bartered or sold and in other places devastated or vacant land was occupied by Europeans. Thus, although a few groups such as the Zulus, Swazi, Basuto and Matabele were able to resist the erosion of their power at least for a time, many other divided and disorganized peoples with an Iron Age culture were no match for the superior power of the trekboers and their commandos or the British army.

For the most part the Bantu-speaking peoples of Southern Africa have retained to the present the homelands they had acquired by the nineteenth century. In detail, however, there are two major exceptions to this and both are the result of the coming of European colonizers to the region. First, as a result of conquest, rebellion or persuasion some large-scale movements of people have resulted directly from European intervention. These will be discussed later in the context of colonial expansion. Secondly, there are today great flows of migrant labourers (mostly adult men) to the centres of industry, mining and plantation agriculture. These are relatively short-term movements and as such are not normally reflected in censuses in which *de facto* populations are counted.

The European Impact

When the Dutch East India Company finally decided to establish a refreshment station on their sea route to India at Table Bay they had no intention of settling there anyone except those company servants necessary for running the establishment: 90 soldiers and sailors in all. Van Riebeeck had instructions to build a fort and lay out a garden, to obtain cattle and sheep from the natives but to maintain good relations with them. In the first three years (1652–5) the establishment endured privations from crop failure and stock theft and also lost soldiers who stowed away on passing ships. Against their better judgment, the Council of Seventeen who directed the affairs of the Company were persuaded by van Riebeeck to make experiments in settling a few colonists to see whether the settlement could become self-sufficient and less of a financial burden to the Company. In 1657–9 volunteers were selected to become *free burghers*, were given 28 acres (11·3 hectares) of land each and were forced to sign a contract which preserved the Company's trading monopoly: the Company fixed grain and cattle prices, took all the surpluses and *inter alia* prohibited tobacco cultivation after Hottentots risked being shot by stealing the plants. Quite apart from removing the economic incentives that would have encouraged the settlers to plant substantial amounts of grain, the Company was anxious to limit both the size of population and extent of the colony in case it got out of their control. But by consenting to permit free colonists in the first place they destroyed the means of controlling the settlement for ever. The size of the settlement grew slowly – by 1679 there were 62 families of colonists – but by then the first generation of children of colonists were petitioning the Company for farms in Hottentots Holland, 30 miles (48 km) inland across the barren sandy Cape Flats. Thus began the outward movement of thinly spread farmers which, after another century, was to come up against the advancing Nguni peoples 400 miles (640 km) east of the Cape of Good Hope (Fig. 32). The next Commander, Van der Stel, sanctioned expansion although he attempted to control it. By 1685 there were about 125 settler families on the land and the Company began actively to encourage immigration to the Cape as a means of holding on to what had become a strongly fortified strategic post guarding the Dutch trade routes to the East. The Council of Seventeen had no difficulty in offering to take some of the Huguenot refugees who came to Holland after the revocation of the Edict of Nantes in 1688. About 200 families of French extraction and Protestant persuasion eventually took advantage of the offer. When they were settled they formed about a quarter of the whole community but such was their education, energy and moral qualities that they soon had a disproportionately great influence (Fouché, 1963: 134). After 1700 no more Huguenots were sent to the Cape and after 1705 the Company ceased to send Hollanders to settle. Although there were a few Dutch and German immigrants during the eighteenth century, opinion in the colony was against increasing the flow as the prospects for the existing colonists were poor enough. In fact, with the exception of a very few years, Southern Africa has never attracted the numbers of immigrants that America or Australia have. As a result the importance of the locally born and brought-up colonist is all the greater. At times, indeed, the latter has feared the prospect of being swamped by uncontrolled immigration even from Europe. (In particular President Kruger, once his republic grew rich from gold, did not wish to see the old order swept away by the numerical and economic superiority of the flood of immigrants pouring on to the Witwatersrand in the 1890's and he passed laws excluding many of them from the franchise.) The European population of the colony rose from 1300 in 1700 to 10,000 in 1778, 22,000 in 1798 and 26,000 in 1806. The remainder of the population was of slave origin or the detribalized remnants of Hottentots who had been decimated by two smallpox epidemics.

After the Cape settlement had finally passed into British hands in 1806 a slow trickle of immigrants from the United Kingdom came to the colony. But, with the exception of a party of Scots privately brought out in 1817, the first important immigration was a government-sponsored scheme for close settlement, most of whose 3,500 participants went to the eastern frontier of the Cape Colony. A party from this latter Albany settlement set up in 1824 as traders with the Zulus in Natal, where they preceded the trekboers who arrived there in 1838. A further British settlement, which introduced 4500 colonists to Natal between 1848 and 1851, was inspired by the colonial reformer Edward Gibbon Wakefield. Among the more important settlement schemes were the ones with which Sir George Grey was associated. As Governor of the Cape Colony (1854–61) he aimed to secure the safety of the eastern frontier where the settlers had been facing the Nguni tribes for upwards of fifty years. He had been influenced by Wakefield's policies for denser settlement and expensive land in South Australia and New Zealand and was encouraged first to accept the disbanded British-German Legion of German mercenaries originally intended for the Crimean war. Soon after they had been settled on the eastern frontier (1856) they were sent to India after the mutiny, so that Grey attempted to secure large-scale immigration of 4000 peasant folk from north Germany. More than half had actually sailed for the Cape before the scheme was disallowed by the Colonial Office in London.

From the beginning of the eighteenth century the Dutch farmers of the Cape had sought grazing farms beyond the mountain barrier east of the Cape Flats. By 1750 they had crossed the Gouritz river and were at the foot of the Outeniqua mountains; by 1770 they were on the Gamtoos, the Sundays and the Bruintjes Hoogte; and by 1775 they had reached a line stretching from the Bushman's river to the upper Fish river and even beyond it in the Tarka district. By the end of a century of trekking they had crossed into the Suurveld and were facing the Nguni tribes across the lower Fish river. Once past the arid barrier of the Great Karoo they were able to fan out northward towards the Orange river in search of still further pastures (Fig. 32). Their occupation of the grazing lands of the Suurveld,

Fig. 32. Southern Africa: Physical Features, Pioneer Movements and Present Political Divisions. Basutoland is now Lesotho.

around present Grahamstown, was not uncontested by the Xhosa tribes, the Nguni peoples who had migrated farthest towards the southwest. The sparsely settled trekboers and their cattle herds were a natural target for the neighbouring Nguni, especially the breakaway branch of Xhosa under Ndhlambi anxious to secure grazing west of the Fish river and away from

Gaika the Xhosa paramount chief. In 1779–81 the trekboers had been allowed to organize a commando to expel the Xhosas, but the East India Company in 1793 had imposed a negotiated settlement on the frontier farmers. Again in 1799 a further Xhosa incursion caught trekboers disarmed and disorganized, as a result of which they had their rights to grazing land south of Graaff-Reinet confirmed at the expense of allowing the Xhosas to remain in the Suurveld. An active British administration cleared the Suurveld of Xhosa tribesmen in 1811 and allowed trekboers to reoccupy their former grazing lands.

This uneasy balance between trekboer and Nguni continued for another twenty years in which time the British settlers were added to the frontier population. In 1798 the great majority of the 21,000 Europeans of the Cape Colony were living in the western districts but thirty years later, such was the shift of farmers towards the frontier, that the eastern districts contained 21,000 of the total of 55,000 Europeans. Then in a few months in 1837 some 2000 trekboers left the Colony, crossing the Orange river on to the empty grasslands of the High Veld. The leaders of the trekkers were perfectly aware that the interior country was in the main free from the encumbrance of a large native population. The Zulu campaigns and their a aftermath had seen to that. The three exploratory *commissie trekke* had established this fact and the nature of the land's resources in places as far apart and as different as South West Africa, the Soutpansberg and Natal. It was to the latter that the trekkers resolved to move in search of fresh pastures. In the course of a decade between 12,000 and 14,000 people trekked out of the Colony, and the distribution of trekboers by the end of the 1840's foreshadowed the extent of the present Republic of South Africa. A large part of the High Veld was occupied and, although a large party of trekkers had left Natal between the Drakensberg and the port of Durban when the British occupied the region, they moved only a short distance across the Tugela river. The Great Trek extended the frontier between the European farmers and the Bantu-speaking tribes from about 200 miles (320 km) to more than 1000 miles (1600 km) in a great horseshoe-shaped curve. From the middle of the nineteenth century these tribes were progressively confined to the arid western periphery of the High Veld or the northern and eastern sub-tropical and tropical plateau slopes and lowlands. A few groups such as the Bataung on the Sand river and the Barolong at Thaba Nchu were left surrounded by trekboers in the Orange Free State. Only in the region between the Great Fish and the Umtamvuna rivers, or Kaffraria as it became known as, was there little interference from European farmers in the affairs of the Nguni peoples. The latter were in any case relatively densely packed in that area, having been driven there by the Zulu depredations.

In the western part of the Cape Colony the Hottentots had trekked through arid Namaqualand and had settled on the better watered grazing grounds of the southern part of South West Africa. This was to become known as Namaland. In the Cape Colony the Hottentots had competed first with the hunting Bushmen and then also with the Dutch for water-holes and fountains (or springs). In Namaland, and farther to the north between the Auas Mountains and the Waterberg (north of present Windhoek), they found grazing for which they did not compete with neighbouring Bushman tribes who hunted in the mountains. But on the plains they had to compete with the Bantu-speaking Herero who had migrated through Bechuana territory and the Kaokoveld south of the Kunene river. At roughly the same time the Bantu-speaking Ovambo moved into northern South West Africa. But all these cattle-owning peoples were initially at the mercy of the Bergdamas, a dark-skinned hunting people of short stature who lived in the highlands and who practised metal-working. The Bergdamas burned the grassland to encourage fresh growth and tempt game on to their hunting grounds. The Herero, who were dependent on large herds of cattle and who already had to contend with periodic droughts, grew desperate at such unfriendly activity. They were also strong enough to invade grassland considered to belong to the Namas. In the second quarter of the nineteenth century the Namas sought the cooperation of Jonker Afrikander, a leader of a band of fugitive slaves and people of mixed ancestry who had left the Cape Colony at the end of the eighteenth century. Superior fighting technique and firepower ensured the defeat of the Hereros and the capture of their cattle. Jonker settled in the Windhoek region roughly on the former boundaries of Namaland and Hereroland. The Namas and Hereros were more or less at war with each other for the whole of the latter half of the nineteenth century. Only the power of the German colonizing forces was able to bring the struggle to an end.

Population movements in Angola and Moçambique are less well known than those farther south. The Portuguese developed an early interest in both territories for trading, transferring their attentions from the Lower Congo region to Angola, from which it is estimated some 3.3 to 3.5 million slaves were taken. The numbers of Portuguese colonists were never great in either territory. Many of them were officials, missionaries or those anxious to begin life again anywhere. Some of them were convicts and criminals who intermarried with locally employed slaves. The territories had so little appeal, however, that even by the end of the nineteenth century there were only 9000 Europeans in Angola and only about 1000 in Moçambique. The settling of wider areas of these Portuguese territories belongs more to the twentieth century, when several colonization schemes on the highlands of

Angola and in settlements such as those at Guija on the Limpopo river were initiated. Even so, only a few hundred families have been involved in these farm settlements: most of the European population today is found in the towns of the two provinces.

The Development of the Political Framework

In inter-tropical Africa Barbour (1961:304) has pointed out that state boundaries are largely the result of the wave of empire building at the end of the nineteenth century. Although this may be true of the northern part of the area now under discussion, in the southern part boundaries are generally of much greater antiquity. It is true that some were established quite late, but, in contrast to the pattern characteristic of inter-tropical Africa, many of the boundaries in the south are not so arbitrary, nor were they drawn so frequently along lines of latitude or longitude. They were in the main drawn up with considerable background knowledge of the areas and peoples they were intended to divide and, in most cases, with reference to the areas occupied by or considered to be owned by tribal groups. Throughout most of the Cape Province, and in the other provinces comprising the Republic of South Africa, tribal groups either had disappeared as recognizable entities occupying distinct tracts of land or had only relatively recently moved to the land they occupied when boundaries were being drawn up. Outside the area of the Republic most boundaries do in fact date from the period of the 'Scramble for Africa'. Their peculiarities reflect rival claims and competing negotiations for treaties with native chiefs by European powers and chartered companies with commercial interests. Yet once these boundaries had been drawn up they acquired a permanence which, assisted by unified administration within them, has helped to engender modern African nationalism.

The southern part of Africa also differs from the rest of inter-tropical Africa in that it is almost the only part of the continent where boundaries have had to divide groups of settlers of European extraction for whom the occupation of land gave them a secure foothold in the continent. Their idea of exclusive proprietary rights over land differed in many cases from the notions of the indigenous peoples of Africa, thus providing fruitful causes of misunderstanding which has been resolved more often by the exercise of force than by negotiations to which both parties came on equal terms. In several instances territory has been acquired by European powers or settlers by conquest or forfeiture, after the inhabitants had rebelled against the administration.

Initially the possessions of the Dutch East India Company were extended by conquest of the Hottentot and Bushman peoples living in the Western Cape. This arose from the need to provide security for the small establishment at Table Bay and to protect the early agricultural settlements. Sovereignty over the area was extended by settlement, although the Company was rarely able to exercise any real authority. Almost all it was able to do was to compel the trekboers to trade with the Company rather than with other foreign powers, although the trekboers continued to spread into the interior and to trade with the Hottentots and Nguni in spite of the *placaats* (edicts) issued by the Company in 1727, 1739 and 1770. The Company also attempted to extend its control by establishing *drostdies* (magistracies) in the frontier districts. But these usually followed settlement. In 1778 the Dutch Governor placed a beacon near Colesberg to mark the northeastern limit of the Colony. Fig. 33A shows how the boundaries were gradually extended towards the east and only defined in the north along the whole length of Orange river in 1847. Immediately to the north of this boundary were the lands of the Griquas whose chief, Andries Waterboer, had entered into a treaty with the British in 1834. The British administration attempted to repeat the policy of the Dutch East India Company and extend the frontier to include those who had taken part in the Great Trek. First, by virtue of the Cape of Good Hope Punishment Act (1835) they claimed the right of jurisdiction in criminal cases over British subjects up to the line of latitude 25°S. Later the Orange River Sovereignty was proclaimed between the Orange and Vaal rivers to south and north and the Drakensberg escarpment between their sources to the east. At first this extension of British sovereignty was backed up by military force; but not long afterwards the impossibility of remote control of frontier farmers who were ranging even farther afield convinced Britain that withdrawal was essential. By the Sand River Convention (1852) the trans-Vaal trekboers were granted independence and two years later, when the Cape Colony achieved representative government, the Orange Free State achieved freedom from British rule. Thereafter the development of the political framework consisted of a series of moves and counter-moves by the land-locked trekker republics and the British government, acting principally through the High Commissioner for South Africa. The former desired access to the coast as well as an expansion of territory for the future increase of population and herds. The latter were equally determined to prevent the coast from being settled, for this would have permitted a non-British power to have had direct dealings with the republics.

Extending Control over Native Peoples
On the eastern frontier of the Cape Colony, which since the end of the eighteenth century had lain along the lower Fish river, the Governor arranged with Gaika, the paramount chief of the Rarabe Xhosas, to maintain a neutral zone between the Fish river boundary and Kaffraria proper;

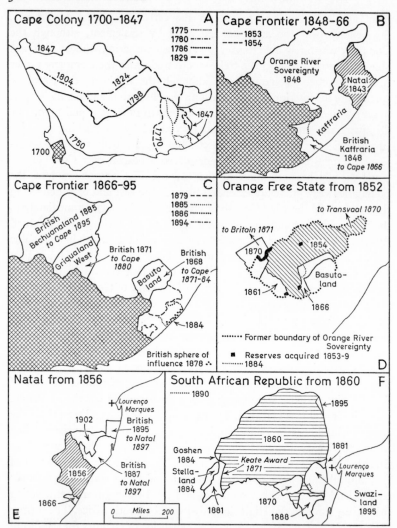

Fig. 33. South Africa: Evolution of the Major Political Units.
(A) Cape Colony 1700-1847; (B) Cape Frontier 1848-66; (C) Cape Frontier 1866-95; (D) Orange Free State from 1852; (E) Natal from 1856; (F) South African Republic from 1860.

which area was considered to lie east of the Keiskamma, a river which rose in the Amatola mountains. Once more uncontrolled contact between the colonists and the Xhosas was forbidden although trade fairs, either at Grahamstown or at Fort Willshire on the Fish river, were sanctioned.

In spite of this 'cordon sanitaire', cattle-raiding among Nguni tribes and between them and the colonists continued. The Fish river frontier did not present a difficult obstacle in the dry months of most of the year and it afforded plenty of cover as well as good grazing and browsing grounds. In 1829 the frontier was extended to include the Kat river basin in the Winterberg foothills. In that basin emancipated Hottentots were settled on small farms. At the same time a body of Fingos (Fetcani from the far east of Kaffraria), who had been defeated by a settler commando, adopted the dubiously protective custody of the Gcaleka Xhosas east of the Kei river. During the almost inevitable frontier war which broke out in 1834 these Fingos were led into the neutral territory from which it had not proved possible to exclude the Xhosas. The settlement after the war at first included the extension of British rule over the territory between the Keiskamma and Kei rivers, as well as the cession of the neutral territory to the Cape, But the former territory, briefly called the Province of Queen Adelaide, was returned to the Xhosas as a result of the combined pressure of humanitarian agitators in London and a natural desire to save the expense of adding an unstable frontier zone to an already expensive commitment on the frontier. This territory finally became British Kaffraria in 1848 and was added to the Cape Colony in 1866, again partly as an economy measure (Fig. 33B).

Further extensions of the boundary of the Cape Colony in the east followed two patterns. The weaker tribal groups which had been in closer contact with colonists would accept a missionary or British resident who was initially representing the law for the community of European traders. Weaker tribes were even willing to pay taxes because they were anxious to come under colonial rule to save themselves from more powerful tribes or from the trekboers. In this way Tembus were located between the White Kei and the Indwe rivers at the foot of the Stormberg in 1853; the Xesibe came under Cape protection in 1878 to preserve them from the Pondos; Fingoland was included in 1879; and the Basuto were saved from the trekboers of the Orange Free State in 1868 by British annexation (Fig. 33c). The Cape Colony was usually persuaded to accept formal annexation on the grounds that the taxes from these areas would help to defray the expenses of administration.

The other pattern of annexation resulted from fractious behaviour on the part of tribes such as both the Gcaleka and Rarabe Xhosas, the Pondos and the Zulus who naturally resented the way in which their former enemies and rivals for grazing were protected by the new colonial power. The Rarabe Xhosas (or Gaikas), like other sections of the Xhosas within British Kaffraria, had been given magistrates. They refused to accept theirs, attacked government forces and sparked off a three-year war, only

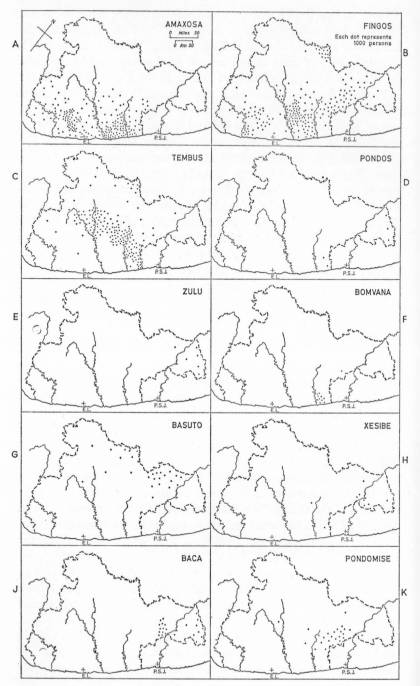

Fig. 34. Distribution of Tribal Groups on the Eastern Frontier of Cape Colony and in the Transkeian territories, 1891 (based on the Census of the Cape Colony, 1891)

to be banished from their mountain home in the forested Amatolas. Another rebellion which they joined in 1877 led to their expulsion beyond the Kei and to the forfeiture of land in what had been the northern part of British Kaffraria. The Gcalekas and the Pondos across the Kei, who reluctantly accepted the peace imposed on them by British and Cape Colonial military forces, submitted to colonial rule in 1885 and 1894 respectively (Fig. 33C). The tribes of Kaffraria proper (now the Transkei) were in the main left in possession of their lands without experiencing the loss of land to trekboers, British colonists or land speculators. Fig. 34 shows the distribution of tribal groups in 1891.

On the eastern side of these relatively densely populated tribal territories the lands below the Drakensberg and between the Umtamvuna and the Tugela rivers was virtually depopulated at the time of the Great Trek. The Republic of Natal had been established here on the strength of a grant of land from the Zulu paramount, Dingaan. This trekker republic was set up only after Dingaan had been driven back across the Tugela in the campaign which followed his treacherous massacre of voortrekkers at Umgungundhlovu in 1838. British military assistance was sent to protect the small beleaguered settlement at Port Natal (Durban), to head off the trek away from the coast, and to establish the rule of law in the area claimed by the trekkers, but this policy proved difficult to carry out. It was not until 1842 that the trekker republic submitted, but not before they had established their own capital at Pietermaritzburg some 56 miles (90 km) inland. The territory was finally annexed to the Cape Colony in 1843, but the Volksraad set up by the trekker republic continued to function for a couple of years until its authority was directly questioned by the new Governor. The British annexation which finally established Natal as a detached district of the Cape Colony in 1845, was on such terms that the majority of the trekboers left for the High Veld or for areas across the Buffalo and Tugela rivers where they obtained permission to live on land acquired in 1848 from the Zulu chief Panda, who had crushed Dingaan with Boer support some years earlier.

Trekboers and Tribesmen: The Struggle for Territory
The acquisition of land given or sold to trekkers by native chiefs is the key to understanding the pattern of territorial expansion in and on the fringes of the High Veld. In the thirty years after the Great Trek the various local trekker leaders independently secured land by treaty, purchase or threat from the chiefs of Nguni and Sotho peoples who surrounded their *lebensraum* on three sides. This process continued virtually unimpeded on the eastern and northern frontiers (Figs. 33D,F). The Swazis sold land on which Lydenburg was founded in 1846. On the High Veld the Bataungs

had in 1836 granted to Potgieter – a trekker leader – land which became the Winburg republic and subsequently the northern part of the Orange Free State. A party of trekkers moving north from Moroko's country near Thaba Nchu met with resistance from Mzilikazi's warlike Matabele tribe across the Valsch river near where Kroonstad now stands. This was over 100 miles (160 km) from Mzilikazi's headquarters in the eastern part of the Magaliesberg, but it showed that the grassy High Veld was not completely depopulated. Having been attacked and with their cattle stolen, the trekker party retired to Thaba Nchu and an expedition was mounted to deal with the Matabele. A trekker victory was followed by a punitive visit from Dingaan's Zulu impis, which confirmed the Matabele in their resolve to move away across the Limpopo into what became known as Matabeleland. The voortrekkers claimed the western part of the Transvaal vacated by Mzilikazi in 1873 as theirs by right of conquest. Some smaller tribes who returned to their former homes appear to have acknowledged this fact, or at any rate they acquiesced in it (Agar Hamilton, 1928: 52). Another group of trekkers settled in the Steelpoort river valley in 1845 on what was apparently vacant land, although it was surrounded by tribes who seem to have resented trekboers visiting them to secure labour for their farming operations. The scarcity of labour would suggest that the area was depopulated, but it may nevertheless have been a hunting ground for neighbouring tribes. Agar Hamilton (1928: 61) considers that much land was acquired as a personal gift from native chiefs to the voortrekker commandant, A. H. Potgieter, and that the rather detailed treaties which they have survived may have been drawn up subsequently to rectify the position and to give the whole trekboer population a stake in the newly won land. Such was the title to the country between the Olifants river, the Portuguese border and 26°S latitude, which recorded an instalment in the purchase of that land from Mswazi, son of the founder of the Swazi nation. In spite of all these acquisitions of territory the trekker republics contained large and significant tribal communities which they were forced to tolerate since they were in secure occupation of certain tracts. For example the Bapedi under Sekukuni, who occupied the Lulu mountains between the Olifants and Steelport rivers, refused to acknowledge that their land belonged to the trekkers by virtue of purchase from Mswazi. The internally divided South African Republic, which was a loosely welded confederation of like-minded trekker republics, was unable to compel Sekukuni's submission. Trekker commandos were defeated and even mercenary soldiers were no more successful. Finally he submitted to a force of British troops during the period when the Transvaal was annexed by Britain (1877–81). Sekukuni himself was captured in 1880 and he was at length forced to come to terms with the republican authorities.

The Basuto were similarly obliged to submit to military force, although they retained their independence in mountainous terrain, deprived of some of their best agricultural land. The campaigns of 1865–67 centred round the perpetually thorny question of stock theft and agricultural land. When the Orange Free State burghers succeeded in capturing both the cattle and the standing crops of the Basuto they had them at their mercy. At this stage a goodly portion of land either occupied or claimed by Moshesh of the Basuto was annexed to the republic. Since much of this was not occupied by Free State farmers and continued to be held by Basuto the paper loss of territory did not prevent the war from continuing. Eventually the British High Commissioner annexed the Basuto country except for the lowlands west of the Caledon river which were retained by the Orange Free State. In this case the threat of annexation of the whole of Basutoland by Natal and the prospect of wholesale removals of population were factors which hastened British action (Fig. 33D).

The western frontiers of both of the trekker republics were established and defined as a result of a nicely balanced series of forces. In the first place the presence of Griqua tribes in the south, Bechuana tribes north of the Orange river and the Matabele to the northwest, limited the easy expansion of scattered grazing communities. In the second place the Missionaries' Road to the interior passed this way, starting on the Orange river at Prieska or at Hopetown. Running through the Griqua states north of the Orange, which had been settled with the support of the London Missionary Society, its routes ran west of the Vaal and Harts rivers to Shoshong and to Sechele on the Zambesi west of the Victoria Falls. It was used by explorers, traders and ivory hunters throughout the nineteenth century. Both the trekker republics attempted to gain control of the road for they feared that the activities promoted by its users would lead to gun traffic and unsettle the tribes on the arid margins of the Kalahari Desert. In the south, after the Bloemfontein Convention of 1854, the process of buying out Griqua land east of the Vaal continued until all the Phillipolis lands were acquired by the Free State in 1861. West of the Vaal a belt of territory was disputed by four parties: the two republics; freelance speculators such as Arnot and Doms who were advisers to Griqua and Bechuana chiefs; and the diggers who had flocked here to search for diamonds since 1869. Wodehouse, the British High Commissioner (and Governor of the Cape), was at first reluctant to intervene. His replacement, Sir Henry Barkly, armed with the knowledge that a new policy had been adopted by the Colonial Secretary in London and forearmed by the Cape Colonial Secretary's campaign to annex the Diamond Fields, met the threats of President Brand of the Free State with counter-threats. Faced with the prospect of having to annex the territory Britain agreed on condition that the Cape Colony would administer the new territory (Griqualand West) and would accept the responsibilities of self-government. Although the Cape declined to administer Griqualand West, it did become responsible for Basutoland in the same year (1871) (Fig. 33D).

Farther north, the Transvaalers had wisely stuck to local arbitration of their disputes. The South African Republic had proclaimed its paper sovereignty over an area between 22½°E longitude in the west, the Lebombo mountains in the east, and from the southern edge of Mzilikazi's Matabeleland and the Limpopo in the north to the Harts river in the south, but excluding the territory of the Batlapin south of Kuruman. This huge republic would have cut right across the Missionaries' Road and included the Tati goldfields on the Shashi river (now in northern Botswana). The Keate Award of 1871, based on arbitration between the tribes and the trekkers drew the boundary of the South African Republic along the Maquassi *spruit* (creek), excluding a number of trekker farms and the embryo villages of Bloemhof and Christiana. In the 1870's the campaign for British control even of Bechuanaland grew, supported by the missionaries and the expansionists in Cape Town. Police detachments were, in fact, placed at intervals with the Bechuana tribes but were withdrawn in 1881. At the same time the British authorities were discussing the question of returning independence to the successfully rebellious Transvaal which had been annexed in 1877. A new line of demarcation farther west than Keate's line of 1871 included farms occupied by Transvaalers which had often only recently been acquired from the divided Bechuanas (Fig. 33F). This was the western frontier agreed to in the Pretoria Convention of 1881, which incidentally reserved to Britain the right of suzerain over the Transvaal's external affairs. No such new line of demarcation could prevent boer freebooters from continuing the subversion of the waning authority of some Bechuana chiefs. Others friendly to the Cape were deprived of ammunition in order to avoid embroilment in the affair and to strengthen Britain's diplomatic protests at the action connived at by the Transvaal authorities. Some of the freebooters set up the mini-republics of Stellaland and Goshen athwart the Missionaries' Road, even blocking mining supplies for Tati and Matabeleland. Mackenzie of the London Missionary Society who had special charge for the Bechuanas in the area was able to summon support in Britain, convincing Joseph Chamberlain of the necessity for British intervention. The revision of the Pretoria Convention took place in London in 1884. This gave the South African Republic a boundary still farther west, including a large part of the settled Stellaland republic (Fig. 33F). However it did not transgress the trade route to the North except at Kunana where it ran through the *stad* of Moshete, one of the Bechuana chiefs who had espoused the Transvaal cause. Further intriguing by the

Transvaal authorities and the annexation of Goshen, which was encouraged by the anti-imperial activities of Rhodes, who replaced Mackenzie as Commissioner in Bechuanaland, finally provoked Britain into sending an armed expedition to the territory. Its purpose was to free the area west of the Transvaal boundary of 1884 and to establish British control over the region. In 1885, therefore, Bechuanaland south of the Molopo river was annexed as British Bechuanaland and until 1895 it was administered by Britain. North of the Molopo river, as far as 22°S latitude, a British protectorate was extended after negotiations with chiefs of the local population including those of the Bamangwato who had been free from Boer interference. (Campbell, 1959: chapters 13 and 14). The latter move appropriately countered the declaration of a German protectorate over South West Africa (1884).

In many ways South West Africa was similar to Bechuanaland and it possessed almost all the requirements for it to pass into the hands of a colonial power. Missionaries, merchants and administrators had tried to interest the Cape Colony in annexation, but it was preoccupied by more pressing problems, and South West Africa was relatively so remote from either Cape Town or the main scenes of activity on the High Veld (Campbell, 1959: 226). Only Walvis Bay, accessible by sea and with a useful anchorage, fell to the Cape Colony because in 1878 Britain had not wished to annex any larger part of the then unknown and turbulent territory in the hinterland.

Apart from the partially successful expansionist move by trekboers to claim a large tract through the lands of the Zulu chief Cetewayo to the east coast at St Lucia Bay (1883–4), the New Republic thus set up in 1886 was recognized by Britain to include only the inland portion of the area claimed. It became part of the South African Republic two years later. British paramountcy on the coast at St Lucia Bay had been declared in 1884 and the work of achieving the isolation of the Transvaal from the coast was completed in two stages. Zululand up to the Mkusi river was annexed in 1887, only a few years after the reinstatement of Cetewayo who had so successfully made war in 1879. Tongaland, between the Mkusi and the southern limit of Portuguese Moçambique, was added to the British dominion in 1895 and both were handed over to the Natal administration in 1897 (Fig. 33E).

Mention has already been made of Rhodes' designs on the area north of the Cape and the Transvaal. He seems to have seized on Sir Harry Johnston's idea of British hegemony from the Cape to Cairo (Oliver, 1957: 143), one of the main links in Rhodes' scheme being Bechuanaland which, in an interesting reflection of his southern and not specifically British viewpoint, he regarded as the Suez Canal of the Cape Colony. The settlement

of the Rhodesias by pioneers in the quarter-century up to 1914 was the last
example of the acquisition of territory by the old methods of concessions
from local chiefs, a show of force and a willing band of pioneer trekkers.
Rhodes' occupation of Mashonaland and the occupation of Matabeleland
by pioneers of mainly British stock prevented further expansion of the
trekboer pattern of life and society north of the Transvaal. The British
South Africa Company allowed 'their land' to be occupied by pioneers,
each of whom had been promised fifteen gold-claims and a farm of 3000
acres (1200 hectares) on the strength of a concession by Lobengula – the
chief of the Matabele (who dominated the Mashona and therefore the
whole of the Zambesi–Sabi–Limpopo watershed) – to the company to
dig for gold in specified places. In fact the Matabele people were unwilling
to see their country taken over, but Lobengula realized the consequences
of resistance to the moves of the Company urged on by Rhodes. The threat
of force compelled him to acquiesce in the march of the pioneer column
from the south to Fort Salisbury (Mason, 1958). Upon rebellion, first
among the Matabele in 1893 and then the Mashona in 1897, measures were
taken to prevent any resurgence of tribal power. The Matabele country
was considered, by the 1894 Order in Council which regularized administration, to belong to the British South Africa Company by right of
conquest. The sphere of operations of the Company lay north of the South
African Republic and British Bechuanaland, east of the German protectorate and west of Portuguese Moçambique and thus effectively filled the
vacuum between the spheres of influence in central Africa. In 1891 the
Company was permitted to extend its operations north of the Zambezi in
the area south of the Congo Free State. The recently appointed Imperial
Commissioner in Nyasaland (H. H. Johnston) was to be paid to administer
the Company's chartered territory north of the Zambezi which, together
with Nyasaland, was to be called the British Central Africa Protectorate.

Southern Africa and the 'Scramble' for Africa

At the same time other boundaries were established, many along lines of
latitude and rivers or watersheds. This phase of delimitation belongs to the
period of the 'Scramble for Africa' and differs markedly from the process
of boundary-making that occurred before the Berlin Conference of 1884–
1885 and south of the tropic of Capricorn. The relative importance of
European power politics and local African questions was quite different
after 1885 and north of the southern tropic. Such considerations led to the
extraordinary Caprivi Strip (*Zipfel*), that projection of the German protectorate over South West Africa along the 18th parallel 'till it reaches the
River Chobe . . .' thence down that river to the Zambezi. 'It is understood
that under this arrangement Germany shall have free access from her

Protectorate to the Zambezi by a strip of territory which shall at no point be less than 20 English miles in width.' (Hertslet, 1896: 645–6). In exchange for this and the cession of Heligoland, Germany withdrew from the Sultanate of Witu on the East African coast and recognized the British protectorate over the Sultan of Zanzibar in respect of that island. At the same time, to appease the French, their interests in Madagascar were recognized as paramount.

This central region which was effectively made a British sphere in the 1890's was in fact a disputed zone. For several centuries the Portuguese had had trading interests on both the east and west coasts and had been in touch with the shadowy Bantu kingdoms of the interior. They had been displaced by the Arabs, but during the middle of the nineteenth century British activities on the middle section of the East African coast and the virtual suppression of the slave trade removed the Arabs from their dominating position. At times the Portuguese seemed keen to establish a trans-African Colony from Angola through to Moçambique. Then in the 1870s a financially embarrassed Portugal tried unsuccessfully to sell Moçambique to Germany. In reality Portuguese authority was uncertain except in limited places on the coast and within reach of the navigable lower Zambezi river. In the relatively inaccessible interior privateer, feudal-like land owners and concessionaires were the only real European authorities. The Scramble, and the need to establish not only the title to territory but an authority sufficient to protect existing rights, prompted the Portuguese to make good their territorial claims by effective occupation. A convention of 1891 had defined the boundaries of Moçambique as they remain today (1966), but the eastern frontier of Angola was not finally settled until 1914 when it was delimited between the extremes claimed by Portugal and the British South Africa Company. In the quarter-century after Portuguese hopes of realizing the African empire depicted on the 'rose-coloured map' a propaganda exercise to impress other European states (Duffy, 1959: 215) there arose the 'new generation' of 1895. They were colonial enthusiasts who established a policy in which the plantation, the chartered company and the use of native contract labour enabled more of the resources of Moçambique and parts of Angola to be developed than any other method of colonization had so far achieved.

In the late 1890s southcentral Africa experienced a wave of treaty-making with H. H. Johnston, Rhodes' indefatigable lieutenants such as Thompson and even some Portuguese like de Carvalho in the lead. In this way the British South Africa Company was able to substantiate its claim to territory between the conventional Congo basin boundary just west of Lake Nyasa and Barotseland. Nyasaland had been an early seat of missionary activity by the Church of Scotland and later, in the 1870's, of commercial activity by the African Lakes Company. In spite of Portuguese attempts to hamper trade at the southern end, and the slave-raiding exploits of powerful tribes at the northern end, of the Lake country, the protectorate declared in 1891 helped to fulfil Rhodes' and Lord Salisbury's design for a British connection from the Cape to Egypt. Rhodes' B.S.A. Company subsidized the administration of Nyasaland for a time, but after 1895 this was taken over by the Foreign Office. However, even Salisbury, like Gladstone before him, was unwilling to become directly embroiled in the annexation of territory in Africa, preferring the indirect methods of the chartered company and the resident consular agent coupled with treaties made with numerous chiefs. The British South Africa Company continued to administer Southern Rhodesia until 1923. It also administered the territory north of the Zambezi until the Jameson raid in 1895 when the manifest lack of control over the region's inhabitants compelled Britain to take over the running of northwestern and northeastern Rhodesia, although the Company still retained a favoured position there.

The Division of Land

Fundamental to any understanding of the changing geography of Southern Africa is the process of land alienation and the enforced adjustment of indigenous concepts of land rights to those concepts characteristic of the colonizing companies or colonial governments. Both because permanent settlement by people of European stock has been relatively recent, and because the pattern of land ownership once established is at the root of regional differentiation at several scales, the way the land is held has an obvious and lasting importance in Southern Africa. The Xhosa proverb 'Land is the Chief' (du Toit, 1954: 259) emphasizes the identity of land and authority. Among the pastoral Hottentots and agro-pastoral Nguni and Sotho, an individual occupied and used land as a member of a community which depended on that land. Individuals could not alienate land. In some cases tribes allowed the European settlers to graze their cattle on what they regarded as their land, thinking that they were only sharing it. A trekboer might follow permission to graze by sowing grain and building a mill, subsequently being granted the exclusive use of that land by the remote Cape Town administration in complete ignorance of the local conditions (Marais, 1939: 6–7). The Voortrekkers' Natal Republic granted farms in land found empty on their arrival. When their presence had become an effective force for peace, many tribal groups who had been driven away by Shaka's and Dingaan's forays returned to their former homes, only to find that they were regarded as squatters. This is understandable in the context of the 1840's; indeed, the voortrekkers always tried to find empty land on which to settle and even moved away from Natal, when it became clear that a substantial proportion of the former Nguni population was returning, because they preferred not to live amongst them. At an early stage, therefore, appears the concept of a White domain in the *platteland*: the rural areas.

The Pattern of European Farms

Southern Africa, like many other tropical or sub-tropical 'new lands', has two main elements in its cadastral landscape: large farms where land use is extensive, for example grazing the veld or bush; and small farms deliberately created to foster closer settlement and more intensive use of land. Among the latter are settlements on irrigated land and mixed farming units in the more favourable areas. Plantations are relatively rare and they usually resemble large farms in terms of their extensive use of land and the number of families they support. These two important types of European agricultural colonization reflect the protean nature of the occupation of new country by immigrants with a cultural background alien to the environment. In the first place, either for defensive purposes or for reasons connected with a prevailing economic theory, small farms were carved out of the available land. Some of the earliest farms were laid out below Table Mountain along the Liesbeeck river, where they were at least protected from the 'south-easters'. These were the 28-acre (11.3-hectare) holdings granted to the Free Burghers. They were able to supply the Dutch East India Company with fresh vegetables, earning the colony the soubriquet of the cabbage patch on the way to India, but the site was still too windy for successful grain production. This small agricultural settlement, some of whose lineaments are still visible in today's landscape, was included within the fortified town on Table Bay and protected by a stout hedge and strong points. In the fourth decade of the settlement somewhat larger freehold grants of land were made in the Paarl and Stellenbosch areas across the Cape Flats to cope with demands made by the first generation of South African-born settlers. The Huguenots were settled among the latter on similar tenure, until by the end of the century most of the beautiful valleys with running water, grazing and sheltered arable land were dotted with farmsteads. Many farms were laid out on the Berg river between Franschoek and the confluence with the Klein Berg river, which gave access through the mountain wall eastward into the Breede (Breë) river valley. From the beginning, grazing by sheep, cattle and goats was permitted in the neighbourhood of the settlements. Grazing licences were issued by the Company to allow stock to be depastured for six or eight months away from the freehold farm. In 1699 the new governor led an expedition into the Tulbagh basin at the head of the Breede valley and the cattle posts which had formerly been scattered around the west of the main mountain walls spread to the interior. At this time the Governor himself had acquired with dubious legality a large farm, Vergelegen, on the eastern side of False Bay and below Hottentots Holland Kloof, which was one of the best routes to the coastal plain beyond. Although this route was blocked for a time, the cattle posts in the Breede valley spread rapidly. Early in the eighteenth century there grew up a system of paying a sum of money as *recognitie* for the licence, and the first records are found of farmers who had grazing licences *without* freehold farms. Starting from the *fontein* where the rudimentary farm buildings were located, the boundaries were marked with stones at the end of half an hour's walk in several directions from the *opstal* (farmsteadings). The local magistrate determined by a field inspection whether the new holding infringed existing grazing rights. A roughly circular holding of about 6000 acres (2450 hectares) resulted from this procedure (Fig. 35A). Although the Company had allowed this expansion of settlement to take place it was powerless to control it, since non-payment of licence fees scarcely ever resulted in eviction. This type of settlement spread rapidly along the coastal belt and the parallel vales north of it, across the Karoo to its eastern and northern limits and towards arid Namaqualand behind the dune-girt coast north of Table Bay. Grazing was the main activity, cattle, and hairy, fat-tailed sheep and boer goats being the principal livestock. In addition, the trekboer on the frontier was in contact with civilization at Cape Town or at a local *drostdy* such as Stellenbosch, Swellendam (from 1745) or Graaff-Reinet (1786) for administrative matters. Alternatively he was able to keep in touch with the remote market through the activities of the *smouse* or pedlars who traded guns, ammunition, bar iron, salt, tea and coffee for the produce of the frontier. This latter was the low-bulk, highly valued produce of the chase (ivory, ostrich feathers and eggs, skins of wild animals) or the partly processed commodities of the livestock industry (butter, tallow, soap) and berry wax from the kannabosch on the veld. Cattle themselves were driven to Table Bay to be slaughtered for the benefit of passing ships and for the growing population of Cape Town. Cape Town was the only market of any importance until the beginning of the nineteenth century when the frontier troubles necessitated the quartering of troops inland from the new port on Algoa Bay (Port Elizabeth). The characteristic type and size of farm extended as far east as the Great Fish river once the Suurveld was finally cleared of Xhosa. However, the *leeningsplaats* (loan-farm) system gradually changed until tenure became less precarious in the direction of permanence and heritability. The system of perpetual quitrent which thus grew up by custom was given official recognition by the Cradock administration in 1813. Loan-farm tenure could be converted to perpetual quitrent tenure, but holdings could not exceed the original limit of 3000 morgen

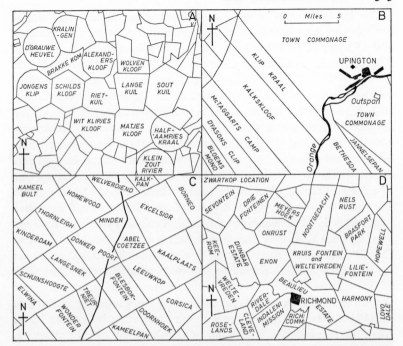

Fig. 35. Patterns of Land Holding by Europeans in South Africa.
(A) Circular, semi-circular and hexagonal farms, originally loan farms
roughly delimited by trekboers before survey. This area settled early in the
eighteenth century lies along the Salt River, south of Riviersonderend and
east of Caledon. (B) Strip farms with riparian frontages; Upington town and
town commonage with a public outspan. (C) Rectilinear farms surveyed for
Afrikaner farmers of the short-lived Stellaland Republic, intersected by the
Transvaal boundary established by the London Convention, 1884. To the
west lies British Bechuanaland, now part of the Cape Province. (D) The
irregular, polygonal farm pattern of Natal with evidence of voortrekker and
English settlement in farm names. Some of the closer settlement on small
holdings are represented by the Dunbar and Beaulieu Estates.
All four maps are based on topo-cadastral maps of the South African Trigsurvey, published by the Government Printer, Pretoria

(about 6100 acres, or 2500 hectares) and were to be surveyed. All further
grants of farms were to be placed on a similar basis. The British administration hoped by this action to regularize land tenure, to reduce the
dispersion encouraged by the uncontrollable loan-farm system and to
increase the revenue of the colony. In practice, although newly settled land
on the eastern frontier was surveyed satisfactorily, the conversion of tenure
and the surveying of existing farms proceeded extremely slowly in the
already settled parts.

The combination of a more determined administration by colonial governors responsible to the British government and the growing pressures of the Xhosa and Tembu tribes on the frontier fathered a reappraisal of the land settlement policy in the Cape Colony. Defence of the frontier and security for its inhabitants demanded closer settlement. Later in the nineteenth century a third justification was added: the need to avoid wasting land. Although there then appeared to be a limited supply of free land for settlement this argument was based more upon unjustifiable comparisons with densely settled Britain. Particularly after 1818, the British government was more than ready to entertain schemes that would reduce the cost of garrisoning the colonies, and the Cape was no exception. If at the cost of a few free passages the colony would become less of a burden to the Treasury, so much the better. Reports of conditions on the frontier and suggestions for the emigration of European colonists had been reaching London since soon after the second British occupation in 1806, Lord Charles Somerset's reports of a land flowing with milk and honey between the Bushmans and Fish rivers (the Suurveld), although exaggerated, were fair in the sense that the Suurveld was better grassed and watered than was the Karoo farther west. It could conceivably carry a denser agricultural population than had been appropriate on those extensive grazing lands. After the renewed Xhosa invasion of the Suurveld and the attack on Grahamstown in 1819 the promotion of emigration to the area 'had come to appear not merely desirable but urgent' (Edwards, 1934: 52). Nearly 5000 British emigrants were shipped to the Cape in 1820 and 1821 to be settled principally in the triangle between Grahamstown and the mouths of the Kowie and Fish rivers, the eastern Suurveld. Each family received a 100-acre (40-hectare) farm at a nominal rent and families were concentrated in parties under appointed leaders in 'locations'. Scattered among them to the north and west were a few of the former trekboer farms; elsewhere there were patches of Crown land. Some of the larger parties banded together to build villages, as at Salem, Cuylerville, Sidbury and Collingham, but in general settlers' houses were scattered throughout the area, being built on their land grants. The villages comprised a few houses on plots laid out in a rectilinear pattern and a surrounding commonage for grazing and firewood. Envy of the large farms occupied by trekboers, and the realization after the failure of several harvests that wheat was not suited to the area, convinced the '1820 settlers' that this scheme for dense agricultural colonization was a failure. Although the acting Governor seems to have promised extensions to holdings, Lord Charles Somerset would not agree to them because it meant the end of his defensive frontier policy. Indeed, when in 1823 a number of settlers were not given their titles to the original grant because they failed to achieve the requisite standard of industry, most of those who had not staked all in the land abandoned their farms. Many moved to Grahamstown or other urban settlements in the Colony. In any case only 55 per cent of the original settlers had been agriculturalists. In reaction to a memorial submitted by the settlers to the Colonial Secretary, a Commission of Enquiry into their grievances recommended that unalienated land adjacent to or near settlers' holdings should provide additional grazing land. Somerset's government accepted the change in policy from a close agricultural settlement to a more extensive pastoral one in 1825. At the same time Dutch farmers who had served the government in the defence of the Colony were given farms north of the Fish river in the 'Ceded Territory'. The closure of the government farm called Somerset was welcomed because it had seriously competed with the settlers for the relatively limited market in agricultural produce through its economies of scale. It was laid out as a village and magistracy and is now known as Somerset East. Finally the labour shortage on the farms was relieved when the settlers were allowed to employ refugee Bechuanas. The prosperity of the settlers improved when they took to merino sheep farming in the late 1820's. Some settlers later found it possible to extend their farming operations by buying farms from Afrikaners who left to go on the Great Trek.

Circumstances permitted another experiment in frontier land policy at the end of the decade in which the Albany settlers had come to the Colony. Maqomo, a Xhosa chief, had been expelled from part of the Ceded Territory on the headwaters of the Kat river. To fill the vacuum it was decided to locate 'surplus' Hottentots (emancipated from servitude since 1828), and the overflow from mission settlements farther west, in an agricultural colony. Each family was given an irrigable plot of between 4 and 32 acres (1·6 to 13 hectares) and a right to communal grazing. Defence and the relief of congestion were the motives, but the scheme failed, not for the same reasons as the 1820 scheme, but because the Hottentots welcomed back Xhosa families as servants and milk suppliers and also because the administration located loyal Fingos among them on equal terms. White farmers and land speculators greedily acquired some of the allotments and bought many more after the Hottentot rebellion during the Kaffir war of 1850–53.

Closer settlement in South Africa, perhaps because of its being castigated by Edward Gibbon Wakefield (1833, Vol. II: 95) as an experiment which failed to attain its object, was tried again both in Natal and at the Cape. After 1831 the British government had yielded somewhat to Wakefield's campaign to reform the practice of colonization by abolishing free grants of land. Although it was the intention of the British government that Crown land should be sold, it was interpreted in the Cape Colony as a desire to sell land at the highest possible price, by public auction. It was Wakefield's idea that revenue thus accruing should be used to finance emigration from the mother country and that by making land reasonably expensive the density of population would be higher, the defence of the newly settled region secured, and the development of the colony ensured through the automatic operation of economic laws. A stratified society which had small farmers who would provide a labour force for the wealthy, large landowners provided the means for development. Robertson (1937: 368) points out that such schemes were bound to fail in South Africa because of the poverty of the environment, the profligacy of previous governments in granting land, and the presence of a large native population which provided an alternate and cheaper source of labour than the immigrants from the mother country. Much land had already been taken up both in the Cape Colony and in the newly annexed territory of Natal, but in both areas mainly by Voortrekkers. In Natal the ease with which title to land was obtained meant that farms were to be found scattered throughout the area in the early 1840's, and many were owned by absentees and speculators. At the same time Zulus who had moved out of the territory to the south, or north across the Tugela river, were returning to live among the scattered white population. The voortrekker republic was in favour of moving the returning native population to areas outside its chosen territory, but fell foul of the Cape's governor, Sir George Napier, who was anxious to avoid unrest between his eastern frontier and Port Natal (Durban). This gave rise to the annexation of Natal by the Crown. Those voortrekkers who could prove continuous occupation of their 6000-acre (2450-hectare) farms had their titles confirmed. Despite concessions made by the Governor of the Cape in allowing many who held claims to large farms to treat them as if they were quitrent titles to land, many voortrekkers left the area below the Drakensberg and speculators were able to buy claims to land. Several of these seized on the possibility of getting a return on their investment by subdividing such land and settling immigrants from Britain thereon. Many of these schemes failed because immigrants could not afford to pay the high prices for small farms. However, land was plentiful and sold at roughly 4s. an acre in the late 1840's so that it was an attractive investment under the Bounty system to entrepreneurs who, in exchange for introducing immigrants to colonial territories and providing them with a passage and land, were able to acquire Crown land for further speculation. One of these entrepreneurs, John Byrne, is credited with having introduced over 3000 immigrants to Natal between 1849 and 1851 (Hattersley, 1950: 109). Many of the immigrants refused the 20-acre (8-hectare) lots as too small to be worth survey, but later schemes were an improvement because they adopted 150-acre (61-hectare) farms. Still others were responsible for sending emigrants from Britain to Natal so that altogether 4144 'approved' emigrants embarked between 1849 and 1851, plus several hundred who came without approval (*ibid*: 136). The Lieutenant-Governor was able to add an extra 25 acres (10 hectares) to the holdings of Byrne settlers who remained on and cultivated their original twenty. In general much land was unsuited to subdivision and only holdings within reach of the markets of Durban and Pietermaritzburg were viable small farms. By the late 1850's, although there was much vacant land, there was a scatter of homesteads throughout the area between the coast and Pietermaritzburg; and these homesteads often served as the nuclei of small towns serving future farming populations. Watts' map (1855) shows that in the 1850s Natal possessed a few areas of small farms, but Mair's map of 1875 indicates that by then the greater part of Natal between the Tugela and the Umkomanzi (Umkomaas) rivers, the Drakensberg and the coast was divided into large farms, many of which possessed Dutch names. Small farms were an important feature of the landscape only between the Umgeni and Tugela rivers along the north coast and between the Umlazi and Umtwalumi rivers along the south coast. A few scattered areas inland had small farms, especially around Pietermaritzburg and Richmond where Byrnetown formerly stood amid an area of 'Immigrant Lots' – now Dunbar Estate (Fig. 35D).

In the republics across the Orange river and the Drakensberg the pattern of land holding is directly descended from that which characterized the Cape until the middle of the nineteenth century. Large polygonal farms, each with its *fontein* (spring), extend over the whole of the High Veld and Middle Veld, an area some 450 miles (720 km) by 250 miles (400 km). Even where the rigid application of laws of inheritance has encouraged piecemeal subdivision of these voortrekker farms during the last century or so, the outline of the original farm is still visible on present-day maps. Indeed, it is often now a landscape feature of some significance, affecting the pattern of growth of modern towns such as Johannesburg and Benoni where street alignments are clearly fitted to portions of original farms, and, in particular, where streets meet at acute angles leaving odd gores of land chiefly on the boundary lines between original farms.

On the margins of the High and Middle Velds and the Kalahari the lower carrying capacity of the grazing encouraged a trend towards larger farms. They also appear more regular in outline, particularly where there are few natural eminences or complicated valley systems, as along the whole southern and eastern margins of the plateau. Much of Griqualand West and British Bechuanaland were divided into rectilinear farms running in great strips up to 100 miles (160 km) long right across all natural features. These are the products of a later phase of settlement when Crown land was surveyed before it was settled. Throughout much of South Africa the reverse is the case, so that the monotonous regularity of the mid-western United States, of the Canadian prairies and of interior New South Wales is generally avoided. It is, however, generally true in South Africa that where survey preceded settlement farms are smaller. The regular farms of the desert fringe between Kuruman and Mafeking are on the whole smaller (about 3 miles or 8 km square) than those occupied by trekboers moving outward from the earliest settlements north of the Vaal river. Those in the present Bloemhof and Christiana districts are often four or five miles (6·4 to 8 km) square and are in a region with a higher carrying capacity for livestock (Fig. 35C). Where near desert conditions prevail, as just north of the Orange river between Prieska and Upington, farms away from the river are much larger still, while those with riparian rights, and the possibility of irrigation from the Orange, forms strips frequently ten miles (16 km) long with a couple of miles of river frontage (Fig. 35B).

Regulated settlement of Crown land is more common on what may be loosely termed the frontiers of white settlement in the Eastern Cape Colony in Natal and Zululand. Farms are again polygonal, making use of identifiable natural points as beacons between which boundaries are normally rivers or straight lines. Although these were drawn on surveyors' diagrams at the time of their occupation they were fenced only gradually. The pattern of farms in the areas where the administration was careful to regulate the supply of land to more adventurous farmers and greedy would-be farmers derives very largely from the conditions under which the land came into the possession of the Crown. As has been mentioned, some land was vacated by migrating tribesmen, other parts were forfeited after war and rebellion, and some became more or less vacant after internecine tribal wars or famines and disasters, such as that which befell the Xhosa in 1857. Once the greater part of the population and their cattle had dispersed, either into the Colony proper as it then was, or into the Transkei, the land – in the view of Governor Sir George Grey – became empty and available for settlement. He had already settled for defensive reasons parties of Germans (ex-legionaries and peasants) along a line of road between Buffalo Harbour (East London) and the interior. In 1858 and subsequent years almost all the rest of the pleasantly rolling and dissected bush-clad grassveld between the Keiskamma and the Great Kei rivers was divided into farms of some 1500 to 3000 acres (600–1200 hectares). Similar territory between the Keiskamma and the Fish rivers had been allocated in the same way a few years previously. At that time considerations of defence of the colony and the peace of frontier districts were paramount so that a higher density of agricultural settlement than prevailed on voortrekker farms west of the Fish river was the aim of official policy. Early grants of land were made on conditions such as those requiring farmers to remain on their farms, or to muster in defensive localities in times of trouble. In the Eastern Cape Colony farms grew larger towards the drier interior and many carry English names given by the surveyors, unlike the farms where settlement preceded survey which trekboers often named after some natural feature: *Doorn Bosch* (thorn bush), *Helder Fonteyn* (clear spring); or romantic, comforting names such as *Weltevreden* (contented), *Eenzaamheid* (solitude) and even *Laaste Stuiver* (last penny)! In fact the names of many of the trekboers' farms are vividly expressive of the nature of the country. Words attached to *fontein*, such as *brak*, *klip*, *groen*, *opgedroogte*, *kruid* and *riet* (brackish, stone, green, dried-up, herb and reed), often give clues as to the nature of the water or the surroundings of the spring itself. Apart from such indications of the trekboers' perception of their environment there are many farm names which refer to wild game, some of which has long since been hunted out but is testified to by early travellers (Botha, 1926: 94–115).

A further aspect of the cadastral pattern which is distinctive to what was formerly termed British South Africa is the device of surrounding a planned urban settlement with a commonage where burghers were able to graze draught oxen and dairy cattle (Fig. 35B,D). Although such commonages are found around towns founded during the rule of the Dutch East India Company (as at Paarl), they are far more commonly associated with towns and villages created after the British occupation. The industrial towns of the southern Transvaal which grew among the huge voortrekker farms have no such commonages. Another element in the rural landscape, formerly more important than in the days of mechanized transport, is the outspan. When survey preceded settlement or there were opportunities to obtain small corners of land near roadways, land with water and grazing was set aside for draught animals to rest and graze on. At such places wagons were outspanned. Such patches of ground were provided regularly along routeways to assist the movement of traffic, although nowadays many may be rented from local councils by farmers for grazing their own livestock.

The pattern of land grants in large farms is very typical of parts of South West Africa and Rhodesia and even extends into Zambia along the line of the railway to Lusaka. It is indicative of the spread of a system of land tenure and occupation which began in the Cape, was formalized by British administration, tempered by local custom, and adapted to the nature of the country. For many years European settlers have owned the farms they occupied rather than renting them from a class of landowners or feudal authorities.

The Portuguese territories have, as might be expected, a rather different system. Moçambique is predominantly a tropical lowland, suited not to pastoralism but to the production of plantation crops. The growth of vast estates there during the seventeenth and eighteenth centuries was partly a reaction to the loss of control in the interior by the Portuguese authorities at Moçambique Island. Missionary activity was largely replaced by commercial activity in which gold and ivory trading was rivalled only by slaving. The feudal *prazo* system of huge exploited domains owned by absentee speculators was the means by which the Portuguese Crown attempted to exert its control. In fact, effective control cannot be said to have existed far from the coast, the navigable Zambezi and the few forts in the interior. The estates made relatively little impression on the landscape except to depopulate areas affected by the slave trade. Most attempts at growing commercial crops such as coffee or coconut palms were thwarted by administrative action until commerce was organized, railways constructed and plantations established by three chartered companies which, backed by British and French capital, became virtual rulers of vast portions of the territory in the 1890's and remained so for half a century. The Moçambique Company, for example, held an area of 62,000 square miles behind the port of Beira.

Although coffee plantations in Angola had been established in the same wave of colonial enthusiasm that had affected Moçambique, Angola is better known for its smaller, close settlements of peasant colonizers from rural Portugal. Many of these are to be found along the railway lines, but most are in the more habitable highland areas of the southwest. One such colony, at Cela, failed when plots of only 30 acres (12 hectares) were made available to peasant families in the recent post-war period. Holdings of between about 125 and 300 acres (50 to 120 hectares) are now the rule and more prosperous peasants are being settled there. Such schemes have as their aim the reproduction of modern Portuguese society in Africa, even to the building of a replica of the church at Santa Comba Dao, the birthplace of Dr. Salazar. Peasant colonization schemes are also to be found in Moçambique although these are limited to a few areas and have little effect on the landscape as a whole. In general the rural areas of the Portuguese provinces are dominated not by Portuguese farmers but by African peasant farming under more or less traditional systems.

South West Africa and Swaziland have considerable tracts of European farmland, and even Botswana has a strip of white-owned farms along its eastern border near the railway line.

The Native Reserves

The occupation of southern Africa by peoples of European descent has brought with it a system of land ownership and usage entirely alien to the

continent and its indigenous peoples. It has not been possible in this essay
to do more than sketch the expansion of European settlement from Cape
Town and the more tropical coastlands, but it has been emphasized that
this expansion frequently took place into territory actually or nominally
under the sway of Bantu and other tribes. The process of accommodation
or adjustment between these two major racial groups has been achieved
by means of the device of the reserve for native peoples. The British
administration in North America had adopted this policy in 1763 and it
was taken up by the United States which began to make reservations in
1784 (Royce, 1892). In South Africa the reserve system, or the location
system as it is sometimes known, had its origins in the spate of treaties with
native chiefs entered into by British governors of the Cape colony. Brookes
(1924: 21) considers that they embodied the principle of territorial
segregation because one of their prime objects was to leave the natives
alone, provided they did not disturb the Queen's peace. This segregation
operated by keeping the native territories outside the colonial boundary.
The location system in a more formal guise with many of its modern
attributes took shape in Natal in the mid-nineteenth century when refugees
from the Zulu chief Mpande returned to the grassveld south of the Tugela
which had held only about 20,000 Bantu when the voortrekker republic
was first set up in 1838. Faced by the prospect of having to rule a much
larger native population than had the Republic, the Lieutenant-Governor
of Natal had the gifted Theophilus Shepstone installed as Diplomatic
Agent to the Tribes and set up a Natal Native Commission (1846–7)
on which Shepstone served. The solution of the establishment of locations
with white superintendents or agents implied partial segregation of territories as an insurance to preserve some of the land for Whites rather than
return it all to Bantu occupation (Brookes, 1924: 30). The voortrekker
republic had suggested complete segregation, but the new scheme, worked
out in changed circumstances, created the beginnings of the patchwork of
native reserves that today characterizes 1.5 million square miles (3.9
million km^2) of southern Africa (Fig. 36).

In the Cape Colony three frontier wars (1834–5, 1846–7, 1850–53)
finally spelled the doom of the treaty system, by which the Cape government attempted to keep Bantu chiefs peacefully on the farther side of the
colonial frontier. The attempt to annex the territory up to the river Kei in
1834 was thwarted by the Colonial Office. However, in 1847 the impetuous
Governor of the Cape Colony, Sir Harry Smith, concluded the Kaffir war
by a complete change in the policy of dealing with the Bantu chiefs. He
annexed the territory up to the Kei and exerted the Queen's authority as
their new Paramount Chief, telling them to behave and to stop buying
wives. He further threatened to destroy them like a wagon of gunpowder

that he exploded before them. By this action the Cape Colony acquired a
sizeable Bantu population and the Crown obtained ownership of the land.
Henceforward the Bantu in the 'Ciskei' held and occupied their land at
the pleasure of the government. In the newly annexed territory – British
Kaffraria to distinguish it from Kaffraria proper across the Kei, the modern
Transkei – European magistrates imposed civilized standards through
martial law. The Bantu remained in unfettered occupation of their land
except that they regarded it as too small for their needs. Something
approaching Shepstone's system of locations under supervision was
adopted in the Peddie district, west of the Keiskamma. On several tracts

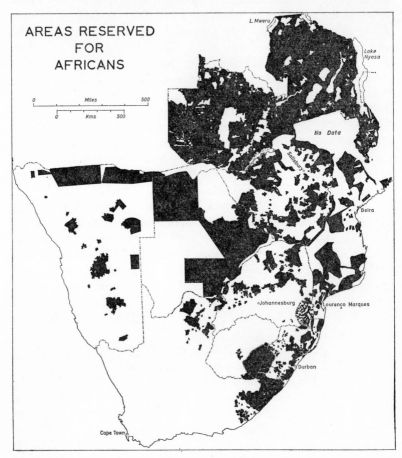

Fig. 36. Southern Africa: Areas Reserved for Africans (after maps in
Wellington, 1955, and the Atlas of the Federation of Rhodesia and Nyasaland)

of land there were located Fingos who had assisted the Government against the Gaikas and others in the war of 1846. They were rewarded with land free from the restraints of native custom and paid £1 a year quitrent to the government for individual allotments. They also had the use of a commonage which surrounded their arable lots. Such a scheme represents the introduction to the Cape Colony of the location system and the spread of the patchwork of native reserves among European farms so characteristic of southern Africa. It was after the creation of locations that the rest of the Peddie district was divided into farms (1854). A similar situation developed in British Kaffraria where originally the whole territory was regarded as Native Reserve. After the catastrophic depopulation which followed the cattle-killing episode of 1857, much good grazing and agricultural land fell vacant. It lay between the Cape frontier zone, where there was pressure among British and Afrikaner farmers alike for more farms, and the restless Gaikas to the north and the Gcalekas and Tembus across the Kei. Sir George Grey, the Governor, who had been modifying the Smith system, seized the opportunity to extend the rule of law and to suppress the unfettered exercise of native law in the territory. He boldly divided the whole territory into European farms of various sizes and native locations. Farther east both the farms and locations were defined simultaneously as part of a regional scheme for settlement of Europeans and natives. In the Government Notice (16 of 1858) setting out the purpose and outline of the scheme, Grey warned the Chief Commissioner who administered British Kaffraria 'to reserve sufficient tracts for the future wants of the former inhabitants of the district who are likely to return there, selecting the localities with a view to the safety of the European population, to the tastes and habits of the Kaffirs, and with a view to their location in villages under the existing system.' The latter is a reference to attempts to concentrate the Bantu population in nucleated settlements so that they would be 'within reach of the arm of good Government' as one adviser put it in 1857 (Board, 1962: 120). Although villages of huts were created, arable allotments were not surveyed except in areas where Fingos predominated or near mission stations. Even the villages had disintegrated as a result of pressures to establish new areas for hut sites at reasonable distances from each other. In fact, throughout the first half of the twentieth century, headmen with the backing of local magistrates or native commissioners have allocated hut sites and arable land in convenient places where locations are unsurveyed. The intense pressure of Bantu population on land resources has led to alterations in this system which is now as rigid as in those locations where hut sites and arable lands are now surveyed. If Sir George Grey's policy of civilizing the Bantu through contact with and working for the Europeans, while they lived next door to them, had been suitable for the partially depopulated Ciskei, it was not feasible in the Transkei, where the Bantu population was altogether more numerous. After a number of abortive attempts to establish Europeans on farms in the Transkeian territories, where it appeared that there was vacant land, the whole tract between the Kei and the Natal border, with the exception of East Griqualand, became a native reserve.

Although the pattern of reserves in other parts of South Africa appears similar to that created in the Cape and Natal, some important differences exist, particularly in the process through which the pattern came into being. In both the Orange Free State and the South African Republics the settlement of the High Veld by voortrekkers was generally achieved without having to resort to the practice of reserving land for native occupation. There are a number of important exceptions, but the greater part of the present area of the two trekboer republics was considered state land by virtue of occupation or conquest by the voortrekkers. In fact, virtually nowhere on the High Veld were the Bantu tribes sufficiently numerous or securely attached to their land for provision to be made for their living space. In practice many stayed where they were and became as it were squatters on the large farms, often as farm servants. In the Transvaal Bantu tribes had no security of tenure and no land rights anywhere until the 1880's. It was not until the Pretoria Convention of 1881 that a Native Location Commission was set up with the object of reserving land for tribes, 'due regard being had to the actual occupation of such tribes' with arrangements for compensation; and that land sales in the outlying districts of Waterberg, Zoutpansberg and Lydenburg were halted until such locations had been laid out. Many groups of natives had corporately purchased farms, the ownership of which was often registered with a trustee such as a missionary. Still other farms were privately bought. In the Orange Free State a similar situation prevailed except that there were two government locations: one at Thaba Nchu where some Baralong farms had been occupied on tribal, communal tenure by natives and became the property of the Free State in 1884; the other between Harrismith and Basutoland, which was called Witzieshoek, and occupied on similar terms by a Msuto chief who became a subject of the Orange Free State in 1867. The government locations defined in the Transvaal were mostly peripheral to the main region of European settlement and lay scattered either on the western border next to Bechuanaland or around Pietersburg in the Middle Veld.

The pattern of government locations in Natal is again peripheral to the main line of pioneer settlement by Europeans – the route between the Drakensberg passes near Harrismith (Van Reenen's) and Volksrust and Durban as well as along the coast (Fig. 32). The locations are generally some miles from the coast in the lower middle sections of rivers dissecting the coastal plain or along the Tugela frontier with Zululand. In the triangle of Natal north of the Tugela, which was formerly part of the New Republic absorbed into the South African Republic, no provision was made by the government for Bantu tribal land. Here some farms were bought for communal occupation by native tribesmen. The location system was, however, extended to Zululand after 1897 when the Imperial government transferred the territory to Natal. Previously there had been no doubt that Zululand was a reserve for the Zulu and other tribes, but in spite of numerous pledges by the Imperial government that the country would not be taken from them, the Zululand Lands' Delimitation Commission established locations for Zulus and the Tongas at an average rate of 85 acres (34·5 hectares) per family of five, and excluded two-fifths of the territory's Crown lands from these locations. This was done in order to throw open some of the then unused or underused land for sale on condition that natives would be allowed to purchase and that they would retain access to forests (Brookes and Hurwitz, 1957: 12–13). In practice the possibility of land purchase by natives in Zululand and elsewhere in South Africa except for the Cape Province was precluded by the Natives Land Act of 1913.

The pattern of locations outside South Africa, at least in Rhodesia and South West Africa, is very similar to that in the Transvaal. In Rhodesia, the land passed finally by the purchase of a concession given by Lobengula to a German called Lippert to the British South Africa Company in 1891. The Company had from the arrival of the pioneer column in Mashonaland in 1890 begun to grant farms of 1500–3000 morgen on quitrent tenure to Europeans of British or colonial extraction. The allocation of farms to pioneers and volunteers in the war of 1893 proceeded with some speed, although there was a lull in occupation during the Anglo-Boer war. Some 7 million acres (2·8 million hectares) were surveyed by 1894, 8 million (3·2 million) by 1899 and 22 million (8·9 million) by 1913. As part of the settlement after the Matabele War and the death of Lobengula the Company and the British Colonial Office compromised on an extension of control by the Company over Matabeleland, but reserved final authority to the British government. The establishment of reserves for the Matabele was part of this settlement. The Matabeleland Order in Council of 1894 set up a Land Commission to assign to natives inhabiting Matabeleland 'land sufficient for their occupation', but the British South Africa Company were to retain mineral rights and the ability to take land for public works on payment of compensation in land. Two reserves covering 2·1 million acres (816,000 hectares) were hastily established late in 1894, but one (the Gwaai) proved to be virtually waterless and remained almost uninhabited. After the risings of 1897 further reserves were established until by 1902 some 21 million acres (8·5 million hectares) had been set aside. This remained the officially reserved land until 1930 (Roder, 1964). The Company's report for 1897–8, reporting on several months of peace following the rebellions, stated that blocks of land have been reserved for the exclusive occupation of natives in the districts of Mashonaland. 'When placed on these reserves the natives are collected in large kraals (villages) under responsible chiefs or headmen. In this way the natives can be better governed, and the authority of the chiefs is strengthened' (B.S.A. Co. Report, 1897–8: 206). It was observed that although natives expressed a preference for living on government rather than private (farm) land it was not necessary to compel them to move as they had often come to 'reasonable arrangements' (*ibid*: 102). Later reports mention the scarcity of labour on European farms, except when hut taxes were due to be paid. It appears that the native population, whether in the reserves or on farms, were not so desperate as to be forced to work for the Europeans. The imposition of a hut tax by the Company soon provided an incentive for the Mashona, Matabele and other tribes to work on mines and farms and in service for the cash they required.

In South West Africa German colonial policy was first aimed at making treaties with groups of indigenous tribesmen and confirming their rights of occupation subject to German sovereignty. Land claims by Nama and Herero peoples were disallowed after their rebellion in 1903–7 and loyal groups such as the Damara were rewarded with land grants. In the north of the protectorate, between the Kaokoveld and the Zambezi at the eastern end of the Caprivi strip, the Bantu and other peoples remained in occupation of their land unaffected by the German occupation. The system inherited by the Union of South Africa in 1915 was thus not very different from that which prevailed in its own territory. The Union proceeded to establish and define reserve for all native peoples throughout the territory until some 51 million acres (20·6 million hectares) had been set aside. To this may be added the 3·2 million acres (1·3 million hectares) belonging to the Basters of the Rehoboth Gebiet, a region which these people of mixed racial ancestry had secured by treaty from Nama and Herero chiefs in 1870 and which was later recognized by the German administration. It consists of surveyed farms and townships with commonages and is therefore quite unlike other areas in native ownership. Some land remained unalienated, that is to say it lay outside the areas reserved for native occupation and had not been divided into farms. It has been suggested that the spirit of the mandate was not being observed when such land was offered as farmland for Europeans. In fact a handbook on South West Africa prepared for the British Empire Exhibition at Wembley in 1925 includes a map distinguishing between farms taken up and those available for settlement.

Reference to the map of Native Areas in Southern Africa (Fig. 36) shows that all other territories are dominated by land owned by or kept in trust for the Africans of that territory. Little has been published on the reserves in Angola and Moçambique but their pattern of native areas differs only slightly from that of Zambia, Botswana or Swaziland where agricultural settlement by Whites is relatively slight and scattered. Again there is a tendency for these reserves to lie away from the corridors of development along railways and from areas settled by Europeans (Fig. 41).

The Emergence of Modern Southern Africa

Economic Development: Transport and Towns

A century ago South Africa was a predominantly agricultural country with a small European population and the other territories of Southern Africa were largely unknown, dominated by indigenous tribes and sometimes loosely administered or ministered to by Europeans. Only south of the Zambezi, and in the immediate vicinity of the long-established colonial settlements on the coasts of Angola and Moçambique, was there any semblance of a modern economy.

In the Cape Colony, reaction to the industrial revolution in Western Europe had stimulated an increase of merino-wool sheep farming in the damper eastern Cape where farmers were less attached to breeding hair sheep for the domestic market and for passing ships than they were in the drier western Cape. However, by 1865, the merino sheep dominated all districts apart from the northwestern Cape. The domestication of wild ostriches by incubating their eggs, which was achieved in the eastern Cape in 1869, for a time made possible a profitable trade based on feathers and prevailing nineteenth century fashions. Wheat was grown in the immediate vicinity of Cape Town and in favourable localities on the plains below the barren mountain ranges between the Berg and Breede rivers. The method of its cultivation and harvesting was extensive in relation to land and intensive in relation to labour, little machinery being employed until the end of the nineteenth century. Irrigation was uncommon and usually restricted to situations where mountain streams could be diverted or where a shallow, ephemeral stream could be dammed at floodtime and seed sown in the saturated mud floor (*saaidam*) of its valley. In Natal plantation agriculture had been established with the help of the unfortunate expedient of bringing indentured Indian labourers to work in the sugar fields from 1860. During the nineteenth century farming in the interior benefited from the introduction of the hardy merino sheep, although exports of wool through Natal amounted only to between one-seventh and one-third of the value of those through Cape ports. Towards the end of the nineteenth century an increasing proportion of wool from the important Orange Free

State grazing lands was exported through Durban. For the most part agriculture on the interior High Veld was geared to subsistence, the only significant exports being hides, skins and wool. During most of the nineteenth century the principal urban markets were the coastal towns and the few administrative and military centres established at no great distance from the coast. The developments of the last third of the century changed this, reversing many of the patterns of travel and trade and outlook, converting South Africa from a wild plateau with a busy and populous margin into a country dominated by a wealthy and expanding central axis.

Until the discovery of diamonds on the Orange river near Hopetown in 1867 there existed no stronger incentive for intercourse between the coast and the interior than trade in agricultural commodities and bare necessities. A network of gravel and dirt roads and some telegraph lines penetrated the trekker republics, as well as interior Cape Colony and Natal, and improvements were slowly being made to the road systems which carried mainly ox-wagon traffic heavily dependent on supplies of grazing and fodder along the route. However, routes parallel with the Cape and Natal coasts radiating from Cape Town, Port Elizabeth and Durban were just as important in holding together the far-flung chains of European settlements and strategic positions. Schaffer (1965: 103) considers that had it not been for the diamond discoveries the railway network would also have followed these lines of settlement. In an age when railways and steam traction provided a considerable advance in the speed and reliability of transport it is easy to realize how the newly developing centres in the interior became the goals of railway construction. By contrast the more rapid transit possible by vehicles powered by internal combustion on tarred, all-weather roads have re-emphasized the links between coastal towns and the lineaments of European settlement.

The development of the railway network proceeded in several stages (Fig. 37). The earliest period of construction aimed at opening up the country adjacent to Cape Town and Durban and took place before diamonds were discovered. After the rush to the Vaal diggings and Du Toit's Pan in the early 1870's, the colonial governments began a series of lines between their ports and the diamond fields in Griqualand West. The lines from Cape Town and Port Elizabeth which joined at De Aar had barely reached Kimberley when, in 1886, gold was discovered in attractive quantities on the Witwatersrand, some 40 miles (64 km) north of the confluence of the Vaal and the Klip rivers. The sudden injection given by the gold discoveries to the economy of the Transvaal made the Witwatersrand a desirable terminus for railways and gave prominence to the drifts (fordable crossings) across the Vaal. Ironically the Cape Colony had rejected a suggestion to extend their railway line from Kimberley into the

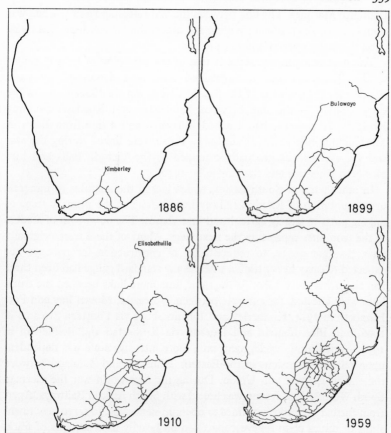

Fig. 37. Southern Africa: Railway Development (after reports of the South African Railways and Harbours)

Transvaal just before gold was discovered. Instead the republican government turned again to the line being brought in from Lourenço Marques which had been begun in 1883 for the traffic from the Lydenburg gold-fields. That line provided for the Transvaal an outlet independent of the British coastal colonies, which profited greatly from customs dues raised on imports to the interior to say nothing of the revenue gained by their government railways. The Orange Free State, pursuing an independent policy and nearer to the Cape ports, allowed extension of the Port Elizabeth line from Colesberg through Norvalspont, Bloemfontein and Kroonstad to the Vaal, and the connection with the Pretoria line was not made until 1892, although still two years earlier than the completion of the line from

12

Lourenço Marques. The link between the Witwatersrand and Durban was completed in 1895, thus providing rail access for the southern Transvaal to all the major ports of southern Africa.

The next recognizable stage is that of the extension of railway routes to the Rhodesian and Bechuanaland hinterland dominated by Cecil Rhodes. By the outbreak of the South African war the 'Suez Canal of the Cape Colony' – the line between Kimberley and Rhodesia avoiding Kruger's Transvaal – had reached Bulawayo and a line from Beira in Moçambique had reached Salisbury. These were linked during the war and the system was gradually extended to the Victoria Falls and into Northern Rhodesia and the Congo by 1910.

In other parts of South Africa, which lacked the stimulus of minerals or the ambition of Rhodes, railway lines belong to the primary stage of linking ports to largely agricultural hinterlands. The outgrowth of feeders to the trun lines represents the next stage. Many of these were originally on a two-foot gauge, to reduce costs of construction for railways not expected to carry heavy traffic, whereas the standard gauge had been three feet six inches since 1880. At the same time more links between the trunk lines were effected, for example between Worcester, Mossel Bay and Port Elizabeth in 1913, Kimberley and Johannesburg via Fourteen Streams in 1906, and Bloemfontein and Durban via Kroonstad and Bethlehem in 1906. Agricultural development on a more intensive scale was dependent upon railway extensions in the Eastern Transvaal and Zululand between the end of the war and Union. During the first world war the German South West African system was linked with South African Railways. Apart from further extensions of lines to open up new areas, to serve new townships or mines or to relieve congestion on heavily used sections of track, changes in the railway system since the first world war have consisted of improvements to existing routes. Beginning in the 1920's suburban lines in the Cape Town area and the steeply graded Natal main line were electrified, and this form of traction was later extended to the Witwatersrand area where commuting traffic had greatly increased. Work is now in progress on the electrification of the line from Pretoria to Lourenço Marques whilst electric traction now runs all the way from Johannesburg to Capetown, except for the section Beaufort West to Beaconsfield. Since most routes consisted of single tracks with passing loops, doubling of the line was undertaken where economically feasible, beginning with lines in the Southern Transvaal until at the present time double track extends from Bloemfontein to Johannesburg and Pretoria and along much of the Natal main line. Other heavily used sections on the Natal coast and parts of the main line between Johannesburg and Cape Town are also being doubled. Further improvements were possible by engineering new routes with better gradients and less sharp curves which required many more earthworks and tunnels than had originally been provided. Since all the main trunk lines from the coast to the interior had to climb long sections with ascents of the order of 500 ft (150 m) for 10 miles of route, regrading has made possible more speedy and economical running. Finally, signalling improvements have increased speeds on single line sections.

These improvements in transport have coincided with a phase of industrial development and urban growth sparked off by the mineral discoveries of the nineteenth century. The latter first introduced indigenous Africans in large numbers to European ways of life, to the market economy and to industrial towns. During the latter half of the century Bantu labour had been increasingly employed on road and railway construction and harbour works, but at distances never far from the workers' homes in the Reserves. It was estimated that there were between 10,000 and 20,000 Bantu labourers employed on the diamond fields in the mid-1880's and 30,000 by the end of the century. However, only 1500 were at work on the Reef (Witwatersrand goldfields) in 1886, although this figure had risen to 96,000 by 1899. Apart from this considerable labour force, requiring at least the basic wherewithal to live, there were also the newly concentrated European populations with higher incomes and more sophisticated wants. This rapidly growing interior market stimulated not only 'transport riding' (i.e. ox-wagon traffic from port or rail-head to the minefields) but agriculture on the High Veld. Although the South African War caused severe damage to farms, crops and livestock, the growing prosperity of mining and associated manufacturing and service industries in Kimberley and on the Rand, together with the political moves towards Union and the confidence thus inspired, encouraged further movements of people to the new cities. Chinese indentured labourers were employed in the Rand mines because of a serious labour shortage (1904–10), but by 1910 some 200,000 Bantu were employed on the mines, over half of whom came from Moçambique. The growth of Johannesburg, which had about 100,000 people before the South African War, to over 600,000 fifty years later, would not then have taken place if the town had been solely dependent upon gold-mining. The deeper levels of payable ore successfully worked from the late 1890's required more labour, machinery, investment and large-scale power supplies. The close proximity of coal supplies in the Boksburg and Heidelberg area reinforced the position of this island of economic activity in the Southern Transvaal. Commerce and secondary industry were soon attracted to the region which has ever since dominated the economy of South Africa. From employing just over a quarter of the labour force in secondary industry in 1916–17, the Southern Transvaal in the mid-1950's employed nearly half of that force (Hobart Houghton,

1964: 133). In the same period the labour force in the Union had risen sevenfold to 855,000. However, whereas in 1916–17 37 per cent of that labour force consisted of Europeans, only 31 per cent were so classified in 1954. Furthermore the contribution made by manufacturing to the national income has steadily increased until in 1963 it accounted for more than a quarter, whereas mining contributed about a seventh and is growing at a slower rate (*Statistical Yearbook*, 1964: U3).

The reasons for this growth are perhaps less important than the effects. In the major industrial areas, but more especially in the Southern Transvaal, the Bantu population has been increasing faster than the European. In the early days of the gold rush the increase of the European population dominated the scene and led to a new sprawl of cities and towns along the outcrop of the gold-bearing reefs and to suburban expansion in coastal cities, particularly in Cape Town, Durban and Port Elizabeth. This half-century of industrial and urban expansion has introduced new urban forms to the South African scene and has brought the racial conflict, formerly on the frontiers of rural settlement, into the dominantly European towns. With large Bantu populations uprooted from their tribal backgrounds now in close proximity to the residence and work place of the Europeans, who had and expected to continue to have a vastly higher standard of living, problems were bound to become more pressing, with the result that racial affairs once again became the dominant political issue. Between the discovery of gold in the Witwatersrand and the first world war the conflict between the trekker republics and residual imperial influence or, too, the commercial and the mining interests identified with English-speaking *uitlanders*, absorbed the energies of the European population of South Africa and neighbouring territories. When the four colonies merged in Union these conflicts appeared to be less important than the preservation of the high standard of living and material civilization of the Europeans in the face of a marked numerical disadvantage. The development of a clearer policy and its effect on the geography of Southern Africa provides the concluding theme in this essay.

The modernization of the 'White' areas of South Africa after the reconstruction begun by Lord Milner's teams and continued after Union by virtue of the developments arising from the first world war, led to subtle changes in the appearance of the platteland (country) and townscape. These changes were felt also in South West Africa and Southern Rhodesia, although to a lesser extent. Shortages of imported goods stimulated domestic industries, and the establishment in 1924 of a Labour-Nationalist government, which adopted tariff protection in 1925, encouraged the setting up of state-supported heavy industry. The key position of South Africa in the second world war, coupled with the expansion of industry to meet the war effort, sustained the progress of modernization. At the same time the gold-mining industry received a fillip from the discovery of deep-lying ores in the Orange Free State and later in the Kinross area of the Transvaal as well as from the production of uranium.

Apart from the coastal towns, which owe their foundation to ports and their growth to the expansion of trade, commerce and industry, and the interior towns created for administrative or defensive reasons, most urban places in Southern Africa owe their origin and growth to mining and industry. The transition from mining camp and native compound to town was sometimes extremely rapid but towns dependent entirely upon gold, diamond or other mining are notoriously ephemeral. In the eastern Transvaal Pilgrim's Rest possessed about 1000 diggers in 1874 and Steynsdorp (Carolina district) once had about 3000. The former had a European population of about 300 fifty years later and Steynsdorp rapidly lost its population to the Witwatersrand, only a post office remaining as an indication of its former importance. However, the Witwatersrand mining towns were able to attract industries where initially the promise of deep mining of southward-dipping reefs encouraged the miners, the financiers, the engineers and the supporting population to stay. Thus heavy industry as well as consumer-goods industries straddle the Reef along its east-west axis forming here a belt between the predominantly residential northern areas and ground underlain by gold-bearing reefs to the south. Continued expansion of industrial activities has perpetuated the impetus first given by gold-mining to immigration, population growth and the spread of residential areas.

In Rhodesia and Zambia manufacturing was to some extent protected by their remote inland situation and was aided by mining, engineering and heavy industry based on local resources, helping Bulawayo, Salisbury and the Copper Belt towns to grow and attract Bantu migrants from rural areas in great numbers.

The rapid growth of industrial and commercial towns in the last half-century has meant that the European population of Southern Africa is now overwhelmingly urban, but, although the Bantu population remains mainly rural, it comprises the largest single racial group in many towns. In fact, the Bantu formed the most numerous single group in all but 28 of the 107 urban places with a population of 7000 or more in 1960, as they did also in the 19 places with more than 50,000 persons in 1960 except for Cape Town and Pretoria which had larger Cape Coloured and European groups respectively. In 1936 only 13 urban places had more than 50,000 and of these only 6 possessed numerically dominant Bantu groups (the mining towns east and west of Johannesburg). 'Dorpstad', the typical South African town, generally possesses a small original core usually on a simple grid plan or consisting of a straight length of street. Cape Town was laid out around the Dutch East India Company's gardens (later to become public gardens) in such a formal grid plan. This set the pattern for almost all other towns except Kimberley whose irregular core derives from the chaotic conditions prevailing during the early mining period (Fig. 38c).

Fig. 38. Street Patterns in South African Towns
(A) Johannesburg, north and east of the centre. The boundaries of farms out of which the city and suburban townships were carved may still be detected. The influence of two hard rock ridges trending east by north on the street pattern is clearly seen. (B) East London: the centre lies within the loop of the railway at an angle to the Buffalo river. The separate townships of which the city is made up are indicated by the open, rectilinear street pattern; at the top of the map the narrow plots of African townships are distinctive. The railway presents a marked barrier to movement and has affected the pattern of growth. (C) Kimberley: showing the old centre of the city between the 'Big Hole' and another deep diamond mine. Later extensions to the town have a more regular street pattern. (D) Orlando and Meadowlands African townships, southwest of Johannesburg: geometrical layout on rolling ground. Note the contrast with the sparse network of rural roads to the northwest. All these maps are on the same scale and are based on the 1:50,000 topographic maps of the South African Trigsurvey, published by the Government Printer, Pretoria.

Many early townships were surrounded by an expanse of town commonage on to which it was possible to extend if local relief permitted. At East London a cramped site and the location of the railway terminus on the side of Buffalo Harbour opposite the original foundation has produced a town plan made up of awkwardly articulated fragments, each on its own grid pattern until the latter became unfashionable in the inter-war period. The process of urban expansion by the establishment of a surveyed township results in individual elements in the town plan being clearly distinguishable (Fig. 38B). The *erven* (plots) are, however, not necessarily all built on at once or even before another section of veld is subdivided for a new township. Except for the biggest cities, the price of land is low enough to encourage those who wish to live in new houses to build on virgin land rather than replace existing, older properties. Urban renewal in the 'White' residential areas of South African towns is usually limited to the replacement of large houses by blocks of flats. This does not apply to the central business districts, however, which have, at least in the larger centres, gradually been transformed from clusters of single-storey buildings with iron roofs and *stoeps* (verandahs), first to two-storey buildings of stone or brick with iron roofs and embellishments and then to multi-storey buildings of brick and stone or, more lately, of ferro-concrete with glass. Such transformations have occurred in Johannesburg within half a century, in Durban over a century. In smaller towns such as Bedford (Cape Province), Dundee (Natal) or Dewetsdorp (O.F.S.) the transformation is beginning with new and modern buildings lying cheek by jowl with older style buildings. In many cases the prosperity of a town may be visually assessed by a study of the character of the buildings used for central functions. In Potgietersrus (Transvaal) virtually the whole frontage of the main street (the National Road to the north) had been reconstructed by the mid-1950's. On the other hand, King William's Town (Cape Province) still contains a large proportion of late nineteenth century buildings housing central functions in its business centre. The latter town was relatively more important in the nineteenth century as a centre for military, administrative and commercial activities, functions now frequently subsumed by East London 36 miles (58 km) away and a port with direct rail links to the interior. Where town centres have been modernized original market squares have frequently become gardens or parks. Old photographs show such squares full of ox teams and wagons, whose use often demanded wide streets. However, by the time Johannesburg was being planned, land cost too much to 'waste' on roads and plots are often smaller, creating the right conditions for the future vertical growth of shops and offices (Fig. 38A). The expansion of central government activities in Pretoria since Union has been responsible for the wholesale replacement of single-storey houses south of the centre by blocks of offices which present cliff-like faces to the remaining early twentieth-century residences.

Starting from the time when Bantu mineworkers lived in compounds at Kimberley, a tradition grew up of residential segregation of the two main racial groups. In the case of the Coloured and Indian groups, however, it was more usual to find them in cheaper, low-rented property adjacent to the business centres or near industrial or port areas. A distinctive region such as East London's North End, which lies just outside the earliest township on the east bank of the Buffalo river, developed a mixed racial composition although at one time it was a high-income suburb occupied by Europeans who built several churches there and whose congregations now live still farther from the centre of the city (Board, 1962: 220). In Durban, views of the sea and exposure to the welcome sea breeze in the town's sticky climate, endowed seaward-facing ridges (e.g. The Berea) with a higher value as residential property and they became dominated by Europeans, whereas the valleys sheltered from the sea-breeze (e.g. Cato Manor) developed as residential zones for non-Europeans. Beyond, still higher ridges again stand out as European residential areas. Although the design of houses is frequently similar in both kinds of area the careful observer can detect the presence of low-income groups, chiefly Indians, by the occurrence of narrower, unmade streets of irregular layout and the bamboo poles and flags of the Hindu religion (Kuper, Watts and Davies, 1958: chapter 4).

The establishment of residential areas largely occupied by non-Europeans tended to confirm their use for those groups, with the result that when towns grew and new residential areas were laid out Europeans leapfrogged the 'undesirable' areas, leaving them incapsulated but nearer the central business districts. Thus public transport services that were developed for European passengers generally had longer journeys to undertake and were most costly unless they were (as in Cape Town) able also to cater for the needs of non-Europeans living nearer the centre of town. In the case of Johannesburg the extremely rapid northward growth of low-density suburbs since the second world war, and the relative affluence of the population, makes bus services uneconomic when so many commute by car and has effectively prevented the extension of trolleybus routes.

Although in general Bantu residential areas are peripheral to residential areas owned and occupied by Europeans, the growth of separate towns in the Witwatersrand conurbation means that many are no longer between the town and open country but form – like the former Sophiatown and Alexandra townships – 'barriers' or 'obstacles' to the unfettered expansion of White residential areas. This phenomenon, although it is perhaps more serious in the Southern Transvaal where township populations are larger, is characteristic of all the larger urban areas in South Africa, Rhodesia, Zambia and the Portuguese provinces. However, areas of temporary housing in the shape of shanty towns for Africans and poor Whites are still significant in cities such as Luanda and Beira (Van Dongen, 1960: 26 and Hance and Van Dongen, 1957: 314).

Political Developments: Land and Population

When the Cape Colony had received self-government in 1872 the policy of identity, of treating different races in the same way, was accepted by the administration, although there was considerable local support for a policy of racial differentiation. The absorption into the Colony of large Bantu populations east of the Kei in the 1870's and 1880's brought home to the mainly White politicians and electorate the possibility of their being swamped by new, Black voters. Between 1887 and 1894 this policy of identity was fundamentally modified through the raising of hurdles in the path of non-European, would-be voters. First a share in communal property was not to count for qualification, then the value of property to be held for qualification was increased and proof of the ability to write was also made a condition. Although these changes affected all races, their incidence was felt more by the Bantu than by others. Both the farmers and mining interests were complaining of labour shortages and put forward the virtue of paid labour as a means of civilizing the 'Kaffirs'. Missionaries and administrators had for some time advocated emancipation from tribal, communal tenure and had recommended individual land tenure as a way of accustoming the Bantu to civilized life. From the beginning, indeed, Transkeian native policy was one of differentiation, of public consultation and of gradual progress towards a form of self-government. It was this policy that was enshrined in the Glen Grey Act of 1894 which set up local councils and substituted individual, quitrent tenure for communal tenure of arable land. The original act contained a provision that those who did not hold land on quitrent title should pay a labour tax of 10s. per annum, unless they could show that they had been in service outside the district for at least three months in the year. The act was quickly applied to four other districts east of the Kei and by 1903 to nine others. Although the labour tax was dropped in 1905 the cooperation between farming and mining interests, both Afrikaner and English that placed the act on the statute book, led the way to a policy of differentiation throughout the Cape and foreshadowed measures undertaken as part of the policy of 'separate development'.

The pattern and speed of urbanization referred to above is, however, undoubtedly one of the most important reasons for the adoption of the

12*

policy of separate development in the Republic of South Africa.[1] Other powerful motives have been the deterioration of the soil and grazing in the Reserves through overpopulation and poor agricultural methods, and the desire of the White South Africans (both English- and Afrikaans-speaking) to maintain their national identities. From time to time government commissions and prominent individuals have commented on the importance of the 'native question' and the tendencies towards the greater urbanization and westernization of the Bantu population in South Africa. At one time attention was focused upon the pressure of population in the Reserves, on the regulation of Native Law in the Reserves and on such social issues as polygamy, witchcraft and drink as they affected the Bantu population. One of the terms of reference of the Native Economic Commission 1930–1932 was to report on the effect on the European and Coloured population of 'the residence of Natives in urban areas and the measures, if any, to be adopted to deal with surplus Natives in, and to prevent the increasing migration of Natives to, such areas.' That Commission viewed the problem as one of a clash between two economic systems whose roots lay in the Reserves containing 'millions of uneducated tribal Natives, held in the grip of superstition and of an anti-progressive social system' (Native Economic Commission 1930–1932: 3). Further commentary on the problem came from the Social and Economic Planning Council at the end of the second world war. Their report insisted that the Reserves could not 'absorb or provide for the whole Native population, or anything like it' (No. 9, 1946: 3) and that their utmost development would still leave large numbers of Natives outside them, raising issues which South Africa could not evade. It was obvious that grave social and economic problems had been created by migration of Bantu to urban areas during the war. The war effort had led to housing shortages and piecemeal attention to the concomitant problems arising from individuals living in temporary accommodation away from the comforts and sanctions of life at home in the Reserves. The attention of two Commissions, reporting respectively in 1948 and 1955, was turned to the question of the permanence of the Native population in the urban areas. The Social and Economic Planning Council had pointed out the drawbacks of the migratory labour system and recommended a more stable and efficient labour force in the mines as well as in industry. The earlier Commission (Native Laws Commission 1946–1948) had considered that many Natives were permanently resident in urban areas from economic necessity, finding that

[1] Although known as *apartheid*, the policy of the government since the mid-1950's has been characterized by the development of Bantu areas and industries to employ Bantu there as well as by restrictions on further mixing of the racial groups implied by the word 'separateness' or 'apartheid'.

camps, shanty-towns and 'sakkiesdorps' were frequently inhabited by those who were unable to find other accommodation near their work (Native Laws Commission 1946–1948: 18). They disagreed with the view that Native labourers ought to be regarded as merely temporarily living in towns in 'White areas'. This latter view had been strongly expressed by the Stallard Commission (1921) and has frequently been expressed by members of the government since 1948: for example during the debates in the South African House of Assembly in 1959 on the bill promoting self-government for Bantu areas. That these views were held by leaders of the National Party was well known to the electorate who voted them into power in 1948. One of the new government's first acts was to set up a commission to report on a comprehensive scheme for the rehabilitation of the native areas 'with a view to developing within them a social structure in keeping with the culture of the Native and based on effective socio-economic planning'. This was done because, once committed to apartheid, the new government could not accept the conclusions of the Native Laws Commission 1946–1948. These had been that the different racial groups in South Africa were so intertwined economically and territorially that they were compelled 'to regulate their contacts, to bridge their differences and to settle their disputes' accepting as fundamental the idea of mutual interdependence. In 1956 the Tomlinson Commission placed renewed emphasis on the development of the Reserves as a method of absorbing the largest possible proportion of the Union's Bantu population. It admitted the existence of about 1·5 million Bantu permanently resident in urban areas in 1951 but considered that, unless the Reserves were developed to their utmost, race relations in South Africa would deteriorate. The commissioners put forward the formula of separate development as a means of giving maximum satisfaction to both the Bantu and European populations by the creation of separate homelands for each group. Because the Bantu were already located in several territorial divisions where respective ethnic groups were dominant, these were to become the new homelands where the Bantu would be able to exercise self-government and have more control over their own economic development. A measure of self-government has since been granted to the Transkei and the South African parliament has voted resources for the industrial, agricultural and urban development of the Reserves.

Against this brief summary of views on and actions taken to cope with the problem of race relations in South Africa it is important to see what geographical changes have been brought about by the exercise of the policies of successive governments. The first action to be noted is the enlargement of the area of the Reserves; the second is a number of territorial exchanges to bring about a greater degree of separation between racial groups; and the third is a programme of land reform in the Reserves. Government policy has set in motion forces that are beginning to modify the population distributions and land use patterns which have gradually evolved within first a colonial and later a commonwealth framework.

When the South African Native Affairs Commission 1903–5 reported on its work throughout southern Africa it suggested that the time was ripe for all land set aside for Natives to be defined and that thereafter no more land should be so allocated. The commissioners were, however, not against selected Natives purchasing land in European areas but thought that such purchases should be limited to specifically defined areas. It was not until 1913 that the Native Areas of the Union were defined in the schedule of the Natives Land Act and some years later that the Commission, set up under the Act to define non-scheduled land for purchase by Natives, was able to report. Even then, in 1916, opposition from Europeans led to legislation being dropped, but local committees were established to define similar tracts of land. Between the publication of the reports of these committees and 1936 the Native Affairs Department was able to advise the Governor-General to permit purchases of land in such areas outside the ones scheduled in 1913 where in effect there was close agreement between local opinion and the commissioners. However, additions to the Native Areas up to 1936 were fragmentary and negligible, whereas the Native population living in them had increased by 1·2 million from 1911 to 1936 when it reached a total of nearly 3 million. Land deterioration was particularly serious in the eastern Cape Province and in the Natal Reserves, but the Transvaal was affected less in spite of the fact that comparatively little land had been scheduled as Native Area in 1913.

After roughly ten years of political manoeuvring the Native Trust and Land Act of 1936 transferred most scheduled areas to a new South African Native Trust. This body was also able to buy land in and adjacent to areas specifically released (and scheduled in the 1936 Act) from the restrictions of the 1913 Act, to add to the Native Area. This enlargement of the Native Area was limited by the Act to 7·25 million morgen[1] and was distributed between the four provinces of the Union so that the Transvaal, which was seriously short of scheduled land, would get the greater part of the 'quota land'. Land was purchased gradually, except during the second world war, until at the end of 1964 less than 2 million morgen remained to be purchased.

A new feature of land purchases which is associated with the positive policy of separate development is the 'rounding off' of Bantu areas 'which jut into White areas' in order to consolidate Bantu areas into unfragmented,

[1] I morgen = approximately 2·1 acres (0·85 hectare); 302·4 morgen = I square miles (2·58 km²).

coterminous homelands, such as were urged by the Tomlinson Commission. The procedure also includes what is known as 'the clearing up of black spots' which are fragments of Bantu-owned land embedded in a matrix of White farms. In the whole of South Africa about 500,000 morgen of badly placed Bantu areas were due for elimination in 1960 and a further 250,000 morgen of black spots were identified. In three years about one-eighth of this land had been dealt with and some 50,000 Bantu living there settled in other areas.

These transfers are in general taking place slowly and as and when land can be disposed of or new land obtained for settlement. As far as can be judged there is no overall regional plan for transfers such as was recommended by the Group Areas Board for the Border (Eastern Cape Province)

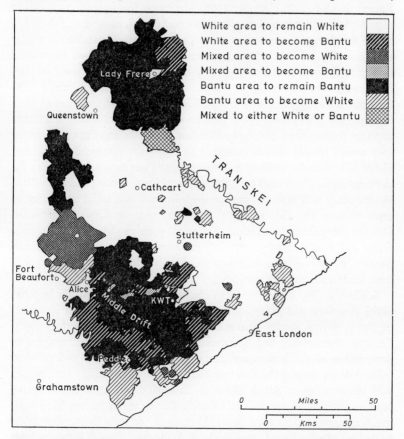

White area to remain White
White area to become Bantu
Mixed area to become White
Mixed area to become Bantu
Bantu area to remain Bantu
Bantu area to become White
Mixed to either White or Bantu

Fig. 39. Exchanges of Land in the Border area of the Eastern Cape Proposed in 1958 (after a map published in the *East London Daily Dispatch*, 28 November, 1958)

in 1958 (Fig. 39). Under the terms of the Group Areas Act, 1957, the regional Group Areas Board set forth a scheme for the division of the Border districts in November 1958 and invited comments from interested parties. If the proposals had been put into effect a belt some 10 to 15 miles (16–24 km) from the Coast between the Fish and Kei rivers would have become group areas for Whites only. Inland, European farmlands lying between tracts of Reserves would have been added to the Reserves. In general the zone some 30 to 40 miles (48–64 km) west of the Kei river, the western boundary of the Transkei, would have become a purely 'White' area. Some tracts which could equally well have been added to Native areas or to White areas were left in doubt. Thus a consolidated Ciskei homeland distinct and detached from the Transkei might have been established. Recent developments (October 1966), stemming from granting a measure of self-government to both the Transkei and Ciskei, suggest that there is a desire for the amalgamation of these two 'bantustans' established under the Promotion of Bantu Self-Government Act of 1959. Both bantustans belong to the southeastern Nguni ethnic group centring on the Transkei. Regional Bantu authorities corresponding with the major ethnic sub-divisions were suggested by the Tomlinson Commission and most of these have already been set up in the Eastern Cape Province. Unless the Bantu areas are consolidated, and, by implication, are made larger than at present, they would remain only appendages to European communities and not viable in economic, social or political terms. Thus runs the argument for the creation of a territorial basis for Bantu self-government and one which, in time, may well radically change the economic and social geography of areas such as the Eastern Cape, Zululand and the Central Transvaal. Despite the deliberate creation of a small-scale patchwork of European farms and Native Reserves by Colonial administrators of the nineteenth century, the forces unleashed by a technically advanced society may well have made such changes inevitable.

While it is only natural to focus discussion of the relationship between political actions and geographical patterns upon the effects of apartheid in South Africa, similar changes have affected countries farther north. Lesotho (Basutoland) and Botswana (Bechuanaland) can be regarded as comparable to the bantustans except that they have achieved political independence despite the fact that they remain economically intertwined with the Republic of South Africa. In Swaziland and Rhodesia the native reserves defined at the time of the first European settlement have been much enlarged so that they may help more of the local Bantu population to derive their livelihood from the land. Such extensions of Reserves have usually come too late to allow the traditional, extensive agricultural systems to provide for the entire Bantu populations, many of whom continue to rely upon earnings made as migrant labourers. Nevertheless, it is only in South Africa where the proportion of the total Bantu population living on farms belonging to Europeans is as high as 20 per cent. In South West Africa the figure is 14 per cent and elsewhere less than 10 per cent of the native population lives on alienated land. This is not to say that the land resources in the Reserves are sufficient for the remainder, but it should also be remembered that the migrant labour system also obtains throughout the whole of Southern Africa. It is not only in South Africa that the Reserves cannot hope to provide the entire livelihood of 11 million Bantu people. Evidence is not lacking in Rhodesia, where it was estimated in 1960 that of 430,000 African farmers only 58 per cent were full-time farmers and over one-eighth were not active at all. These conditions prevail despite the fact that the area of Reserves had been doubled since 1925, over 10 million acres (4 million hectares) having been added between 1950 and 1960.

Such population pressure from the outdated methods of agriculture in the Reserves of South Africa and Rhodesia has prompted the launching of programmes of agricultural restoration and rehabilitation. It is recognized that the control of soil erosion by engineering works does not counteract land deterioration and that the solution lies rather in the creation of a stable peasantry which values livestock as a commercial resource and is prepared to employ modern techniques of cultivation and grazing. In South Africa the Tomlinson Commission calculated that 51 per cent of the families living in the Reserves in 1951 would be considered surplus to the carrying capacity of the land if land utilization were reformed and the remaining families were to be capable of earning a minimum of £60 per annum (1951–1952 prices). It is considered that were this situation brought about the development of a more commercialized agriculture could ultimately yield double that income per family with the same density of settlement. Although soil erosion and overgrazing has been checked over wide areas, so far little impression has been made on the fundamental problem of there being too many people on the land to transform the bantustans into modern societies with a varied economic base. The plain fact is that there is nowhere else for the families to go unless they attach themselves to urban centres in White areas (which migration is now strictly controlled) or are moved to new rural townships in the Reserves. In any case, for the foreseeable future supplementary work and income for many Reserve families will have to be furnished by employment offered by industries and services in White areas. Although the government encourages investment in industry within the Reserves through the Bantu Investment Corporation, which had loaned R565,000[1] to individuals by 1963, the major effort is being made to attract industry to 'border areas'. These are in White-owned regions adjacent to

[1] R1 (one rand) = 10 shillings sterling.

the bantustans and, with the exception of the Durban and Pretoria regions, they are not highly industrialized at present, The advantages of the decentralization of industry from the ports and Southern Transvaal were argued by the Viljoen Commission in 1958. They were particularly concerned with the heavy social costs of the continuing growth of industry in areas away from the Reserves, but accepted that the balance of advantage lay in continuing concentration of industry in existing areas. They recommended that the government should neutralize the disadvantages of smaller centres and help to stimulate industrial growth where it was needed. By attracting labour-intensive industries to border areas the government hopes to make it possible for short-term commuting to take place from the Reserves, and so to reduce permanent settlement by Bantu within White areas and to provide employment for the inhabitants of the hard-pressed Reserves near at hand. If these developments take place on a sufficient scale, the recent increases in the Bantu populations of the Western Cape Province and the Port Elizabeth which have continued between 1951 and 1960, may be stemmed. But this will only be at the expense of increases in the population of Reserves immediately adjacent to zones of industrial development, for example the southern Ciskei and the Natal coast. In situations such as these it is possible to take advantage of the fact that corridors between towns linked by main roads, railways and services in many cases lie within a few miles of the Reserves. The provision of better roads and feeder bus services into such corridors of development as identified by Fair (1957) is a relatively simple matter, contrasted with the developments of brand-new industrial centres by Bantu entrepreneurs in the heart of the Reserves, which is the only other conceivable policy.

Separate development has also been applied to South West Africa in that a government commission of enquiry (the Odendaal Commission 1964) recommended the extension of the system of Bantu homelands there as well as in the Republic (Fig. 40). This was justified by the argument (quoted by Wellington, 1965) that the economic and social progress of the Non-Whites might well be hampered by the creation of a central authority in which all Non-White groups were represented. Instead it was recommended that separate authorities be established for each population group. In several cases the proposed homelands were very much larger than the existing Reserves, but in general the better farmland already occupied by Europeans has been left unchanged. According to Wellington (1965) the extensions to existing Reserves are either short of water or are not suited to settlement by European farmers, who, in some cases, have been bought out by the administration, which has already started to put the proposed changes into effect, some R8 million having been paid out in compensation.

In Swaziland only 37·6 per cent of the country had been reserved in 1907

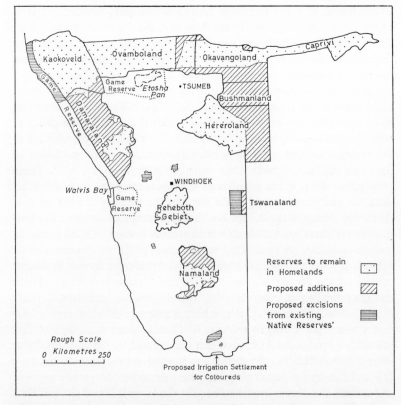

Fig. 40. Proposed Exchanges of Land in Southwest Africa (after Figures 16 and 37 in the Odendaal Report, 1964)

for the exclusive use of the Swazi themselves. Figure 36 shows that it is fragmented into blocks of varying size. Over the last half-century the area of land available for communal occupation by the Swazi has been expanded, partly by the efforts of the Swazi nation and partly by the administration improving the ratio between the number of farmers and the cultivated area. The Swazi nation purchased a further 7·25 per cent of the area of the Colony mainly from Europeans who had acquired farms there. About another 7 per cent was added by buying more farms and allocating Crown land to a Native Land Settlement area. Altogether the Swazi nation has control of just over half the area of the territory, but constitutional developments have differed from those in South Africa in that a single legislative body has been established. The economic development of the territory, which has considerable resources of coal, asbestos, iron ore and timber, has meant the extension of hard-surfaced roads from South Africa and the establishment of a rail link with Lourenço Marques. Although at least 13,000 Swazis are employed in the Republic, the export of produce from farms, plantations and mines which is now possible on the new railway through Moçambique has relieved Swaziland's dependence upon the Republic, from whose political development it is now diverging.

Changes of land ownership associated with the resettlement of Bantu in the major urban areas of the Republic and South West Africa have taken place in the last ten years. Such moves, carried out under the policy of separate development of areas for the different racial groups, have led to the creation of vast new, open-planned townships both southwest of Johannesburg and outside other metropolitan areas (Fig. 38D). Large proportions of the Bantu populations of these centres have been rehoused since the end of the second world war and the creation of what are new dormitory areas on virgin veld has in many instances required the construction of short spurs of double-track railway to cope with the increased commuter traffic. By controlling the direction of future expansion of all suburbs it will be possible to avoid the social problems created by having densely packed Bantu townships between the city centres or inner suburbs and the more recent, outer suburbs. The Portuguese territories, to judge from Luanda, have no strict racial zoning of property or living accommodation within their cities. In the case of Luanda there is an area of flats primarily intended for Africans which was erected by the municipality at some distance from the city centre and beyond the main residential area. It is amid an area of poorer property where the streets are mainly unpaved and services not always available, but like the latter it is well situated for a projected industrial area. In Rhodesia and Zambia on the other hand the presence of politically influential Europeans has secured the segregation of African residential areas on the lines of the locations typical of South African towns. As was formerly the case in the Republic, Indians, Cape Coloureds and others of mixed racial origin who generally belong to the lower income groups lived in the decaying inner parts of towns and cities in poorer property and normally at densities much higher than those prevailing in the 'garden suburbs' occupied by Europeans. In Salisbury, for instance, the oldest part of the town laid out below the Kopje in the early 1890's is now characterized by commercial activities and residences for the poorer groups in the community. About half a mile away lies the modern business centre and beyond that the university and high-class residential areas which now reach several miles into what was farmland only fifteen years ago.

A Synoptic View of Southern Africa

Considerations of space and the selection of topics which focus on the unique racial situation of Southern Africa have led to the neglect of many aspects of its changing geography in this essay. Many of the themes touched upon are reflected in the map of the proportions of the three major racial groups in the region (Fig. 41). Although the salient aspects of this complex pattern will be mentioned, readers will undoubtedly find that the map asks many questions which are not answered. The map is designed so that the relative numerical importance of the racial groups may be seen either together or separately.

Perhaps the most striking feature in the pattern of the races is the dominance of Native populations everywhere north and east of a line from just north of Walvis Bay to Aliwal North (Cape Province) and thence south to Cape Padrone just east of Port Elizabeth. With a few important exceptions the Native population makes up more than 75 per cent of the total beyond that line. Southwest of it is the foothold of the Europeans and their related peoples of mixed racial origin in the drier and extra-tropical parts of South West Africa and the Cape Province. Even more impressive is the huge area dominated by Native population lying between the plateau edge in Angola and the Moçambique coast and penetrating southward to the Limpopo river and its major tributary the Crocodile. Here again, with significant exceptions, there are tracts of Africa not dissimilar from those farther north where Natives predominate to such an extent that no other racial group amounts to 1 per cent of the total population. In these regions subsistence agriculture or hunting has made little impression on the landscape, except to change the vegetation in areas where shifting cultivation, grazing and the gathering of brushwood have persisted for a long time. Occasionally when flying across this area the observer can make out a small township which is a local centre for exchange and administration, an occasional plantation of export tree crops, sugar, or timber in higher areas, and the faint but straight lines of roads or railways. Within this most northerly zone the exceptional areas where non-Natives are to be found in significant proportions are scattered in two main regions. Along the Angolan coastal belt and plateau slopes is an important European population scattered in cities, towns and on agricultural settlements and coffee plantations. A band of European settlements follows the railway line from Lobito Bay towards the Congo, a relationship seen in Zambia, Rhodesia and central Moçambique where it would have been difficult to have established European farms, estates or plantations without the access to markets provided by modern transport. Although the rural European population is important, because it occupies large tracts of land at low densities, it is in the towns and cities where European and Asian populations are sufficiently numerous to dominate the scene. The towns are fundamentally European in form except for the multi-racial crowds in the

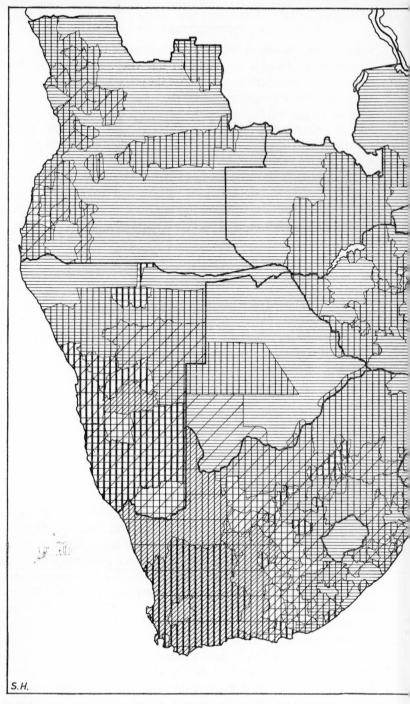

S.H.

Fig. 41. Southern Africa: Europeans, Natives and Other Racial Groups, each as a Percentage of the Total Population (after censuses of population taken in 1956 for Lesotho and Swaziland; in 1960 for Angola,

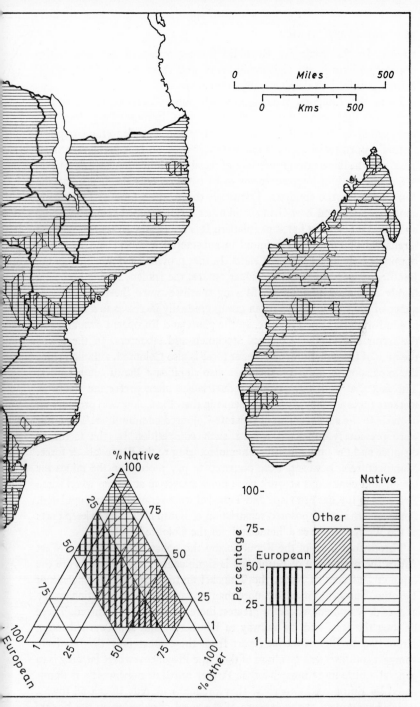

Moçambique, South Africa and South West Africa; 1961 and 1962 for
Rhodesia; 1961 and 1963 for Zambia; 1962 for Malagasy; 1961 for Malawi;
and 1964 for Botswana)

streets. In the Malagasy Republic three-quarters of the non-Native population lives in the eight main towns and there are too few 'French' *colons* (peasants) to dominate any large areas.

From the Limpopo river southward, almost everywhere there is a significant European element in the population. In most of the Transvaal, northern Natal, the northwestern Free State and Swaziland the complication of a third racial group is not generally present. It is perhaps in these areas that the more extreme versions of racial discrimination have developed where the clash of interests seems to be between only the Bantu and the Europeans. In the southern Transvaal, the western Orange Free State, southern Natal and East Griqualand other racial groups begin to make up an important element in the population. It is only in the larger towns of the Transvaal that Indians are found in substantial numbers and they predominate only in the towns of Natal. In that province it is now mainly the Bantu who work on farms and sugar estates, the Indians having become a highly urbanized community. Moving southwestward the relative dominance of the Coloured and Asian group gradually increases to a maximum in southwestern Cape Province. In the platteland Europeans own and run the farms and employ Coloured stockmen and labourers. In the towns the bulk of the non-European labour force is also Coloured, although since the expansion of industry, there are also significant Bantu communities. The fact that both farmers and industrialists often prefer the Bantu as workers (because they are less demanding than the Coloureds) provides an obstacle to the advancement of separate Coloured communities. The latter were previously protected against such competition by the factor of distance and the unfamiliarity of manufacturing to the Bantu labour force. Manufacturers, however, were prepared to pay more than the mines for labour and conditions at work were more attractive at a time when some Reserves in the Eastern Cape and Transkei were seriously over-populated. Some government-sponsored repatriation of Bantu is helping to keep parts of the Western Cape as a 'homeland' for the Coloureds.

Throughout most of the Republic and the policed zone of South West Africa the proportion of Europeans is significant. The exceptions are the remoter Reserves in Natal, the Transkei and, of course, the enclave of Lesotho. Europeans make up more than a quarter of the population on the axes of development where the greatest increases have also occurred. These lie long the Reef and the railway to Kimberley and southward through Kroonstad to Bloemfontein. Apart from these areas only the relatively compact southwestern quadrant of the Cape Province – where farming is in general a little more intensive than farther north or northwest – is dominated by Europeans. Otherwise they predominate only in coastal towns, which have grown at the expense of the rural populations in the hinterlands. In the heart of the Republic serious depletion of the rural European population has given rise to official concern, the view being expressed that the platteland is the pivot of Western civilization and the preserver of the traditional culture of the nation (Du Toit Commission, 1960). The cities are viewed as the home of 'foreign elements' and the 'breeding ground of foreign schools of thought such as atheism, international liberalism, materialism . . .' In some parts of the southern Free State and western Natal over a quarter of the farms, although owned by Europeans, were occupied solely by Bantu families. Undoubtedly the economic and social attractions of city life for the Europeans of a new generation may ultimately help to make the Republic more like the other countries in Southern Africa. Hitherto it has, with South West Africa, been distinctive for its large rural, conservative and mainly Afrikaans-speaking European community. Were this to disappear the possibility of anything but a one-sided territorial apartheid with exclusively Bantu homelands and mixed 'White' areas would vanish for ever.

References and Select Bibliography

AGAR-HAMILTON, J. A. I. 1928. *The Native Policy of the Voortrekkers, 1836–1858*, Maskew Miller, Cape Town.

BARBOUR, K. M. 1961 in *Essays on African Population*, ed. K. M. Barbour and R. M. Prothero, Chapter 15. A geographical analysis of boundaries in Inter-Tropical Africa, Routledge and Kegan Paul, London.

BOARD, C. 1962. *The Border Region: natural environment and land use in the Eastern Cape*, edited by E. D. Mountain and J. V. L. Rennie, Oxford University Press, Cape Town.

— 1964. The rehabilitation programme in the Bantu areas and its effect on the agricultural practices and rural life of the Bantu in the Eastern Cape, *South African J. of Economics*, 32: 36–52.

BOTHA, C. G. 1926. *Place Names in the Cape Province*. Juta & Co., Cape Town.

BROOKES, E. H. 1924. *The History of Native Policy in South Africa from 1830 to the Present Day*. Nasionale Pers, Cape Town.

BROOKES, E. H. and HURWITZ, N. 1957. *The Native Reserves of Natal*, Vol. 7 of the Natal Regional Survey, Oxford University Press, Cape Town.

CAMPBELL, W. B. 1960. *The South African Frontier, 1865–1885: a study in expansion*. Archives Yearbook of South African History, 22nd year, Vol. I, Government Printer, Cape Town.

DU TOIT, A. E. 1954. *The Cape Frontier: a study of Native Policy with special reference to the years 1847–1866*. Archives Yearbook of South African History 17th year, Vol. I, Government Printer, Cape Town.

Du Toit Commission. 1960. (Commission of Inquiry into European Occupancy of the Rural Areas). Report to the Governor-General of the Union of South Africa. Government Printer, Pretoria.

DUFFY, J. 1959. *Portuguese Africa*, Harvard University Press, Cambridge, Mass.

EDWARDS, I. E. 1934. *The 1820 Settlers in South Africa: a study in British Colonial Policy*. Longmans, Green & Co., London.

FAGAN, B. M. 1965. *Southern Africa during the Iron Age*. Ancient Peoples and Places Series. Thames and Hudson, London.

FAIR, T. J. D. 1957. A pattern of development regions for South Africa, *Commerce and Industry*, Pretoria, 15(7): 348–352.

FOUCHE, L. 1963. *The Cambridge History of the British Empire*, Vol. 8. 2nd edition, ed. E. A. Walker, Chapter 5. The Foundation of the Cape Colony 1652–1708: 113–146. Cambridge University Press.

GREEN, L. P. and FAIR, T. J. D. 1962. *Development in Africa: a Study in Regional Analysis with Special Reference to Southern Africa*. Witwatersrand University Press, Johannesburg.

HANCE, W. A. and VAN DONGEN, I. S. 1957. Beira, Mozambique Gateway to Central Africa, *Annals Assoc. American Geographers*, 47: 307–335.

HATTERSLEY, A. F. 1950. *The British Settlement of Natal, a study in Imperial Migration*, Cambridge University Press.

HERTSLET, E. 1896. *The Map of Africa by Treaty*, Vol. II, H.M.S.O.

HOBART HOUGHTON, D. 1964. *The South African Economy*, Oxford University Press, Capetown.

KUPER, L., WATTS, H. and DAVIES, R. 1958. *Durban: a study in racial ecology*. Jonathan Cape, London.

MALINOWSKI, B. 1938. The anthropology of changing African cultures, in *Methods of Study of Culture Contact*. Oxford University Press, London.

MARAIS, J. S. 1939. *The Cape Coloured People 1652–1937*. Longmans, Green and Co., London.

MASON, P. 1958. *The Birth of a Dilemma: the conquest and settlement of Rhodesia*, Oxford University Press.

Native Economic Commission 1930–1932, Report to the Governor-General of the Union of South Africa, U.G. 22, 1932. Government Printer, Pretoria.

Native Laws Commission 1946–48, Report to the Governor-General of the Union of South Africa, U.G. 28, 1948. Government Printer, Pretoria. Stallard Commission (Transvaal Local Government Commission) 1922, T.P.1 1922, Pretoria.

Odendaal Commission 1964. (Commission of Enquiry into South West African Affairs 1962–1963). Report to the State President of the Republic of South Africa, R.P. 12/1964. Government Printer, Cape Town.

OLIVER, R., 1957. *Sir Harry Johnston and the Scramble for Africa*, Chatto and Windus, London.

ROBERTSON, H. M., 1938. The Cape of Good Hope and 'Systematic Colonisation', *South African J. Economics*, 5 (4): 367–411.

RODER, W., 1964. The division of land resources in Southern Rhodesia, *Annals Assoc. American Geographers*, 54 (1): 41–52.

ROYCE, C. C., 1899. *Indian land cessions in the United States* with an introduction by Cyrus Thomas. Part 2 of the 18th Annual Report of the United States Bureau of American Ethnology, 1896–97, Government Printing Office, Washington D.C.

SCHAPERA, I., 1963. *The Cambridge History of the British Empire Vol. 8*, 2nd edition, ed. E. A. Walker, chapter 2, The Native Inhabitants: 21–50, Cambridge University Press.

SHAFFER, N. M., 1965. *The Competitive Position of the Port of Durban*, Northwestern University Studies in Geography, 8, Evanston, Illinois.

Social and Economic Planning Council (Union of South Africa) Report No. 9, *The Native Reserves and their Place in the Economy of the Union of South Africa*. U.G. 32/1946, Government Printer, Pretoria.

South African Native Affairs Commission 1903–5, Report to the High Commissioner and Governments of the Colonies and Territories in British South Africa, Vol. 1, Cape Times, Cape Town.

Statistical Yearbook Republic of South Africa, 1964, Bureau of Statistics, Government Printer, Pretoria.

TALBOT, W. J., 1961. Land Utilization in the Arid Regions of Southern Africa, in L. D. Stamp, ed., *A History of Land Use in Arid Regions*, Part I South Africa, Unesco, Paris.

Tomlinson Commission, 1956. (Commission for the Socio-Economic Development of the Bantu Areas within the Union of South Africa). Summary of the Report, U.G. 61/1955, Government Printer, Pretoria.

VAN DONGEN, I. S., 1960. The port of Luanda in the economy of Angola, *Boletim da Sociedade de Geografia de Lisboa,* 78 (1–3): 3–43.

VEDDER, H., 1938. *South West Africa in Early Times,* translated and edited by C. G. Hall, Oxford University Press, London.

Viljoen Commission, 1958. Report of the Commission of Enquiry into Policy relating to the Protection of Industries. U.G. 36/1958, Government Printer, Pretoria.

WAKEFIELD, E. G. 1833. *England and America: A Comparison of the social and political state of both nations,* 2 vols., Richard Bentley, London.

WALKER, E. A. 1922. *Historical Atlas of South Africa,* Oxford University Press, London.

WELLINGTON, J. H. 1965. South West Africa: the facts about the disputed territory, *Optima* 15 (1): 40–54.

Epilogue: *Problems and Prospects of African Unity*

Epilogue: *Problems and Prospects of African Unity*

By THE EDITORS

The current preoccupation of many writers with the idea of African unity – both on a regional and on a continental scale – is a natural consequence of the rapid devolution of power from European to African hands over the last decade. In the political flux that has accompanied the transition of Africa from colonialism to independence, several movements for unity have arisen; and they have been both stimulated and sustained by the persistence of white minority governments and colonial régimes in the southern part of the continent. The excessive political fragmentation of Africa has also brought home to its peoples the urgent need for inter-state cooperation. Few African states have sufficient demographic and economic strength to form viable and prosperous political units on their own, and it has already become clear that independence is no guarantee of improved living standards or even of individual political liberties. But grouped together the new states of Africa represent a politically powerful bloc which commands nearly one-third of the total voting strength of the United Nations.

The phrase 'African unity', however, has many different connotations. One of its meanings is expressed in *Pan-Africanism*, which began in the 1930's under the inspiration of Americans of African descent. As yet it is little more than a vague concept – an 'emotion felt subjectively' – which defies objective analysis, but it has clearly helped to provide the philosophical framework for such ideas as a 'United States of Africa', an 'African Federation', and a 'Union Government of Africa'. In the 1930's, too, the idea of *Négritude* was born 'out of the revolt of African culture against the French policy of cultural assimilation' (cited in Harrison Church, 1963:93). Senghor, the originator of Negritude, has spoken of it as 'the whole complex of civilized values – cultural, economic, social and political – which characterizes the black peoples, or, more precisely, the Negro-African world. . . . The sense of communion, the gift of myth-making, the gift of rhythm, such are the essential elements of Negritude' (*ibid*: 93). Yet another vaguely defined but emotive concept is that of the *African Personality*, with its combination of self-assertiveness and sense of an underlying continental unity (Davidson, 1964: 71–8).

All these expressions are similar in being conceptual notions of, rather than practical programmes for, African unity; all are based on the idea that Africans have 'something in common'; and all have developed out of a desire to give positive meaning to African independence. But as yet they have made little impact on practical cooperation between African states and what little political unity has developed seems rather to be an expression of combined opposition to vestigial colonialism or neo-colonialism than to be the result of a positive desire for African unity as such. The Organization of African Unity (*O.A.U.*), with its headquarters at Addis Ababa, was set up in 1963 with the aim of integrating African opinion and forging common policies of political and economic action. It has so far met with little success, but this provides no justification as yet for dismissing the *O.A.U.* as a potentially effective instrument for fostering one form or another of African unity.

The positive motives underlying attempts to bring about African unity fall into two main though not mutually exclusive categories. First, there is the desire to reduce the excessive political fragmentation and national parochialism of African states and to eliminate friction between them. Armah (1965), for instance, argues that following the replacement of colonialism by nationalism there should be a United Government of Africa, for in no other way can he see an end to past political struggles and the beginnings of effective collaboration. Secondly, there is the wish to achieve economic advance, it being argued that economic development in Africa can come only from cooperation and coordination between states and not from fostering the growth of autarchic national economies.

This distinction is important because it bears on the two contrasted ways commonly envisaged for the achievement of African unity. One is the rapid and wholesale political approach, in which national sovereignty is subordinated to the needs of Pan-African unity, from which it is expected that economic and social cooperation will ultimately follow. The other approach is that which encourages economic and social cooperation in the belief that this alone can form a realistic basis for eventual political unity. In the late 1950's and early 1960's, these different viewpoints were expressed through two groupings: the Casablanca bloc, which supported a sweeping, political approach; and the Monrovia group, which supported a gradualist, economic approach. Neither approach, however, has yet resulted in any considerable measure of unity.

The essays in this book have indicated some of the practical difficulties – both political and economic – that stand in the way of African unity. The great size and political fragmentation of the continent; the relatively small population; the forces of tribalism; the differing past and present associations with European powers of the new African states, with all the economic, cultural, educational and linguistic differences this implies; the continuance of white-minority governments in southern Africa; the persistence of a few colonial régimes; and the uneven pattern and widely differing levels of economic activity: all these factors make African unity peculiarly difficult to achieve. Furthermore, the fundamental division of African countries into those lying to the north and south of the Sahara is already expressing itself in a number of new ways. Each Pan-African meeting appears to widen the cleavage between northern Africa – Arab, Moslem, and increasingly part of the Arab League community of the Middle East – and Africa south of the Sahara, where the dominant unifying force is Negritude and from which the Arab north is necessarily excluded. This remains true even for those parts of Africa south of the Sahara where Islamization is proceeding most rapidly.

It is in fact pertinent to ask whether the goal of African unity is really either desirable in theory or attainable in practice. It is perhaps surprising that there should be so much talk of unity in Africa when, after all, little attention is paid to the prospects of Asian or South American unity. Much of the contemporary interest in African unity may be only an extension of the illusion, mentioned in the Introduction, that Africa is a continent lacking in diversity. But if, as concluded earlier, there is no justification for assuming that it is markedly more uniform – physically or culturally – than other continents, then it is difficult to argue that there is today any compelling basis for African unity.

Seen in the long perspective of African history, the transition of most of the continent from colonial status to independence has taken place with extraordinary speed. But the impetus for rapid political change appears to be dwindling and a further transition towards unification on a continental scale is likely to be achieved – if at all – only very slowly.

References and Select Bibliography

ARMAH, K. 1965. *Africa's Golden Road*, Collins, London.

CARTER, G. M. 1966. *National Unity and Regionalism in Eight African States*, London.

CHISIZA, D. K. 1963. The outlook for contemporary Africa. *Journal of Modern African Studies*, Vol. 1: 25–38.

DAVIDSON, B. 1964. *Which Way Africa*, Penguin, Harmondsworth.

DECREANE, P. 1961. *Le Panafricanisme*, Hachette, Paris.

HARRISON CHURCH, R. J. 1963. *Environment and Policies in West Africa*, Van Nostrad, Princeton.

LEGUM, C. 1962. *Pan-Africanism, A Short Political Guide*, Praeger, New York.

NYERERE, J. 1963. A united states of Africa. *Journal of Modern African Studies*, Vol. 1: 1–6.

SELASSIE, H. 1963. Towards African unity. *Journal of Modern African Studies*, Vol. 1: 281–291.

Index

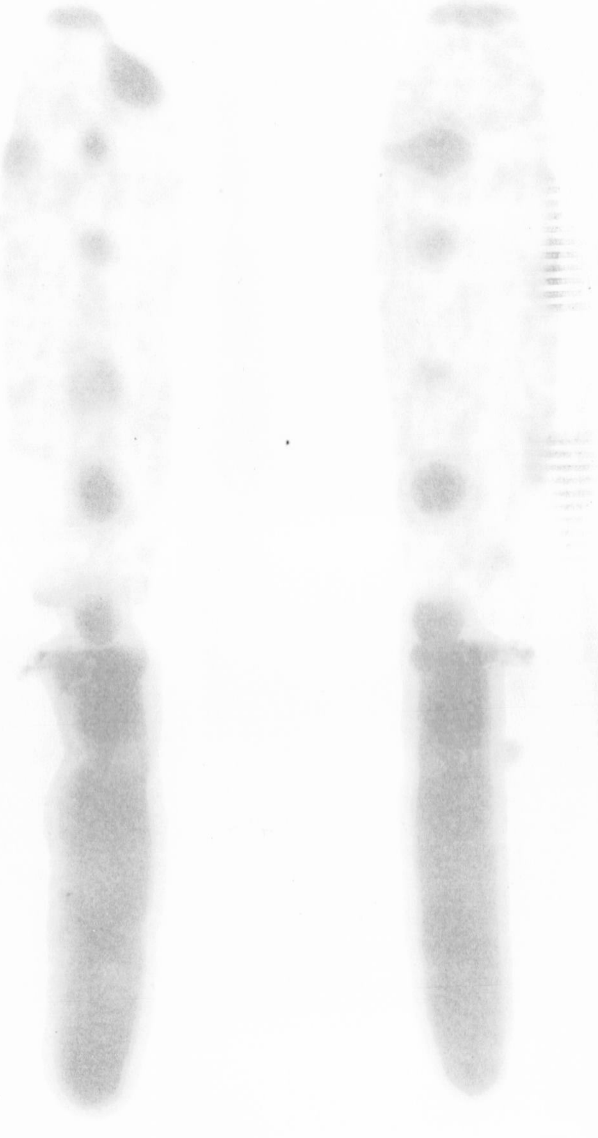

DATE DUE
